THE NOVA SCOTIA BOOK OF LISTS

VERNON OICKLE

MACINTYRE PURCELL PUBLISHING INC.

MacIntyre Purcell Publishing Inc.
194 Hospital Rd.
Lunenburg, Nova Scotia
B0J 2C0
(902) 640-3350

www.macintyrepurcell.com
info@macintyrepurcell.com

Printed and bound in Canada by Friesens

Design and layout: Greg Tutty Design
Cover design: Denis Cunningham

ISBN: 978-1-77276-109-2

Library and Archives Canada Cataloguing in Publication

Oickle, Vernon, 1961-, author   The Nova Scotia book of lists / Vernon Oickle.

ISBN 978-1-77276-109-2 (softcover)

     1. Nova Scotia--Miscellanea. 2. Nova Scotia--History--Miscellanea.
     I. Title.

FC2311.O43 2018   971.6002   C2018-903461-0

MacIntyre Purcell Publishing Inc. would like to acknowledge the financial support of the Government of Canada and the Nova Scotia Department of Tourism, Culture and Heritage.

Dedicated to all the Virgos in the world.
We were born to make lists.
It's in our nature.

The List of Lists

Welcome to The Nova Scotia Book of Lists

I love lists. They're quick and easy to read, and they succinctly capture the subject. With that in mind, I've compiled a collection of lists all about Nova Scotia, including the best fishing holes, top places to go sledding, best burgers and seafood chowder, the top weather events, the most influential people in the province's history, the worst crimes ever committed here, 10 famous Nova Scotians well worth inviting to a dinner party at your house, and Nova Scotians who would be the best interview subjects.

I must thank all the contributors who said yes when I asked them to participate in this project. This book would not be possible without your lists and I am forever grateful for your input.

There is no better way to kick off a book of lists than with a list. So here you have my 25 reasons why I love Nova Scotia:

#1. Nova Scotians are kind, caring, generous and supportive of others.

#2. Neighbours are willing to help their neighbours, especially those who are less fortunate, or those who may have fallen onto hard times.

#3. Nova Scotia is a safe place to live and raise a family.

#4. Unspoiled beauty abounds in Nova Scotia.

#5. The natural, pristine environments in Nova Scotia are second to none.

#6. Our rich and diverse heritage creates an interesting setting in which to live and raise a family.

#7. The eclectic mix of cultures creates a diverse and rich society.

#8. I've always been inspired by the resiliency of the people to keep on fighting in the face of adversity and seemingly insurmountable odds.

#9. I am perpetually impressed by our people's ingenuity, their ability to create their own solutions to their problems.

#10. The can-do attitude that permeates the entire province is often contagious.

#11. The determination that has pulled the province through some tough times and will do so again, is palpable.

#12. The unique and traditional food we enjoy, such as Rappie pie, blueberry grunt, sauerkraut and Lunenburg pudding offers something for everyone.

#13. The abundance of folklore and traditions add layers of culture to our lives.

#14. The ease with which rural and urban communities meld together makes living in Nova Scotia a unique experience.

#15. The natural talent that abounds in Nova Scotia, most notably in the arts, is truly inspirational.

#16. The fact that Nova Scotia is a natural habitat for so many birds and wild animals, and further that as a society we place great emphasis on protecting their habitats, inspires us.

#17. For the most part, and despite the occasional occurrence that draws negative attention, the majority of Nova Scotians are tolerant and accepting of people who are "different."

#18. Nova Scotia is the cradle of democracy and freedom of speech in North America, something for which we should all be immensely proud.

#19. Nova Scotia has produced a long line up of outstanding and distinguished political, business and civic leaders throughout its history that should inspire us all.

#20. Even though the weather can be harsh at times, by and large it is one of the most moderate regions in the country.

#21. We live in a place of relative safety, free of exploding bombs, errant bullets and dissidents wanting to do us harm.

#22. Nova Scotia is well positioned to provide any type of outdoor experience one desires, from experiencing the ocean or a freshwater lake, to enjoying the ski slopes and the inland, wooded regions.

#23. Nova Scotia has a diversified economy that has been built on natural resources,

agriculture, construction, industrial and the arts that has provided many opportunities to attract and build success.

#24. I like the fact that Nova Scotia is one of the oldest regions of Canada. That gives us bragging rights that the roots of our great nation begin right here.

#25. And finally, I am proud and happy to call Nova Scotia my home because my family roots and those of my wife's family are firmly planted in the province. It's also the place where Nancy and I raised our two wonderful children, so Nova Scotia is not only an important link to our pasts, but also to our futures.

It is my hope that you not only enjoy this book of lists but also learn things about the province, and are inspired to do start your own lists.

— **Vernon Oickle**

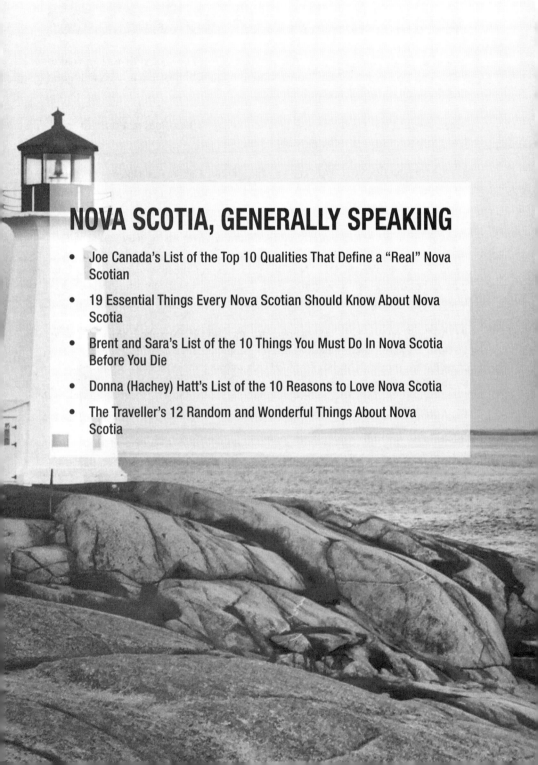

NOVA SCOTIA, GENERALLY SPEAKING

- Joe Canada's List of the Top 10 Qualities That Define a "Real" Nova Scotian
- 19 Essential Things Every Nova Scotian Should Know About Nova Scotia
- Brent and Sara's List of the 10 Things You Must Do In Nova Scotia Before You Die
- Donna (Hachey) Hatt's List of the 10 Reasons to Love Nova Scotia
- The Traveller's 12 Random and Wonderful Things About Nova Scotia

Joe Canada's List of the Top 10 Qualities That Define a "Real" Nova Scotian

In honour of all things Nova Scotian and to kick off our book of lists, I wanted to know what constitutes a "real" Nova Scotian. Who better to help us with that quest than Joe Canada (Jeff Douglas) himself?

When we asked Joe Canada to give his list of the top 10 qualities that define a "real" Nova Scotian, this is what he gave us:

#1. A REAL NOVA SCOTIAN knows what a Dinky Car is. This Hot Wheels crap is for Upper Canadians.

#2. A REAL NOVA SCOTIAN will lend you their truck for two months without drawing up an Agreement, clarifying Terms or even ever asking why you need it.

#3. A REAL NOVA SCOTIAN will never mispronounce Musquodoboit, Tatamagouche, Antigonish or Kejimkujik … No matter how many Annapolis County Ciders they've had.

#4. A REAL NOVA SCOTIAN knows that the KITCHEN is the FAMILY ROOM, and that no party worth mentioning ever happened anywhere else. Unless it was around a fire pit. A REAL NOVA SCOTIAN knows that you should never have a fire pit in your kitchen.

#5. A REAL NOVA SCOTIAN couldn't give less shits what you do for a living, so long as you're a decent person.

#6. A REAL NOVA SCOTIAN knows that things will never make you happy — people, pets and places always will.

#7. A REAL NOVA SCOTIAN will always offer to pick up the tab. This can lead to difficulties when two or more REAL NOVA SCOTIANS go out for a pitcher. A REAL NOVA SCOTIAN knows the only solution is another pitcher.

#8. A REAL NOVA SCOTIAN will never think of anywhere else on Earth as home — even if they've lived away for the vast majority of their life. A REAL NOVA SCOTIAN will also always be scheming as to how they can get back, for good, and be telling everyone, everywhere, how much better life is BACK HOME.

#9. A REAL NOVA SCOTIAN remembers their dad talking to strangers while they were filling empty jugs with real spring water, from a real spring, at nine o'clock on a July night in Victoria Park. A REAL NOVA SCOTIAN also remembers that, after three minutes of conversation, that stranger is no longer a stranger.

#10. A REAL NOVA SCOTIAN doesn't have a cottage. A REAL NOVA SCOTIAN has a camp.

Joe Canada's alter ego, Jeff Douglas, is a Canadian presenter, actor and television personality whose work has been seen by audiences in more than 160 countries. His combination of irreverence, enthusiasm, warmth and humour has endeared him to viewers around the world. Jeff was the recipient of the prestigious Kari Award (2001) for his performance as Joe Canadian in the well-known Molson commercial, "The Rant". Born in Truro, he currently lives and works in Toronto, where he is the co-host on CBC Radios One's As It Happens.

19 Essential Things Every Nova Scotian Should Know About Nova Scotia

#1. ORIGIN OF NAME: Latin for New Scotland. In 1621, King James I of England (James VI of Scotland) claimed the land as a part of the kingdom of Scotland.

#2. LICENSE PLATE: "Canada's Ocean Playground" was adopted on the Nova Scotia license plate in 1972.

#3. MOTTO: *Munit Haec et Altera Vincit* (One defends and the other conquers.)

#4. NICKNAME: Bluenoser. There is a great deal of debate about exactly why Nova Scotians are called Bluenosers. Some say it's because the sailors' mittens were blue and the dye got on their noses when they rubbed them; others, because Nova Scotians' noses turned blue from the cold. And one story has it that the nickname was given to the crewmen of schooners that carried blue-skinned Nova Scotia potatoes to New England in the late 1700s.

#5. COAT OF ARMS: At the centre on a shield is the provincial flag (a combination of St. Andrew's Cross and the Royal Arms of Scotland). To the left of the arms is a unicorn, while a seventeenth-century approximation of a 'native North American' stands to the right. The motto is illustrated directly below with two hands shaking; one, bare, holds a laurel branch, symbolizing peace, while the other, clad in armour, holds the thistle of Scotland. At the base is Nova Scotia's floral emblem, the mayflower, entwined with the thistle of Scotland, which was added in 1929.

#6. TARTAN: The blue and white in the tartan stand for the sea; the green represents the forests; red for the royal lion on the shield of arms; and gold for the royal charter of the province.

#7. PROVINCIAL FLAG: The province's flag is the flag of Scotland with the colours reversed. The Arms (the lion rampant) in the centre of the flag is a symbol of the Crown. Nova Scotia was the first overseas British colony to receive its own flag.

#8. PROVINCIAL FLOWER: Nova Scotia was the first province to adopt a flower. The mayflower, named because it blooms in May, was officially designated in 1901.

#9. PROVINCIAL BIRD: The osprey was designated the official bird of Nova Scotia in 1994.

#10 PROVINCIAL DOG: Nova Scotia's official dog, the Duck Tolling Retriever, is native to Yarmouth County. Also known as the Little River Duck Dog, the Toller was recognized as a pure breed by the Canadian Kennel Club in 1945.

#11. PROVINCIAL BERRY: The blueberry was officially designated our provincial berry in 1996. Nova Scotia is Canada's top producer of blueberries.

#12. PROVINCIAL TREE: The most common tree species in Nova Scotia, the red spruce, became the province's official tree in 1998. It grows to a height of 25 m and its lifespan can reach 400 years.

#13. PROVINCIAL STONE: Stilbite is found in abundance along the Bay of Fundy and the Minas Basin. It became the provincial stone in 1999. Nova Scotian Stilbite is widely known in geographic circles for its bright colours (grey, white, brownish-red, or yellow) and its beautiful crystalline shapes.

#14. PROVINCIAL GEMSTONE: Agate is commonly found in the Jurassic basalt flows along the Bay of Fundy. Although most commonly found in greys and whites, this beautiful, translucent gemstone is also found in shades of blue and a few other colours. Agate is the birthstone for the month of May. Adopted as the provincial stone in 1999.

#15. SAILING AMBASSADOR: Launched in July 1963 from the Lunenburg shipyards of Smith and Rhuland, Bluenose II is a worthy replica of the world-famous Bluenose. The original Bluenose, also built by Smith and Rhuland in 1921, while performing as a fishing vessel for 25 years (the average lifespan of ships at that time was only 10 years), also became a world-class racing yacht in six international competitions. When diesel power became more prevalent at the beginning of the Second World War, the Bluenose was sold to the West Indian Trading Company in 1942. Sadly, she sank in 1946 when she was run aground on a reef near Haiti.

#16. TIME ZONE: Atlantic

#17. AREA CODE: 902

#18. VOTING AGE: 18

#19. LEGAL DRINKING AGE: 19

Brent and Sara's List of the 10 Things You Must Do In Nova Scotia Before You Die

One question we get asked repeatedly is, "What do you recommend I do when I visit Nova Scotia?"

This list — 10 things you must do in Nova Scotia before you die — is composed of our absolute favourite activities to recommend in our home province. They capture our history, culture and are quintessential Nova Scotia. We know this list could be expanded to include hundreds of other experiences. That's the beauty of our marvelous province. But you *must* get these in before you die ... so hurry up!

#1. SAIL ON BLUENOSE II: Lunenburg is the birthplace of the original Bluenose, an undefeated racing champion and Canadian icon. The South Shore town is also home to Bluenose II, a replica of the famous vessel that's featured on the back of the dime. Visitors can experience a harbour cruise on this tall ship in various ports throughout Nova Scotia during the sailing season.

#2. TRAVEL THE CABOT TRAIL: The Cabot Trail is a scenic roadway that winds its way through the majority of Cape Breton Island and is one of the most famous drives in Canada. This trail boasts many scenic look offs, cultural sites, excursions, hiking trails and campgrounds. When planning your trip be sure to give yourself a couple of days to soak it all in.

#3. RELIVE HISTORY AT FORTRESS OF LOUISBOURG: This landmark is a reconstruction of a French town and fortifications from 1713. During the 18th century it served as one of busiest seaports in North America. Visitors come from around the world to see this amazing fortress complete with occupants in traditional dress, traditional food and drink and, of course, the cannon and musket firing.

#4. MARVEL AT PEGGY'S COVE BEAUTY: Peggy's Cove is a quaint fishing village about

40 minutes from Halifax. This community's landscape was transformed by glaciers some 12,000 years ago and is home to unique vegetation and wildlife. The famous lighthouse is what most visitors flock to see and for good reason. Built in 1915 and still operational, it is the most photographed lighthouse in Nova Scotia.

#5. KAYAK THE BAY OF FUNDY: Home of the highest tides in the world according to the Guinness Book of World Records the Bay of Fundy withstands 160 billion tonnes of seawater, twice a day, flowing in and out of its shores. Experiencing a guided kayak tour really captures the magnitude of these tides while getting up close and personal with the remarkable sea stacks.

#6. GO TIDAL BORE RAFTING: The tidal bore is the first wave of the incoming tide that forms a wall of water travelling up a narrow bay against the direction or the river's current. This phenomenon leads to 3 to 4-meter waves and we capitalize on that here in Nova Scotia. Jump in a zodiac and get up close and personal with the tidal bore!

#7. WALK THE HALIFAX WATERFRONT: A visit to Halifax is not complete until you take a stroll on the waterfront boardwalk. The unique shops, historic properties and marvelous restaurants will leave you in awe. Keep an eye out for the numerous events and festivals that take place throughout the year to truly experience the Halifax waterfront.

#8. VISIT WINE COUNTRY: A trip to "The Valley" is one of our favourite things to do in Nova Scotia. This area is known for producing the best wine in the province. Whether you prefer a guided or solo tour, this is a wonderful way to learn about and sample the unique Nova Scotia wines. Amazing restaurants with picturesque views are scattered throughout, so be sure to bring your appetite and your camera.

#9. TAKE A SOUTH SHORE ROAD TRIP: The South Shore of Nova Scotia is full of remarkable experiences. Whether it be the white sand beaches, rich culture or the famous lobster, this is a must-do road trip. There's plenty to do but be sure to leave time for Kejimkujik National Park, Tancook Island, Petite Riviere and Oak Island. For the active road tripper, there are plenty of options including sea kayaking to hiking and if it's festivals you favour, don't miss Privateer Days in Liverpool or the region's newest festival, the South Shore Lobster Crawl.

#10. ENJOY THE CELTIC COLOURS INTERNATIONAL FESTIVAL: This famous festival is held every year in October in communities all over Cape Breton Island. Hundreds of musicians, dancers and performers come from all over the Celtic world to participate in this celebration of music and culture. This magnetic event connects communities, showcases local talent and nurtures the Gaelic tradition.

Brent and Sara are full-time travel writers, customer experience consultants and adventure junkies. When they're not travelling the world and making videos for the travel blog, Dashboard Living, they're working closely with business owners to grow and elevate their brands through world-class customer experiences. Check them out at these social media sites: www.dashboardliving.com/work-with-us/ www.facebook.com/dashboardliving/ www.instagram.com/dashboardliving/

Donna (Hachey) Hatt's List of the 10 Reasons to Love Nova Scotia

Narrowing down a list to only 10 Reasons to Love Nova Scotia is a difficult task. Having had the honour of exploring and visiting nearly every edge of Canada's Ocean Playground, I'm always in awe of her beauty, not only of the landscape and people, but her history and gifts.

Nova Scotia, there are so many more reasons than 10 to love you. You are my home and I hope all Nova Scotians love you in so many more ways than these 10.

#1. FOUR REASONS IN ONE — WE HAVE SEASONS: Can you imagine if we didn't have seasons? How boring would that be — and what would we use as our conversation starters if it weren't for our weather! While the dividing line may be blurred, we have "four" seasons that guide everything from our clothing to recreational activities, what we eat and even drink. The fact that we have four seasons with unique conditions and differing temps means we're always ebbing and flowing, like the ocean. And speaking of ocean, it's one of the key influencers on our weather. If you want a winter with less snow and warmer air temps, head for the South Shore — Nova Scotia's Banana Belt. If you prefer snow — head north of the Cobequid Mountains and into the Highlands of Cape Breton. We have it ALL.

#2. LIFE'S A BEACH: We're surrounded by the Atlantic Ocean. Thanks to the continental shift millions of years ago we're like a patchwork quilt of beaches, and I love them all. Along the edge of the Northumberland Straight you'll find not only the warmest ocean water north of the Carolina's, but also kilometres of rippled red sand bars that stretch out to greet the sun as she rises, perfect for beach strolls — as kids we loved playing touch football out there. Now, you'll have to keep an eye on the timing of the tides, but head out on the ocean floor along the Bay of Fundy. The reddish clay cliffs reveal everything from rich clam beds and dinosaur artefacts to the highest tides in the world. Did you know that the amount of water moved in and out with just one tide would fill the Grand Canyon? And then there are the spectacular, sweeping stretches of white-sand beaches along the Atlantic Ocean. The water there is famous for its "tropical" turquois tones. It is here where you'll hear the ocean surf symphony roar, more and louder than any other in Nova Scotia as the white-capped crests collapse on themselves. It's an endless orchestra. Best of all, they're accessible in all seasons — every day is a beach day in Nova Scotia, after all. It's not like we swim in the ocean all that often anyway.

#3. IT'S ALWAYS LOBSTER SEASON: Thanks to the rotating lobster fishing season, in Nova Scotia it's always lobster season. I love lobster. Thanks to my Grandpa Hachey and parents, I was taught at an early age how to eat a lobster so as not to waste any of it, fresh from the shell. Growing up we thought it was a summer thing as we made regular pilgrimages to Chase's Lobster Pound near Pugwash. When I moved to the South Shore, I discovered to my delight that it was lobster season throughout winter and spring. I willingly embraced the holiday traditions of my surroundings, adopting lobster as a family Christmas Eve event. Yes, my summer-season-lobster family has come to enjoy this new tradition too. Did you know that 40 per cent of all lobster landed in Canada comes from fishing Areas #33 and #34 on Nova Scotia's Southwest shore and is home to the Lobster Capital of Canada: Barrington. So go ahead, make Nova Scotia Lobster a part of your family traditions, year-round.

#4. WE SMELL GOOD: Go ahead, take a deep breath, fill your lungs with *Nouvelle-Écosse*. There's nothing like the smell of a blueberry field ready for picking in Cumberland Country in August (spent many summers raking those fields), being among the orchards in the Valley when they are ripe for the picking or strolling along our sea-salty shorelines draped in seaweed. Eau de Nova Scotia seeps into our pores, soaks into our soul. If you really want to make a relocated Nova Scotian feel homesick, whip out a bag of dulse and give them a whiff. I love seeing the reaction on their faces when they smell it, you can almost see the memories dancing through their minds. And no, most refuse my invite to eat some. All the more for me.

#5. THE WELCOME MAT IS ALWAYS ROLLED OUT: We hear it over and over. Guests from around the world and our neighbours echo the sentiment — Nova Scotians are such friendly people. We are kind, compassionate and generous in so many ways. We care and deep down; we want folks to feel welcome. From giving directions to recommending the best place to get seafood chowder, we're known to be one of the most charitable per capital in Canada — and no we won't laugh at how guests pronounce Kejimkujik or Tatamagouche… ok, we might chuckle a bit.

#6. WE'RE ROOTED IN CULTURE: For such a small province we're a potpourri of founding ancestors, including those arriving and evolving cultures that give us deep roots — and connect us, including the Mi'kmaq whose presence reaches back more than 10,000 years. Our ancestry is also a mix of European (including German) settlers, Acadians, Planters and Black Loyalists, to name but a few. Today, with the welcome mat rolled out to newcomers from across Canada and around the world, we are cultured in the truest sense of the word — you just need to be open to it, to embrace it.

#7. SURF'S UP: While you may associate surfing with California, Hawaii and other destinations, you can put Nova Scotia on this list of the places to surf in the world. Even Surfer Today named us one of their top places to surf. While summers offer more gentle breaks, it's the winter storms that kick up the great surf. Surfing is growing in popularity as a year-round sport for all ages. Head to the edge of the North Atlantic Ocean at Lawrencetown, Cherry Hill, Western Head, White Point or Yarmouth — or maybe you'll stumble across one of the surfing community's secret spots. Watching these water dancers gracefully moving to the rhythm of the ocean is beautiful. They make it look so easy, until you give it a try for the first time. Surfing is a lot of work but what an incredible way to experience and appreciate the power and saltiness of the ocean, and yes, it's very refreshing.

#8. WE'RE ILLUMINATING: Peggy's Cove is certainly the most well known lady of light around these parts, but we're surrounded by ocean with a coastline dotted with some 150 lighthouses. While many no longer serve as aids to navigation by sea, they certainly invite us to navigate, discover and explore our coastline. If you haven't soaked in sunset on Brier Island at the West Point Lighthouse, or taken in Dumping Day at Cape Forchue Lighthouse, or climbed the tower at Fort Point Lighthouse in Liverpool to toot the horn, or watched the sunrise perched at Peggy's Cove, promise me you'll visit at least one lighthouse each year. Go on do it. There are 150 reasons to visit our lighthouses. Why there's even one inland, where Nova Scotia connects to Canada via New Brunswick.

#9. WE'RE LOVELY, NATURALLY: Shaped and sculpted by 7,600 kms of coastline, as the second smallest province in Canada covering only 55,284 square kilometres, our landscape is lovely — naturally. From Meat Cove to Cape Forchu and out to Sable Island, there are more than 260 parks, wilderness areas and nature reserves where you can get off the highways and explore everything, from hiking the Highlands and the Skyline Trail to camping along the Atlantic at T.H. Raddall Provincial Park. Nestled within the heart of the interior is a real jewel, Kejimkujik National Park and National Historic Site. It's the only dual designated National Park in Canada and it is cherished for its wilderness. Keji is also the protector of rare and precious petroglyphs of Mi'Kmaq ancestors. The park has even become a Dark Sky Preserve.

#10. WE SOUND LOVELY, FROM THE OCEAN'S ORCHESTRA TO OUR ACCENTS: Close your eyes and just listen to the soundtrack of Nova Scotia. You'll hear the thunderous roar and smash of the sea symphony, the cobblestone rumbles and clatters as the ocean surf shakes and shifts them along our shoreline. Listen also to the beat of the drum at a Mawi'omi, or give in to the call of the bagpipes, both will move you to your soul. Listen to the wind dance in the trees, or a brook trickling. Listen for the endangered Piping Plovers who check into our shorelines from April to August to nest and raise their chicks before heading south again. Add to that the distinct accents of the fishermen in Southwest Nova, the uniquely Acadian or Gaelic dialects, the sound of the Mi'Kmaw language, a touch of German, and an ever-growing montage of Arabic, Mandarin and more.

If you just listen, you'll hear our orchestra play old favourites and new ones inspired, created and savoured. If you really want to listen, head outside at night — maybe guided by a full moon, or a rare blue moon (or a Ceilidh!) — and listen … just listen. You'll love what you hear.

The more I explore, the more I discover. Every day I am adding another place to visit, a festival to take in, a hike to tackle, a craft shop or gallery to appreciate and even more neat places to eat. I'm proud to be a Nova Scotian. I'm proud of who we are, what we stand for and for how much we have to offer willingly to each other, and to those who visit – or relocate to our shores.

Donna (Hachey) Hatt is Marketing and Product Development Manager at White Point Beach Resort. She says she gave up hyphenating many years ago because it sounded too much like a sneeze!

The Traveller's 12 Random and Wonderful Things About Nova Scotia

I have recently (summer 2017) returned from two weeks of travelling through Nova Scotia. Apart from biking the Cabot Trail on Cape Breton Island a few years ago, I had not been to what I call mainland Nova Scotia in more than 25 years, despite having lived there on two occasions in my life. It was interesting to see the province with fresh eyes and as a mature adult.

Here are 12 random observations I made about Nova Scotia.

#1. You can find homemade butter tarts in almost every cafe or even gas station you stop at.

#2. There is no shortage of antique stores. I love the old pieces of Nova Scotia pine that are much in evidence in these places.

#3. There are one heck of a lot of used lobster traps for sale around Nova Scotia. Some were offered for as little as $2.50.

#4. The best lobster roll I had was at The Rope Loft in Chester. I savoured every mouthful and went back twice.
#5. I've only ever seen signs offering pickled eggs and Solomon Gundy for sale in Nova Scotia. I didn't know people still ate pickled eggs.

#6. In June, lupines are everywhere. I never got tired of seeing field after field of them.

#7. People in Nova Scotia still hang out their laundry to dry; I think that's great. What a treat it is when you get to a place and sleep between sheets dried by sea breezes.

#8. Bear River is a small village where some of the stores and houses are built on stilts because of the tide. This might be an idea for those people in Calgary living along the river.

#9. You can get a big glass of wine in restaurants for $5 – and I'm not talking gut-rot kind of wine here. What a treat to pay those kinds of prices.

#10. You might think you're in Scotland when you go into cafés looking for food. Oats are big — and oatcakes seem to be *De Rigeur* as an offering.

#11. You can get amazing bowls of fish chowder in the most unlikely looking places — I especially liked the one from The Deck, on a rural road near Hubbards.

#12. The people I ran into in Nova Scotia were unbelievably friendly and very proud of their province. It was a breeze to be travelling solo, and surprisingly social, especially since I mostly stayed in B&Bs.

*Known as The Traveller, Leigh McAdam is founder of the blog, Hike Bike Travel (**http://hikebiketravel.com**). The preceding list was reprinted with permission from her post, "45 Random Thoughts About Nova Scotia" at **https://www.hikebike travel.com/ 26539/45-random-observations-nova-scotia.***

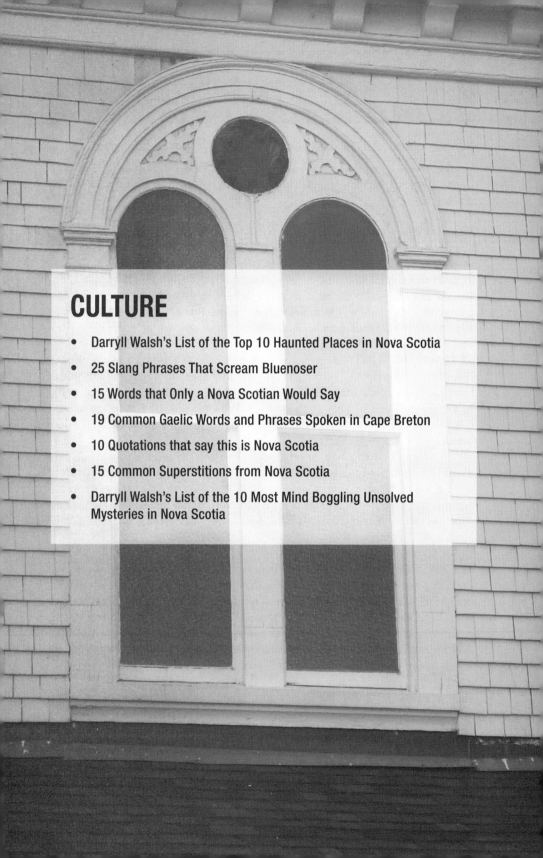

CULTURE

Darryll Walsh's List of the Top 10 Haunted Places in Nova Scotia

Being the birthplace of Canada (1605), Nova Scotia has an embarrassment of riches when it comes to haunted places. We've benefitted from a rich collage of cultural histories, superb researchers and an unending hunger for the supernatural among our citizens.

Here are the Top 10 Haunted Places in Nova Scotia — they include whole counties, lonely roads, dark woods, mystery islands and a bay of phantoms and treasure.

#1. CAPE BRETON ISLAND: Yes, the whole island. Arguably the most haunted place in Canada and unarguably the most varied in its horrors. Cursed land, witches, devils, forerunners, ghost ships, spook lights, horrible phantoms, fairies, ghostly animals and buried treasure are a traveller's nightmare, but a folklorist's dream.

#2. LUNENBURG COUNTY: Be prepared for the most haunted stretch of coastline in Nova Scotia. A potpourri of the strange and mysterious can be found not just in famously supernatural Mahone Bay but all along the Lunenburg coast. Think you'd be safer in the interior? That won't save you. You can't hide from marsh phantoms, witches, beckoning wraiths and ghostly lights trying to lead you astray into the dark woods.

#3. URBAN HRM: Not surprisingly, the urban centres of Halifax, Dartmouth, Bedford and Sackville boast the most densely concentrated ghostly phenomena in the province, with more being created everyday by those who see dollar signs rather than delicious fear in the guise of a phantom. Second only to Cape Breton Island for the variety of phenomena.

#4. BRUNSWICK STREET, HALIFAX: An unrecognized fact about one of the oldest streets in the city and once its western most boundary, is the number of haunted sites along, or close to, its course from North Street to Spring Garden Road. A number of haunted houses, pitiable phantoms, unearthly cries in the night and spook-infested older buildings such as Citadel Hill, The Town Clock, the old NFB building, the Memorial Library and, across from it, the Provincial Courthouse, all make this street the haunted heart of the city.

#5. THE SPOOK FARM, GUYSBOROUGH COUNTY: Four-and-a-half kms from the hamlet of Caledonia Mills the province's most powerful fire poltergeist reigned over this land and cursed it for well near a century. Frosh from St. Xavier University make a yearly pilgrimage to where they mistakenly believe the cursed land is located in order to usher in a new school year with a large bonfire. However, a careful eye is kept towards the dark woods where phantom black dogs once roamed, a vampire graveyard was said to have existed, mysterious fires occurred and a curse is still on anyone who dares remove any relic of the old McDonald Homestead where evil reigned for a few months in 1922.

#6. DAGGER WOODS, ANTIGONISH COUNTY: Hearing awful cries and unearthly screams — first from far away and moving gradually and unnervingly closer — is a common experience in these woods. Possibly related to a murderer who hid here once, or perhaps those of a demon, the famous Baucan or Bochdan, who calls to travellers and outdoor enthusiasts unaware of the evil in these dark woods. Nearby, strange sights of a fiery barrel flying across the sky near a salt water spring and the phantom of the Gray Man can be seen when the conditions are just right.

#7. BEECH HILL, ANTIGONISH COUNTY: The Gray Man, with his horrible features of pain and anger, wanders around Antigonish County and is often encountered here. So too the Bochdan from Dagger Woods can be seen when his usual haunts are lacking in human prey. Years ago, many a peddler or settler who ventured too far from the safety of hearth and home disappeared. This may have something to do with the strange odours, rattling chains and the frightening visage of a floating coffin that can still be seen on quiet nights when the air is still and the night its blackest.

#8. THE BLACK GROUND, GRAND A'NSE, RICHMOND COUNTY: The Black Ground is an uninhabited open space with the ruins of old foundations and ancient paths now overgrown and forgotten. Out of the dense overgrowth come piercing cries of unseen birds of prey. Strange grunts from unknown animals emanate from it. Human shapes, often of women in black, suddenly appear out of a strange mist. There are rumours of hidden treasure and maybe this is what the mysterious apparitions are searching for.

#9. OAK ISLAND, MAHONE BAY, LUNENBURG COUNTY: The world's most famous treasure isn't the only thing that haunts this island. A curse that says the secret of the treasure won't be discovered until seven men have died, phantom soldiers and sailors are seen prowling the woods, strange lights dance in the trees and a human skeleton at the bottom of one of the treasure shafts make this island one of the most haunted in Nova Scotia. Even a ridiculous reality television show can't kill the thrill most people get when they dream of what might be on the island.

#10. HIGHWAY 354, HALIFAX COUNTY: This section of the Beaver Bank Road from Kinsac Corner to the Beaver Bank Villa rates as the most unnerving stretch of road in Nova Scotia. They used to hang criminals at Kinsac; their death moans and cries can still be heard. Bigfoot as well as another creature, part dog and part wolf, with long white hair and glowing red eyes prowl the area. The Devil's footprints can be seen along a trail from the highway to Grand Lake. The Phantom, a figure in a long white cape that floats over the road at night, can be seen with its insane red eyes by unlucky drivers. Ghostly forms roam the Villa's abandoned grounds, and strange lights that many believe to be UFOs crisscross the sky near the old decrepit radar base.

Darryll B.D. Walsh, Ph.D. is an author and parapsychologist who has been investigating and analyzing trends in the paranormal for more than 20 years. The author of Ghosts of Nova Scotia *and* Legends and Monsters of Atlantic Canada, *Walsh is also the co-producer on various documentaries such as* Zombie Mania *and* City of the Dead: Halifax and the Titanic Disaster. *He has conducted major research projects on Bigfoot as well as the supernatural in Canada. His next efforts are an analysis of the supernatural element in the Jack the Ripper mystery as well as the study of the overlooked connections between witchcraft and vampirism.*

25 Slang Phrases That Scream Bluenoser

Every region of the world has its own distinct language. Words and expressions, nurtured and given meaning over time, inform the jokes we tell and provide those of us living here with a collective shorthand that identifies us as Nova Scotians or true Bluenosers.

Nova Scotia is blessed with a rich language. It is littered with words and expressions that vary from county to county and town to town. However, if you've ever really listened to a Nova Scotian speak, you may be left scratching your head and wondering what you've just heard. Sometimes, the words are so twisted that the phrase sounds foreign, but they're all ours.

Here is a list of 25 phrases that scream Bluenoser:

#1. A FACE ONLY A MOTHER COULD LOVE: Describing someone really ugly, as in, "The child has a face only a mother could love."

#2. A FLAT: Describing a flat tire or 24 cans of beer.

#3. ARE YOU COMING WITH?: Are you coming along with me when I leave?

#4. BED-LUNCH: Something you eat before going to bed at night.

#5. BETTER TO BE SAFE THAN SORRY: Always take precautions.

#6. BORN IN A BARN: Used to describe someone who never closes the door when they enter a house.

#7. CALM BEFORE THE STORM: A period when everything seems to be going well but you anticipate things will take a turn for the worse.

#8. CHEWING THE FAT: Having a casual conversation.

#9. DONE IN: Exhausted.

#10. DON'T POKE A PIG: Don't continue to argue with an angry person.

#11. DON'T BLOW A GASKET: Don't lose your temper.

#12. DUMPING DAY: The first day of the lobster fishing season, the day when lobster traps can be deployed.

#13. FISH OR CUT BAIT: Describing someone who has to make a decision.

#14. GIVE YOU AN INCH AND YOU TAKE A MILE: Describing someone greedy or who is never satisfied.

#15. HALF CUT: Used to describe someone who has been drinking but is not yet fully intoxicated.

#16. I COULD STRETCH A MILE BUT I AM TOO LAZY TO WALK BACK: Feeling tired.

#17. IT IS WHAT IT IS: Just accept things as they are.

#18. KNOCK WOOD/TOUCH WOOD: Said to maintain one's good luck.

#19. LET THE STINK BLOW OFF: Telling someone, mostly kids, to go outside and play and "let the stink blow off."

#20. MUD SEASON: Mid-March to mid-April when back roads and unpaved driveways become virtual tank traps. Sometimes Nova Scotians will say they have four seasons — winter, mud season and construction season, and hunting season.

#21. NO GRASS UNDER MY FEET: I don't waste time; I know how to get things done.

#22. ONCE IN A BLUE MOON: Describing something that happens only on rare occasions.

#23. POOR MAN'S FERTILIZER: A snowstorm that occurs later in March.

#24. RIGHT OUT STRAIGHT: Extremely busy.

#25. SOCKED IN: Really thick fog.

15 Words that Only a Nova Scotian Would Say

As with our expressions, Nova Scotians have a set of their own, distinct words. It's like we have our own language. The following are 15 words that only a Nova Scotian would say:

#1. ANTSY: Someone restless

#2. BIFF: To throw something as in, "Say that again and I'll biff this Timmy's cup at you."

#3. BOILING: Getting really angry or upset.

#4. CEILIDH: Common on Cape Breton, these informal social gatherings feature Scottish/Irish dancing, music and storytelling.

#5. CHESTERFIELD: Couch.

#6. DONAIR: A sandwich wrapped in pita bread that features spicy meat, tomatoes, onions and a distinctly Nova Scotian sauce which is sweet, creamy and garlicky.

#7. DRUNK: Describing a major party or someone who has had too much to drink.

#8. GIT: Get going.

#9. HARDSHELL: A lobster that hasn't molted yet.

#10. ISLANDER: Someone from Cape Sable Island.

#11. JEET: A question: did you eat yet?

#12. LOBSTAH: Mispronunciation of the word lobster.

#13. LUMPING: To remove scallops from a boat.

#14. PRITNEAR: I almost got it done.

#15. SUPPA: Lazy way of saying supper.

19 Common Gaelic Words and Phrases Spoken in Cape Breton

According to the Nova Scotia Museum, here are 19 common *Gaelic* words and phrases spoken in Cape Breton:

#1. CIAMAR A THA THU? : How are you?

#2. THA MI GU MATH: I'm well

#3. THA MI GLÉ MHATH: I'm great

#4. CIAMAR A THA THU FHÉIN? : How are you, yourself?

#5. BEANNACHD LEAT.: Goodbye

#6. DÉ AN T-AINM A TH'ORT? : What is your name?

#7. IS MISE... : My name is...

#8. CÓ ÁS A THA THU? : Where are you from?

#9. THA MI Á... : I'm from...

#10. TAPADH LEAT: Thank you

#11. 'SE DO BHEATHA: You're welcome

#12. SIN THU FHÉIN: Good job

#13. SUAS E! : Drive 'er! (said when you're enjoying someone's singing or playing)

#14. FÀILTE : Welcome

#15. THIG A-STAIGH: Come in

#16. DEAN SUIDHE: Have a seat

#17. GABH ÒRAN: Sing a song

#18. GABH PORT: Play a tune

#19. SIN AGAD E! : That's it!

10 Quotations that say this is Nova Scotia

Some of Canada's most influential politicians, writers and trendsetters have come from Nova Scotia and many of them have left their mark through the words they have written and spoken. Here is a list of quotations from 12 famous Nova Scotians that will resonate throughout history.

#1. JOSEPH HOWE, journalist and politician, was born in Halifax and said:

"My public life is before you; and I know you will believe when I say, that when I sit down in solitude to the labours of my profession, the only questions I ask myself are: What is right? What is just? What is for the public good?"

#2. THOMAS H. RADDALL, multi award-winning author, who was born in England and resided in Liverpool, Queens County, said:

"In the frantic world of today, with everything in a ceaseless uproar like a forest in a hurricane, it's a good thing to see that your roots go a long way down."

#3. SIR CHARLES TUPPER, politician, was born in Amherst and served as the Premier of Nova Scotia from 1864 to 1867. He led Nova Scotia into Canadian Confederation and went to become the sixth Prime Minister of Canada. He said:

"A privilege may not be a right, but, under the constitution of the country, but I do not gather that any broad distinction is drawn between the rights and privileges that were enjoyed and that were taken away."

#4. WANDA ROBSON, sister of early civil rights activist Viola Desmond, was born and raised in Halifax. She said:

"What happened to my sister is part of our history, and needs to remain intact. We

must learn from our history so we do not repeat it. If my parents were here today, it would warm their hearts to see Viola recognized as a true Canadian hero."

#5. ANGUS WALTERS, Bluenose captain, born in Lunenburg, said:

"The wood ain't growin' yet that'll beat Bluenose."

#6. SIR ROBERT BORDEN, Canada's Prime Minister from 1911 to 1920, lead the country during the First World War, and was the third Nova Scotian to hold the office. He was born in Grand-Pré, Kings County, and said:

"Let us never forget the solemn truth that the nation is not constituted of the living alone. There are those as well who have passed away and those yet to be born. So this great responsibility comes to us as heirs of the past and trustees of the future. But with that responsibility there has come something greater still, the opportunity of proving ourselves worthy of it; and I pray that this may not be lost."

#7. ROBERT STANFIELD, 17th Premier of Nova Scotia and the leader of the federal Progressive Conservative Party of Canada, was born in Truro and said:

"There's only one me, and I'm stuck with him."

#8. ALEXANDER GRAHAM BELL, inventor, was born in Edinburgh, Scotland but resided in Beinn Bhreagh, Victoria County. He said:

"Before anything else, preparation is the key to success."

#9. ANGUS L. MACDONALD, 14th Premier of Nova Scotia, was born in Dunvegan, Inverness County, and said:

"Nova Scotia is not the most prosperous part of Canada, but it is still, I hope, and always will be, I trust, a land where the higher things of life preserved inviolate, where religion is venerated, where education is cherished, where justice is fairly administered, where law is duly observed, where time-honoured virtue of hospitality is not for forgotten, where 'stranger' is still a sacred name."

#10. RICKY, from the Trailer Park Boys, played by actor Robb Wells, said:

"Once a trailer park boy, always a trailer park boy."

15 Common Superstitions from Nova Scotia

Red sky at night, sailors delight;
Red sky in the morning, sailors take warning.

This is, perhaps, the best-known superstition in Nova Scotia, but there are many others.

Superstitions are part of our heritage. These traditions are hand-me-downs from earlier generations and they are an important part of our heritage. They permeate our everyday existence, often on a subconscious level, but they are part of our lives nonetheless. Oftentimes, you just don't realize how superstitious you truly are and those of you who do realize, don't really want to admit it.

Following are 15 of the most common superstitions found in Nova Scotia:

#1. Knock on wood for good luck.

#2. It is said that one crow is bad luck.

#3. A bird hitting the window means someone you know is going to die.

#4. Seeing a forerunner (which is essentially someone who isn't there) is a sign of impending death.

#5. Dropping a dishtowel on the floor is a sign that a stranger or someone you have not seen for many years is going to visit your home.

#6. Women, redheads and pigs are not allowed on boats because they are all considered bad luck.

#7. It is bad luck to give the gift of an empty wallet or purse. Always make sure it contains money, even if it is just a few coins.

#8. If you kill the first snake you see in the springtime, it is said that you kill your worst enemy.

#9. Always sweep the dirt out the back door and not the front, or you will sweep away your friends.

#10. Always leave a house using the same door through which you entered or you will encounter bad luck.

#11. It is bad luck to walk under a ladder.

#12. Rocking a rocking chair with no one sitting in it means a certain death in the family will soon follow.

#13. If the bottom of your feet itch, it means somebody has been walking over the ground that will someday be your grave or it might also mean that you are soon going to walk on strange ground.

#14. Stabbing your knitting needles through your balls of yarn will bring bad luck to anyone who wears something made from that yarn.

#15. If spiders build their webs high off the ground in the summer and fall, it means lots of snow in the winter.

Darryll Walsh's List of the 10 Most Mind-Boggling Unsolved Mysteries in Nova Scotia

Nova Scotia is unique among Canadian provinces for its diversity in folklore and mysteries. Here are 10 of the most mind-boggling mysteries to be found in Canada's Ocean Playground.

#1. OAK ISLAND MONEY PIT: The question of treasure on Oak Island is Nova Scotia's oldest, and in terms of money spent (wasted?), its greatest mystery. Known worldwide, it's attracted the rich and famous, and spawned dozens of theories. The only thing buried for sure on the island is many men's dreams.

#2. SHAG HARBOUR PART 1: In October of 1967 lights were seen in the sky over southwestern Nova Scotia and witnesses believe something crashed into the waters off Shag Harbour. Some people believe it was an extraterrestrial craft while others believe it was meteorites or flares. The exciting debate continues annually at the Shag Harbour UFO Festival each October.

#3. SHAG HARBOUR PART 2: Days later a huge military presence was seen off Government Point, 25 miles from Shag Harbour. Those who believe in the alien theory of Shag Harbour think the crashed spacecraft moved up the coast and was discovered near one of the most sensitive military posts in the world at that time. Others believe that a Soviet submarine on an espionage mission was discovered and forced to retreat.

#4. IS NOVA SCOTIA THE VIKING'S VINLAND?: The Vikings had a settlement on Newfoundland at L'anse aux Meadows around the year 1000 CE. They also had butternut and wild grapes that are only found together in Northeastern New Brunswick, and thus would have likely been aware of Nova Scotia and Prince Edward Island as they explored the rest of the Gulf of St. Lawrence. Though no evidence exists for any settlement outside Newfoundland, the question of the extent of their territory, which they called Vinland, has been one of hot debate. Will some bemused farmer one day dig up the archaeological find of the century on a farm along the Northumberland Strait of Nova Scotia?

#5. THE AMHERST MYSTERY: Perhaps the most famous poltergeist in the world and found in most books on supernatural phenomena. Though a tame poltergeist in comparison to many others, it does have a catchy phrase associated with it, one guaranteed to send a shiver up the spine: "Esther Cox, you are mine to kill." Recently, author Charlie Rhindress has spearheaded efforts to commemorate the Esther Cox story in Amherst.

#6. MARY ELLEN SPOOK FARM: This more complex poltergeist occurred near Caledonia Mills in 1922. Fires, thrown knives, phantom black dogs and rumours of a vampire make this story perhaps unique among worldwide poltergeist reports. A recent book, Fire Spook: The Mysterious Nova Scotia Haunting by journalist Monica Graham, gives a balanced and in-depth account of this fascinating story.

#7. HALIFAX'S SECRET UNDERGROUND: A running debate in Halifax revolves around the exact nature of a series of tunnels running underneath the city's streets. A popular theory is that they were secret military tunnels to aid in the deployment of troops or in the retreat of the same from strong points such as Citadel Hill. That they exist is beyond question. Those who dismiss them out of hand say they were sewers and that the geology of Halifax is not conducive to a tunnel system, yet the facts would seem to indicate otherwise. The British were the best tunnellers in the world and the idea they would not have had created tunnels only in Halifax is patently ridiculous. But what were they for?

#8. THE MYSTERY HOUSE: Built in 1845, this house on King Street in Dartmouth has a connection to pirates, ghosts and the mysterious disappearance of Dr. John McDonald, Justice of the Peace and Governor of Dalhousie College. One winter evening, Dr. McDonald went out and didn't return. His disappearance piqued the interest of the neighbourhood, as some people reported a trail of blood in the snow. It was also believed that on the night of his disappearance, Dr. McDonald had in his possession a large sum of money. A skull was later found in a well, which was hidden under the floor in the basement. Though unconnected to his disappearance, the skull may be related to the famous Saladin mutiny. Even today the house is said to be haunted, but by who remains a terrifying mystery.

#9. MONSTERS IN THE NIGHT: Though not hospitable for hidden monsters, Nova Scotia does generate some amazing reports of Bigfoot, Phantom Cats, Devil Dogs and even our own version of the 1970s era Dover Demon that terrorized Pennsylvania, USA. They appear and disappear across the province from year to year. How could they get here? And where do they go?

#10. DID PRINCE HENRY SINCLAIR DISCOVER NOVA SCOTIA?: Long before Christopher Columbus landed in the New World in 1492, Prince Henry 1 Sinclair, Jarl of Orkney and Baron of Roslin is believed by some to have "discovered" North America by landing in Chedabucto Bay in 1398. He's often connected to the Knights Templar and their alleged search for the bogus Holy Grail. There is a granite monument to Sinclair's supposed landing at Halfway Cove and it is a popular and scenic place for picnicking as you ponder who was the first European to set foot on Nova Scotian soil.

Darryll B.D. Walsh, Ph.D. is an author and parapsychologist who has been investigating and analyzing trends in the paranormal for more than 20 years. The author of Ghosts of Nova Scotia *and* Legends and Monsters of Atlantic Canada, *Walsh is also the co-producer on various documentaries such as* Zombie Mania *and* City of the Dead: Halifax and the Titanic Disaster. *He has conducted major research projects on Bigfoot as well as the supernatural in Canada. His next efforts are an analysis of the supernatural element in the Jack the Ripper mystery as well as the study of the overlooked connections between witchcraft and vampirism.*

THE OUTDOOR EXPERIENCE

- Gerry Doucet's List of the Top 10 Fishing Holes in Nova Scotia

- Pam Wamback's List of the Top 10 Spots to Picnic in Nova Scotia

- Len Wagg's List of the 10 Best Places in Nova Scotia to Photograph

- The Top Seven Places to Surf in Nova Scotia

- Blackrattle's List of the Top 10 Geocaching Locations in Nova Scotia

- Alain Bossé's List of the Best Places To Go Fly a Kite In Nova Scotia

- Tristian and Angharad's List of the Top 10 Canoeing Spots in Nova Scotia

- Patricia Nelder's List of the Top 10 Places To Go Sailing in Nova Scotia

- A List of 19 Great Places To Go Sledding in Nova Scotia

- Astro Wayne's List of the Top 10 Favourite Places in Nova Scotia to View the Moon, the Stars, the Solar System or Anything Else That Happens to be in the Night Sky

- Scott Cunningham's List of the 10 Best Sea Kayaking Routes in Nova Scotia

- Joshua Peters' List of the Top 10 Best Dive Sites in Nova Scotia

- The Halifax Adventurer's 10 Best Beaches in Nova Scotia to Go Searching for Sea Glass

- David Currie's List of the Top 10 Places to Go Birdwatching in Nova Scotia

- Michael Haynes' List of the Best Trails in Nova Scotia

- Adam Barnett's List of the Top 10 Bike Rides in Nova Scotia

- A List of the Top 11 Places to Go Snowmobiling in Nova Scotia

Gerry Doucet's List of the Top 10 Fishing Holes in Nova Scotia

Although Nova Scotia is the second smallest province in Canada, it is surrounded by 7,500 kilometres of coastline. No wonder fishing plays an integral role in the hearts and habits of Nova Scotians.

I grew up on Cape Breton Island, the grandson of an inshore fisherman from Cheticamp. As a consequence, my earliest memories involve wharfs, boats, giant codfish and fishing gear. When I was small, we lived near the Canso Causeway and this contributed significantly to my growing fishing habit. In elementary school my brother and friends spent countless hours exploring local brooks and creeks with nothing more than fishing line wrapped around a stick, a couple sinkers, a hook and a bobber. This all fit comfortably in our back pockets. Net result — simple childhood joy that would continue into adulthood.

I have fished my whole life. I have worked on a commercial fishing boat as a mate. I have been a deckhand on charter boats. I'm a licensed fishing guide. Mostly I'm a recreational fisherman. My fishing travels have brought me all over Eastern Canada, but Nova Scotia has a special place in my psyche. Here are the places that are most meaningful, and as such, belong in my Top 10.

#1. CANSO CAUSEWAY: The gateway to Cape Breton Island or, as some Cape Bretoners say, the way to get to Nova Scotia. This is the place of my youth, steps away from my house. The fishing season began in June but July through September was peak season. We fished for Pollock, mackerel, perch, cod, smelts, hake, eels – pretty much anything that swam around the locks of the canal. Whales and seals were often nearby and the piers off the causeway gave a great platform to many recreational fishers. I still fish there today and have spent many wonderful hours with my children and wife.

#2. MARGAREE RIVER (INVERNESS COUNTY): This majestic river is a visual splendour, a gift to the Earth. It is Nova Scotia's premier Atlantic salmon river with anglers from across the planet making an annual trek to try their luck with the King of Fish. It is imbibed with a fine run of sea trout accompanied with a commercial run of gaspereau as well. In recent years, the feisty striped bass has found refuge in these clear waters. You can use gear and bait, but generally the river is restricted to artificial fly for the majority of the season, with peak salmon fishing from July to October.

#3. ST GEORGE'S BAY: North of the Canso Causeway separating Cape Breton and mainland Nova Scotia. Home of giant bluefin tuna, this large saltwater bay offers many fishing options — mackerel, smelt, cod, hake, herring, striped bass and flounder to name a few. Many pleasure boats enjoy the bay because it is relatively sheltered and offers access to viewing marine species such as harbour seals, grey seals, harp seals, pilot whales, minke whales, humpback whales and porpoises. The reigning world-record bluefin tuna was caught in these waters. Ken Fraser successfully wrestled this leviathan, weighing an outstanding 1,496 pounds in October of 1979. Primetime for fishing this body of saltwater is July through October.

#4. OCEAN LAKE (GUYSBOROUGH COUNTY): Located in what I believe is one of the most rural areas in mainland Nova Scotia islies Ocean Lake, where you can fine excellent brook-trout fishing. When many trout lakes become stale in the mid-summer heat, Ocean Lake continues to produce great fishing because it is spring fed, keeping the water temperatures moderated. I have a fishing camp on one of the islands that dot this large lake and throughout the years it has produced many quality fish and memories. Great fishing can be found during the entire fishing season.

#5. ST. MARY'S RIVER (GUYSBOROUGH COUNTY): The St. Mary's River is the largest drainage basin on the Mainland. Fifty years ago it was considered among the world's best Atlantic salmon rivers. The river was the central heartbeat of the local economy. Many celebrities cast a fly here, including baseball great Babe Ruth. Today the salmon fishing is closed, but the river is open to tremendous sea-run trout, shad, gaspereau and other migratory species. The river is characterized by a meandering course that drains four counties. Grassy undergrowth undulates and on bright summer days offers iridescent reflections in her currents. Today, the St. Mary's River Association is hard at work developing and executing a multi-year plan to enhance habitat, stabilize banks and deepen channels. This long-term plan aims to reestablish the mighty Atlantic salmon to historic levels last seen in the 1980s. I am particularly enchanted by the East Branch of the St. Mary's, but the river is very large and I still have much to explore. The best fishing experience under current regulations is found in June and July.

#6. SHUBINACADIE RIVER (CENTRAL NOVA SCOTIA): This Bay of Fundy river is located in the middle of the province and anglers can find easy access to its waters as the major highway between Truro and Halifax crosses over it. A wide river with characteristic red muddy banks, it provides a world-class stripe bass fishery along with an exciting American shad experience. Prime fishing is in the spring and early summer. This long river is characterized by its extreme tides. Dramatically changing water levels in the lower reachescan be dangerous to the inexperienced fisher. The mid-river and upper reaches of the Shubie flow in a consistent manner, which poses no safety threat to the angler. Unfortunately, the once mighty run of the Atlantic salmon has been all but decimated by the aquaculture farms in the Bay of Fundy.

#7. WEST RIVER ANTIGONISH: This river system offers a variety of angling experiences. It sources its water from the Highland areas of Antigonish County and it meanders its way through Antigonish County. Running directly through the heart of the Town of Antigonish, it slows its pace as it reaches the long estuary of

Antigonish Harbour, eventually emptying into St. George's Bay. Many species of fish are found in the West River including brook trout, brown trout, rainbow trout, Atlantic salmon, striped bass, shad, smelts and a few others. Trout fishing has been managed by the province with "Special Management Regulations," with the net result producing very large trophy fish. The Atlantic salmon fishery is amongst the best on the mainland. In 2012, I successfully battled the largest Atlantic I have ever landed, measuring 48 inches and nearly 40 pounds. The river has many fishable pools that are easily waded due to the even substrate, which is primarily gravel. Access is easy; there are roads on both sides of the river. Extensive habitat restoration has allowed for enhanced spawning for trout and salmon, resulting in excellent fishing opportunities. Primetime is the spring and the fall.

#8. RIVER PHILLIP (CUMBERLAND COUNTY): The waters of the River Phillip run through the Town of Oxford, considered the blueberry capital of North America. The river crosses the Trans-Canada Highway and has secondary roads that run up and down. Blessed with a long estuary, the Phillip eventually empties into the Northumberland Strait. This small-to-medium stream offers excellent angling throughout the full fishing season, from April to the end of October. Early season offers great trout fishing along with other migratory species including striped bass. In August, if the conditions are appropriate, the mighty Atlantic salmon arrive and continue arriving until the season closure on Halloween. Due to extensive efforts from local groups and volunteers, considerable habitat enhancements have occurred over the past few decades. Not surprisingly, the fishery has responded in a very positive manner. The River Phillip and the West River Antigonish are probably the two healthiest river systems on mainland Nova Scotia.

#9. BARNEY'S RIVER (PICTOU COUNTY): The Barney's (or as some of us call it, The Barnyard) is one of the wildest rivers left on mainland Nova Scotia. Located at the Pictou-Antigonish County line, its headwaters come from the surrounding Highlands. There is very little commercial or residential development on the river, nor is there any farming, thus allowing for its wild nature. Every year, considerable meandering occurs, ever changing the course of this small river. What is constant is a tremendous run of brown trout, many brutes in the 10 to 15 pound range. Accompanying these trophies, the Barnyard is blessed with a healthy run of fall Atlantic salmon. This is a high-water river, so when other nearby streams are unfishable after large rain events, the Barnyard is prime. This river is difficult to fish; it is only crossed by three bridges and the remainder if the river is challenging to access. Extra time and local knowledge is a must when taking on this Northumberland stream. Primetime is August to October, with some exceptional early-April fishing.

#10. MY BRAIN: As I write this overview in the closing days of February, I happily reflect on all the wonderful places I have fished in Nova Scotia. There are so many more places that are not included on this list, and I struggled with some of my selections. It is somewhat like being asked, "Who is your favourite child!"

THE OUTDOOR EXPERIENCE **41**

Because I grew up in Cape Breton, the places I outlined above are primarily in the north and eastern parts of the province. It should be noted that a disproportionate number of provincial records come from this part of the province, including one that belongs to my son. Hence, I am happy to live in this area. Nonetheless, the reader should be aware there are many other quality lakes, rivers, streams and shorelines to be found in this province that is peppered with lakes and marbled with rivers and streams.

I've had wonderful experiences chasing trout and salmon on the Musquodoboit River; fishing during a total solar eclipse on the Avon River; being surprised to find great urban fishing in the Halifax/Dartmouth area on Lake Loon, Albro Lake, Elbow Lake, Lake Major and many more.

Equally important, I think about all the conversations I've had with other anglers and their favourite waters. Many of these I have yet to wet a line in, but I continue to dream, on this February day, of the joy and comfort in the warming days of spring, the floating and drifting in a boat during the dog days of August and the exciting river migrations of trout and salmon in the fall. As Nova Scotians we are blessed to have this rich resource.

Gerry Doucet was born in Antigonish in 1965 and grew up on Cape Breton Island. He attended St. FX and after a stint in British Columbia he married his university sweetheart, Cyndy. Together they moved back to Antigonish to raise their four children. Fishing has always been a central theme throughout his life and he is never far from his fishing rod. Fly fishing, especially for Atlantic salmon, is his greatest thrill. He is actively involved in provincial fish policy and regulation and is an active member of local river associations.

Pam Wamback's List of the Top 10 Spots to Picnic in Nova Scotia

I have a cool job. I get to show off my home to hundreds of travel-media professionals from around the world on an annual basis. I get to tell them that while we may look small on the map, we are big on what we have to offer as a travel destination. They can experience changing landscapes, engage with a variety of cultures and dine on some of the best and freshest seafood in the world — all easily doable in the course of a day, no matter what part of the province they visit. I'm constantly filled with pride when I introduce them to the people and the places I am lucky enough to call home. And no wonder — with more than 7,600 km of shoreline, and an area of 55,284 square km, there's a lot of great adventures packed into Nova Scotia. I quite often get asked to share my "favourites" — favourite town, place for lobster, winery, park, live-music venue, favourite spot to photograph, etc.

It's never easy to answer. It's like trying to pick a favourite child — but there are some places I feel are quite magical in and of themselves that I'm always happy to share, like my favourite places for a picnic! I'm a person who loves the sound of the ocean, so quite often my favourite spots are not far from the sea or beach.

#1. POINT PLEASANT PARK, HALIFAX: It's easy to feel you are in the middle of nature here, when in actuality you are just minutes from the bustling streets of downtown Halifax.

#2. CRESCENT BEACH, LUNENBURG COUNTY: Crescent Beach is a 2 km long, 40 to 65 m wide crescent-shaped beach, with white sand, not far from the community of LaHave. The beach is known for its sandy dunes and windsurfing. Automobiles are permitted on the beach, which is rare in Nova Scotia. It's easy to find a spot all to yourself, pop the tailgate and enjoy a leisurely lunch as you watch the waves roll in.

#3. BLUE ROCKS, LUNENBURG COUNTY: I love the authenticity of this small fishing village. Quite often, I will pack a bagged lunch and head here for the afternoon to sit on one of the "blue rocks," catch up on my reading and watch the kayakers navigate the small coastal islands or, if I'm lucky, see the Bluenose II sail into Lunenburg Harbour.

#4. CLARK'S HARBOUR, CAPE SABLE ISLAND: It's one of the most southwesterly points of the province and I think one of the most authentic as well. I love to grab a lobster roll from Captain Kat's Lobster Shack and head to a nearby wharf to watch the fishermen unload their daily catches. You'd be surprised how many picnic tables you can find at the Living Wharves.

#5. CAPE FORCHU LIGHTHOUSE, YARMOUTH COUNTY: Peggy's Cove is a gem but I often tell my guests that we have dozens of Peggy's Coves around the province. Cape Forchu is one of them and the walking trail is easily accessible with great spots along the way for stopping and taking a break. I suggest making this one a dinner picnic stop and going as the sun sets. Finish your picnic as you gaze at the stars in this Starlight Tourism Destination.

(*Bonus*: A close second is Fort Point Lighthouse in Liverpool where Lane's Privateer Inn now offers a Lighthouse Picnic Lunch program daily in season. The lighthouse lunch comes packed in a wooden crate with cloth napkins, porcelain dishes and stainless cutlery. Choose from healthy and delicious selections that include lobster rolls, sandwiches on house-made breads, market salads, blueberry lemonade and house-made desserts. They offer kids lunches too.)

#6. LISCOMB RIVER TRAIL SYSTEM, GUYSBOROUGH COUNTY: This was one of the first projects I worked on when I started my tourism career, so it holds a special place in my heart. There are more than 20 km of inland and coastal trails, featuring beautiful waterfalls, a fish ladder and a swinging bridge — all great spots for a picnic lunch.

#7. INVERNESS BEACH, INVERNESS COUNTY: One of the best spots to find mermaid tears (aka beach glass) and the little take-out shack nearby makes a wicked good crab roll.

#8. GRAND PRE NATIONAL HISTORIC SITE: Okay, not exactly by the water but I love the beauty of the landscape in this UNESCO Heritage Site with Cape Blomidon in the background and farmland as far as you can see. Plus, knowing the history of this place always makes me pause, reflect and give thanks for what the people before us sacrificed so that we could call this place home.

#9. GREEN HILL PROVINCIAL PARK, PICTOU COUNTY: Green Hill Provincial Park, in the Northumberland Shore region (off Highway 104, 9 km east of West River), is a picnic park with magnificent panoramic views of the farmlands of Pictou County.

#10. SKYLINE TRAIL, CAPE BRETON HIGHLANDS NATIONAL PARK: With the Cabot Trail as your background you can't go wrong. Plus, Parks Canada now offers a picnic program so all you have to do is place your order and pick up your picnic basket and you're all set! Picnics are prepared from a choice of local favourites, such as The Bean Barn Café & Deli (Ingonish), Harbour Restaurant and Aaucoin's Bakery (Chéticamp), and Danena's Bakery & Bistro (South Harbour). Once you've had your fill, keep your souvenir Parks Canada picnic blanket and box to use again and again.

Pam Wamback is a Media Relations Specialist (Editorial) with the Nova Scotia Department of Tourism and Culture.

Len Wagg's List of the 10 Best Places in Nova Scotia to Photograph

The visual journey that Nova Scotia offers is as vast and varied as the changing weather. Not only do we have a diverse ecosystem but our geographical location, hanging on to the continent, means our weather and light change day by day, even hour by hour.

The different weather and geology means we can shoot a picture along the Fundy shore and miles away shoot a totally different landscape that looks like they are thousands of miles apart. It's the geology, along with the changing light, that make the province a clean canvas every day. You can be at one spot one day have it look bland while later on you can go to the same spot and have a stunning image. That said, there are a few spots that you can go to and be almost guaranteed to get a good image. These are some of my favourites.

#1. CAPE SPLIT PROVINCIAL PARK: I was in my early teens when I first made my way out to what has become a rite of passage for every Nova Scotian. Not only does the two-hour hike reward you with stunning views of the Bay of Fundy from hundreds of feet up, it also provides wonderful flora-and-fauna images along the way. Besides hiking there are boat tours you can do from the Parrsboro side, which give a totally different perspective. This perspective will also give you a better understanding of why you should stay away from the edges of the cliffs, which are actively eroding.

#2. LISCOMB RIVER/SHERBROOKE VILLAGE: This section of the province is stunning. The Liscomb River has a hiking trail that crosses a waterfall and it looks fantastic. There are numerous beaches to visit along the way. Sherbooke Village during the Christmas holiday becomes something from 100 years ago, lit up with tens of thousands of lights. A great place to go in the evening!

#3. CAPE CLEAR: While not on many roadmaps, this location is one of the best spots to take in the Cape Breton Highlands. After a drive on a wooded road that feels like it will go on forever, you reach the parking spot and in seconds are gazing down over a sheer cliff that takes in parts of the Margaree Valley. Watching the shadows of the setting sun along the valley below is truly a sight to see. If you go in the fall, the hardwood trees will not disappoint. The only way there in the winter is by snowmobile and there are signs that will show you the way.

#4. DUMP DAY AT CAPE FORCHU: One of the most spectacular cultural events happens in late November when lobster season starts. The sight of hundreds of lobster boats, motoring out together, slowly, as people line the shore at 6 a.m., gives you an understanding of the relationship this province has with the sea. It is a fantastic night/dawn image that has a great story to it.

#5. LUNENBURG: Everything about Lunenburg is great. The UNESCO town with lots of older buildings and colours make it a treat to shoot. The evenings make it really good as the setting sun bathes the town in a wonderful golden light.

#6. GRAND PRE AND SURROUNDING MEADOWS: The spire of St. Charles Church surrounded by massive trees with Cape Blomidon in the background is a fantastic image of the province's history. The story of the Acadians, and their expulsion, is a tragic tale. The memorial church and the gardens around it are a place you can photograph apple blossoms, ponds, wild birds, and massive willow trees.

#7. MAVILLETTE BEACH: Located between Metaghan and Yarmouth, Mavillette Beach is a fantastic place to lose yourself shooting. When the tide goes out you are left with kilometres of sand that have amazing rippled shapes. The beach is surrounded by dunes that are home to many birds and wildlife. The area is relatively dark so it is a great place for night images of stars as well.

#8. HALIFAX WATERFRONT: Walking the waterfront at dawn brings opportunities galore. There are the reflections of the buildings, ships at dock, early morning light on the entire scene, ships (including the ferry) moving back and forth. The options are endless.

#9. AMHERST SHORE COMPLETE WITH A HIKE THROUGH THE WETLANDS: The area is excellent for anyone looking for big-sky-type pictures. Grasslands that are teeming with birds make for an amazing experience. I've come across beavers, muskrats and foxes along this area. For those who look to the modern approach, there is a wind farm that makes for some interesting shots as well.

#10. PEGGY'S COVE: The go-to place for anyone visiting Nova Scotia. It is a draw for people wanting to experience the wild Atlantic Ocean along with the charm of a working fishing village. I don't go when there are crowds. My best advice is to get out there before sunrise or to stay until sunset; that's when the best light is. Also, there are numerous hiking trails that are just outside the town that provide some amazing vistas for shooting.

Len Wagg's photographs have appeared in newspapers, magazines and books all over the world. He is author of seven books on Nova Scotia and in 2008 won the Award for Excellence in Illustration for his book Wild Nova Scotia.

The Top Seven Places to Surf in Nova Scotia

According to a national list released by the Canadian Surfing Association in January 2018, here are the top seven places to surf in Nova Scotia:

#1. SUMMERVILLE: Located near Port Mouton, Summerville is a beach break located near a river mouth. It works best with Atlantic E/NE/SE swells, and winds blowing from NW.

#2. WHITE POINT BEACH: Located in front of a resort with the same name, White Point Beach is one of the busiest surf breaks in the region. The place is idyllic, and the multiple peaks offer a lot of options. It works best with Atlantic E/NE/SE swells, and winds blowing from NW.

#3. WESTERN HEAD: Located near Liverpool, Western Head is a reef break ready to pump long and big left-handers. For perfect conditions, get there when an NE swell meets NE/N winds.

#4. POINT MICHAUD BEACH: Located at Michaud Cove, this long sandy beach is capable of producing the finest waves in Canada. For pristine surf sessions, get to it with an E/NE/SE swell, and W/NW winds.

#5. OSBORNE: Located at Cow Bay, Osborne is a consistent right-hand point break protected from onshore winds. Despite the occasional strong rip currents, it offers decent surfing conditions all-year-round. Go for it with S/SW/SE swells and windless conditions.

#6. LAWRENCETOWN BEACH: Located 20 kms east of Halifax, Lawrencetown Beach is a popular south-facing, sand-and-cobble beach with strong rip currents, and several peaks. On big swell days, the left-hander opens a sizeable barrel. At the center of the beach, there's a wave for longboarders and beginners.

#7. MARTINIQUE BEACH: Hailed as the longest sandy beach in Nova Scotia, Martinique Beach is a five-kilometer white sand sanctuary located south of Musquodoboit Harbour. It is one of the best breaks in the region during summer.

Blackrattle's List of the Top 10 Geocaching Locations in Nova Scoita

First of all, my real name is Dave Brown. We all use nicknames online and Blackrattle is my name. My wife, Melinda, and I have been geocaching since April 2009.

To compile this list, I talked to many geocachers and did an online survey to find the top 10 geocaching locations in Nova Scotia. The overall theme I see is that most gave spots that are a combination of cache density (number that can be found in a day), uniqueness of caches and the quality of the scenery at the location.

I will give the top 10 from the online poll, which seems to track pretty well with what people told us in person, with one exception. The very first geocache in Canada is located in Nova Scotia, near East River. I think it is one of the most visited geocaches in the province but it did not make the list because it is a single cache and may not have been perceived as a location. I think it needs to be on the list as it is a must visit for many serious geocachers.

Geocaching is a sport/hobby that uses a GPS to find containers hidden by other players. The coordinates of the containers are found on the website geocaching.com. The website was made possible when on May 1, 2000, the built-in error of most civilian GPS units, selective availability, was eliminated. On May 3, 2000, Dave Ulmer decided to test the new system's effectiveness by placing a container in the woods and uploading the coordinates to a message board. It was found within hours. A new sport was born.

On June 28, 2000 the first geocache in Canada was placed near East River. The name of this cache is GCBBA and was the 51st cache placed worldwide. This cache is now the 20th oldest cache in existence. It is a must-visit cache for both locals and visiting geocachers.

The following list was compiled through chats with other geocachers as well as from our personal experiences. Most of these spots are of the "unique geocache" or "scenic area" variety. Enjoy your hunt for geocaches.

Here are the Top 10 geocaching locationsand the reasons they are so popular:

#1. TANCOOK ISLAND (27 VOTES): Beautiful scenery, unique caches and a good number of caches.

#2. COSBY'S LIVERPOOL SCULPTURE GARDEN (19 VOTES): Unique scenery, unique caches and dragons.

#3. CAPE BRETON HIGHLANDS (14 VOTES): Beautiful scenery and lots of caches.

#4. CAPE FORCHU NEAR YARMOUTH (11 VOTES): Beautiful scenery, iconic lighthouse, lots of caches, unique caches and tourist gateway.

#5. BLUE ROCKS/STONEHURST IN LUNENBURG COUNTY (10 VOTES): Beautiful scenery, unique landforms and lots of caches to find.

#6. KEJIMKUJIK NATIONAL PARK (9 VOTES): Beautiful scenery, backcountry caches and accessible to all levels and ages

#7. BRIER ISLAND (9 VOTES): Beautiful scenery, lots of lighthouses and lots of caches.

#8. CAPE SABLE ISLAND (9 VOTES): Beautiful scenery, lots of caches and unique caches.

#9. MCNAB'S ISLAND (7 VOTES): Beautiful scenery, lots of history, lots of caches and seclusion.

#10. LUNENBURG (6 VOTES): Lots of caches, lots of restaurants and great scenery.

Alain Bossé's List of the Best Places To Go Fly a Kite In Nova Scotia

My love affair with flying kites came as a fluke when I was looking for ideas on how to do something to increase gift-shop revenue at the Pictou Lodge Resort. I decided one day to start selling a few kites and thanks to our waterfront location it was an instant hit.

I followed the festivals and I was hooked. I now have more than 100 kites in my collection, ranging from a 20-foot lobster to basic deltas. They all give me the pleasure of flying and total relaxation. Flying a kite always brings out the kid in me. I love it. There are so many places to fly a kite in Nova Scotia in all four seasons but these are my top picks. Enjoy!

#1. THE KILTED CHEF FARM: Pictou County.

#2. THE QUARTERDECK BEACHSIDE VILLAS & GRILL: Summerville Beach, Queens County.

#3. TANTRAMAR MARSH: Amherst.

#4. CITADEL HILL: Halifax.

#5. INGONISH BEACH: Inverness.

#6. JOGGINS CLIFFS: Near Joggins.

#7. CAPE D'OR LIGHTHOUSE: Advocate Harbour.

#8. GREENHILL LOOK OFF: Greenhill Provincial Park in Pictou County.

#9. BELLE COTE: Inverness County.

#10. FORTRESS OF LOUISBOURG: Cape Breton.

#11. PEGGY'S COVE: St. Margaret's Bay.

Alain Bossé, also known as the Kilted Chef, has travelled the world from kitchens to convention centres sharing his expertise and love for buying and eating local ingredients with people near and far. With his signature tartan kilt, proud Acadian heritage and undeniable flair for cooking with local ingredients, he has earned a reputation as Atlantic Canada's culinary ambassador.

Tristian and Angharad's List of the Top 10 Canoeing Spots in Nova Scotia

Canada's Ocean Playground is not the first region that comes up when talking about freshwater canoeing in Canada, but Nova Scotia has some fantastically wild waterways that are underappreciated and easily accessed. Canoeing is a very low-impact form of wilderness travel and is a traditional way to explore the backwoods of our province.

This is a list of 10 great places to go canoeing in Nova Scotia. We have included a range from easy day-trips suitable for beginner canoeists or families to remote wilderness areas with opportunities for multi-day trips; there is something for everyone.

#1. KEJIMKUJIK (*KEJIMKUJI'JK*): Central Nova Scotia
Difficulty: Beginner-Advanced (depending on the trip)
Season: May-November, while the park is open

Kejimkujik National Park and Historic Site is focused around several beautiful lakes and rivers. Visitors can stay at the car-access campsites in the park and rent a boat from the park outfitter for a day trip on Keji Lake to explore some more peaceful parts of the front-country. There are also many options for multi-day canoe trips, in some of the beautiful backcountry campsites. There are a series of well-maintained portages that allow canoeists to access the more remote lakes (and islands of old-growth hemlock), and there is a lake-loop route that is possible if you are a brave portager. The park also offers the lake loop as a guided trip for those who are keen to experience the backcountry but not confidant enough to take it on independently.

#2. ANNAPOLIS RIVER: Annapolis Valley
Difficulty: Beginner
Season: Summer-Fall (high water in spring makes this river more difficult to navigate)

The Annapolis river canoe route is 80 km long, beginning as a meandering stream in woodlands near Kingston and flowing down the centre of the Annapolis Valley past towns and agricultural fields, ending as a large and deep river where it meets the sea at Annapolis Royal (Tewopskik). While the river picks up speed as it approaches the sea, even the tidal section of this river (below Paradise) is relatively calm and slow-moving. That said, the lower section becomes quite exposed and paddling there on windy days should be avoided. Because the river passes through so many towns, there are plenty of opportunities to put in and take out a boat, so paddlers can make their trip on the Annapolis River as short or long as they like.

#3. BLUE MOUNTAIN BIRCH COVE LAKES WILDERNESS AREA: Halifax Reginal Municipality (HRM)
Difficulty: Beginner-Intermediate (depending on how much portaging you do)
Season: Anytime the lakes aren't frozen

This wilderness area is surprisingly large and wild considering its proximity to Halifax (kjipuktuk) and, remarkably, is known to be inhabited by mainland moose. There is an ongoing effort to protect it as a regional park, but as of yet it remains a wilderness area, with relatively minimal infrastructure. It is a perfect place for canoeing, with many lakes that can be explored as day-trips (especially handy for HRM residents), and a solid six to eight-hour portaging loop if you want a workout. Camping is also allowed in the wilderness area, although there are no established campsites.

#4. SHUBENACADIE CANAL AND RIVER SYSTEM (*S K PNE'KATIK*): Fundy/HRM
Difficulty: Beginner-Intermediate (depending on the section)
Season: Anytime the lakes aren't frozen

This route takes travellers clear across the province from the Bay of Fundy to the Halifax Harbour. It was used for centuries by the Mi'kmaq before an early settler government decided to develop the route by building a canal system to eliminate portages. Start in Shubie Park in Dartmouth, where there are boat rentals available, and paddle upstream to Lake Charles for an afternoon of exploring. To do the whole route, start in Lake Banook and make your way up through a series of lakes, eventually reaching the Shubenacadie River, which meanders down to the Fundy (this is a comfortable two-day trip). Keep in mind that the end of the Shubenacadie River is tidal and could be considered class IV or V due to the tidal bore — make sure that you take out before the tidal section or carefully plan your timing with an outgoing tide.

#5. MARGAREE RIVER (*WIAQAJK*): Cape Breton
Difficulty: Intermediate (Class II)
Season: Spring/Fall or after a heavy rain

The Margaree River, designated a heritage river in 1998, is a long river with two branches that flow from the Cape Breton Highlands, join at Margaree Forks, and reach the sea at Margaree on the west coast of Cape Breton. There are many places to put in and take out your boat, so this river is well suited for single or multi-day trips. The river is relatively fast moving but features many deep pools and is well known by sport fishermen for its healthy population of Atlantic salmon, which spawn in the clear and cold waters of its upper reaches.

#6. ST. MARY'S RIVER (*NAPU'SAQNUK*): Eastern Shore
Difficulty: Intermediate (Class II)

St. Mary's River is a beautiful wild river on the Eastern Shore and a well-known Atlantic salmon spawning ground. It flows with a moderate current through a hilly landscape of Acadian forest, smooth paddling interspersed with some class I and II rapids. The river has three branches, but the 77-km trip down the west branch beginning in Trafalgar is most highly recommended. That route takes two to three days to complete, though there is plenty of opportunity to modify the trip length since the river mostly follows the road and as such has many accesses.

#7. MUSQUODOBOIT RIVER (*MUSK TO'PUKWEK*): Eastern Shore
Difficulty: Intermediate (Class II, possibly Class III in high water conditions)
Season: Summer, ideally

The Musquodoboit River is a long, relatively easy river to paddle, and is another traditional and ancient Mi'kmaw transportation route. The river flows through rolling wooded hills and farmland and makes for a fantastic three-day trip, passing by some impressive granite escarpments on the last day. The main section of the river begins near Middle Musquodoboit and ends just above the rapids at Musquodoboit Harbour., Paddlers can start farther upstream in Upper Musquodoboit if water levels are high.

#8. TANGIER GRAND LAKES WILDERNESS AREA (*WOSPEGEAK*):
Region: Eastern Shore
Difficulty: Advanced

The Mi'kmaq name for this area, *Wospegeak*, means "sunshine is reflected from water." Like most of the Eastern Shore the Tangier landscape is wild and rugged, with an undulating glacial landscape of old-growth hemlock stands and hardwood hills interrupted by lakes, streams, bogs and barrens. The trip is 35-km long and has 19 portages that link the many streams and lakes, including Tangier Lake, which is the largest lake in Nova Scotia without a road access. Because this wilderness area is so infrequently travelled, some of the portages can be difficult to find or follow, so it is critical for travellers to bring a GPS or map and compass to help with navigation. This is a trip for the adventurous.

#9. TOBEATIC WILDERNESS AREA (*TUPSIA'TUKJI'JK*): Southwest Nova Scotia
Difficulty: Advanced

The Tobeatic Wilderness Area, adjacent to Kejimkujik National Park, is the Maritime's largest expanse of wilderness, touching five counties and covering a total of 120,000 hectares. It contains an incredible diversity of landscapes, from rich Acadian forests to harsh acidic bogs, calm clear lakes to exciting white-water rivers. Parts of the current wilderness area have been under some form of wildlife management since the 1920s, and in the 30s several warden cabins were built so that the area could be monitored. Recently, two of them have been restored, and are open for the public to stay in (marked 'C' on the map) — if you can get there. The Tobeatic can be accessed via logging roads from the Annapolis Valley, or through Kejimkujik. With more than 100 lakes (and at least 50 established portages) there is nearly endless potential for trips ranging from a day to over a week in length.

#10. ANYWHERE THERE IS WATER: Nova Scotia (or elsewhere)
Difficulty: Various

It turns out you can go canoeing just about anywhere. Maybe there's a lake you've seen from the highway, a protected ocean cove you've always wanted to explore, or an unnamed creek that runs through your backyard. Best-of lists only go so far; part of the fun of canoeing is exploring new places and getting away from developed areas. While crossing private land requires permission, all bodies of water in Canada belong to the crown and citizens have the right to travel on them, if they can get to them. Many lakes and rivers have public accesses, and many more are within crown land to begin with. Finding a new route can be really rewarding and exciting, so get out there and enjoy the water.

Tristan Glen loves all things outdoors. With a background in environmental science and engineering he has worked in renewable energy, conservation, and as a hiking, rafting, and cycling guide.

Angharad Wylie has been canoe tripping, hiking and camping since she was a kid in Ontario and Quebec. She works as a GIS technician and cartographer at an urban planning and design studio in Dartmouth, NS.

Patricia Nelder's List of the Top 10 Places To Go Sailing in Nova Scotia

So you like to sail but you really have no idea where to go. I suggest you try anyone of these locations. They are perfect for the novice or the most experienced sailor:

Cape Breton Island

#1. CRAMMOND ISLANDS: West Bay, Bras D'Or Lake

#2. ST. PETER'S INLET: St. Peter's Marina

#3. THE ST. PETER'S CANAL AND BATTERY PARK

#4. THE MUNICIPAL WHARF: Baddeck

5. D'ESCOUSSE ANCHORAGE OR TOWN WHARF: Isle Madame

Lunenburg

6. ZWICKER WHARF: Town of Lunenburg

Mahone Bay

7. TANCOOK ISLAND

8. CHESTER: Back Harbour

9. ATLANTICA: Oak Island Marina

10. MAHONE BAY ISLANDS: Any of the the Mahone Island Conservation Association Stewarded Islands in Mahone Bay

Patricia Nelder is the Executive Director of the Atlantic Marine Trades Association/ Boating Atlantic.

A List of 19 Great Places To Go Sledding in Nova Scotia

After a big snowfall, kids and kids-at-heart love zooming down the fresh powder of a nice, steep slope. If you're not lucky enough to have a huge snowy hill in your own background, here are some great sledding destinations across the province:

Halifax

#1. CITADEL HILL: It's a natural first choice because it's easy to find with lots of parking and it's right in beautiful downtown Halifax. But be careful and look before you slide so you don't wind up careening into traffic! There are also lots of nearby cafes to visit for a hot drink when you're done.

#2. ASHBURN GOLF CLUB: This is a long-time favourite in Halifax's west end and you'll often see a large crowd here on a snowy afternoon. You're safely away from the road and there's even a spot for snowboarders who want to do tricks.

#3. THE MOTHER HILL: Located behind Mount Saint Vincent University, this hill has a few different access points and a nice steady incline. It's undoubtedly one of the top sledding spots in the neighbourhood.

#3. GORSEBROOK JUNIOR HIGH SCHOOL: This south-end sledding mecca has multiple inclines for sledders of different abilities — from timid preschoolers to thrill-seeking teens and adults. You can find the school at 5966 South St.

#4. BRIGHTWOOD GOLF CLUB: A popular sledding spot in Dartmouth is Brightwood Golf Club — located at 227 School St. — which has multiple hills that get plenty of snow.

Northumberland Shore Region and Cape Breton

#5. KEPPOCH MOUNTAIN: Located minutes from exit 30 on Highway 104, the Keppoch recreation facility is open year-round for a variety of activities, including a big hill and a kiddie hill for tobogganing in addition to its extensive 20-km trail system, also used for cross-country skiing and snowshoeing. Because it is a private facility, visitors are asked to sign a consent form located on site or on their website. A lodge with amenities is open on site on winter weekends.

#6. MCCULLOCH HILL: Pictou area residents refer to McCulloch Hill on the lands of McCulloch House Museum and Genealogy Centre on Haliburton Road, across from the Maritime Odd Fellows Seniors home and just down the road from the town's hospital. The parking lot is cleared in the winter although it may take a bit longer after a big storm. The museum and genealogy centre is open during the week.

#7. STELLARTON: Albion Baseball Field is the only sledding site the municipality of Stellarton promotes. It's a popular destination. The hill is adjacent to Allan Park on Albion. The site is inspected regularly for safety and the marked area gives coasters a pretty long run. Helmets are recommended.

#8. MIRA: Two Rivers Wildlife Park offers winter frolics from coasting to sleigh rides. There are several hills on open fields that allow for all ages and abilities. The canteen and amenities are open only during special occasions like Winter Frolic in February, but park admission prices ($7 adults, $5 students/seniors, free for children under two years) allows you to also access the wildlife park and trails.

#9. NEW WATERFORD: Colliery Lands Park on Ellsworth Avenue is where locals go in New Waterford. There is a playground and off-leash dog park too. The park opened to mark the site of two former collieries and pays tribute to the men who died in the Island's worst mining explosion in 1917.

#10. SOUTH BAR: The coast is clear on this popular hill since the former South Bar School was demolished this past fall, but the CBRM property is expected to be redeveloped for the port's use. But for now, when the snow falls, the sleds all come out, say the locals.

Valley, Tri-County and South Shore

#11. RIVER HILLS GOLF COURSE IN CLYDE RIVER, SHELBURNE: In Shelburne County, a favourite sledding spot for locals is the River Hills golf course in Clyde River. The hilly terrain well off the road is a little bit of a trek, but the thrill of the downhill ride makes the effort worthwhile. Many families and children take advantage of the recreational opportunity on winter afternoons when a blanket of snow covers the fairways.

#12. FORT ANNE, ANNAPOLIS ROYAL: While it's not promoted as a sledding destination by Parks Canada, the super-steep embankments of Canada's first national historic site is sure to create some memorable moments in sledding history, as they have for generations. The grounds are open year-round, but there is no winter maintenance of the parking lot except a small fire lane. Much of the fort's ramparts are tucked safely away from road traffic and clear of trees. A visit to some of the town's quaint cafes is a warming experience, too.

#13. HANTSPORT: The Hantsport Memorial Community Centre encourages coasting on the hill behind Churchill House. There are only a few trees on the side to avoid. Parking is available about 100 feet from the hill, in the upper parking lot, with overflow available in the lower lot by the outdoor ice rink, about a two-minute hike away.

#14. MUNICIPAL ACTIVITY & RECREATION COMPLEX, DAYSPRING: The MARC, as it is known locally, is managed and maintained by the Municipality of the District of Lunenburg. It has two popular toboggan runs nestled in a scenic area. The runs end at each side of a frozen pond used for family skating.

#15. YARMOUTH LINKS GOLF COURSE: When it snows in Yarmouth, kids and families head to the golf course in Yarmouth — a tradition that dates back many generations. It's a safe area to sled with a clear treeless path to the bottom of the hill. The only downfall is the walk to get back to the top. It can be a bit of a workout.

Amherst and Truro

#16. AMHERST: Technically, Fort Beausejour is in New Brunswick, but close enough to Amherst for hosting the coasting for adventure-seeking Nova Scotians. On your way back, you can stop into the Aulac Big Stop to fill those hungry bellies with some heart-warming favs, or any number of restaurants and shops in Amherst.

#17. PARRSBORO: A popular spot for tobogganing is at the Don Yorke Memorial Ballfield on Upper Main St., where coasters slide down a medium-grade hill and right through the field. The parking lot is usually plowed. The site is across from the Home Hardware, handy in case you need repairs to your toboggan.

#18. TRURO: You may not find Legion Hill on a map because it's named for its location behind the Royal Canadian Legion off Brunswick Street. A steep hill, which can get icy and makes for an accelerated coast and a slower walk back up. It's handy to downtown Truro's shops and restaurants for post-coast activities.

#19. BIBLE HILL RECREATION PARK: Located on Guest Road, just off College Road, the Cobequid trail system wraps around the hill that is visible and close to the plowed parking area. Coasting areas are clear and there are some gentler areas for smaller children. Picnic shelters and a playground make this park a popular spot for families. Signs are posted requesting that sledders wear helmets.

This list, which appeared in Tidings *in December 2017, was compiled by Lindsey Bunin, Manager, Custom and Community Publishing. It is reprinted with permission from* The Chronicle Herald, *A member of the Saltwire Network.*

Astro Wayne's List of the Top 10 Favourite Places in Nova Scotia to View the Moon, the Stars, the Solar System or Anything Else That Happens to be in the Night Sky

I based my picks for these sites on their accessibility, low horizon and relatively dark skies, free of stray light. My last pick shows that dark skies are not a necessity to enjoy the sky.

These are just a few picks but Nova Scotia offers so many beaches, ball fields and parks that are all waiting for you to visit so LOOK UP!

#1. KEJIMKUJIK NATIONAL PARK: Keji is a Dark Sky Preserve that offers some of the darkest skies in Nova Scotia. Two areas within the park for viewing are

Merrymakedge Beach and the Sky Circle at Jeremy's Bay. Arrive at the beach as the sun is setting and watch as the stars take over the sky or take a seat the large circular platform in the Sky Circle and enjoy the overhead skies. There is also a cement pad located here to set up a telescope.

#2. BEACH MEADOWS BEACH: The beach is located in Queens County and is a personal favourite of mine. The boardwalk down to the beach has a seating platform for relaxing and enjoying the dark star-studded sky, with either your naked eye or optical aid like binoculars or telescope.

#3. SWISS AIR 111 PEGGY'S COVE MEMORIAL: This one comes recommended for its dark skies and superb southern sky views.

#4. TWO RIVERS WILDLIFE PARK: Located in Cape Breton on the Mira River, this site offers dark sky views to the south and east. An observatory on site for night sky programs is available.

#5. TUSKET: Located on Tittle Road on Surrette's Island. This one comes recommended also because of its inky black skies.

#6. NELSON MEMORIAL PARK: This park, located in Tatamagouche, is recommended because of its easy accessibility and views of the north sky.

#7. BLOMIDON LOOK-OFF: Go up the mountain in the valley and enjoy the unobstructed, superb views of the sky.

#8. GRAVES ISLAND: This beautiful park with high ground located in Chester offers excellent views of the southern sky.

#9. FIVE ISLAND PARK: Splendid views of the sky can be seen from the east to the southwest in this park located near Parrsboro.

#10. FORT ANNE HISTORICAL SITE: This recommendation many not be the darkest site but it offers a chance to see bright objects such as the moon, brighter planets like Jupiter, Saturn and Venus, or brighter stars.

Wayne Mansfield, better known as Astro Wayne to those in the astronomy world, has had an interest in astronomy since he was a young boy growing up in the Space Race era in the 1960s. Among his collection of telescopes and binoculars is the first scope purchased for him at age 12, more than 50 years ago.

Scott Cunningham's List of the 10 Best Sea Kayaking Routes in Nova Scotia

If you're looking for a unique way to discover the biology, geology and human history of the pristine wilderness of this province then sea kayaking is the best way to do it and these 10 routes are the best in Nova Scotia.

#1. TANGIER HARBOUR: The waters between Murphy Cove and Tangier Harbour are known as Shoal Bay, and as the name implies, it is a shallow basin with numerous reefs, islets and islands. These create diversity as well as some protection from the open sea. It is close to Halifax but offers a degree of the seclusion common to more remote areas. All the islands in the Tangier grouping are crown owned and have a variety of exceptional campsites. Several interesting day-long and weekend excursions are possible and you can put in or take out at many different spots. Beautiful sand beaches, protected lagoons, seal and sea bird colonies and hidden homestead remnants will make this a charming and fascinating paddle route. Mussel beds and clamflats can add to the evening meal. Although not yet inundated with paddling visitors, this has become one of the more popular locations.

#2. BAY OF ISLANDS: I first explored this neglected paradise in 1975 and it was my introduction to our coastal islands. It seemed worlds removed from the inland waterways and planted the seed for my eventual circumnavigation of the province in a canoe. The Bay of Islands is appropriately named. It has one of the largest concentrations of islands, islets and shoals along the entire coastline and was known to explorers as early as Champlain (who gave them their name: Baye des Isles).
Fishermen built shanties and lobster-trap depots on some islands, but permanent settlers never arrived. It was far too rugged and inhospitable and the isolation contrasts sharply with Tangier Harbour. The tiny remote islands attract the seabirds and some of the outer islands have been designated sanctuaries.

#3. CANSO ISLANDS: Because of its distance from Halifax, this route will probably be one of the last along the Eastern Shore that a coastal paddler will visit. However, it is well worth the long drive. In many ways, its rugged beauty is reminiscent of remote shores in Newfoundland, consisting of rugged granite, much like the Peggy's Cove barrens but without the people. Trees are scarce and stunted and there are numerous shallow lakes and bogs. Glacial erratics perched in various unusual places and positions makes it seem as if it was only recently that the ice sheet scoured the region. The islands, some no larger than a house, hug the highly indented shoreline, often coalescing at low tide and its hidden coves, narrow channels, offer something different around each corner. Most of this route borders public land (one of the provinces protected areas) and there are numerous campsites.

#4. LOUISBOURG TO MAIN-A-DIEU: Sometimes I stumble upon a new gem and this was the case along the northeastern tip of Cape Breton Island. Between Louisbourg and Main-a-Dieu the wide beaches, sand spits and drumlin headlands have mutated into a serrated shoreline where little glacial till remains. Indentations of exposed volcanic bedrock present a broken shoreline where, in a calm sea, you can weave in an out of these rock gardens in a seemingly endless progression of passages — a paddler's delight where you can pick and choose depending on your skill and interest. This route is exposed (although here there are plenty of landing options) and should be avoided in a rough sea. Most of the perimeter is public and the open terrain has some great hiking trails and extraordinary campsites.

#5. CAPE BRETON HIGHLANDS: The Cape Breton Highlands have long been the favourite destination for visitors to Nova Scotia and its tourism status is well deserved. The Cabot Trail is a scenic drive, rivalling any on the continent, where a winding path clings to a rugged terrain separating the Gulf of St. Lawrence from the Atlantic Ocean, and an ancient plateau erupts from the sea. The rich hardwood forest flanking the Highlands belies the fact that it is much farther north than the stunted woods surrounding my abode on the Eastern Shore. The shoreline is relatively linear and the ancient igneous bedrock alternates with deformed sedimentary strata to create the imposing cliffs that slide under the gulf waters in enormous sheets. Sea caves, arches and overhanging crescent amphitheatres are carved into the escarpment. Shoals and spires litter the perimeter and bald eagles peer from protected vantage points onto the numerous reefs below, where the seals haul out. Most impressive of all, the pilot whales range close to shore in pursuit of mackerel and squid. From the perspective of the paddler, you will touch a geological and biological variety that car camper's only dream of. This is one of the most imposing coastal regions in eastern North America.

#6. CAPE CHIGNECTO: The weathered cliffs of Cape Chignecto contain a diversity of formations seldom found in such a compact area. Precambrian gneiss, schist and slate are intruded by the granites and clothed by the recent sandstones and conglomerates, all intermixed in a myriad of colours, textures and forms. This imposing scenery is rendered more striking by over 12-m (40-ft.) tides that have produced amazing pinnacles, arches and sea caves. The deep green rockweeds are at eye level one moment and high above your head a few hours later. It is a strange world, especially for those used to a more moderate tidal differential along the Atlantic coast. The southern escarpment overlooks the highest cliffs on mainland Nova Scotia, more than 200-m (650-ft.) high in some places. On the western shore, the elevation is somewhat lower, but cliffs and pocket beaches continue and the coastline is a jagged combination of shoals and rock spires inset with tiny coves and waterfalls. Seals are common, as are sea birds, such as cormorants and guillemots. There are several small spots, which provide for a stopping spot for lunch, or for longer if the weather dictates. This is a region of the province seldom seen by either tourists or Nova Scotians and the route has always been one of my favourites.

#7. FIVE ISLANDS: According to the Mi'kmaw story, Five Islands were formed when Glooscap, the demi-god, stopped his arch enemy the giant beaver from building a dam across the Minas Channel by tossing huge boulders from Blomidon — and they are a geological fantasy land. Imposing black basalt contrasts with deep red sandstone; vertical, often unassailable, cliffs descend onto soft sand and mud flats and rock spires, caves and arches adorn the perimeter. Add to all this a land- and seascape that is continually transformed by 12-m (40-ft.) tides and strong currents and you have a story that few places can equal. If you are lucky, you might discover semi-precious stones, such as jasper, agate and amethyst embedded in the volcanic basalt, or even fossils on the park beach. Except for clam diggers, few have cause to venture close to their shores and for the sea kayaker; experience and caution are in order.

#8. LAHAVE ISLANDS: The LaHave Islands are a collage of white-sand beaches, granite rock, eroding drumlins, sheltered salt marsh, oldfield, layered slate and exposed shoals. Variety is the norm and although one of the province's most popular beaches (Rissers) is nearby, few venture where the road does not. You will seldom have to share these deserted beaches and salt marshes with more than migratory shorebirds and white-tailed deer (although it has become popular in recent years). This compact group of offshore islands is partly linked by a road to the mainland. Their importance in the fishing industry predates the founding of Halifax. Samuel de Champlain mapped and named them and French fishermen visited during the summers. The English moved in after the Acadian Expulsion but they too left by the early part of this century. Today, only seasonal inhabitants reside on the outer islands.

#9. BLUE ROCKS: The name, Blue Rocks, is derived from the greenish-blue slate, which predominates in the area. The extensive laminate of parallel striations are the result of eons of geological evolution, beginning with the deposition of sand and mud on the ocean floor and followed by heat, pressure and uplifting. The direction of the crustal folding is clearly apparent by the lay of the inner islands. At low water the tiny islets are draped with brown algae (rockweed and knotted wrack) that turn a brilliant golden-yellow by mid-summer. This is one of our most spectacular paddling routes. The islands were settled but, as is the case elsewhere, they are used now only as a summer retreat, if at all. Small-boat traffic is common due to the proximity of Lunenburg, a large fishing port, and the tourist appeal of Chester. Several seabird nesting sites and an unmanned lighthouse will be found on the outer islands.

#10. LOWER PROSPECT: The coastline between Terence Bay and Prospect Bay is near the metropolitan area but it offers a "wilderness" saltwater paddle. Other than a few summer homes and hunting cabins, the islands are uninhabited and the shoreline, except for that bordering the village, is undeveloped and public. The topography contrasts sharply with the coast east of Halifax/Dartmouth. Instead of eroding headlands of loose glacial debris, long shallow inlets and extensive salt marshes, this shore is characterized by stark granite outcrops, of which the most famous example is found at Peggy's Cove. It is an austere but compelling landscape. Soil is sparse and glacial erratics compete with shrubs and stunted trees for a place on the pitted surface. Beaches and good campsites are not plentiful.

Dr. Scott Cunningham, biologist and writer, is the author of Sea Kayaking in Nova Scotia *and numerous magazine articles. He has paddled coastal waters extensively and he circumnavigated Nova Scotia in 1980. He has also kayaked in Europe and is a BCU Coach 4 (Sea) and a Paddle Canada Senior Instructor Trainer. He operates Coastal Adventures, which is Atlantic Canada's foremost sea kayaking operation, and 2018 is their 38th year of offering coastal paddling excursions.*

Joshua Peters' List of the Top 10 Best Dive Sites in Nova Scotia

To some, the idea of diving around Nova Scotia may not seem very appealing. You might think there isn't much to do or see. You would be wrong. Once you get past the cold temperature, there is a whole new world of life below the surface of the waters around the province.

With plenty of shipwrecks to explore, old artifacts to find and, on rare occasion, tropical fish to see, you'll soon discover a hobby that will have you hooked for life, and even in that time it may not be enough to dive everywhere. To help you narrow down your choices, here is a list of the Top 10 dive sites to see while in Nova Scotia:

#1. HMCS SAGUENAY, LUNENBURG: The number one dive location has to go to the HMCS Saguenay. The *HMCS Saguenay* was a St. Laurent-class destroyer that served in the Royal Canadian Navy and later the Canadian Forces from 1956–1990. The ship is 366 feet long and is now 100 feet below the surface, as it was sunk to be made into an artificial reef in 1996. Monthly tours can be booked from Torpedo Rays Scuba in Halifax: *torpedorays.com*.

#2. SS ARROW, CHEDABUCTO BAY: Built in 1948, the SS Arrow ran aground on Cerberus Rock in Chedabucto Bay in February of 1970. The wreck is split into two parts and after a successful oil cleanup this dive is now safe. This is one of the best dives outside the Halifax area and can be completed with the correct training.

#3. BEAR COVE, HALIBUT BAY, HALIFAX: Bear Cove is an ocean shore dive and is the quintessential Nova Scotia dive. This popular site is conveniently located in Halifax Regional Municipality and offers the opportunity to see marine life and explore portions of the wreck of the *USMS Humboldt*. The site encapsulates everything that is Nova Scotia diving.

#4. PEGGY'S COVE, MOUTH OF ST MARGARET'S BAY: While Peggy's Cove itself is not fully accessible, due to the high tourism traffic and large surges, two nearby coves will allow you to enjoy the scenic views while avoiding the tourists. These are Cranberry Cove and Polly's Cove. The area generally has great visibility when the conditions are right, with an abundance of marine life including sea perch, skate, lobsters, lumpfish and even a small cod from time to time. Both these coves are often secluded and very peaceful dives.

#5. SANDY COVE, TERRANCE BAY: Sandy Cove is a unique site. The entrance and exit points are at different sides of the peninsula, allowing for an interesting 40-minute swim between the two. See if you can spot the Wolfish that lives there along the way!

#6. HERRING COVE, HALIFAX: Herring Cove, a small cove located near Halifax, is usually sheltered from the weather. It is frequently used by divers year round, day or night. It is well suited for the skill level of a novice diver, but should be experienced by all types of divers. This site is also very good for photography, as its relative shallowness allows good light penetration and it hosts a variety of marine life. Herring Cove boasts an easy entry and exit point, slight or no surge, good visibility for this region, possibly six inches of fresh water on top and a gentle sloping bottom. It also allows for access to a small shipwreck called the Solerno, if you don't mind a surface swim beforehand. It's an all-round great site with loads to do.

#7. BIRCHY HEAD, ST. MARGARET'S BAY (WEST SIDE): Birchy Head is a small, secluded dive area appropriate for experienced open-water to advanced-level divers. Divers can reach depths of up to 140 feet here. Birchy Head boasts a variety of marine life and has an interesting rock bottom that includes boulders and ledges. There's always lots to see while diving there.

#8. WHALING STATION, SOUTH OF BLANDFORD: Dive in this active harbour and see whale bones! Take a giant stride off the lower sections of the dock if the boats are gone. Otherwise enter and exit at the slipway; watch your step. Whale bones are in the middle of the harbour and resemble driftwood. Swim around enough and you'll find them easily.

#9. ARCTIC STATION, SHEET HARBOUR: The *Arctic Trader* is a shipwreck located in Sheet Harbour. The wreck lies in relatively shallow water and is just off the edge of a wharf. This site provides an excellent opportunity for new divers to experience wreck diving without being restricted by depth limits. The surrounding marine life and condition of the ship make it an interesting and enjoyable site for experienced divers. Penetration of the wreck is also possible. However, this should only be attempted by divers with special training. Divers without a wreck diver certification should never attempt to enter a wreck. The site also offers simple entry and exit points and typical to above-average visibility

#10. PORTUGUESE COVE, HALIFAX: Portuguese Cove is a secluded cove just south of Halifax. While the site itself is small, the diving is often clear with very still waters, contrasting most of the Nova Scotia coastline, which is typically anything but calm. Plenty of wildlife can be found in this nook and it is well worth a visit, even more so if you aren't quite used to the harsher conditions of Canada.

Joshua Peters has been diving for more than a decade, diving multiple times a week around Nova Scotia. He currently works at Torpedo Rays Scuba Adventures in Halifax and is part of the Sea Wolves Dive Club in Halifax, whose members helped contribute to this list with ideas and inspiration.

The Halifax Adventurer's 10 Best Beaches in Nova Scotia to Go Searching for Sea Glass

I grew up near beaches, walking them was always an exhilarating thing to do. Finding sea glass and other treasures was just an added bonus. When asked to contribute to a top 10 list many locations came to mind. To narrow it down was difficult but fun, and personal exploration and the generous feedback from fellow sea glass hunters helped … and it all came together.

Nova Scotia offers up many beaches of bountiful treasures from sea glass, bottles, bottle lips, marbles, glass doorknobs, pottery shards and so much more. The best beaches are pebbly sandy shores to larger rocks where the beach glass gets trapped.

Twice a day, new treasures wash in. Some are easy to see with just a walk by. More commonly, you have to work for your treasures. Moving the pebbles and rocks around, you'll be amazed at what you may find. The best time to go for your walkabout is when the tide is falling to low. Arrive about an hour after high tide and peruse the shore as the tide goes out. That way you're bound to find all the newly washed-up treasures. Another good time to go is at the first low tide after a storm.

#1. INVERNESS BEACH: Located at the end of Beach Rd #1 in Cape Breton, Inverness Beach has a 1.5-km sandy beach. It is one of Nova Scotia's most beautiful sea-glass beaches, although at first glance you may not see what's there. Only after moving the rocks around will you realize that the amount of beach glass is astonishing. Nicely tumbled pieces of white, green, brown, aqua, mauve, and even some blue-beach glass can be found in small to large pieces. This location has even been known to offer the rarer pieces of orange, red and cobalt-blue, not to mention the pottery and other treasures.

#2. BRIER ISLAND: Located in Digby County, this a must-go spot for sea glass. The variety of colours, shapes, sizes and textures is available only here.. Lots of pottery, marbles, stoppers and bottles can be found. There are purples, pinks and blues, etched and tumbled beautifully. You never know what you're going to find. Check out the area around the Brier Island Lighthouse at low tide, especially after a storm.

#3. POINT PLEASANT PARK: Located on the southern tip of the Halifax peninsula, thei park once hosted several artillery batteries, some of which are still present today. If you check out the beach where the coastal artillery batteries are, you'll find the beach is hiding many pieces of sea glass. You must dig around the rocky shore to find your treasures, although sometimes you may just come upon them in plain sight. Mostly you'll find small pieces including whites, browns and greens, nicely tumbled. In my search, I did come across a lot of pieces that were sharp and not glazed over. If you find pieces like that, throw them back into the ocean to cook some more.

#4. BIG TANCOOK ISLAND: Located in Mahone Bay, Lunenburg County, this island is the largest of the Mahone Bay islands. There are a couple locations you can check for sea glass on the island. One is Southeast Cove, which is located along Beach Road. Another option is Fossil Beach, adjacent to the ferry wharf. You'll be amazed at the amount of sea glass, pottery and other interesting beachcombing finds you will come across. Pieces range in size from very small to medium size. Quality of glass is nicely tumbled frosted pieces of browns, greens, whites, aqua and cobalt blue.

#5. DOMINION BEACH PROVINCIAL PARK: Located in Dominion in Cape Breton, this picturesque park offers a 1.5-km beach with boardwalks and dunes. It's a long sandbar that catches the waves from Indian Bay and beyond that the Atlantic Ocean. Dominion Beach is known for its bottle stoppers, marbles and other wonderfully shaped sea glass. A wide variety of blues can be found, along with reds, pinks, yellows, white, browns and even orange. A bountiful cornucopia of colours.

#6. INDIAN BEACH: Located in North Sydney next to the Marine Atlantic Ferry Terminal on Purves Street, this popular beach offers a natural sandy peninsula that juts out into the Sydney Harbour. The pieces are small but plentiful. Nicely frosted and tumbled whites, greens, browns and blues can be found. Dig around, as they are not always visible on a walk by.

#7. SANDY COVE BEACH: Located along the Digby Neck, this 500-metre crescent-shaped beach is well hidden away. It's known by the locals as Fundy Beach and there's actually a small sign that points the way off Highway 217. It's a popular spot where you can find a good mix of tumbled sea glass and pretty pebbles. There's a downside to this beach though; because of its crescent shape it's also a catchall for a lot of trash.

#8. LOCHMAN'S BEACH: This beach can be found at the end of Cable Street in Sydney Mines. Somewhat of a crescent-shaped beach, you can explore for quite a distance, all the way to Chapel Point Battery Site. A historical site that was built in 1939, it played an important role during the Second World War. Nicely tumbled pieces of green, white and teal, brown, mauve and the rarer blue and orange. Pottery chards as well as fossils have also been found here.

#9. FORT POINT: Located in LaHave in Lunenburg County, this small beach packs a big punch. Next to the Fort Point Museum, where the river meets the sea, you'll find 400-year-old sea glass — nicely frosted tumbled pieces, small to medium in size. There is lots of sea glass to go around for everyone.

#10. SPINDLER BEACH: This beach in Feltzen South is also known as sea-glass beach. It's a very popular beach and has been well picked over but that didn't stop me from checking it out and I'm glad I did. There were many people but there was also a lot of sea glass to go around, including frosted pieces, small to medium in size of white, green and brown. I even found a red.

Every beach, every day offers a whole new batch of surprises, so if you didn't find much yesterday, try again tomorrow or the next day after that. — The Halifax Adventurer

Cheryl Campbell is the Halifax Adventurer. She created Halifax Adventure in 2013 and she posts articles and photos that she believes will be of interest to others. She also loves and writes about history. "Today it's just me enjoying life the best way I know how. Catching a beautiful sunset or watching a squirrel bite into an apple while still on the tree. I enjoy photography and most of my photos are of nature and landscapes," she says.

David Currie's List of the Top 10 Places to Go Birdwatching in Nova Scotia

I remember being curious and noticing birds and other animals at a very young age. My most vivid memories of childhood are of animals, but birds in particular seemed to hold a much stronger fascination. In my late teens I was lucky to live close enough to Point Pelee, Ontario to visit there on weekends. I met influential people such as the world-famousRoger Tory Petersen and Canadian author and historian Pierre Berton. These people and others added fire to my passion and helped make birding a lifelong vocation.

Since moving to Nova Scotia, my involvement with birding has grown to include being the coordinator for the Audubon Christmas Bird Counts for the Atlantic region and president of the Nova Scotia Bird Society. Nova Scotia is one of the foremost places in North America to experience birding at its best. For me it adds to my sense of good fortune for living here.

With some of the most picturesque places in the world, Nova Scotia has long been considered a bird watcher's paradise. If you're an experienced or novice birdwatcher, you must check out these locations:

#1. THE HAWK: Located in one of the most southerly place in Nova Scotia, Cape Sable Island, "The Hawk" is an excellent birding stop for shorebirds, brant and snowy owls, and a multitude of smaller migrating birds in Spring and Summer.

#2. CAPE FORCHU: This picturesque headland near Yarmouth is one of the first and last stops migrating birds use to navigate the Gulf of Maine. The laneways and trails here can produce any number of rare birds during May-June and August-September.

#3. BRIER ISLAND: Noted as one of Canada's few places to view whales, this small piece of real estate is also one of the premier places for birding. Thousands of migrating hawks can be seen here in September. Watching for passing puffins, razorbills, murres, kittiwakes, loons and ducks can be impressive at almost any time of the year.

#4. THE GUZZLE: If not just for the name, this wonderful part of the dyke land near Evangeline National Historic Site is a must and can be extremely good for witnessing masses of shorebirds in August and September, inclusing the short-eared owl, eagles and hawks. In winter, it is often one of the best locations to find the snowy owl, horned larks, sparrows, snow buntings and Lapland longspurs.

#5. MINER'S MARSH: This lovely little park in the middle of downtown Kentville is worth a visit almost any time of year. The freshwater marshes are great for blackbirds, grebes, ducks and shorebirds. The surrounding woodlands are often "traps" for migrating birds as well as resident birds such as cardinals and catbirds.

#6. HARTLEN POINT: Probably the most visited birding area in the metro Halifax/Dartmouth area, the mixture of habitats on this headland can't help but have migrating birds stopping here. As good as it can be in spring and fall for migrants, it is one of the few places to find the rough-legged hawk and snowy owl in winter months.

#7. CHEBUCTO HEAD/DUNCAN'S COVE: A short hike to the Chebucto Head Lighthouse will provide you an awesome vista of the Halifax Harbour and this side of the Atlantic Ocean. Gannets, jaegers, harlequins and other ducks, as well as loons add to the species you may have seen while walking there. Nearby Duncan's Cove has a wonderful hiking trail over headland barrens with panoramic views of the ocean for sea-watching.

#8. AMHERST POINT BIRD SANCTUARY: The Amherst area and border region between New Brunswick and Nova Scotia can keep a birder busy for days. The Amherst Point Bird Sanctuary, part of a Ducks Unlimited marshland development, can be exciting for not only the varieties of marsh and water birds but also smaller resident and migrating birds among the bordering forest areas.

#9. CANSO: In spring and fall, Canso's geographical location makes it a truly remarkable birding area. There are several trails to explore. Be prepared for exciting rarities as they tend to pool up at the last bit of the mainland in that part of the province.

#10. TAYLOR HEAD PROVINCIAL PARK: Those looking to find the more boreal species, including black-backed woodpecker, spruce grouse, boreal chickadee, fox sparrow, blackpoll warbler and winter finches should try this provincial park. The trails range from easy to challenging and provide an ideal location to experience our coastal Acadian forests. The rocky shorelines can be a very good location for the harlequin duck and common eider as well as a variety of shorebirds in late summer.

David Currie has been president of the Nova Scotia Bird Society since November 2012.

Michael Haynes' List of the Best Trails in Nova Scotia

Making a list of the "best" of anything is always a challenge. In trails, one route can provide a thousand experiences, with weather, season and time of day all contributing to making each walk or bike ride exceptional.

However, there are some paths that I find I enjoy most at a particular time of year, and because I believe we should all strive to be active and outdoors year-round, I decided to provide one suggestion for each month. Of course, any of these trails can be enjoyed in any season: so get outdoors and explore!

#1. GHOST BEACH (JANUARY): Starting at the Cape Breton end of the Canso Causeway, the Celtic Shores Coastal Trail follows the former rail bed 90 km to the community of Inverness. For the first nearly 4 km, however, the trail traverses a slender finger of land with the Canso Causeway on one side, the large Long Pond on the other.
I enjoy Ghost Beach for two reasons. First, so close to the causeway and all its human activity gives it the feel of a walk in a city park — until the wind howls down and dashes waves completely over the narrow land bridge that is your route. The second reason is that, despite its proximity to these busy communities, when a rain or snow squall descends, which often happens, the exterior world disappears and it is easy to imagine that you are trekking on the edge of the Earth.

#2. VICTORIA PARK (FEBRUARY): Even before Truro's creation of Victoria Park in 1887, the waterfalls on Lepper Brook were an attraction. Although pleasant to visit at any time of year, in winter, when ice glazes the rocky slopes flanking them, and the spray thickens into a freezing fog, these cataracts are enchanting. While Waddell Falls is only a short walk on an excellent pathway from the Park Road entrance, more than 20 km of groomed cross-country trail are available for use.

#3. FRANEY (MARCH): For those who snowshoe, the Cape Breton Highlands are a fantastic destination well into April. And after February, the snow, while still deep, is usually surfaced with a firm crust that enables relatively easy walking. One location that should be explored is Franey, near Ingonish in the Highlands National Park. From near sea level, the trail climbs to a look off nearly 425 m above the Clyburn Brook canyon. On a clear, crisp day, you can see Cape Smokey, Middle Head and the Keltic Lodge and deep into the interior of the Highlands. The entire loop is less than 8 km, but be prepared for a four to five-hour trek.

#4. SEASIDE ADJUNCT (APRIL): While thousands flock to this popular detached fragment of Kejimkujik National Park during the warm summer months, I have always enjoyed it earlier in the year. April is a particular favourite, not only because it is usually empty of other walkers, but because this is when the migratory seabirds pass through on their way to their nest grounds in the arctic. St. Catherine's Beach, several kilometers of gleaming white sand, is often host to hundreds of sandpipers, plovers, and 'peeps' of various sizes and descriptions, resplendent in their breeding plumage. And even if there are few avian visitors that day, it is still a magnificent beach walk.

#5. CAPE SPLIT (MAY): Quite possibly the most well-known hike in Nova Scotia, the 16 km return hike to Cape Split, near Scots Bay, is most famous for the towering sea stacks and cliffs at its apex. For me, the most special time to visit is during a brief period in May, when the ground vegetation is bursting forth but before the leaves on the hardwoods unfurl. In that brief two- to three-week window, the ground on the top of the cape is carpeted by a brilliant layer of purple trillium and spring beauties. Spring might feel tentative or uncertain in other parts of the province, but on the top of Cape Split it exists in riotous assurance.

#6. COASTAL TRAIL (JUNE): One of the best seaside trails in Nova Scotia is the Coastal Trail in Cape Breton Highlands National Park. Tracing the rugged, rocky shoreline between Black Brook Cove and Neils Harbour, this 13-km (return) walk requires some fitness to complete. I enjoy it most in June because spring arrives later on the Cape Breton coastline, so flora and fauna are lively and at their most vibrant. Colourful harlequin ducks are common sights, and more than once male spruce grouse, their red eye combs brilliant in the sunshine, swagger past.

#7. TAYLOR HEAD PROVINCIAL PARK (JULY): During the summer heat, a walk on the Atlantic coastline can be refreshing and invigorating. At Taylor Head Provincial Park, near Sheet Harbour on the province's Eastern Shore, can be found the best coastal trail network in the province. Located on a slender, rocky finger of granite, the park offers 18 km of footpath, organized into a series of loops that permits shorter or longer hikes as desired. And as a reward after your walk, sheltered Taylor Head Beach, more than 1 km of dazzling sand, is available to rest, relax and enjoy a picnic before you leave.

#8. POLLETT'S COVE (AUGUST): Some trails/hikes have attained almost legendary status in Nova Scotia. One of these is Pollett's Cove in Cape Breton. The rough but adequate footpath takes you through the finest in Cape Breton's highland scenery. Situated on the western shore of the island, Polletts Cove can be reached only along a sinuous and unofficial footpath that negotiates its way along cliffs and through ravines deeply incised into the sheer slopes, which provides access to the isolated wilderness north of Cape Breton Highlands National Park. This is a route only for the experienced and I recommend completing it over two days. The land around Pollett's Cove Beach is private property, although the landowner generously permits public access. Treat it well.

#9. CAPE CHIGNECTO PROVINCIAL PARK (SEPTEMBER): There are few multi-day hiking trails available in Nova Scotia. Of these, the three-day, 51-km trek around Cape Chignecto is perhaps the most challenging, and most popular. Structured in a triangular loop beginning and ending in the community of Advocate Harbour, two sides skirt the Bay of Fundy coastline, providing breathtaking ocean views — and breath-robbing climbs. This train is rarely busy. In September there are fewer people still who choose to camp out in the cool fall evenings. Those who do are rewarded with fall foliage colours, energizing ocean breezes and blissful solitude. Perhaps best of all: no mosquitoes!

#10. KENOMEE CANYON (OCTOBER): At 21 km, the Kenomee Canyon Trail can be completed in one day. But why rush, when several delightful remote campsites are available? Starting near the impressive Economy Falls near the village of Economy, this trail loops through the 6,000+-ha Economy River Wilderness Area. This can be a demanding hike requiring fording the river several times. Fortunately, the water level in October is very low and the cool, crisp fall air energizing. Best of all, the fall colours can be achingly impressive.

Should this distance seem too daunting, shorter and equally scenic routes are available in the same area — with no river crossings required.

#11. HEMLOCK AND HARDWOODS (NOVEMBER): For many, cold and cheerless November is their least favourite time to hike. For me, when the leaves have fallen but the snow has yet to arrive, it seems as if it is only then when the bones of the Earth are visible. It is then that the texture of the terrain, which lies hidden most of the year in a shroud of green vegetation, is revealed. One location that looks much the same in November as it does in July is the grove of old-growth Hemlock in Kejimkujik National Park. Towering high above the needle-carpeted ground, living pillars of a natural cathedral, these 300-year-old trees always evoke feelings of awe and wonder in me. Hemlocks are conifers, and their acid-rich needles inhibit understory growth, so the ground surrounding them looks similar year-round — though the approach over hardwood-covered ridges looks quite different. This short 5-km hike is worthwhile at any time of year.

12. THE BLUFF LOOP (DECEMBER): Halifax is one of a few major Canadian cities with a long-distance wilderness hiking trail that can be reached by city transit. Situated within the Five Bridge Lakes Wilderness Area on the Chebucto Peninsula, The Bluff Trail offers a series of four loops that are connected to permit routes of varying distance, with the longest exceeding 30 km. The trail runs through ecologically sensitive barrens, including large areas of open rock. It is scenic, but rugged. December is an excellent time to hike it, especially if enough snow has fallen to cover the ground.

Michael Haynes is considered one of the leading authorities of the outdoors in Eastern Canada. His book titles include: Hiking Trails of Mainland Nova Scotia, Hiking Trails of Cape Breton, Hiking Trails of Ottawa, Trails of Halifax Regional Municipality, Hiking Trails of Montreal, *and most recently* Trails of Prince Edward Island. *He has been a regular contributor to CBC Radio in Halifax, Sydney and Ottawa. In addition to his books and radio appearances, Haynes has published numerous articles about Canada's outdoors, both locally and nationally.*

Adam Barnett's List of the Top 10 Bike Rides in Nova Scotia

Riding a bicycle is one of the best ways to explore an area. You can cover distances easily while experiencing the feel of the land, smelling the scents of the season and taking the time to stop and explore when something piques your interest. Nova Scotia is special spot to ride a bike. The landscape changes wherever you go around the province and there are many quiet roads and coastal routes to explore.

The routes featured here were selected by the cycling community. A survey was sent around and people wrote in with their favourites. Of course there were many more than 10 routes so they had to be pared down. The routes were ultimately chosen for: the beauty of the area, often coastal; towns to visit along the way; relatively quiet roads or trails, and, beautiful locations and landscapes.

Road Rides:

#1. CABOT TRAIL: Nova Scotia's best-known cycling route. This is an incredible ride, following both coasts of Cape Breton and cutting through the Cape Breton Highlands National Park. World-class scenery. Epic climbs. Great chowder.

#2. ASPOTAGAN LOOP: This is a classic. A short drive from Halifax, this loop follows the coastline of the Aspotogan Peninsula, weaving between small fishing villages, with lots of incredible views and undulating hills.

#3. EASTERN SHORE: #4. Sheet Harbour to Canso: The Eastern Shore of Nova Scotia is often overlooked but it has some beautiful cycling. Ride low-traffic roads while following the coastline, smelling the sea air and experience some of Nova Scotia's fishing heritage. The road can get a bit isolated at times but there are sufficient amenities to take on this long-distance ride with a bit of planning.

#4. SAMBRO / PURCELL COVE LOOP: This is a popular ride starting in Halifax. Mostly on paved shoulders, it provides great ocean views and takes you down to Crystal Crescent Beach, a popular beach destination.

#5. ADVOCATE TO PARRSBORO:
This route is known as the "mini-Cabot Trail" and has lots of fun hills, twisty roads and great views. Pass by Five Islands Provincial Park, visit the Old Dutchman's Cheese Farm and check out the historic Cape D'or lighthouse.

#6. LUNENBURG TO LIVERPOOL VIA LAHAVE: Start your ride in historic Lunenburg, one of Nova Scotia's most beautiful towns. Take the ferry to LaHave (being sure to visit the La Have Bakery) and follow the coast, passing by incredible white-sand beaches and picturesque communities.

Rail Trails:

#7. SALT MARSH TRAIL: Start your ride in Cole Harbour and find yourself transported from the city to beach country in just a couple of hours. This is a popular ride that takes you through some beautiful salt marshes, ending up at the popular Lawrencetown Beach where you can rent a surfboard, enjoy a swim or just take in the view.

#8. CELTIC SHORES COASTAL TRAIL: This trail was designated as Nova Scotia's first Destination Trail, a status designated by Tourism Nova Scotia as a world-class ride. The trail is mostly flat and is around 90 km long, connecting Port Hawksbury to Inverness. This is a beautiful coastal ride, connecting you to many vibrant and authentic Cape Breton communities.

#9. RUM RUNNERS TRAIL: The Rum Runners Trail connects the City of Halifax to Lunenburg via an old rail bed. This trail is separate from traffic, making it a safe and comfortable ride. Ride over old trestle bridges, take in the view and stop in Mahone Bay, easily one of the prettiest towns in Nova Scotia.

#10. HARVEST MOON TRAIL: This is an incredibly popular rail trail that connects historic Grand Pre to Annapolis Royal. Visit the wineries in and around Wolfville while cycling past the famous Acadian Dykes. There is easy access to many communities along the way with a diverse range of views and environments.

Adam Barnett has always loved riding a bike and does his best to find ways to incorporate cycling into his life and work. He spent over four years as a guide, leading people on bike tours around the Maritime Provinces and has spent the last few years working with Bicycle Nova Scotia, an organizing dedicated to all things cycling. He loves Nova Scotia and is passionate about highlighting all the incredible things happening in the area.

A List of the Top 11 Places to Go Snowmobiling in Nova Scotia

The following is a list of places to go snowmobiling in Nova Scotia as recommended by members of the Nova Scotia Snowmobiling Association.

#1. Take a trip from Collingwood to Five Islands, up toward Lynn Mountain. Take the trail to Moose River, go through Parrsboro and up Kirk Hill; follow the trail to Advocate, return through the Chignecto Game Sanctuary/ Kelley River WPA, pass through Southampton and Springhill and back to the start. Food is available in Parrsboro, Advocate and Springhill. Gas is available in Advocate and Springhill and can be obtained in Parrsboro.

#2. Why not get away from it all and come to beautiful Pictou County? The trail system located in the eastern half of the county encompasses approximately 350 kilometres of trails.Check out the state-of-the-art clubhouse located at 994 Brookville

Road. It is the heart of their system. To complement it they have four warming shelters located throughout. The newest shelter is on the 104 at Black Pit Road. Perch Lake offers another shelter, the Swinging Bridge in Sunnybrae, and the last one is in the Garden of Eden Barrens.

If you choose to depart from the clubhouse then you have to decide which way you wish to travel. If you wish to head towards the Antigonish trails, go east. This system will have you sledding through some beautiful hardwood stands and along the edge of Eden Lake. From Sunnybrae onwards you are travelling along the Trans Canada Trail on what was once the Guysborough Railway. You will travel though rock cuts that had to be blasted out to make the railway. Take a moment to consider the effort to construct this rail bed so long ago. Throughout the barrens you will find other trails groomed. From this end of the system the trails for the neighbouring club, Antigonish Sno-dogs, await you.

If your choice is to go west, more scenic trails await you. Portions of this system leave Pictou County and enter both Colchester and Guysborough counties. Travelling on these trails takes you through new growth plantations to East and West Loon Lakes, which are a cottage-country area. These trails are divided between old trails and pulp roads. The 104 will take to the Stewiacke River. Once you cross it, you enter the system of a sister club in the county, Dalhousie Mountain. These trails offer a diverse amount of scenery, hardwood stands, groves of pine trees and open blueberry fields. (They ask that you respect the landowners and follow the marked trails through their fields). The clubhouse is just a short distance from New Glasgow. There you will find hotels, restaurants and shopping.

#3. From Southampton to Advocate Harbour via the Welton Lake through Kelly wilderness area, this is an excellent route for snowmobiling. Start at the Highway 209-302 intersection. You can unload there. Head west on 30-30a along 30 to Advocate, or take 33. It is an excellent ride with good snow. The trail takes you right to the local store, gas and food. The maps are available on the SANS website.

#4. Leaving from Whycocomagh and heading towards Inverness is one of the nicest trails in the province. It's also beautiful going from Whycocomagh to Margaree. Cape Breton has numerous beautiful spots, but these two trails top the list.

#5. One place with great accommodations, which isa big snowmobile supporter, is Smith Rock Chalets in Scotsburn. They have a website and Facebook page for details. The chalet is in the heart of the Dalhousie Mountain Snowmobile Club's trail system and offers some of the best views of the towns close by, as well as the Northumberland Strait.

#6. From the Hants SnoDusters come these suggestions:

Tennycape: Little trail off of #52. Looks out over the beautiful Minas Basin.

View the South Canoe Lake Wind Farm from Round Mountain or travel through the wind farm on the Ellershouse Trail system.

Travel Trail 30, which has views ofthe Atlantic Ocean.

Falmouth Trail System features various trail types. Wide highway-like trails, old-fashioned twisty trails and trails through deep wooded areas and over mountains.

"We have to include our favourite destination of all, the Farmers' Family Diner (1256 Ward Rd., Aylesford)." This location is a long-time supporter of snowmobilers that provides not only a hearty home-cooked warm meal after a long day on the trails, but also tops it off with amazing dessert. The trail system leads right to their restaurant; no matter the trail conditions it is always worth the trip.

#7. One of the main destinations in the Annapolis Valley is called the "Not So Swinging Bridge," located on the Hants SnoDusters Snowmobile Club Trail System. The bridge is over 70 feet long and spans the canal that feeds Black River Lake. Before this bridge was installed by landowner Ken Long, there was a swinging bridge that use to span the river. When the new bridge was installed it didn't swing anymore and a member of the Hants SnoDusters called it the "Not So Swinging Bridge." The name stuck and now it is one of our main destinations.

#8. Snowmobiling in the Cobequid Mountains, which includes the North Shore Snowmobile Club, has to be one of the best places to ride in Nova Scotia. A portion of the trails covers more than 150 km and a large section of that is the 104 main trail. There is a warming hut that has dry wood for the wood stove, a picnic table and a 110-volt LED light that is very comfortable. This hut is located in Nuttby, between two large wind turbines, which are part of a 22-turbine wind farm. The trail has good signage and leads to the Warwick Mountain Recreation Clubhouse, which is open to the public on winter weekends has the best fresh-never-frozen hamburgers on the trail. High-test gasoline is available. It is a fun time to sit by the fire and meet new people. The trails start in East Mountain, which is very close to Truro, and go all the way to Belmont Mountain and Warwick Mountain. The trails connect with the Dalhousie Snowmobile Club in the east and in the west with the Fundy Trail Snowmobile Club. A great group of volunteers manages and looks after bridges, trail clearing and signage all year long.

#9. Snowmobile trails in Cape Breton are mostly in the highlands. Trail-staging areas on the east side of the island include Wreck Cove, North River and Baddeck, including Hunters Mountain. These areas have ample parking for snowmobilers.
On the west side of the island staging areas include Wycocomagh, Port Hastings, Creignish, Judique, Port Hood, Mabou, Inverness, Margaree and Cheticamp. There are more than 1000 km of groomed trails. Throughout the highlands of Cape Breton, there are more than 4,000 km of forestry roads, which provide a wonderful

experience of snowmobiling and off-groomed trail riding. Snowmobile maps are available through the local snowmobile clubs.

#10. From the Annapolis Valley Ridge Runners (AVRR) come these suggestions: The approximately 600 kms of maintained trails of the AVRR have three distinct areas, each deserving of mention.

The Annapolis Valley floor, with its wide sweeping trails along rivers and through farmland, towns and villages, offers an easy ride for beginners and families, with lots of potential loops and plenty of services along the way. The main corridor trail is the 101. The abandoned rail line runs from Coldbrook to Bridgetown and offers access to the trails on the North and South Mountains.

The North Mountain of the Annapolis Valley offers narrower, twistier trails with beautiful lookouts over the Annapolis Valley. Best access is from the Coldbrook area.

The South Mountain — everyone's favourite. It has many access points from the valley floor. When snow levels are low, park and ride from the trails near Aylesford Lake, Loon Lake, or Salmon Tail on the #12 highway. Often there is riding available in the Lake Paul area when other areas are closed. Trail 101 arrives from the east, from the Hants SnoDusters trails, and exits to the west, where it joins the Crossburn Trail System. Services are found by travelling to the valley floor on the #2, #3 or #22. Trials for all riding experiences are available, with very few road crossings. The views from the hilltops of the lakes makes the ride very enjoyable.

#11. One of the most popular locations for snowmobiling in Nova Scotia has to be the Sutherland's Lake area, located near the top of Westchester Mountain in southern Cumberland County. The SLTGA trail system boasts approximately 160 km of groomed trails, traversing some of the most scenic wilderness areas found on mainland Nova Scotia. Plenty of free parking is available at the club parking lot, just off North End Road, Sutherland Lake. Trails leave directly from the clubhouse and connect to Trail 104, the trans- provincial main trail. Fuel and canteen services are available on weekends throughout the snowmobile season at the Clubhouse. Destinations reachable within an easy day's run from there include Collingwood, Oxford, Spring Hill, Tatamagouche, Folly Lake and even Amherst or Pictou. Visitors are always welcome and seasonal passes, as well as three-day passes, are available on site (weekends only).

PEOPLE

- Rick Howe's List of 10 Nova Scotians He Would Like to Interview
- John Boileau's List of the 10 Most Important People in Nova Scotia's History
- Denyse Sibley's List of the 11 Funniest People from Nova Scotia
- John Boileau's List of the 10 Most Influential People in Nova Scotia's History
- A List of Canadian Super Centenarians Born in Nova Scotia
- Richard Crouse's List of the 10 Most Influential Nova Scotians and Their Impact on the World
- Sheldon MacLeod's List of the 10 Nova Scotians He Considers Heroes
- Heidi Petracek's List of the 10 Nova Scotians She Would Invite to Her Dinner Party
- The List of Nova Scotia's Female Trailblazers
- The List of 12 Other Nova Scotian Women of Distinction

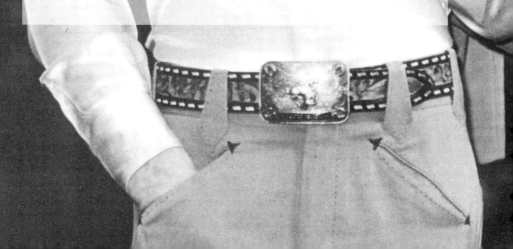

Rick Howe's List of 10 Nova Scotians He Would Like to Interview

I interview people for a living, at times eight to 10 interviews a day on my radio program. Over the years I have had the opportunity to talk with some pretty interesting people, from Johnnie Cochrane, who represented O.J. Simpson, to hockey great Gordie Howe and his wife Colleen, to Wheel of Fortune letter turner Vanna White. Throw in a few former prime ministers, well known musicians and sports greats, and it has certainly been an interesting career.

I've been asked to prepare a top 10 list of famous Nova Scotians, alive or not, I would like to interview. Here's who I'd put on that list. Some I have already interviewed.

#1. EDWARD CORNWALLIS: I know he's not a native Nova Scotian, but he is Halifax's founder and he has become the focus of a huge debate over naming public landmarks for notorious public figures. Indigenous groups and their supporters were successful in demanding his statue in the south-end Halifax park that bears his name be removed. The park will likely be re-named. There's also an effort to re-name the Cornwallis River in the Annapolis Valley and Pastor Rhonda Britton plans to rename her Cornwallis Street Baptist Church in Halifax. Cornwallis' detractors accuse him of genocide against the province's Mi'kmaq. I think it would be very interesting to hear his defence when faced with the criticisms and his explanation for his actions against the Mi'kmaq and previous to his arrival in Nova Scotia, his suppression of the Jacobite Rebellion in Scotland.

#2. JOSEPH HOWE: This Halifax lawyer, politician and journalist is credited with defending the rights of journalists and I would certainly touch on his now famous court case defending his newspaper from charges of libel, but Howe was also initially an opponent of Nova Scotia joining Canada's confederation. He was a rebel who later changed his mind and got on the confederation bandwagon. It would be fascinating to hear him explain why the change of heart. I'd also love to hear the story of his duel in Point Pleasant Park. He accepted a challenge and allowed his opponent to shoot first. The shot missed. Howe then shot his pistol into the air, which won him the right to refuse any future challenges. A great story.

#3. ANGUS L MACDONALD: He was premier of Nova Scotia from 1933 to 1940, when he was called on to serve in the federal government, then returned to Nova Scotia and was premier again from 1945 to 1954. He also served in the First World War. He was known affectionately as Angus L; the L by the way stands for Lewis. He's considered one of this province's greatest politicians and during his time in office Nova Scotia saw new roads and bridges built and improved public education. In the

1945 provincial election, his Liberals won all the seats in the legislature. Their campaign slogan was "All's well with Angus L." He died in office in 1954.

#4. ROBERT STANFIELD: Nova Scotia's 17th premier. He led the Conservative Party to power in 1954 and served three straight terms as the province's premier before becoming leader of the federal Conservative Party. Stanfield is described as the best prime minister Canada never had and had the unfortunate situation of butting heads with Liberal leader Pierre Trudeau. He lost three elections. I'd love to hear firsthand his thoughts on those political fights and his explanations for those federal losses after so much success at the provincial level.

#5. HENRI MEMBERTOU: The Grand Chief of the Mi'maq nation, born in 1507. He established relations with the French and met Jacques Cartier and Samuel Champlain. He was believed to have powers of healing and prophecy and died at the age of 104. It would be an experience to hear his thoughts on the European invasion of Nova Scotia by both the French and the English and whether, looking back at that time today, he had any regrets.

#6. JOHN BUCHANAN: Nova Scotia's three-term premier was first elected in 1978, defeating the Liberal government of Gerald Regan. I've interviewed Buchanan on several occasions and always enjoyed the feisty exchange. Buchanan's nickname was "Teflon John" and despite several controversies during his tenure nothing really seemed to stick to this down-home populist premier. People loved him and his wife Mavis. The two would stand by the Armdale Rotary the morning after election wins carrying a thank you sign and waving to the motorists on their way to work. But his free-spending ways also drove Nova Scotia deep into debt with bailouts for failed industries like Sydney Steel. Buchanan went on to become a federal senator before retiring from politics. I'd love to ask him what he thought the secret to his political success was.

#7. HALIFAX POLICE CHIEF VERNON MITCHELL: He was chief of the Halifax force in the 50s and 60s during a period of time when this port city was a rough and tumble place with gambling dens, brothels and bootleggers. He was chief in December 1955 when businessman Michael Resk was gunned down, a murder that continues to be unsolved today. Resk's murder is one of dozens noted at the Halifax police department's unsolved-murders link on its website. There are several rumours associated with Resk's death, including police involvement or even a mafia hit. Newspaper accounts indicate the chief, who later took his own life, took a special interest in the case. It would be fascinating to hear his thoughts on who might have been responsible for Resk's murder.

#8. GLORIA MCCLUSKEY: The "iron lady" of Nova Scotia politics. Dartmouth G was the City of Dartmouth's last mayor before amalgamation and she served several terms after that as a member of the Halifax regional city council. She is another on my list who I have interviewed. She's been a guest on my radio show many times. A staunch defender of everything Dartmouth, Gloria holds back on nothing. She's got a quick wit and a sharp tongue and no matter the topic she is always on mark and entertaining. I would love to hear more from her on the days leading up to the amalgamation of Dartmouth, Halifax, Bedford and Halifax County, a shotgun marriage pushed by then-premier John Savage despite much opposition, including Gloria's.

#9. ANNE MURRAY: Springhill's singing superstar got her big start on Don Messer's Jubilee television show, a mini-skirt wearing, barefoot songstress with the golden voice who has gone on to have a huge and successful international career. I've seen her in concert, but never had the opportunity to sit down and talk about her career and her continuing devotion to her hometown of Springhill and her home province of Nova Scotia. From hits like "Snowbird" to "Danny's Song," Murray has been a tremendous entertainer and a great ambassador for Nova Scotia.

#10. SIDNEY CROSBY: Nova Scotia's Sports Hall of Fame has put together a list of the top Nova Scotia athletes with stars ranging from boxing's Sam Langford to track's Johnny Miles along with many other great athletes. But the kid from Cole Harbour tops my list of the province's greatest athletes and what an opportunity it would be to sit down with the Pittsburgh Penguins captain and talk hockey. I did interview Crosby when he was 14 and just back from Los Angeles, where he had skated with the likes of Wayne Gretzky. Even then he presented himself as a young man with a good head on his shoulders. Was the golden goal in Vancouver his most treasured hockey moment? Or was it a Stanley Cup win? Another moment in his glorious career? And how worried is he about his string of concussions? I'd love to hear his frank comments.

There are many other Nova Scotians who could be on this list, but these are some of the people I think are or would be great interviews. Everyone has a story, famous or not, and talking to and questioning people is something I truly love to do.

Rick Howe has been in the radio business since 1972 with stops in Campbellton, Newcastle and Saint John, New Brunswick before moving to Halifax in October 1978. He has been a labour and police reporter, on air anchor and news director before becoming a talk show host in 1998. He currently hosts the Rick Howe Show on News 95.7 in Halifax. He lives in Fall River with his wife Yvonne. He has three grown sons, Jason, Greg and David and two granddaughters, Brihanna and Madeline.

John Boileau's List of the 10 Most Important People in Nova Scotia's History

Important (adjective) 1. of great effect or consequence; significant. 2. (of a person) having high rank or status, or great authority (Canadian Oxford Dictionary).

Important, like influential, is a relative term and often depends on whose criteria are used to decide "importance." For the purposes of this list, important means a person who has had a great and direct impact on the history of Nova Scotia. The individuals below are listed in chronological order, without any attempt to rank their importance.

#1. PIERRE DUGUA, SIEUR DE MONS (C.1558-1628): French merchant, explorer and colonizer who, along with fellow explorer, geographer and cartographer, Samuel de Champlain (c. 1570-1635), founded Port Royal on the Annapolis Basin in 1605, the first permanent European settlement in North America north of the Spanish possessions in Florida.

#2. HENRI MEMBERTOU (1507-1611): Mi'kmaq Grand Chief who established good relations with the French when they established Port Royal, guarded their fort and belongings carefully during their absence from 1607-10 and became the first Indigenous leader to be baptised, choosing the Christian name Henri.

#3. JEAN-BAPTISTE LOUIS-FRÉDÉRIC DE LA ROCHEFOUCAULD DE ROYE, DUC D'ANVILLE (1709-46): French nobleman and naval officer who led a disastrous 65-ship armada in 1746 in a failed attempt to recapture Louisbourg and Annapolis Royal from the British, which resulted in his death at Birch Cove in Bedford Basin.

#4. COLONEL EDWARD CORNWALLIS (1713-76): British army officer appointed governor of Nova Scotia (1749-52), who founded Halifax with about 2,500 settlers in 1749 as a counter to Louisbourg, but failed in his attempts to make a lasting peace with the Mi'kmaq.

#5. BRIGADIER-GENERAL CHARLES LAWRENCE (1709-60): British army officer appointed administrator (1753-54), lieutenant-governor (1754-56) and governor (1756-60) of Nova Scotia, and who directed the settlement of the "Foreign Protestants" at Lunenburg in 1753, ordered the Expulsion of the Acadians in 1755, oversaw the subsequent settlement of New England Planters on Acadian lands and reluctantly instituted representative government for the colony.

#6. GENERAL GEORGE RAMSAY, 9TH EARL OF DALHOUSIE (1770-1838): Scottish-born British army officer appointed governor of Nova Scotia (1816-20), who founded Dalhousie College (later University) in 1818 as the first non-sectarian college in the colony, using funds appropriated from customs duties collected during the British occupation of eastern Maine during the War of 1812.

#7. REVEREND RICHARD PRESTON (1791/2-1861): Former slave from Virginia, who became a religious leader and abolitionist, founded the African Baptist Association and assisted in establishing 11 Baptist churches across the colony.

#8. JOSEPH HOWE (1804-73): Journalist, poet, politician and premier (1860-63) who successfully defended himself in court against a charge of seditious libel after he published an anonymous letter in his newspaper (1835) attacking politicians and police for pocketing public money — a landmark in the struggle for a free press. He was later instrumental in the establishment of responsible government in the colony, but also led the anti-Confederation movement.

#9. CHARLES TUPPER (1821-1915): Physician, politician, founder of the Confederation Party and premier (1864-67), who led Nova Scotia into Confederation before going into federal politics.

#10. EDITH JESSIE ARCHIBALD (1854-1936): Writer, activist, reformer and suffragist who championed the right of women to vote and led a 1917 delegation of women to convince Premier George Murray not to block a suffrage bill, which the legislature passed the next year.

Retired army colonel John Boileau is the author of more than a dozen books of historical non-fiction, as well as more than 500 magazine and newspaper articles on a variety of subjects, book reviews, op-ed columns, travelogues and encyclopedia entries.

Denyse Sibley's List of the 11 Funniest People from Nova Scotia

Nova Scotia is blessed to have many talented people. We have produced a long list of world-class singers, actors, writers, artists and entertainers but what about funny people? Coming up with a list of the 11 funniest people from Nova Scotia is no easy task, but here are my picks.

#1. LOU LEBLANC: Former co-worker and radio personality from the South Shore. Lou has always been one of my favourite people. We shared a Halifax morning show for over a decade. We were like family. Ask anyone who knows him what comes to mind when you say his name and they'll reference his sense of humour.

#2. MARK CRITCH FROM THIS HOUR HAS 22 MINUTES: Yes, I know he is a Newfoundlander, but the cast is local wherever they go. Watch just one episode of the show and you'll be going back for more. I realize of course they have writers, but look at the twinkle in his eye.

#3. BJ, KATE AND BOBBY FROM Q 104: These guys and gal are the real deal. It's like a well-oiled machine. I don't hear them often, but I've lived in this world for many years and it's grassroots humour.

#4. JIMMY FLYNN: (He lives locally, although he's from Newfoundland.) A lot can be learned from this comedian. He knows how to connect with an audience. I was honoured to have him as a morning-show feature for a few years. I will always think of him as a friend first and co-worker second.

#5. ELLEN PAGE: Funny, talented AND local. Enough said. I don't have a personal connection, but I've watched her being interviewed on a few occasions and she's a hoot.

#6. JOHN DUNSWORTH AKA MR. LAHEY: Of course he's funny. Have you ever watched the Trailer Park Boys? He slipped into the drunken character with such ease and every time I met up with him at local events, he made me laugh. What I found the funniest was that he was a big Denyse fan. I was flattered for sure. He will be missed.

#7. MAGICIAN AND MASTER HYPNOTIST, IAN STEWART: He's my friend and pilot, so we're connected in a couple different ways. I've watched his shows many times and been in his company at events. #Hilarious #Amazing

#8. CBC REPORTER BRETT RUSKIN: A good sport, who carries out some of the wackiest assignments with a smile on his face. You can't help but laugh.

#9. FRANK CAMERON/DOUG SAUNDERS: These two are friends of mine and former co-workers. Seldom an exchange that isn't in good humour. They can easily bring on the belly laughs.

#10. ANDREW DOUGLAS, FRANK MAGAZINE: Dry, sarcastic humour. Talk to him, read his columns and follow his social pages.

#11. MIKE SAVAGE: Had him join me on-air and been in his company at many different local events and I'm always impressed that he's polite and kind and when he addresses the crowd, he never forgets to inject a degree of humour that makes him 200 percent relatable and likeable.

Denyse Sibley is a Halifax-based radio personality.

John Boileau's List of the 10 Most Influential People in Nova Scotia's History

Influential (adjective) 1. having a great influence or power (Canadian Oxford Dictionary).

Influential, like important, is a relative term and often depends on whose criteria are used to decide "influence." For the purposes of this list, influential means a person who has had a great and direct impact not only on the history of Nova Scotia, but also outside the province. The individuals below are listed in chronological order, without any attempt to rank their influence.

#1. SIR SAMUEL CUNARD, 1ST BARONET (1787-1865): Halifax merchant, entrepreneur and shipping magnate who completely revolutionized trans-Atlantic shipping with the establishment of regularly-scheduled steamship crossings in 1840.

#2. ABRAHAM PINEO GESNER (1797-1864): Physician and geologist from Cornwallis Township, King's County, who developed a method of extracting a liquid from coal, bitumen and oil shale in 1846, creating a new fuel, which he named kerosene.

#3. GEORGE MERCER DAWSON (1849-1901): Geologist and surveyor from Pictou whose field work in Canada's west and north laid the foundations of much of our knowledge of the geology and natural history of these regions.

#4. SIR ROBERT LAIRD BORDEN (1854-1937): Lawyer and Conservative politician from Grand Pré, who, as Prime Minister (1911-20), successfully led Canada through the First World War and its immediate aftermath.

#5. REVEREND DR. MOSES COADY (1882-1959): Roman Catholic priest and social activist from Margaree Valley, Cape Breton, who founded the Antigonish Movement, which blended adult education, co-operative business ventures, microfinancing and rural community development to assist small, resource-based communities in the Maritimes and led to the establishment of credit unions.

#6. CYRUS EATON (1883-1979): Investment banker, businessman and philanthropist from Pugwash, Cumberland County, who became one of the most powerful financiers in the American Midwest and financed the first Pugwash Conference on Science and World Affairs in 1957 to bring together scholars and public figures to reduce the danger of armed conflict.

#7. ISAAK WALTON KILLAM (1885-1955): Financier and philanthropist from Yarmouth, whose wealth established the Killam Trusts (held at five Canadian universities to fund scientific research and artistic ventures), the Isaak Waltham Killam Hospital for Children in Halifax, the Montreal Neurological Institute and the Canadian Council for the Arts (the latter with Sir James Dunn).

#8. FRANK SOBEY (1902-1985): Businessman from Lyons Brook, Pictou County, who was the primary builder of the Sobey's chain of supermarkets and Empire movie theatres, and later established the Sobey Foundation to provide funding for initiatives that have a positive impact on health, education and communities, as well as the Sobey Art Award for young artists.

#9. VIOLA DESMOND (1914-1965): Businesswoman and civil rights pioneer from Halifax who challenged racial segregation in a New Glasgow theatre in 1946 and was jailed for sitting in the whites-only section (by refusing to pay the one-cent difference between the upstairs segregated seat she paid for and the downstairs one she used), which helped start the modern civil rights movement in Canada.

#10. DONALD MARSHALL, JR (1953-2009): Mi'kmaq from Sydney, who was wrongly convicted of murder in 1971, largely because he was Indigenous and spent 11 years in jail before being acquitted, which resulted in changes to the Evidence Act with regard to full disclosure by the prosecution. He was also the primary petitioner in a landmark Supreme Court of Canada case, which upheld the treaty rights of Aboriginal people to catch and sell fish.

Retired army colonel John Boileau is the author of more than a dozen books of historical non-fiction, as well more than 500 magazine and newspaper articles on a variety of subjects, book reviews, op-ed columns, travelogues and encyclopedia entries.

A List of Canadian Super Centenarians Born in Nova Scotia

Anne Adele Samson was born on February 27, 1891 in Richmond, Nova Scotia, to parents Thomas and Philomene (née Bourque) Samson. She had nine siblings, four of whom were brothers and five were sisters. After she finished school, she became a teacher in 1912, teaching at a school in Truro.

In 1917, she took her final vows as a member of the Filles de Jesus. She then returned to Nova Scotia and continued teaching for another 30 years, retiring in 1947. She then moved to Quebec and stayed there for 10 years. She returned to the Maritimes to do part-time jobs until 1976, when she moved into the Motherhouse of the Order in New Brunswick.

In her later years, she enjoyed writing poetry and songs. Samson broke her hip when she was 95, which rendered her unable to walk, but she was writing and composing well beyond her 100th birthday. For her last few years, she was bedridden, but was said to still love chocolate even though she had no teeth. When Anne Samson passed away on November 29, 2004 at the age of 113 years, 276 days, she was the oldest nun in the world and the oldest Nova Scotian on record. However, there have been others who have lived past 110 years and the following is a list of Nova Socotian-born super centenarians.

#1. ANNE SAMSON
Born: February 27, 1891
Died: November 29, 2004
Age: 113 years, 276 days
Died in New Brunswick

#2. LOUISE GIBSON
Born: August 7, 1883
Died: January 2, 1995
Age: 111 years, 148 days
Died in the United States

#3. VIRGINIA MUISE
Born: July 28, 1893
Died: November 2, 2004
Age: 111 years, 97 days
Died in the United States

#4. ALINA MORTON
Born: November 10, 1878
Died: April 20, 1989
Age: 110 years, 161 days
Died in Nova Scotia

#5. MARGUERITE ROBERTSON
Born: May 13, 1907
110 years, 260 days as of January 28, 2018
Resides British Columbia

#6. LAURA ROLLOCK
Born: November 16, 1878
Died: December 29, 1988
Age: 110 years, 43 days
Died in Nova Scotia

#8. CHESTER PUSHIE
Born: June 24, 1884
Died: July 22, 1994
Age 110 years, 28 days
Died in Nova Scotia

#9. ROSE MCDONALD
Born: September 5, 1890
Died: September 16, 2000
Age: 110 years, 11 days
Died in Nova Scotia

Richard Crouse's List of the 10 Most Influential Nova Scotians and Their Impact on the World

Nova Scotia's influence spreads far and wide. From the Billboard charts and bookshelves, to movie screens and U2 concerts, the ingenuity of folks from Canada's second-smallest province in art and industry is integrated into the everyday life of millions around the world. Narrowing it down to a list of 10 influential Nova Scotians and their impact on the world is no easy task, but here are my picks.

#1. MAUD LEWIS: In her lifetime, folk artist Maud Lewis's rough-hewn paintings gained an international audience. Richard Nixon hung two of them at the White House and more recently Maudie, a biography of her life and art, starred Sally Hawkins and Ethan Hawke.

#2. TERRENCE "TIGER" WARRINGTON: Terrance "Tiger" Warrington was a Canadian light-heavyweight and heavyweight divisions champion who fought all over Canada, the United States and in Cuba.

#3. HANK SNOW: Hank Snow's 140 albums and 85 Billboard country hits include the self-penned chart toppers "I'm Moving On" and "The Golden Rocket" and hit cover versions of "I Don't Hurt Anymore," "I've Been Everywhere" and "Hello Love."

#4. JERRY LONECLOUD: Entertainer, ethnographer and medicine man for Nova Scotia's Mi'kmaq people Jerry Lonecloud became famous in the 1880s as a member of Buffalo Bill Cody's Wild West Show and later as the author of the first Mi'kmaq memoir, Tracking Dr. Lonecloud: Showman to Legend Keeper.

#5. GEORGE ELLIOTT CLARKE: Much of poet and playwright George Elliott Clarke's socially aware work documents the experience and history of the Black Canadian communities of Nova Scotia and New Brunswick. In 2016 he was named Canada's Parliamentary Poet Laureate and in 2017, U2 featured two of his poems on screens at their Joshua Tree at Thirty concerts.

#6. ANNE MURRAY: Anne Murray has sold more than 55 million albums worldwide. Her hit "Snowbird" made her the first Canadian female solo singer to reach No. 1 on the U.S. charts and to earn a gold record.

#7. BRIAN MACKAY-LYONS: Architect Brian MacKay-Lyons' inventive and beautiful designs earned him an international reputation as "the poet of place." From the Ship's Company Theatre in Parrsboro, Nova Scotia to the Canadian High Commission in Dhaka, Bangladesh he has left his distinctive mark the world over.

#8. ELLEN PAGE: Nicknamed "the tiny Canadian," Ellen Page parlayed acting on locally shot television shows, including Trailer Park Boys, into a Hollywood career that saw her star in Inception, X-Men: Days of Future Past and Juno, which earned her Best Actress nominations from the Academy Awards, BAFTA, Golden Globe and Screen Actors Guild Awards.

#9. ALFRED CARL FULLER: Industrialist Alfred Carl Fuller was the original "Fuller Brush Man." The door-to-door brush and cleaning company was so successful it inspired two movies, The Fuller Brush Man and The Fuller Brush Girl. Fuller even recorded an album, Careers in Selling: An Interview with Alfred C. Fuller, which became a bestseller.

#10. RITA JOE: Mi'kmaw poet and songwriter Rita Joe is often referred to as the Poet Laureate of the Mi'kmaq people. As her seven volumes of poetry acquired a worldwide audience, she was made a Member of the Order of Canada and became one of the few artists ever appointed to the Queen's Privy Council for Canada.

Richard Crouse is the regular film critic for the 24 hour news source CTV's News Channel and CP24 and hosts the talk show Pop Life for Bell media. His syndicated Saturday afternoon radio show, The Richard Crouse Show, originates on News Talk 1010 in Toronto. He is also the author of 10 books on pop-culture history including the bestselling Raising Hell: Ken Russell and the Unmaking of The Devils, *and* Elvis is King: Costello's My Aim is True. *He also writes a weekly column for* Metro *newspaper.*

Sheldon MacLeod's List of the 10 Nova Scotians He Considers Heroes

It's not as easy as you might think when someone asks you to come up with a list of Nova Scotia heroes. Or at least it wasn't for me.

What makes a hero? Is it about saving lives or defeating an enemy? Or is it about ordinary people faced with choices that seem to force them down paths they hadn't intended to travel, compelling them forward?

These are just some of the people I found when I started this list.

#1. CARRIE BEST: Her mother used to tell a story that when Carrie was only four, she didn't turn her eyes away when the white lawyer her mother sometimes worked for walked past and spoke to her. In the early 1900s in New Glasgow, a Black family held a different place in society. She later found her voice writing letters to the editor. As a young mother, Best no doubt had many things to say when she was arrested with her son for sitting in the whites-only section of the Roseland Theater. She was convicted and a few years later there was a similar story about another young Black woman facing the same charge. Carrie Best chose to start the first black-owned and operated newspaper and her coverage of the Viola Desmond story helped lead to the end of the Jim Crow Laws of segregation in Nova Scotia.

#2.VIOLA DESMOND: She was already a young woman determined to find success in the world and car troubles that day were likely a bit frustrating, but only a small setback. Since the parts wouldn't arrive until the next day, she may as well see a movie in the Roseland Theater. She was born of a white mother and Black father, and later the management said she'd been sold "the wrong ticket" and would have to move to the balcony. Viola was a successful beautician in spite of having to travel out of Nova Scotia because there was no school a Black woman could attend. It's no surprise she didn't just walk out that day. And she didn't listen when her husband and others told her to let it go. She couldn't. Eventually she was recognised for that stand she took over a seat in 1946.

#3. FIREFIGHTERS EDWARD CONDON, WILLIAM BRUNT, WILLIAM BRODERICK, MICHAEL MALTUS, JOHN DUGGAN, WALTER HENNESSEY, FRANK KILLEEN, JOHN SPRUIN, FRANK LEAHY: In 1917, the Fire Service in Halifax was already more than 160 years old, but technology was only just moving into the modern age, away from horse and carriage. When the alarm sounded that early December morning for a ship on fire in the harbour, the fate of the crew of the city's first motorized pumper was sealed, but there was no hesitation. They arrived at a nearby pier, when the blast from the munitions ship claimed all but the driver of The Patricia. In all, nine firefighters died in the line of duty that morning. Their heroismled to several monuments being placed around the city to remember their sacrifice. These nine men are named and remembered at the monument at the Station on Lady Hammond Road: Fire Chief Edward Condon (age 60), Deputy Fire Chief William Brunt (age 41), Captain William Broderick (age 32), Captain Michael Maltus (age unknown), Hoseman John Duggan (age 34), Hoseman Walter Hennessey (age 25), Hoseman Frank Killeen (age 21), Hoseman John Spruin (age 65) and Hoseman Frank Leahy (age 35).

#4. WALTER HENRY BROMLEY: Born in England just two years before the Declaration of Independence, Walter Henry Bromley was in Nova Scotia from 1810-1811 as a soldier with the 23rd Regiment of Foot. After retiring on half pay he did return to Halifax as a social reformer. Bromley worked with the poor and the Mi'kmaq were among the poorest in society. He founded the Royal Acadian School and dedicated himself to educating low and middle-class children including girls, Blacks and immigrants. Although he was convinced that Indigenous Peoples should be farmers and argued they could be integrated, he spoke out against their treatment in speeches in Halifax and to the people of Great Britain.

#5. ANGUS WALTERS: One of 12 children born to a fishing captain and growing up in Lunenburg it was inevitable that Angus Walters would go to sea. His legacy as a Canadian icon was not as easy to predict. Working his way up from a 14-year-old sea hand on his father's schooner, he eventually became captain of his own vessel by the age of 23. He became well known for how quickly he could fill his ship and get back to port. That was enough to get him involved in the first ever International Fishermen's Race between Lunenburg and Gloucester, Massachusetts. A broken mast meant he lost a chance to qualify for the event, but a race committee was formed and Bluenose was built for the next year's race. Walters won. He and the schooner went

on to be undefeated in five consecutive races giving the country something to cheer for during the Great Depression.

#6. DONALD MARSHALL JUNIOR: Spending more than a decade in prison would change anyone's outlook. And even more so if you weren't guilty of the murder they accused you of. Donald Marshall Junior was just 17 when he and a buddy decided they were going to "roll a drunk" that night in Sydney. After the death of his buddy, police focused on Marshall and he was convicted of murder. It was only after a person came forward 11 years later that the conviction was overturned and a settlement was given to Junior for the miscarriage of justice. Two decades later Marshall was charged with fishing eels. His case went all the way to the Supreme Court of Canada, with the court upholding the treaty of 1760 that guaranteed the right for Mi'kmaq to fish and sell their catch, ultimately changing the rules for all Indigenous Peoples across Canada.

#7. WILLIAM HALL: The son of slaves who escaped the U.S. during the war of 1812 and were brought to Nova Scotia as part of the Black Refugee Movement, William Hall was born in Kings County. As a teenager, he went to work in the shipyard near his home. He went to sea on merchant ships at the age of 17 and later served as with the U.S. Navy during the Mexican-American war, and then as a volunteer with the British Navy, where he rose to the rank of Captain of the Foretop aboard HMS Shannon. It was during a mission on that ship in India where Hall and another officer — the only ones to survive — continued to fire the ship's cannons until the wall of a fortification was breached. For that, Hall became the first Black person, the first Nova Scotian and only the third Canadian to be awarded the Victoria Cross for bravery.

#8. GLADYS PORTER: More people should know about the first woman elected to the Nova Scotia Legislature. Gladys Porter was born in Sydney, in 1893, where her father had been the town's first mayor. By 1943 she was living in the Valley, where she was elected to Kentville town council. When she ran for mayor in 1946, not only did she win, she became the first woman mayor in Atlantic Canada. She held the job for 14 years before running for, and getting elected as as the Progressive Conservative representative for Kings North, in the process becoming the first female MLA. She won re-election in 1963 and was still in office when she passed away in 1967.

#9. ROSE FORTUNE: Rose was just 10 years old when she arrived in Nova Scotia as a Black Loyalist. She was born into slavery in Philadelphia but made history in Annapolis Royal. She must have been as outgoing as she was ambitious, starting her own business by carting luggage between the ferry and the homes and hotels in her wheelbarrow. As a young, Black entrepreneur she eventually grew the company that stayed in the family for a century. Fortune was known to impose and enforce curfews at the local wharves and many consider her Canada's first Black Female Police Officer. The ferry MV Rose between Digby and Saint John is named in her honour.

#10. ALEXANDER KEITH: Born in Scotland, he was already brewing beer before he arrived in Halifax in 1817. Three years later, Alexander Keith founded the brewing company that bears his name. He was proud of his Scottish heritage and was well known as a Freemason. He was charitable, influential and political. He was the fourth mayor of Halifax and served as President of the Legislative Council of Nova Scotia, appointed by Queen Victoria. He was a supporter of Confederation and worked at helping Canada become a country 47 years after establishing the brewery.

A seasoned broadcast reporter and news anchor, Sheldon MacLeod has worked in markets across the country during his 25 years in the radio industry. He is a volunteer deputy fire chief, a passionate home cook and is proud to call Nova Scotia home. A husband to Patricia and father to Connor and Kaylee, he's committed to making his community a better place to live. Each weekday afternoon from 12:30 p.m. to 3:30 p.m., Sheldon's special brand of talk radio offers NEWS 95.7's listeners a daily adventure and a compelling afternoon drive home. Get news, opinion, lifestyle and more on The Sheldon MacLeod Show and find out what's right and what could be better in our great city of Halifax.

Heidi Petracek's List of the 10 Nova Scotians She Would Invite to Her Dinner Party

So, you're throwing a dinner party and you have the opportunity to invite 10 Nova Scotians (living or deceased) to join you. Who would you invite? Here are my picks:

#1. VIOLA DESMOND: What a fascinating dinner guest she would be! As someone who makes a living talking to interesting people, this would be a real treat for me — to talk to someone who stood up and made a powerful point at a crucial time in Nova Scotia (and world!) history. I would love to talk to her about why she chose to make a stand back in 1946 at the Roseland Theatre — and about how she feels about the ripple effect her actions had for decades to come when it comes to race relations in Nova Scotia.

#2. SYDNEY CROSBY: A selfish choice, I admit it! But how fun would it be to talk to "Sid the Kid" about what it's like to be one of the most celebrated figures in modern-day hockey? I'm sure he could tell a few interesting tales about life in the Penguins' locker room and on the ice. He also just seems to be a genuinely nice guy who spends a lot of his time giving back to the community — in Cole Harbour and beyond. He never broadcasts the fact when he participates in a charitable activity. In the current world of over-sharing on social media, Crosby is a refreshing change.

#3. RODNEY MACDONALD: I actually played a bit of hockey with MacDonald when he was premier of Nova Scotia and found he was that rare kind of politician who knows when to just leave partisanship at the sidelines and have a little fun. We met on the ice for a shoot with a television show I was hosting at the time, and he was a really good sport. Not only could he talk about his love of hockey with Crosby, but he could also play a fiddle tune or two with dinner. He's an accomplished player who would definitely add some extra entertainment to the night!

#4. JOEL PLASKETT: Plaskett is one of the nicest, most genuine and most humble musicians you will ever meet. I've interviewed him numerous times and he's always passionate about his music and the people he plays with, and he really appreciates his fans. Plaskett would represent the City of Lakes at the table quite nicely. He's also a consummate songwriter and maybe he could even bring along his father, Bill, to play some folk tunes with him.

#5. SHERI LECKER: This is a name that probably isn't familiar to most Nova Scotians, but Lecker is a woman who should be recognized for the work she does as executive director of Adsum House for Women & Children, a non-profit organization that helps women and children experiencing homelessness. Lecker is a petite woman, probably just over five feet tall, but she is a force of nature who works tirelessly to help the community! I don't know how she finds the energy. Her drive and dedication is to be admired and her knowledge of the practical and social needs of people in the community is unquestionable.

#6. BARB STEGMANN: Stegmann is an entrepreneur, a trailblazer, a force to be reckoned with — and her smile lights up any room! I've had the pleasure of meeting her several times and it's always fascinating to hear her talk about her many adventures and journeys in her bid to help combat violence in Afghanistan through her perfume company, The 7 Virtues. She is the first woman to be named Honorary Colonel at 14 Wing Greenwood, and she is an example of what being "on a mission" really means.

#7. LUCY DECOUTERE: Actress Lucy DeCoutere is a woman I admire so much. Not only because she was brave enough to stand up to sexual harassment in a cultural climate that doesn't always treat victims kindly, but also because she has always been one to speak her mind. Even before her name hit headlines during the Jian Gomeshi court trial, Decoutere was known for cutting through any artifice to get right to the heart of any matter. When I see her on the street, she always looks me straight in the eyes and asks how I'm doing. And I know she wants an honest answer.

#8. RITA JOE: I wish I could have had the chance to have dinner with Rita Joe — a warrior for Mik'maw rights and women's dignity. Her life wasn't easy, but what amazing work she produced. The fact that she died with a poem in her typewriter — what an amazing end to an incredible legacy. Her words live on, both for her own people and for those of us who need to remember those lessons of the past. If she came to dinner, I would ask if she would so kindly recite one of her poems. What an amazing moment that would be.

#9. CYRIL LUNNEY: What can I say, it's not just because I work with the guy! Cyril has a story for every occasion and his tales always have us busting a gut here at the CTV Morning Live office. There are few people in the Maritimes who have done as much as he has. From water skiing, boxing, acting, dancing, becoming a drag queen and so much more. Just when you think he's done everything, Cy finds another activity to try. With Cy at the dinner table, I'm not sure anyone would be able to finish their meals, they'd all be laughing so hard!

#10. ANN MURRAY: The favourite daughter of Springhill, Nova Scotia and one of the biggest adult-contemporary artists of all time has been on stage, in the recording studio and backstage with some pretty incredible artists. She must have some revealing tales to share. She's also incredibly grounded for someone who has had such time in the spotlight, so I can imagine it would be a lot of fun to dine with her. She's also a great golfer, so maybe she could pass along some tips (I could use a few!).

Former co-host and producer of CTV Morning Live, Heidi Petracek has been bringing her energetic, witty and engaging personality to radio and television for more than 17 years. She is now a reporter for CTV News in Halifax. Heidi started her career as a television news reporter in her home province of Saskatchewan, before moving on to work in Calgary, Toronto, Corner Brook and St. John's. Heidi was named Media Person of the Year by the Tema Conter Memorial Trust for her coverage about PTSD among first responders in Canada. She has also been nominated for "Media Person of the Year" for both the Nova Scotia Music Awards and the East Coast Music Awards.

The List of Nova Scotia's Female Trail Blazers

The group of 12 Nova Scotian women who appear on this list must be revered and honoured as trailblazers. Through sheer determination, skill, talent, courage and inner strength, these women knocked down barriers. Often fighting a less-than-hospitable social and political structure, these women rose above the oppressive society that would keep them down, lighting the way for all those who came after them.

#1. VIOLA DESMOND: Today, Viola is known as an icon for in Canada, but decades earlier she was ostracized and persecuted because of the colour of her skin. In New Glasgow on November 8, 1946, when this Black woman refused to give up her seat in the "whites only" section of a movie theatre, she spent a night in jail, was fined and set off a chain of events that, 60 years later, led to a formal apology from the Province of Nova Scotia and a Royal Pardon that affirmed that there had been a miscarriage of justice and that Viola Desmond had committed no crime.

#2. MAUD (DOWLEY) LEWIS: Maud Lewis was born in South Ohio, Yarmouth County, on March 7, 1903. She died in Marshaltown, Digby County on July 30, 1970. She remains one of Canada's best known and most loved folk artists. Maud was afflicted with polio as a child and it left her with crippled arms and deformed hands. Both her parents died while she was still dependent on them. At that time she moved to Digby to live with an aunt. At the age of 18, she married Everett Lewis. They were quite poor and lived in a small 10-by-12-foot shack. Everett continued to live in that house after Maud died in 1970 but was killed there by an intruder 10 years later. The Art Gallery of Nova Scotia reconstructed the Lewis House and installed it in their gallery as part of their permanent Maud Lewis Exhibit.

#3. GLADYS MURIEL PORTER: Kentville made history on Tuesday, February 5, 1946, by electing Gladys Muriel Porter as the first woman mayor of a town in Nova Scotia, adding emphasis to the fact by giving her the highest majority in the town's history, and in the largest vote ever polled there, 970 citizens having marked ballots for the successful candidate and 442 for her opponent, former councillor W. C. Vincent. During her campaign for mayor, Porter told the voters in her election message that she wanted nobody to vote either for or against her as a woman, but to consider her only as a human being.

A native of Sydney, Nova Scotia, Gladys Porter moved to Kentville upon her marriage. In 1943 she became a town councillor in Kentville and three years later won the election for mayor, making her the first woman in the Maritime Provinces to do so. She was re-elected for a total of 11 years and only resigned after winning King's Centre in the provincial election of 1960, becoming the first woman to be elected to the Nova Scotia Legislature. At her death in 1967 she was still a Member of the Legislature.

#4. MARY HELEN CREIGHTON: The career of prominent folklorist Helen Creighton spanned several decades. During that time, she collected more than 4,000 traditional songs, stories and beliefs, and published many books and articles on Nova Scotia folk songs and folklore. Born September 5, 1899 on Portland Street in Dartmouth, Creighton developed an early interest in folklore and the supernatural. Between 1914 and 1916 she attended Halifax Ladies College and earned a junior diploma in music at McGill University in 1915.

Creighton began searching for literary material in 1928 when she met with Dr. Henry Munro, the Superintendent of Education for the Province of Nova Scotia. Munro showed her a copy of *Sea Songs and Ballads from Nova Scotia* by W. Roy MacKenzie and suggested Creighton attempt to find more songs. She began to travel around Nova

Scotia, collecting songs, tales and customs of Gaelic, English, German, Mi'Kmaq, African and Acadian origin. Frequently, she had to walk or sail to remote regions to satisfy her interest, all the while pushing a metre-long melodeon in a wheelbarrow. Among Creighton's many contributions was the discovery of the traditional *"Nova Scotia Song,"* widely called *"Farewell to Nova Scotia,"* which has become a sort of provincial anthem.

Between 1942 and 1946, Creighton received three Rockefeller Foundation fellowships to collect songs in Nova Scotia. The second of these fellowships was used to collect songs with equipment loaned by the Library of Congress. She also made recordings for the Canadian Museum of Civilization from 1947 to 1967. As she collected songs, Creighton also became interested in the ghost stories and superstition in Nova Scotia and the Maritimes. She presented these stories first in the themed collection of ghost stories *Bluenose Ghosts*, published in 1957, and later in an additional book Bluenose Magic in 1968. She received numerous honorary degrees for her work and was made a Member of the Order of Canada in 1976. She died on December 12, 1989.

#5. ALEXA ANN MCDONOUGH: Born on August 11, 1944, McDonough made history in 1980 when she was elected leader of the Nova Scotia New Democratic Party, becoming the first woman to lead a major, recognized political party in Canada. McDonough served as a member of the Nova Scotia Legislature from 1981 to 1994, representing the Halifax Chebucto and Halifax Fairview electoral districts. She stepped down as the NSNDP's leader and as a member of the legislature in 1994. She subsequently ran for, and was elected, leader of the federal New Democratic Party (NDP) in 1995. She was elected the Member of Parliament (MP) for the federal electoral district of Halifax in 1997. She stepped down as party leader in 2003, but continued to serve as an MP for two more terms, until 2008, when she retired from politics altogether. In 2009 she became the interim president of Mount Saint Vincent University and was appointed an Officer of the Order of Canada in December of that year.

#6. CARRIE M. BEST: Carrie Best was born in New Glasgow on March 4, 1903, was a pioneering Black Canadian journalist and social activist. A daughter to James and Georgina Ashe Prevoe, she married Albert T. Best in 1925. In 1943, Carrie Best confronted the racial segregation of the Roseland Theatre New Glasgow when she purchased two tickets for the downstairs seating of the theatre and attempted to watch a film with her son, James Calbert Best. Both were arrested and fought the charges in an attempt to challenge the legal justification of the theatre's segregation. Their case was unsuccessful and they had to pay damages to Roseland's owners. However, the experience helped motivate Carrie Best to found The Clarian in 1946, the first Black-owned and published Nova Scotia newspaper. It became an important voice in exposing racism and exploring the lives of Black Nova Scotians. In the first edition of *The Clarion* she broke the story of Viola Desmond who also challenged racial segregation at the Roseland Theatre and whose story became a milestone human rights case in Canada. In 1952, Carrie Best started a radio show, The Quiet Corner, which was aired for 12 years. From 1968 to 1975 she was a columnist for *The Pictou Advocate*, a weekly newspaper in Pictou.

In 1977, Best published her autobiography, *That Lonesome Road*. In 1974, she was made a Member of the Order of Canada and was promoted to Officer in 1979. She was posthumously awarded the Order of Nova Scotia in 2002. She is commemorated on a postage stamp issued by Canada Post on February 1, 2011. Best died July 24, 2001 at the age of 98 of natural causes in her hometown of New Glasgow.

#7. ROSE FORTUNE: Rose was born into slavery in Philadelphia, PA, on March 13, 1774, her family subsequently being relocated to Virginia by the Devones family. Escaping slavery during the American Revolution, the family was relocated to Annapolis Royal, Nova Scotia, as part of the Black Loyalist migration, when Rose was 10 years old. In 1825, she started her own business, carting luggage between the ferry docks and nearby homes and hotels. She became entrusted with safeguarding property and maintaining order on the wharves and warehouses of Annapolis Royal, acting as the town's waterfront police officer, and in so doing became the first female police officer in Canada.

Rose Fortune died on February 20, 1864, in the small house she owned at the engineer's lot near Fort Anne. The business she founded was continued by her grandson-in-law Albert Lewis as the Lewis Transfer Company and continued for several generations, remaining in business until 1980. Rose Fortune was buried in Annapolis Royal in the historic Garrison Cemetery. Her grave is unmarked, but a plaque in the Petite Parc on the Annapolis Royal waterfront commemorates her life and contribution to Nova Scotian history. Her direct descendant was Daurene Lewis, who was elected Mayor of Annapolis Royal in 1984, becoming the first African-Canadian woman to attain that position. In May 2015, the name *MV Fundy Rose* was given to the ferry that crosses the Bay of Fundy from Digby to Saint John, New Brunswick.

 # 8. DR. MARIA LOUISA ANGWIN: An educator and physician, Dr. Angwin was born September 21, 1849 in Blackhead, Conception Bay, Newfoundland. Nothing is known of her childhood except that her father, a Methodist minister, was transferred to Nova Scotia during the mid 1850s and by 1865 had settled permanently in Dartmouth. Maria was sent to the ladies' academy of Mount Allison Wesleyan Academy at Sackville, New Brunswick, in 1866, and she graduated three years later with a mistress of liberal arts diploma.

Although she had initially contemplated becoming a lawyer, Angwin gradually changed her mind, deciding instead to become a doctor. Canadian medical schools were not then admitting female students, but a degree could be obtained from several American institutions, notably Woman's Medical College of the New York Infirmary for Women and Children, established in 1868 by doctors Elizabeth and Emily

Blackwell. Such training was expensive, however, especially for a Methodist minister with four sons to educate. Angwin solved the problem by raising the necessary funds herself. On September 20, 1884 Maria Angwin became the first woman licensed to practice medicine in Nova Scotia, although others from the province had earlier taken medical degrees in the United States. She initially saw patients in both Halifax and Dartmouth, but after 1886 she confined herself to a joint residence and office in the central part of Halifax.

Late in 1897, in declining health, she returned to the New York infirmary for additional post-graduate work. She was expected to resume her Halifax practice, but while visiting in Ashland, Mass., she died suddenly following minor surgery.

#9. PORTIA WHITE: The renowned operatic contralto Portia White was born on June 24, 1911 in Truro, the third of 13 children born to Izie Dora and William Andrew White. Her mother was the descendant of Black Loyalists, while her father was the son of former slaves from Virginia, and on his graduation from Acadia University in 1903, he became the university's first Black graduate. He later became the minister of Cornwallis Street Baptist Church in Halifax, where Izie Dora White was the musical director. Portia White began her musical career there as a choir member at the age of six. She made her national debut as a singer in Toronto in 1941, and her international debut in New York City in 1944. A three-month tour of Central and South America followed in 1946 and she sang in France and Switzerland in 1948. Vocal problems later forced her to retire from singing in 1952, and she settled in Toronto where she taught some of Canada's foremost singers of the day. White briefly left retirement to perform for Queen Elizabeth II, at the opening of the Confederation Centre of the Arts in Charlottetown in 1964. This was to be one of her last major concerts. She died in Toronto on February 13, 1968, following a long battle with cancer.

#10. ANNE MURRAY: Born on June 20, 1945, in Springhill, Anne Murray is a multiple award-winning singer in pop, country and adult-contemporary music whose albums have sold more than 54 million copies worldwide as of 2012. A physical education teacher, Murray got her big break in the 1960s when she appeared on the television show Singalong Jubilee. In just a few years, she became the first Canadian female solo singer to reach No. 1 on the U.S. charts, and in 1970 also the first to earn a gold record for one of her signature songs, "Snowbird." Murray has received four Grammys, a record 24 Junos, three American Music Awards, three Country Music Association Awards and three Canadian Country Music Association Awards. Murray has been inducted into the Canadian Country Music Hall of Fame, the Juno Hall of Fame and The Songwriters Hall of Fame. She is a member of the Country Music Hall of Fame Walkway of Stars in Nashville, and has her own star on the Hollywood Walk of Fame in Los Angeles and on Canada's Walk of Fame in Toronto. In 2011, Billboard ranked her 10th on their list of the 50 Biggest Adult Contemporary Artists Ever.

#11. DAURENE ELAINE LEWIS: Born in Annapolis Royal on September 9, 1943, Lewis was trained as a registered nurse and held a diploma in teaching in schools of nursing from Dalhousie University, a Master of Business Administration from Saint Mary's University, and in 1993 was awarded an honorary doctorate in humane letters from Mount Saint Vincent University. Her first formal political involvement was in 1979, when she ran for town council in Annapolis Royal. She was appointed as deputy mayor in 1982. In 1984, Lewis was elected mayor of Annapolis Royal, making her the first female Black mayor in Canada. Lewis attempted to enter provincial politics in the 1988 election, making an unsuccessful bid to represent Annapolis West in the Nova Scotia Legislature for the Liberal Party. She was the first Black woman in Nova Scotia to run in a provincial election. Following her political life, Lewis became the executive director of the Centre for Women in Business at Mount Saint Vincent University. She was principal of both the Institute of Technology and Akerley Campuses of the Nova Scotia Community College. In 2001 she became the first African Canadian senior administrator in the history of the college. Lewis died in a Halifax hospital on January 26, 2013.

#12. MAXINE COCHRAN: Maxine was first elected to the Nova Scotia Legislature as a Progressive Conservative in the June 5, 1984 provincial election for Lunenburg Centre and held the seat until September 6, 1988. She was the first woman appointed to the Cabinet when she became Minister of Transportation on November 26, 1985. Born in Lawrencetown, Annapolis County on August 5, 1926, she was a respected teacher, healthcare provide and community volunteer. Cochran died at the age of 87 on July 8, 2014 in Halifax.

The List of 12 Other Nova Scotian Women of Distinction

#1. MONA LOUISE PARSONS: Born in Middleton on February 17, 1901, Mona Louise was an actress, nurse and a Second World War resistance fighter. She was the only Canadian woman to be imprisoned by the German army, yet her story remains unfamiliar to most Canadians. The daughter of a successful businessman, Parsons was known as a fiercely independent woman. She studied acting and moved to New York City in 1929, where she became a Ziegfield showgirl. Her theatrical pursuits did not take her far and she became a nurse.

In 1937 she married millionaire Willem Leonhardt, a Dutch businessman. The couple moved to Holland and lived a life of privilege until the Nazis invaded in 1940. She and her husband joined a resistance unit that rescued downed Allied airmen, but their involvement was short-lived. A Nazi informer betrayed them to the Gestapo in 1941.

They were arrested — first Mona in September and then Willem in December — and held in separate prisons. A Nazi tribunal was held the day after Leonhardt's arrest and Parsons was condemned to death. She appealed and her sentence was commuted in 1942 to life in prison. In 1945, Parsons was moved to Vechta Prison, which habeen a reform school. There she met Baroness Wendelien van Boetzelaer, with whom she planned to escape when an opportunity arose, which happened during an Allied bombing raid. The men's side of the prison was bombed and the women were taken outside. The warden, the former principal of the school, left the gates open and told the women they could take their chances with the Allied bombs or German bullets. Parsons and van Boetzelaer made a break for it. For three weeks they made their way to the Allies posing as German sisters, with Mona feigning a speech impediment to cover her accented German. The women became separated and Parsons eventually reached a Canadian battalion, the North Nova Scotia Highlanders. She received a commendation for her war efforts from British Air Marshal Lord Tedder and US President Eisenhower.

Parsons and Leonhardt were reunited after the war, but he never fully recovered from his imprisonment and died in 1956. She returned to Nova Scotia in 1957, where she became reacquainted with a childhood friend, Harry Foster. They married in 1959 and lived in Halifax. Foster died in 1964 and Parsons moved back to Wolfville in the late 1960s, where she remained until her death on November 28, 1976.

#2. RUBY KEELER: Although she was known as an American actress, dancer and singer, Ethel Ruby Keeler (who was billed professionally as Ruby Keeler) was actually born in Dartmouth, on August 25, 1910. Keeler was perhaps most famous for her on-screen coupling with Dick Powell in a string of successful early musicals at Warner Brothers, most notably the 1933 hit *42nd Street*. Following the success of that film, legendary film producer Jack L. Warner gave Keeler a long-term contract and cast her in *Gold Diggers* in 1933, *Footlight Parade, Dames and Colleen*. From 1928 to 1940, she was married to actor and singer Al Jolson. She and Jolson starred together in *Go Into Your Dance*, which was their only film together. Jolson and Keeler appeared on Broadway one last time together, for the unsuccessful show *Hold On To Your Hats* in 1940.

Keeler retired from show business in the 1940s, but in 1963 she appeared in *The Greatest Show on Earth*, Jack Palance's television series, and made a brief cameo in the 1970 film *The Phynix*. She made a widely publicized comeback on Broadway in 1971, and in 1972 she was acclaimed as a star again in the successful Broadway revival of the 1920s musical No, No, Nanette. Keeler starred in the musical for two seasons on Broadway, followed by two additional years touring in the show. After suffering a brain aneurism in 1974, she became spokeswoman for the National Stroke Association. In 1992, a Golden Palm Star on the Palm Springs Walk of Stars was dedicated to Keeler and she has a Star on the Hollywood Walk of Fame at 6730

Hollywood Blvd. Keeler died of kidney cancer on February 28, 1993, aged 82, in Rancho Mirage, California.

#3. THERESA MCNEIL: Theresa was the first female high sheriff in Canada. She entered the workforce to support her 17 children after her husband died suddenly in 1973. She became high sheriff of Annapolis County four years later. She is the mother of Nova Scotia Premier Stephen McNeil.

#4. MYRA AVA FREEMAN: Born May 17, 1949, Myra is a philanthropist and teacher. She was also the 29th and Lieutenant Governor of Nova Scotia and the first woman to hold the position. Freeman, who was actually born in Saint John, New Brunswick, graduated from Dalhousie University with a Bachelor of Arts and a Bachelor of Education. She started teaching with the Halifax Regional School Board in 1971, where she remained until her appointment. She was appointed Lieutenant Governor of Nova Scotia in 2000 by Governor General Adrienne Clarkson, on the advice of Prime Minister Jean Chrétien. She served as lieutenant governor until September 7, 2006. On July 1, 2008 Freeman was appointed as a member of the Order of Canada.

#5. CARROLL BAKER: Carroll Baker was born March 4, 1949, in Bridgewater and lived in Port Medway, Queens County until, at the age of 16, when her family moved to Ontario. She began her recording career in Thunder Bay in 1970. In 1972 she went to Nashville for her first session, producing her first top-10 hit, "Ten Little Fingers." The song peaked at number three on the RPM Canadian Country Music Charts. In 1975 Baker recorded "I've Never Been This Far Before." This was the beginning of 12 consecutive number-one records in Canada for Baker, a streak that has never been broken. With more than 20 number one records, gold and platinum record sales, numerous TV shows and a list of honours, including three Juno Awards for Female Vocalist of the Year, Baker is one of the most accomplished stars Canada has ever produced. Although she still resides in Ontario, she frequently returns to Port Medway, where she still has family and to revisit her South Shore roots.

#6. RITA MACNEIL: A native of Big Pond, Cape Breton, Rita MacNeil was born May 28, 1944, and achieved international fame as a country and folk singer. Her biggest hit, "Flying On Your Own," was a crossover Top 40 hit in 1987, although she had hits on the country charts throughout her career. In 1990, she was the bestselling country artist in Canada and she was also the only female singer ever to have three separate albums chart in the same year in Australia. MacNeil hosted a CBC variety show, *Rita and Friends*, from 1994 to 1997. She co-wrote her memoir, *On a Personal Note*, in 1998. MacNeil died April 16, 2013, from complications of surgery after a recurrent infection.

#7. ELLEN PAGE: Ellen Page was born in Halifax and started her career in Canada with roles in the television shows *Pit Pony*, *Trailer Park Boys* and *ReGenesis*. Page ventured into films in her home province but earned widespread attention after starring in the 2005 drama Hard Candy. Her breakthrough role came in 2007's Juno, for which she was nominated for an Academy Award for best actress, a Gold Globe Award and a BAFTA. Her other notable films have included *Smart People*, *Whip It*, *Inception, X-Men: The Last Stand* and *X-Men: Days of Future Past*, in which she played the mutant Katherine "Kitty" Pride or Shadowcat, a girl who can walk through walls. Most recently, she was seen in the remake of *Flatliners*.

#8. ELIZABETH BENSON GUY: This World-famous soprano was born in Halifax in December 1925 but was raised in Bridgewater. She studied first with her mother, Sarah Louise Anderson, a European-trained singer, and later at the Juilliard School. She made her opera debut in 1947 as Marie in the Royal Cons Opera School production of *The Bartered Bride*. As a concert artist she made debuts at Carnegie Hall, New York, on May 10, 1959, and at Wigmore Hall, London, October 31, 1967, and gave several major recitals in Toronto. Guy retired from public performance around 1974. She retired from teaching and musical activities in 1979.

#9. HOLLY COLE: Holly was born November 25, 1963, in Halifax. She is a popular jazz singer known for both her versatile and distinctive voice. In 1983, Cole travelled to Toronto to seek a musical career and in 1986 she founded a trio with bassist David Piltch and pianist Aaron Davis. The Holly Cole Trio was offered a record deal in 1989. A succession of releases followed through the early 1990s but in 1995 the label dropped the Trio and Cole began her solo career. Cole was also a part of the 1998 groundbreaking Lilith Fair tour. Her newest studio was released in late 2012 on Universal Music Canada.

#10. NATALIE MACMASTER: Natalie is an award-winning fiddler from Troy in Inverness County who plays Cape Breton fiddle music. MacMaster has toured with many of today's contemporary artists including the Chieftains and Carolos Santana, and has recorded with Yo-Yo Ma. MacMaster was born on June 13, 1972, and is the niece of renowned Cape Breton fiddler Buddy MacMaster.

#11. JOYCE SEAMONE: Female country artists appeared more frequently on the country hit charts in the 1970s than their male counterparts. But only one of more than 50 who made their chart debuts during the entire decade earned a number one debut hit. That feat was achieved by the South Shore's own Joyce Seamone.
With her 1972 indie release, "Testing 1-2-3," Seamone received a gold record for sales in excess of 80,000 albums and 10,000 eight tracks. After three LPs, Seamone signed with Boot Records, owned by Stompin' Tom, and managed to make the Canadian Country Music Charts with each release. In 2004, Seamone was inducted into the Nova Scotia Country Music Hall of Fame. In 2009, she received the Stompin' Tom ECMA award for Mainland Nova Scotia.

#12. BARBARA HANNIGAN: Barbara is an award-winning soprano who has commanded audiences from stages in New York, London, Paris and Berlin. She grew up in Waverly and became the first Canadian to win one of the most important awards in French music, Prix de la personnalité musicale the l'année (Music Personality of the Year).

GEOGRAPHY

A List of 25 Fascinating Facts About Nova Scotia's Geography

#1. Described on the provincial vehicle-license plate as Canada's Ocean Playground, the province is almost surrounded by water and as such, the sea is a major influence on Nova Scotia's climate. The province is surrounded by four major bodies of water — the Gulf of Saint Lawrence to the north, the Bay of Fundy to the west, the Gulf of Maine to the southwest and the Atlantic Ocean to the east.

#2. The Bay of Fundy's tides are the world's highest. In fact, the highest tides on the planet occur near Wolfville in the Minas Basin. The water level at high tide can be as much as 52.5 feet higher than at low tide. The greatest difference between high and low tide ever recorded was at Burntcoat Head at 53.38 feet in the Bay of Fundy's Minas Basin on September 12, 1775.

#3. The Bay of Fundy's twice daily tidal change is equal to the daily discharge of all the world's rivers combined — 100-km cubed of water. It makes sense then, that Nova Scotia has North America's only tidal power plant.

#4. The Annapolis Valley's beautiful and unique Acadian Dykes Drive (near Wolfville) dates to the 1680s to hold back the rising tides.

#5. The coldest temperature recorded in Nova Scotia was 41.1 below zero in Upper Stewiacke on January 31, 1920.

#6. The hottest temperature ever recorded was 38.3 on August 19, 1935 in Collegeville.

#7. The most snowfall on record was 101.2 cm that fell on February18-19, 2004 in Yarmouth.

#8. The wettest month on record was August 1971, when 387.1 millimetres of rain was recorded.

#9. In Nova Scotia, there have been at least three tornadoes on record — January 30, 1954 near White Point Beach; June 24, 1997 in Lantz and August 18, 1999 in Pugwash.

#10. One common landform the United States shares with Nova Scotia is the Appalachian Mountains.

#11. Cape Breton Island is the missing west coast of present day Scotland.

#12. The Bras d' Or Lake in Cape Breton is one of the world's biggest saltwater lakes.

#13. The largest fresh-water lake in all of Nova Scotia is Ainslie in Cape Breton Highlands National Park. The lake was named after George Robert Ainslie who was Lieutenant Governor of Nova Scotia from 1816 to 1820.

#14. The largest fresh-water lake in mainland Nova Scotia is Lake Rossignol.

#15. The White Hill in Cape Breton's north highlands is Nova Scotia's highest elevation point, with its highest point being at 532 m (1,745ft).

#16. The Margaree and the Mira are the province's largest rivers. In 1991, with the active support of the Margaree River Advisory Committee, the Margaree-Lake Ainslie System became the first river in Nova Scotia to be nominated to the Canadian Heritage Rivers System.

#17. The longest river in Nova Scotia is the St. Mary's. It is 95 km or 59 miles long.

#18. Martinique Beach is a public, 5-km long, sandy beach. It is the longest beach in Nova Scotia.

#19. Stewiake is halfway between the Equator and the North Pole.

#20. Nova Scotia is in the Atlantic Time Zone.

#21. Halifax is closer to Dublin, Ireland than it is to Victoria, British Columbia.

#22. Halifax boasts the second largest ice-free natural harbour in the world after Sydney, Australia.

#23. The oldest tree ever found in Nova Scotia — a 418-year-old eastern hemlock — was discovered by a university student studying environmental science. While its exact location has never been publicly revealed to protect the tree, it is known that it stands somewhere in southwestern Nova Scotia.

#24. The Isthmus of Chignecto borders New Brunswick and Nova Scotia and connects the Nova Scotia peninsula with North America. The isthmus separates the waters of Chignecto Bay from those of Baie Verte. The isthmus stretches from its northerly point at an area in the Petitcodiac River valley near the city of Dieppe, New Brunswick, to its southerly point at an area near the town of Amherst, Nova Scotia. At its narrowest point between Amherst and Tidnish, the isthmus measures 24 kilometres wide.

#25. Spanning parts of five counties, the Tobeatic Wilderness Area covers 103,780 hectares and is the largest remaining wild area in the Maritimes. The region is characterized by unique barren and semi-barren landscapes with outstanding undisturbed glacial landforms including esker fields, moraines, kettles and outwash plains. It protects remote and undisturbed wildlife habitat, expansive wetlands, pockets of old-growth pine and hemlock forest, and the headwaters of nine major river systems flowing to both the Atlantic and Fundy coasts.

Mayor Mike Savage's List of the Top 10 Qualities That Attract People to Halifax

When you ask Mayor Mike Savage to give you a list of the top 10 qualities that attract people to Halifax, here's what he'll tell you:

#1. More than 30,000 post-secondary students make us a fun, youthful, smart and ever-changing city.

#2. 3.7 million passengers fly through Halifax Stanfield International Airport each year, connecting us with the world and the world with us, and yet you can still come here to get away from it all.

#3. At the Emera Oval you can skate all winter and roller skate all summer, all for free.

#4. Our mass transit includes the oldest saltwater ferry service in North America; what a way to commute.

#5. We mark noon with the boom of a cannon from Citadel Hill, a nationally historic fort that has never had to defend the city.

#6. From late-night donairs to oysters on ice, food trucks to fine dining, we have something for foodies of all kinds.

#7. We are one of the top cities to "party in before you die," according to Matador Travel, and we're one of the top 20 friendliest cities in the world (and the only one in North America) according to Conde Nast.

#8. Water, water everywhere: from the great paddling lakes of Dartmouth to our stunning harbour and sandy stretches of ocean beaches.

#9. We are Canada's Ocean City, building a new economy tied to our oldest and greatest asset. From Irving Shipbuilding to the Centre for Ocean Ventures and Entrepreneurship (COVE), to the Dalhousie-led Ocean Frontier Institute.

#10. Our culture reaches back more than 13,000 years to the great Mi'kmaq Nation and now includes people from around the globe, all working to build a city for all.

Mike Savage was first elected Mayor of Halifax Regional Municipality on October 20, 2012. Mayor Savage ran on a platform to make Halifax the most liveable, entrepreneurial and inclusive city in the country, principles that continue to shape his work at City Hall and in the community. On October 15, 2016, Mayor Savage was elected to a second term based on a platform of sustained progress in making the Halifax region a place where residents can live, belong and thrive. Mayor Savage and his wife Darlene have two children, Emma and Conor, and continue to make their home in Dartmouth, where Mayor Savage grew up and attended school before graduating from Dalhousie University.

Dr. Tim J. Fedak's List of the Nine Most Important Minerals or Gems in Nova Scotia

Ever wonder what's under the ground or in the Nova Scotian soil? Well, here's a list of nine of the most important minerals or you'll find underfoot, so to speak.

#1. STILBITE: Nova Scotia's Provincial Mineral. A zeolite mineral that is commonly found on the shores of the Bay of Fundy and associated with the basalt headlands.

#2. AGATE: Nova Scotia's Provincial Gemstone. Agate is a microcrystaline form of quartz that comes in many forms (eg. banded, flame) and is often used for jewelry. Agate has also been commonly used for forming Mi'kmaq points.

#3. CHABAZITE: Another zeolite mineral that is common on the Bay of Fundy shore, forms cubic crystals and is often brown/red in colour. Although collected for their beautiful shapes and colours, the zeolite minerals are important in industry as well, acting as filters by absorbing and releasing water from their crystal structure.

#4. AMETHYST: A purple quartz crystal, found in several locations around the Bay of Fundy. Some amethyst found in Nova Scotia was kept by Henry IV and included in the crown jewels!

#5. JASPER: Another form of microcrystaline quartz, found associated with the basalts.

#6. GYPSUM: An evaporite mineral that is found in several locations around the province, which formed during the evaporation of ancient oceans about 300 million years ago. It is an important industrial mineral with rich deposits in Nova Scotia.

#7. COPPER: Found associated with the basalt headlands of the Bay of Fundy, native copper can occur as thin strands of mineral within the basalt. Obviously, an important industrial mineral.

#8. CALCITE: A carbonate mineral that is transparent or opaque. Forms naturally and also biologically as part of the shells of snails and bivalves.

#9. SMOKY QUARTZ: Quartz crystal with a dark tone while remaining transparent. Often used in jewelery.

Dr. Tim J. Fedak is Director/Curator of Fundy Geological Museum in Parrsboro.

A List of the Top 10 Creepiest Location Names in Nova Scotia

Not surprisingly, with all the richness of folklore and history of the province there have been many places that have gained unsavoury, mysterious or downright creepy monikers. In fact, Ghost Project Canada found that Nova Scotia has the most supernatural sounding names of all the provinces. Here is a list of the Top 10 creepiest location names in Nova Scotia:

#1. SACRIFICE ISLAND: Lunenburg County

#2. PHANTOM COVE: Halifax County

#3. HELL LAKE: Lunenburg County

#4. DEVIL'S HILL: Cape Breton County

#5. SKULL BOG LAKE: Annapolis County

#6. DEATH MEADOW: Digby County

#7. DEADMAN'S ISLAND: Halifax County

#8. GRAVEYARD COVE: Shelburne County

#9. HOODOO HILL: Annapolis County

#10. GHOST BEACH: Inverness County

There are 32 land and sea forms with an essence of the supernatural in Nova Scotia. There could be many more, including those of back roads, lanes and pathways. If you have any information you wish to add to the official list of supernatural stories and place names from around the country you may contact the Ghost Project at *ghostprojectcanada@gmail.com*.

A List of the 50 Most Unusual Road Names in Nova Scotia

You could spend days, weeks, perhaps even months driving around Nova Scotia and musing at the many unusual road names found throughout the province. The following is partial list of some of the most unusual road names in Nova Scotia:

#1. PIG LOOP ROAD, Chester

#2. OLD KETTLE ROAD, Mill Village, Region of Queens

#3. FLAT IRON ROAD, Mill Village, Region of Queens

#4. KISSING BRIDGE ROAD, Lunenburg

#5. CANDY LANE, Hebron

#6: EASY STREET, Greenwood

#7. DOC, GRUMPY, HAPPY, SLEEPY, DOPEY, BASHFUL AND SNEEZY LANES (Snow White and Seven Dwarfs), Lake Echo

#8. BLINK BONNIE TERRACE, Halifax

#9. SLEEPY HOLLOW ROAD, Martins River

#10. NECUM TECH, Ecum Secum, Eastern Shore

#11. CHERRY LANE, Bridgewater

#12. DAGGER WOODS ROAD, Antigonish County

#13. PETTICOAT LANE, Barrington

#14. PUFFY CUP DRIVE, Lunenburg

#15. TROLLOPE STREET, Halifax

#16. THIS STREET, Porter's Lake

#17. THAT STREET, Porter's Lake

#18. THE OTHER STREET, Porter's Lake

#19. BALLS CREEK, Cape Breton

#20. BOBOLINK STREET, Halifax

#21. HAUNTED BOG ROAD, Milton (near Liverpool)

#22. BOOTLEGGER'S LANE, Liverpool

#23. FRONT STREET, Mabou, Cape Breton

#24. BACK STREET, Mabou, Cape Breton

#25. KILL DOG COVE ROAD, Cornwall

#26. LITTLE DYKE ROAD, Little Dyke

#27. BERRYLAND DRIVE, Hebbville

#28. HARDSCRATCH ROAD, Yarmouth

#29. GOOSE CHASE ROAD, New Germany

#30. THE BOAR'S BACK ROAD, River Hebert

#31. GALLOWS HILL ROAD, Kentville

#31. WAKE UP HILL, Marriot's Cove

#33. LOIS LANE, East River

#34. GRIMM ROAD, Lunenburg

#35. MEADOW POND LANE, Liverpool

#36. FIVE POUND ROAD, Wentzell Lake, Lunenburg County

#37. SUCKERS BROOK ROAD, Sackville

#38. BLUE SAC ROAD, Five Islands

#39. FLYING POINT ROAD, Lawrencetown

#40. ROUND TUIT ROAD, Prospect

#41. RABBIT TOWN ROAD, Pugwash

#42. SQUIRREL TOWN ROAD, Route 10 (New Germany to Middleton)

#43. HARSCRABBLE ROAD, Bridgewater or Joggins

#44. ALL HALLOWS DRIVE, Near Prospect

#45. DEVILS HILL ROAD, Off of Route 253

#46. TRITTLE ROAD, Surette's Island, Yarmouth County

#47. LONG STRETCH ROAD, Port Hastings in Cape Breton

#48. ROOSTER HILL ROAD, Cape Breton

#49. EGYPT ROAD, Cape Breton

#50. YANKEETOWN ROAD, Hammond's Plains

TAKE FIVE: Darryll Walsh's List of Five Ghoulish Road Names in Nova Scotia

#1. HELL LAKE ROAD: Off the #103 onto Camperdown Road near Middlewood in

Lunenburg County, just past the meeting Of Camperdown and Crouse Settlement Roads on your left. (Very short.)

#2. LAKE TORMENT ROAD: Annapolis County, runs off the #8 about halfway between South Milford and Maitland Bridge.

#3. NORTH SALEM ROAD: East Hants, starts at Mill Village on the West Indian Road from Shubenacadie and goes nowhere.

#4. SALEM ROAD: Both at Green Hill in Pictou County and Enon Lake, Cape Breton County.

#5. PIRATE HARBOUR ROAD: Guysborough County, runs from Pirate Harbour to a crossroad near Boylston.

Pam Mood's List of the Top 10 Most Notable Nova Scotian Landmarks

Nova Scotia is sprinkled with villages, communities, towns, cities and more, the boundaries of each touching another. Each section of real estate has its own landmark that allows "bragging rights," and every single one is as amazing and important as the next one, together telling the beautiful story of Nova Scotians — our history, our culture, lifestyle, difficult times and our proudest moments: a resilient people who have been through much but always rise to the occasion to celebrate life to the fullest.

#1. CAPE FORCHU LIGHT STATION: Located in Yarmouth County, the veritable beacon to Canada stands 23 metres tall above volcanic rock. Named one of Canada's Great Public Spaces, the "apple-core" lighthouse, surrounding park and museum remind us of our sea-faring history.

#2. CABOT LINKS AND CABOT CLIFFS: Right here in Nova Scotia, two world acclaimed, Top 100 walking-only golf courses bring together world-class golf and an ocean view from each hole that heightens the senses in a way that ensures this surpasses all other golf experiences. And the fact that they're on Cape Breton Island adds culture and beauty to the encounter.

#3. CABOT TRAIL: Just saying the name of this Cape Breton jewel musters up a sense of adventure. And the longer you take to do the trail, the more you'll feel the spirit of Cape Breton and the more you'll understand just how blessed we are in this beautiful province.

#4. CITADEL HILL: Standing proud, watching over her city and province, this hilltop fortress is steeped in history. She has many layers from the Prince Edward-commissioned clock to the reenactments to underground tunnels.

#5. PORT ROYAL NATIONAL HISTORIC SITE: A reconstruction of the 17th-century buildings known as the Habitation, Port Royal is the site chosen by French explorer Samuel de Champlain for European settlement. It is also home to the Order of Good Cheer, which saw the men enjoying lavish meals and festivities in the early 1600s – and the Order is still alive today!

#6. THE RED PHONE BOOTH: The fun of taking pics with the phone booth is surpassed by Luckett Vineyard's open-air restaurant overlooking the vineyards and the Annapolis Valley. Breathtaking, inviting, it screams "Tuscany at home — with off-the-charts hospitality!" Cheers!

#7. LONG POND: On the beautiful Howard Dill Farm in Windsor, you'll find Long Pond, the birthplace of hockey. We Canadians live and breathe hockey and a trip to the very spot where it evolved is a must. On a cold winter's day, bring your stick and lace up your skates… and take a trip back in history!

#8. CAPE SPLIT: For the bold, outdoor spirits who are willing to do the four- to five-hour, 12-km return hike, the reward is a stunning view of the Bay of Fundy and her highest-in-the-world tides. The constantly eroding cliffs require an extra dose of adventurous spirit, but the breath-taking view it is well worth the trip.

#9. JOGGINS FOSSIL CLIFFS: At this UNESCO World Heritage Site, the world's highest tides have uncovered fossils that pre-date even the dinosaurs. What fun for everyone … what will you discover?

#10. PIER 21: In a province where we celebrate our rich and diverse culture, Pier 21 is filled to the brim with the stories of ancestors, who came to Canada to ensure better lives for their families. From the tossed-at-sea stories to the celebrations of immigrants through newcomer stories and more, this is a must for each of us to experience. We will each walk away richer for it.

Pam Mood is a born-and-bred Nova Scotian, coming to us from what she describes as the "best piece of real estate on earth" — the seaside town of Yarmouth. As serving mayor of her community, she understands the beauty of the entire province and its diverse people. Of Lebanese descent, she appreciates all that is Nova Scotia and takes every opportunity to share the rich stories of our history and never misses a chance to talk about the potential of this amazing province. She is a proud Acadia graduate, leadership expert, professional speaker and loves nothing more than a good cup of tea, a great conversation and a good belly laugh.

Joan Dawson's List of the 10 Most Memorable Backroads She's Ever Travelled in Nova Scotia

As a history buff, I have selected roads that reflect aspects of Nova Scotia's past. But many of them also have stunning views and all are worth exploring. In no particular order, here's my list:

#1. RIVER DENYS MOUNTAIN ROAD: If you turn left from Highway 105 just after Glendale, you come to this rough dirt road winding steeply uphill, with a deep gorge to one side and a wooded hill on the other. (Don't say you haven't been warned!) At the top, there is an intersection. The road to the left leads down to Judique, but if you turn right, you come suddenly to a clearing where there is a graveyard and a little white church. This is the simple wooden Roman Catholic Church of St. Margaret of Scotland, the only remaining building of a community that once farmed and cut lumber in this remote place. It was established in the early 1830s by a group of Gaelic-speaking settlers from the highlands and islands of Western Scotland, led by Donald MacDonald and his family. They built their church and school at the centre of their scattered homesteads. I found the church open, and it is worth a visit.

The population reached its peak in the late 19th century, but declined as people abandoned the isolated settlement for more lucrative work in the coalmines or in Western Canada. The last families left in the early 1950s, but to this day many descendants of the pioneer families are laid to rest in this graveyard. The road continues down towards Melford and is equally daunting, so I would recommend a vehicle with four-wheel drive, but the experience is worth the effort.

#2. THE POST ROAD FROM WEST LAHAVE: Driving from Bridgwater on Route 331, just beyond the LaHave River Yacht Club at West LaHave, a sign indicates the Post Road leading to the left, towards the river. It is a short dirt road down to the shore, where there is an old stone wharf. This is the spot from which John Pernette, whose father received a large grant of land here in the 1760s, established the first ferry across the LaHave River at the end of the 18th century. The ferry and the road formed part of the main route from Lunenburg to western Nova Scotia, and the Post Road is so named because it was used by the mail carrier who crossed on the ferry with his horse. The route continues past St. Peters Church along what is now the Mount Pleasant Road, and on towards Liverpool. The last section before you reach Petite

Riviere is still unpaved, and probably looks much as it did in the days when it was used by farmers in buggies, pedestrians and the postman and his horse. At Petite Riviere, the road rejoins Route 331.

#3. LOCH BROOM LOOP: As you drive along Highway 376 (the West River Road) on the way to Pictou, a sign points to Alma Road and Loch Broom, to the right. Just beyond the bridge over the West River, with its lovely scenic view, the Loch Broom Loop turns off to the left. The road passes through woodland to open farmland, where a sign points left to an historic log church. This is a replica of one of two churches that were built in 1787, by Scottish Presbyterian settlers, for their first minister, the Rev. James MacGregor. It was made of logs, like many of their homes. The seats are also made of logs with one side flattened. There is a gallery, reached by a ladder, for the younger members of the congregation. Here, long sermons were preached both in English and Gaelic. Many of the present residents of this area are descendants of the pioneer settlers of Pictou, and the replica church was once again built by local volunteers. It is still used for special events, and a Gaelic service is held each August. The church is recognised as a National Historic Site, and is well worth the detour along Loch Broom Loop.

#4. LOWER LAHAVE ROAD: Most people driving through Riverport are on their way somewhere and stay on Route 332, but it is worth making a side trip through the old village of Riverport, with its former stores and warehouses, and carrying on along the Lower LaHave Road. At first, the road clings to the shore where there is a stunning view of Ritceys Cove to the right. On the left are the former schoolhouse, now the community centre, and several magnificent old houses built in the days of prosperous merchants and ship owners, as well as more modest homes of various periods including some lovely examples of the "Lunenburg Bump." Also on the left is the Keith M. Mosher Memorial Park, established in memory of a former resident killed in action in the Second World War. Shortly afterwards, there is a fork in the road. The dirt road to the left leads to Kingsburg, but we cross the bridge to the right. The paved road passes the ponds and marshes behind Oxners Beach, where livestock belonging to the 17th century French settlement across the river once grazed, before coming to an end at the beach. This peaceful road, with its well-kept homes and gardens, and varied scenery, is well worth visiting.

#5. THE OLD SACKVILLE ROAD: Long before Highway 101 was established, the Old Sackville Road formed part of the main road from Halifax to Windsor. Today, it forks off to the left from Route 1 just by the Fultz House Museum. In the early 19th century, roads were only beginning to replace water as an important method of travel. What was known as the "Great Road" from Halifax to Windsor was the first of what would later be a network of roads linking different parts of the province. It was used by pedestrians, horses and buggies, private carriages, and from 1816, stage coaches that also carried mail. In winter, the wheeled vehicles were replaced by sleds. This road was also an early settlement site as the population of Halifax began to spread outside the city. Land was granted to would-be settlers, on condition that they cleared and developed it. Farms were established on the meadows along the Sackville River. As it became an established travel route, inns were built to serve travellers along the way. The journey between Halifax and Windsor was slow and tedious, particularly in bad weather, and people were glad of places to stop for refreshment, and to rest or change their weary horses. Today, the road is quiet, serving mostly local traffic, and it eventually rejoins the newer Route 1 by way of the Lucasville Road. It makes an interesting drive, though there are few traces of its former importance.

#6. DYKE ROAD, FALMOUTH: Dyke Road is reached by turning off Highway 101 at Exit 7 towards Falmouth, right on Route 1, left at the first fork, and left again at the second intersection. The road has many points of interest. It takes its name from the Acadian farms that were established along the Avon River in the late 17th century by dyking the marshes along the river. The land is still farmed. The road runs through the former Acadian parish of Ste. Famille, established in 1698 to serve the Acadian families on the east side of the river. It was later settled by New Englanders, whose descendants built the beautiful Baptist church at the intersection with Town Road.

Continuing on Dyke Road, a little further along to the left is Gabriel Road, and a short distance along this road is the old Ste. Famille cemetery, the burial place of the people who first farmed this land.When you return to Dyke Road, the landscape quickly opens up with a view to the left across the dyked meadows to the Avon River and the Martock ski area in the hills beyond. A few minutes later, the vineyards and buildings of the twentieth century Sainte Famiile Winery, also built on Acadian land, come into view on the right. Beyond the crossroads a short distance ahead lies Castle Frederick, the former site of a mansion built by Joseph Frederick Wallet DesBarres, hydrographer and governor of Cape Breton during its brief period of separation from Nova Scotia. This, too, was once an Acadian farm owned by the Landry family, and now home to the Bremner family farm, with hiking and snowshoeing trails. Few roads in Nova Scotia have such a long history encompassed in a few short kilometers. Returning to the crossroads, the Sangster Bridge Road past the Anglican church takes you to Route 14.

#7. TOWN PLOT ROAD, STARRS POINT: A few kilometres along the road from Port Williams to Starrs Point, a sign points to Town Plot Road on the right. This road is all that remains of the town that was laid out in the early 1760s for a group of settlers from New England, known as Planters. They were invited to come to Nova Scotia to take over the abandoned Acadian farms after the Acadian Expulsion. The town was designed as the centre of Cornwallis Township, established on the site of the former Acadian parish of St. Joseph-des-Mines that extended from the Cornwallis River to the North Mountain. Farm and water lots were granted to the new arrivals, and the town was to be the administrative centre, consisting of a grid of streets with town lots and a parade square. It was linked by a ferry across the Cornwallis River to Horton Township on the south side. The road to the ferry on the Horton side was poor, so the ferry was unsatisfactory. The town site proved to be too isolated, and was abandoned as people preferred to live on their farms or in less convenient settlements like Port Williams. Today, the road forms a square, with one side close to Willowbank farm. A track leads along the riverbank to the old burial ground. The only remaining traces of the town are a cairn on the upper road, and the old Planters' Barracks building that is now a B&B.

#8. OLD POST ROAD, GRAND PRÉ: The Old Post Road crosses the Grand Pré Road that leads to the Grand Pré National Historic Site from Route 1. Today it is just a short detour off the main road, but this stretch of road is full of history. In the late eighteenth century it was used by mail carriers on horseback who would have called at the Horton Post House, an inn run by John Fowler, to drop off and pick up mail. In the nineteenth century, it was still the main road to Yarmouth, and stagecoaches carried both mail and passengers along it before it was altered to its present route. But its story goes farther back. If you turn right at the intersection, the road leads to Horton Landing, on the shore of the Minas Basin. Here, the Deportation Cross marks the spot from which the Acadians were forced into exile in 1755. At this same spot, the New Englanders who replaced them came to Nova Scotia. Turning left, at the top of the hill is the viewpoint established to overlook the park of the National Historic Site, and the huge area of dyked farmland beyond, created by the Acadians who came here at the end of the 17th century. The view is spectacular, and interpretive panels explain the significance of this place. Shortly after this, the road rejoins Route 1, and our detour is over.

#9. THE ROAD TO BEAR RIVER: Most people travelling along Highway 101 between Annapolis Royal and Digby are in a hurry but, for those with time to spare, it is worth leaving the highway at Exit 24 and taking a detour along the road to Bear River. The road runs parallel to the river for six kilometres, with tantalizing glimpses of the water, until you reach the village of Bear River in its deep valley, and cross the bridge on the right. The river is tidal, with a difference of 17 feet between high and low tides. Now you find yourself on the main street, with a beautiful riverside park on the left, beside an inviting art and craft shop. Farther along the street are more interesting shops. A café near the bridge has a deck overlooking the river, where if you are lucky you may witness the tide turning. There are several other interesting shops. Bear River is known as "the village on stilts" because many of the buildings near the river actually overhang the water to save space in the narrow valley. At the top of the hill on the far side there are vineyards, one of which is said by some to be on the site of one established by Louis Hébert who was at Port Royal with Champlain. You have probably spent more time than you expected in Bear River, and you can rejoin the highway either by retracing your steps, or return on the other side of the river along Chute Road at the top of the hill, to Exit 23 on 101.

#10. FORT LAWRENCE ROAD, AMHERST: Just north of Amherst along Route 2, close to the border with New Brunswick, Fort Lawrence Road turns off to the left. It passes through farmland and woodland until you come to a clearing where there is a parking lot and a gazebo with interpretive panels. You are at the site of the former Acadian village of Beaubassin, destroyed during the fighting between the British and the

French for control of Nova Scotia. Beaubassin was a border town and it was destroyed not by the British but by the Mi'kmaq, on orders from a French missionary priest, Father LeLoutre, who stirred up their hostility to the British. LeLoutre's aim was to compel the Acadian inhabitants of Beaubassin to cross to the French side of the Missaguash River that formed the boundary between British Nova Scotia and French Canada. The British built Fort Lawrence close to the deserted village site, across the river from where the French built Fort Beauséjour. In 1755, British forces seized control of Fort Beauséjour, renamed it Fort Cumberland, and abandoned Fort Lawrence. Nothing remains above ground of either the fort or the village, but both are designated National Historic sites.

Joan Dawson was born in London, England, in 1932, attended English schools and received an MA in Modern Languages from French at Oxford University, where she met her future husband, Robert Dawson. She came to Canada in 1954, spent five years in Winnipeg and has lived in Halifax since 1960. While raising their two sons she took a master's degree (MLS) in what was then called Library Services at Dalhousie. She has worked as a teacher, a librarian and a freelance researcher and translator. As a volunteer at Fort Point Museum at LaHave, she became interested in local history and cartography, which resulted in the publication of a number of books, including The Mapmaker's Eye *(1988) and* The Mapmakers' Legacy *(2007). Her 2009 book,* Nova Scotia's Lost Highways, *was followed by* Nova Scotia's Historic Rivers *in 2012, which was nominated for the Dartmouth non-fiction book award in 2013. Her most recent publication was* A History of Nova Scotia in 50 Objects *(2015).*

Brent and Sara's List of the 10 Most Unusual Things to Discover in Nova Scotia

Nova Scotia, Canada's Ocean Playground, is full of amazing things to see and do. However, sometimes we yearn for something different, unique or even unusual. When we discover these rare gems, we brag about them! This list — The 10 Most Unusual Things to Discover in Nova Scotia — is just that.

#1. PICTOU ISLAND: Located between Nova Scotia and PEI, Pictou Island is unique in so many ways. This off-the-grid island is home to only a few permanent residents and summer homeowners and is accessible only by boat. The white-sand beaches and turquoise waters rival some of the most beautiful in the world and there are surprises around every corner.

GOOD TO KNOW: The island is also home to a large blue-heron colony, seal colony and a car graveyard, which is one of the most surprising things we've ever seen!

#2. POLLET'S COVE: We knew a hike had to be on this list and it was a difficult choice because Nova Scotia is famous for its hiking trails, which are often compared to those on the west coast of Canada. Pollett's Cove makes the list because the reward at the end is only matched by the effort it takes to complete. A 16-km long hike over difficult terrain isn't for beginners but it's well worth it.

GOOD TO KNOW: The hike has many steep inclines and declines but when you reach the end, the forest opens up to one of the most magical sites in all of Nova Scotia. Pollett's Cove looks like a scene straight out of a fairy tale and if you're lucky, you'll meet the horses that call this little peninsula home!

#3. STEINHART DISTILLERY: Steinhart Distillery is located in Arisag, Nova Scotia. Well known for their unique vodkas and gins, what makes this particular distillery so special is that guests can stay on site in one of their country cottages and actually brew their own vodka.

GOOD TO KNOW: The accommodations aren't listed on their website so you'll have to call if you want to book.

#4. CONCRETE CREATIONS: Concrete Creations is located in Liverpool and is the brainchild of local artist Ivan Higgins. A winding, wooded trail leads you through a collection of intricate concrete sculptures, some of which stand well over 10-feet tall. The impressive collection is constantly growing, now with more than 25 sculptures!

GOOD TO KNOW: The concrete garden is found behind the Cosby's Garden centre and would be easy to miss if you didn't know what you were looking for.

#5. SABLE ISLAND: Located about 175 km off the eastern coast of Nova Scotia, Sable Island is, in essence, an oversized sandbar and home to some 400 wild horses. Famous for its white sand, unpredictable weather events and shipwrecks, the island is protected and managed by Parks Canada.

GOOD TO KNOW: Visitations to the island are becoming more and more accessible for the general public through various tour operators and promotions through Parks Canada.

#6. VICTORIA PARK: We couldn't complete this list without including a true gem that lies in our hometown of Truro. This 1,000-acre park, located right in the centre of town contains an extensive trail system, two waterfalls and the famous Jacobs Ladder, which is 175 steep steps!

GOOD TO KNOW: Victoria Park is limited to day use only and also has biking trails, groomed cross country trails in winter months, an outdoor public pool, playground, baseball diamond and much more.

#7. COAL MINE TOURS: There are several museums around the province that pay tribute to Nova Scotia's rich history of coal mining but our pick for this list is the Miner's Museum. Located in Glace Bay, Cape Breton, tourists can visit the museum during the summer months and take a tour into a coal mine and learn about life underground.

GOOD TO KNOW: What makes these tours really special is that the guides are retired miners themselves, some of who spent upwards of 30 years underground and their knowledge of life in the mines is extensive.

#8. 100 WILD ISLANDS: This archipelago of more than 100 islands that stretch over 30 km along the Eastern Shore of Nova Scotia are home to over 100 species of birds and have been largely untouched by humans for more than 10,000 years. The dramatic landscape and white sand beaches are truly astonishing and whether you visit by boat or enjoy the short hiking trail to shelter cover, it's worth a visit.

GOOD TO KNOW: The area is protected by the Nova Scotia Nature trust who host several events each year to take visitors out to the islands to explore the bogs, barrens and boreal rainforests in a safe and respectful way.

#9. OYSTER PICKING: Whether you like to eat them or not, oyster picking is something we think everyone should experience. There's something about rolling up your pants and trudging around in the water for a couple of hours hunting for these little treasures that's just quintessential Nova Scotia.

GOOD TO KNOW: Oyster picking is highly regulated in Nova Scotia so you either have to get a license (which is easy and inexpensive to do) or go with a tour. We recommend both! The two best spots we've found are Caribou Island and Brule shore.

#10. BURNTCOAT HEAD PARK: Burntcoat Head Park is still one of the most magical things we've seen in Nova Scotia. As you descend the stone staircase and step out onto the ocean floor, it's hard not to be amazed. What was filled with up to 53 feet of water just hours before, now opens onto 360 degree panoramic views of the Bay of Fundy. Witnessing the extreme contrast of low and high tide is something everyone should experience but few actually have!

GOOD TO KNOW: Plan your day to see both low and high tide and be sure to mind the time as you explore the ocean floor. Leave plenty of time to get back up the stairs before the tide turns — it comes in quickly!

Brent and Sara are full-time travel writers, customer experience consultants and adventure junkies. When they're not travelling the world and making videos for the travel blog, Dashboard Living, they're working closely with business owners to grow and elevate their brands through world-class customer experiences. Check them out at these social media sites: **dashboardliving.com/work-with-us** **facebook.com/dashboardliving / instagram.com/dashboardliving**

Denyse Sibley's List of the 10 Most Romantic Places in Nova Scotia

So you are looking for a romantic place to take your sweetheart but where in Nova Scotia should you go? Here are a few of my favourite places:

#1. BLOMIDON PROVINCIAL PARK: It's a storybook getaway and it would be tough to leave this beauty off the list for a romantic spot. One look and you're in love. I could stay here forever.

#2. THE EMERA, HALIFAX SKATING OVAL: Hand in hand and if you can't skate or you need help, all the happier. Nothing says romance better.

#3. HELICOPTER RIDE OVER THE NORTH SHORE OR SCENIC WENTWORTH VALLEY: There is something about a rotary-wing chopper and the accompanying g forces. Snuggle up and enjoy the ride. This romance is between me and the machine.

#4. DOLLAR LAKE: I grew up in Meagher's Grant. I was only a few miles from this lake, so all my teen life I took it for granted. I remember going there with two of my close friends from high school and JUST CHILLIN. I now appreciate the beauty so close to home.

#5. THE CHICKEN BURGER IN BEDFORD: Have to dig that Jukebox. It's the old hits, the '60s sock-hop feel. I always think of the soundtrack to Dirty Dancing with Patrick Swayze and Jennifer Grey is amazing and the food is delicious.

#6. SKYDIVING AT ATLANTIC SCHOOL OF SKYDIVING: Located in Waterville. Don't you think it's a romantic first or second date?

#7. BOAT RIDE ON LEWIS LAKE, MOUNT UNIACKE: It's my backyard and you can't beat it on a hot summer day. Lazy, hazy… enough said.

#8. TRURO FLYING CLUB IN DEBERT: Book a scenic flight anywhere in Nova Scotia and you're in love. I was thrilled to become a licensed pilot in the late 90s and you really can't appreciate the true beauty of Nova Scotia until you see it from the air. You get a view worth bragging about and I do... often.

#9. KEJIMKUJIK NATIONAL PARK: Not just a favourite place of mine, but also my four kids would be hard pressed to say anything negative about this park — even during black-fly season. There is no way I could leave it off the list.

#10. PURCELL'S COVE ROAD LOOKOUT: It can easily take your breath away and although it may not match the thrill of tidal-bore rafting it's serene — sailboats and midnight kisses.

Denyse Sibley is a Halifax-based radio personality.

FOOD

- 16 Foods That Define the Taste of Nova Scotia
- Pete Luckett's List of the 10 Top Nova Scotian Products (Grown or Produced) He Likes to See on the Menu When He Dines Out
- Joan McEllman's List of Five Things She Likes About Cooking in Nova Scotia
- Elaine Elliot's List of Nova Scotia's Top 10 Pickles and Savoury Jellies
- Jared Hochman's List of His 10 Favourite Burger Joints in Nova Scotia
- Jared Hochman's List of His 10 Favourite Places to Find Comfort Food in Nova Scotia
- The Pizza Queen's List of the Top 10 Places to Get Pizza in Nova Scotia
- Elisabeth Bailey's List of the Top 10 Seafood Chowders in Nova Scotia
- Elisabeth Bailey's List of the Top 10 Fish-and-Chip Joints in Nova Scotia
- The Bologna Lover's List of the Top 10 Ways Nova Scotians Eat Bologna
- The Kilted Chef's List of the 10 Best Ways to Eat Lobster
- Virginia Lee's List of the Top 10 Food Items Grown or Made in Nova Scotia

16 Foods That Define the Taste of Nova Scotia

With an eclectic mix of cultures, Nova Scotia is a virtual melting pot of traditions and nothing illustrates that diversity more than the foods we eat. Here are some of the tasty dishes that have been made in local kitchens for decades, if not centuries, and they truly define the taste of Nova Scotia.

#1. HODGE PODGE: A mid-to-late summer ritual in Nova Scotia, this dish is usually made when the produce can be taken fresh from the garden (or a farmer's market). For a traditional Hodge Podge, you'll need potatoes, carrots, beans (yellow and green) and peas as well as cream, butter (preferably the real thing), pepper and salt. In some kitchens, some cooks have been known to add salt pork fried to a golden brown, which you throw into the pot before adding the cream.

#2. CHOW CHOW: Some people call this green-tomato relish. This side dish is often served with the Saturday night baked beans that many Nova Scotians love. You'll need green tomatoes, onions and a variety of spices if you plan on making this traditional dish.

#3. SOLOMON GUNDY: A very old traditional recipe originating from the Lunenburg area. Solomon Gundy, pickled herring and raw onions, is usually served as an appetizer or side dish.

#4. LUNENBURG PUDDING AND LUNENBURG SAUSAGE: Nothing says the South Shore of Nova Scotia more than Lunenburg pudding and Lunenburg sausage. Lunenburg pudding is more in keeping with the old English definition of pudding. It contains beef, pork, liver and spices all stuffed into an edible casing. Since it's already cooked, it can be eaten directly from the fridge. Lunenburg sausage is a raw, all-beef product. Most people fry it up to serve with potatoes and vegetables. It can also be boiled.

#5. RAPPIE PIE: A truly Nova Scotian dish with the tradition originating in the Acadian communities of southwest Nova Scotia, mostly in the Clare, Pubnico and Wedgeport areas. Initially, the dish was served for special occasions and celebrations, but it is served up in most households in the region. Although it's unquestionably a French-Acadian dish, there are different views about its origin. Some suggest that Rappie Pie was introduced to the Acadian communities after The Deportation in 1755 but prior to the Acadians returning. After they returned to Nova Scotia, the Acadians grew lots of potatoes and it was a natural thing for them to use what they had access to.

#6. SAUERKRAUT: The word sauerkraut means sour cabbage. For the last 200 years, Tancook Islanders have been growing cabbage for the art of making sauerkraut, making it a truly local treat. To make sauerkraut, you pack cabbage into barrels along with a healthy amount of coarse salt. The sauerkraut must age in the barrels for several weeks. A weight is used to push the mixture down. According to Tancook Island tradition, as the cabbage ages, the volume of juice rises and falls in the barrel. All the work was carried out in special cabbage buildings. In the 1800s and early 1900s the cabbage was stomped by using bare feet before it was put into the barrels. You can still buy original Tancook sauerkraut in some Lunenburg County stores or directly from Tancook producers. Traditionally, in Nova Scotia, sauerkraut as a meal is served with mashed potatoes and pork (or wieners). Many people enjoy as a condiment on their hot dogs or sausages.

#7. BLUEBERRY GRUNT: A delicious Nova Scotian dessert of stewed dumplings mixed with berries that dates back to the earliest settlers. Over the years, apples, rhubarb and strawberries were used, but blueberries are, by far, the favourite. It may be called blueberry buckle.

#8. FISH CAKES: This is another simple, but tasty dish from Nova Scotia. Simply cook and mash a pot of potatoes. Cook your fish (normally cod, but haddock or any fish could be used) with onions and pork scraps. Mix all the ingredients together and form patties. Fry the patties in a little oil or margarine.

#9 CAPE BRETON PORKPIES: Traditionally served on Christmas Eve, mostly on the eastern tip of Cape Breton Island, porkpies are not pies at all. They are tarts and they are not made of pork either. The filling in porkpies is made of dates and the shells are made of flour, butter and brown sugar, and the icing contains maple extract. All together there are about five ingredients in a porkpie. Aside from Christmas, porkpies are also eaten at special occasions such as weddings, anniversaries and baptisms.

#10. APPLES: Did you know that Nova Scotia used to be a major apple producer for not just North America but Britain as well, and that several varieties were developed at the research station in the valley?

#11. SEAFOOD CHOWDER: It is a Christmas tradition in many Nova Scotian homes to serve seafood chowder that includes, along with potatoes, lobster, scallops, clams and haddock, but it is a delicious meal that can be served any time of the year.

#12. PAN-FRIED HADDOCK: Simple but delicious when served with boiled potatoes and vegetables.

#13. KAT: Basically smoked eel, this is a traditional Mi'kmaw dish.

#14. HOUSE BANKIN: Also known in Nova Scotia as a Dutch Mess, this dish basically consists of salt cod, potatoes, onions and bacon.

#15. CLAPSHOT: The basic ingredients of this dish are potatoes mashed with rutabagas. It originated in Scotland.

And for desert ...

#16. GRAPE-NUT ICE CREAM: Grape-nut ice cream is a popular regional dish in the Maritimes, but especially in Nova Scotia. One origin story is that it was created by Chef Hannah Young at The Palms restaurant in Wolfville in 1919. According to the popular story, she created it when she ran out of fresh fruit to add to ice cream and decided to throw in some cereal. It proved popular at the restaurant and the Scotsburn Dairy Company began mass producing the ice cream variety, and it sold across the region.

Pete Luckett's List of the 10 Top Nova Scotian Products (Grown or Produced) He Likes to See on the Menu When He Dines Out

I believe any such list should showcase the diversity of Nova Scotia products and the best of what our province has to offer. All of the items I will mention are also sustainable, which is something I always consider when determining my favourite products.

We can really make use of the "farm to table" approach in our province, because there is an excellent selection of everything you need! We have high-quality meats, seafood, vegetables, fruits and craft beverages that encourage us to eat seasonally, learning and educating others on what items are best to eat and when.

When I dine out, this is my list of the top 10 choices of Nova Scotian-grown or produced products that I like to see on a menu.

#1. Nova Scotia's own Tidal Bay appellation wine.

#2. Nova Scotia lobster, scallops and incredible oysters.

#3. Nova Scotia apples (old varieties like Cox's and Orange Pippins and new varieties like Ambrosia and Honey Crisp).
#4. Nova Scotia beer.

#5. Nova Scotia Cider (hard or not).

#6. Nova Scotia distilled products (I love that local gin).

#7. Nova Scotia foraged items like mushrooms, fiddleheads and samphire.

#8. Uncommon vegetables like romanesco, kohlrabi and celeriac.

#9. Nova Scotia honey.

#10. Nova Scotia raised beef.

Pete Luckett crossed the Atlantic in 1979 and settled down in Atlantic Canada. He grew from a single retail outlet in New Brunswick in 1982, to one of Atlantic Canada's best known and loved brands...Pete's Frootique. He launched Pete's Fine Foods in Nova Scotia in 1992 with locations in Halifax and Bedford. For 14 years Pete appeared on the national television program, Midday, where he extolled the flavour and health virtues of exotic fruits and vegetables. His weekly newspaper column and books feature exciting recipes. His food-adventure television series, The Food Hunter, aired internationally for three seasons and enticed consumers from the comfort of their armchairs. In 2011 Pete launched Luckett Vineyards in the Gaspereau Valley, and sold his grocery retail and wholesale business to Sobeys.

Joan McEllman's List of Five Things She Likes About Cooking in Nova Scotia

Being a transplant from the Okanagan Valley of B.C., we have found Nova Scotia to be so similar in so many ways and it's just getting better. I love the fall, when all the produce is readily available and everything is fresh and crisp. Here are five things that I like about cooking in Nova Scotia:

#1. Fresh fruits and vegetables.

#2. Farm markets along the roads, everywhere you travel
#3. Fresh seafood

#4. Incredible dining experiences

#5. And of course, all the local wineries.

Joan McEllman is the host of EastLink TV's Welcome to My Kitchen and author of a cookbook by the same name.

Elaine Elliot's List of Nova Scotia's Top 10 Pickles and Savoury Jellies

Walking into one of the heritage cottages of the Eastern Shore's Sherbrooke Village recently, I was assailed by cooking odours from my past. They had to be making the cucumber pickles that mother used to make! And while I've not tasted one of those pickles for probably 30 years, I was immediately back in my grandfather's dining room on a Sunday evening with cousins, aunts and uncles enjoying a Nova Scotian family dinner. I'm sure you remember those gatherings — the impromptu meals when whoever was around brought something to add to the table, the adults at the large dining table and the children nearby at makeshift children's tables. Suffice to say, I searched old cookbooks but finally had to rely on the Internet to find the recipe for Peeled Cucumber Mustard Pickles.

Ah, that bygone era when all country folk had a kitchen garden and everything was used or shared with neighbours. And the Peeled Cucumber Mustard Pickles? Why, they were made with cukes that had grown too large, the ones that missed picking at their prime, and called out to our frugal Scottish background of "waste not, want not." Peeled, seeded and cut in wedges, these overripe cucumbers were cooked in a sweet mustard sauce to be enjoyed during the long winter months when last summer's garden was snow covered and seed catalogues were awaiting perusal.

I tend to favour savoury over sweet condiments and my list reflects the accompaniments my family has come to expect with certain meals. Sunday's roasts of beef are served with green-tomato chow, cod fish cakes need the pungent bite of cardamom found in the rhubarb chutney, and Reuben sandwiches cry out for garlicky dill pickles. The cranberry sauce I serve at Thanksgiving and Christmas may take longer to prepare than simply opening a can, but is so worth the effort.

This summer check your local farm markets, pick the freshest produce you can find and follow a canning recipe — I guarantee the satisfaction you feel when you serve your homemade treats will turn you into an avid preserver. Here is my top 10 list of preserves made from products grown right here in Nova Scotia:

#1. PEELED CUCUMBER MUSTARD PICKLES

#2. CRANBERRY SAUCE WITH ORANGE LIQUOR

#3. GREEN TOMATO CHOW CHOW

#4. DILL PICKLES WITH GARLIC

#5. SWEET ZUCCHINI RELISH

#6. PICKLED BEETS

#7. RHUBARB, APRICOT AND ALMOND CHUTNEY

#8. ZESTY RED PEPPER JELLY

#9. SWEET MUSTARD PICKLES

#10. BREAD AND BUTTER PICKLES

Elaine Elliot is a food writer who has spent countless hours seeking out new and exciting food ideas. The author of several cookbooks and magazine articles, she has also worked as a cooking team with her sister, Virginia Lee gathering, testing and adapting recipes for their hit series, Maritime Flavours — Guidebooks and Cookbooks. She resides in Wolfville with her husband in Nova Scotia's lush Annapolis Valley.

Jared Hochman's List of His 10 Favourite Burger Joints in Nova Scotia

Does any food cause a more existential discussion than a burger? I mean, it's some sort of patty between a bun (which is two pieces of bread), does that make it a sandwich? Or is it something distinctly different? Perhaps it has that burger-like je ne sais quoi that puts it in a class of its own. Either way… Sorry. Got off topic there. It doesn't matter how you want to classify a burger, what's important is that we can all agree they are delicious. And Nova Scotia abounds with places offeringmouth-watering interpretations.

Narrowing this list down to only 10 was near impossible. With so many great locations from Yarmouth to Sydney, some hard decisions had to be made. I personally have not visited all 10 locations on this list, but I have it on good authority — from friends, colleagues, reviewers and good old word of mouth — that these spots truly embody what it means to serve a burger.

So, don't look at this as just my list … look at it as our list. The people's list. For burgers.

#1. COASTAL RESTAURANT & PUB: (36404 Cabot Trail, Ingonish) Situated along the eastern coast of Cape Breton's Cabot Trail, The Coastal Restaurant & Pub offers a full menu, but they offer a burger which is particularly renowned — The Ringer Burger. Featured on The Food Network's You Gotta Eat Here, Coastal's signature burger combines a 6-oz lean-beef patty, grilled and served with their smokey homemade Ringer sauce, onion rings, bacon and melted mozzarella cheese. Plus, how often do you get to eat something famous!

#2. APPLESEED MODERN DINER: (33 MacGregor Avenue, New Glasgow) Located on the outskirts of New Glasgow, just off the Trans-Canada Highway, The Appleseed opened its doors in July 2014. The menu is BIG — there's definitely something for everyone — and that extends to their burger options as well. With nearly 10 different choices, you can try something traditional, or ones with toppings such as chili, peanut butter and Sriracha aioli, or even Granny Smith apples!

#3. BROWNSTONE CAFE: (244 Main Street, Antigonish) Craving a burger with maple syrup and maple bacon? A burger with cheese curds or a black bean and mushroom veggie burger? Make your way to downtown Antigonish, where the Brownstone Cafe offers all those selections and more. A cozy spot with indoor and outdoor seating, hanging out on Main Street in Antigonish tackling a Mac n' cheese burger (yes, that's correct, it's a burger with macaroni and cheese on it), is a pretty good way to spend a day.

#4. BLACK ROCK BISTRO: (151 Main Street, Parrsboro) A little different than your standard burger shop or pub, Black Rock proudly offers an Indo-Moroccan atmosphere for customers, ranging from the restaurant's colours and the furniture to the flavouring of each dish. Have your burger with lean ground beef or vegetarian, with a Caesar salad or black bean and corn pilaf. Flavour is front and centre with these burgers, whether it's their signature burger with a spicy tomato jam and dijonnaise sauce, or a burger with smokey bacon jam and That Dutchman's Dragon Breath blue cheese.

#5. PORT PUB & BISTRO: (980 Terry's Creek Road, Port Williams) Uniquely (yet purposefully) designed so a spectacular view of the Cornwallis River is available virtually wherever you sit, The Port Pub has now surpassed a decade of offering incredible meals, with a heavy focus on locally-sourced products. A staple of the Annapolis Valley, their commitment to great, local food is no more evident than in the Starr's Point Burger, with grass-fed Starr's Point beef, a brioche bun and all the delightful toppings that make any burger aficionado content.

#6. UNION STREET CAFÉ: (183 Commercial Street, Berwick) Classic pub food, reimagined favourites and some pretty outside-the-box burgers, the Union Street Café has been doing food a little different since first opening in Y2K. Whether it's a local beef and bacon burger, handmade almond and chickpea burger, or a Vietnamese Pork Burger, The Union Street Café is always a good choice to stop at. They offer more than just food too — they're considered one of the top live music venues in the province … because who doesn't love a good show with a great burger?

#7. GRAND BANKER BAR & GRILL: (82 Montague Street, Lunenburg) As if noting that the Grand Banker was opened by the same person who helped create Halifax's famed Your Father's Moustache pub wasn't enough, there is also this: The Lunenburger. A 6 oz. beef burger with smoked mozzarella, smoked bacon and spinach. Oh, and it's topped with fresh lobster meat. And a tarragon butter sauce. And picked with a bacon-wrapped scallop. You're welcome.

#8. LANE'S PRIVATEER INN: (27 Bristol Avenue, Liverpool) A true pioneer to the Nova Scotian food scene (they were a charter member of Taste of Nova Scotia), Lane's Privateer Inn is nothing short of iconic for Liverpool — and the South Shore overall. With a nautical name, it's only proper that good seafood is their specialty, so if you're craving a quality fish burger (haddock, in this case), I'd say a visit here is warranted (although a local Italian-sausage burger with pickled red onion and gouda sounds quite delightful too).

#9. KRAVE BURGER: (5680 Spring Garden Road, Halifax) There is no shortage of gourmet burger restaurants in Halifax, so for one to come along relatively late in the game (2014) and quickly make an impression as one of the city's best says a lot about the quality and innovation of their burgers. Using 100 percent locally sourced beef, an ever-rotating selection of burgers and plenty of toppings, Krave's selections are plenty creative enough, especially when it's Burger Week.

#10. DARRELL'S: (5576 Fenwick Street, Halifax) I simply cannot talk about the top burger places in Nova Scotia without having Darrell's front and centre. In the heart of South End Halifax, Darrell's has hit 25 years as one of the city's premier burger places. But you don't need me — or their endless accolades — to tell you that. The proof is in the pudding. Or in this case their world-famous (I swear) peanut-butter burger. Or the Hen Den. Or the Pepper Burger. With a province full of incredible hand-held sandwiches, Darrell's is among the true royalty.

Nova Scotian born and raised, Jared Hochman has a love of food and beverage (created from more than years in the restaurant industry) and a passion for communication (founded in his journalism degree from the University of King's College). After 29.5 years on the East Coast, Jared moved to Toronto in 2016 to find new adventures — and restaurants. Follow his journey on Instagram @thejlhochman.

Jared Hochman's List of His 10 Favourite Places to Find Comfort Food in Nova Scotia

Ask 10 different people what comfort food means to them, and you'll get 10 different answers. Some believe it's food that tastes great. Others will say it's how it makes them feel. Then there's the group that believe comfort food is not just about the now, but how it brings back old memories and the familiar good times you've had with that meal. And finally, some folks find comfort in where they eat their food — the sights and sounds that accompany a meal are sometimes as important as the meal itself.

That's why, when I asked different friends and valued foodies about where their favourite spots for comfort food are and I thought about the places that immediately came to my mind, the criteria were truly all over the board. But these 10 spots stand out — not for the same reasons, but they do all find ways to fulfill the mind, soul and stomach.

In no particular order then, here are my suggestions for the top places to find comfort food in Nova Scotia.

#1. RED SHOE PUB: (11573 Route 19, Mabou) Cape Breton has no shortage of beautiful sights — the Bras d'Or Lakes, the Cabot Trail and crossing the causeway to name a few — but another is the beautiful drive through the twisty roads of Western Cape Breton, especially in Mabou. And when in Mabou, there's a familiar comfort in grabbing a bite at the Red Shoe Pub. Perhaps it's the fact that it's owned by the Rankin Sisters. Perhaps it's the lively atmosphere. Or perhaps it's a menu that takes as much pride in offering wings, chili and beef tips as it does pan-seared scallops, char-grilled salmon and daily seafood specialties. Regardless of how, you'll feel right at home at the Red Shoe, whether Mabou is actually your home or not.

#2. LE GABRIEL: (15424 Cabot Trail, Cheticamp) Nova Scotia's history is deeply intertwined with that of Acadian culture, and traditional Acadian fare is exactly what Le Gabriel serves up. Named after Acadian icon Gabriel (from the Henry Wadsworth poem "*Evangeline*"), Le Gabriel is more than just a restaurant; it's a symbol for where Acadian culture has been, where it has come and where it is going. The menu items may look familiar: fillet of cod, liver and onions and sautéed scallops, but they all have a little something extra added to them — soul.

#3. BIG G'S PIZZA: (111 Main Street, Guysborough) *Full disclosure*: I was born and raised in Guysborough, so Big G's has a special place in my heart. For everyone else, this cozy spot, which overlooks the Chedabucto Bay, offers wonderful pizza, donairs, wraps and way-too-filling-but-it's-worth-it panzerottis. What makes Big G's even better, however, is the hospitality from owner Gandhi Mohrez, who takes the time to make each and every visitor feel welcome. It's comfort food, but also a comfort atmosphere.

#4. CHOWDER HOUSE: (265 Main Street, Tatamagouche) There's an age-old saying that "chicken soup is good for the soul." That may well be true, but in Nova Scotia nothing cures an ailing soul more than a hearty bowl of seafood chowder. And at the Chowder House, a quaint little spot that sits along Waughs River, their chowder certainly is comforting. Stop for a bowl (or five) and indulge in any of their healthy-choice daily lunch specials, or anything on their unassuming-yet-delicious menu (but with a name such as Chowder House, I mean, you gotta have chowder).

#5. CRUSH PAD BISTRO @ LUCKETT VINEYARDS: (1293 Grand Pré Road, Wallbrook) While the array of dazzling small plates, salads, sandwiches and main courses are delectable, and their seasonally-inspired menu keeps things fresh, for this little bistro at Luckett Vineyards, aesthetics is everything. They just might have one of the most stunning views of any restaurant in the province. Sit at the top of a hill and gaze upon the Gasperau Valley and across the Minas Basin for as far as your eyes can focus. It's a view that is breathtaking and would almost make you forget about the food in front of you (key word is "almost").

#6. EVANGELINE CAFE: (11668 Hwy 1, Grand Pré) An iconic stop along the Evangeline Trail, next to the Grand Pré National Historic Site, the Evangeline Café again provides more than just food — it's another window into Acadian culture and history, albeit a perspective entirely different from that which you'd find on the eastern end of the province. Come for some impressive burgers, fish cakes, appetizers and more. Stay for the culture, the nature and the beauty of the area. Have some seafood and THEN explore the rest of the Valley. It's a rich history explained (partly) through food.

#7. MERN'S FAMILY DINER: (82 Main Street, Yarmouth) Come in. Feel like family. Eat well. Don't leave hungry. Those basic/simple truths have established Mern's as a muster station for tourists, locals and everything in between. From lobster straight from the wharf and delicious fish and chips, to what many consider the best seafood chowder in town, you walk into Mern's knowing a generous heaping of good food is headed your way.

#8. RIVER PUB: (750 King Street, Bridgewater) Armed with a beautiful patio overlooking the LaHave River, and a menu featuring classics such as poached garlic and dill haddock, steamed mussels, Rueben sandwiches and more, River Pub has been a community go-to place to eat for more than 10 years. With a combination of the food you love, the people you like and a comfort at-home feeling, a good meal here does seem to just put you at ease.

#9. KING OF DONAIR: (6420 Quinpool Road, Halifax) You know when you're having a bad day — the weather is brutal or your car broke down—and you just really need to eat something you know will bring a smile to your face? We've all had those, and thankfully, King of Donair is there when we need it the most. Take your pick for how to brighten your spirits — their namesake donair (official food of Halifax, by the way), the first ones in Canada. Or maybe you'll open an aromatic box of garlic fingers (something the folks in Ontario have yet to truly discover). Or maybe even just a pizza, poutine or mozza sticks. It's scientifically impossible to make a bad decision.

#10. JOHN'S LUNCH: (352 Pleasant Street, Dartmouth) It's really hard to beat a good plate of fish and chips. Like, extremely tough to do. And it just so happens that John's Lunch has, oh you know, what many consider the best fish and chips in Canada. That's right: in the entire country. I guess that shouldn't be a shock, considering this little spot nestled in Dartmouth has been open since 1969. Nearly half a century of experience will turn into some pretty amazing food, and whether it's haddock tips, whole clams, calamari or the seafood platter, just know that when you're eating something getting thrown around as the best in Canada, that's going to bring a smile to your face!

*Nova Scotian born and raised, Jared Hochman has a love of food and beverage (created from more than years in the restaurant industry) and a passion for communication (founded in his journalism degree from the University of King's College). After 29.5 years on the East Coast, Jared moved to Toronto in 2016 to find new adventures — and restaurants. Follow his journey on **Instagram** @thejlhochman.*

The Pizza Queen's List of the Top 10 Places to Get Pizza in Nova Scotia

#1. BRAMOSO PIZZERIA & BEER BAR (6169 Quinpool Road, Halifax) When you think Bramoso, think variety. This place does it all. White or whole-wheat dough? Traditional or thin crust? Gluten-free, dairy-free or vegan? However you like your pizza, they'll make it just the way you want it and cook it in their brick oven. You can even find them at the Halifax Seaport Farmer's market every Saturday. They even make a breakfast pizza. But the biggest thing to note is that Bramoso is all about quality. They partner with the best farms, vineyards and specialty kitchens to ensure things are done right. If you haven't tried Bramoso yet, now you have dinner plans!

#2. TOMAVINOS: (1113 Marginal Road, Halifax) At Tomavinos they only use the finest local organic ingredients and are constantly searching for exciting ideas for their menu. Tomavinos is the proud recipient of The Coast magazine's "Best Pizza in Halifax Award" four years running. I like to call this place a hidden gem. Due to its location I feel it can go unnoticed but mark my words, I tell people loudly and proudly just how delicious this pizza is.

#3. ALEXANDRA'S PIZZA: (1263 Queen Street, Halifax) The first Alexandra's opened in 1991 on Queen Street in downtown Halifax and it has since expanded to 10 other locations. There are nine locations in the province including Halifax, Dartmouth, Spryfield and Sackville.This year, they opened their first store ever in Ontario, in downtown Toronto on Yonge Street. Over the years their poutine has been voted "Best in Town" by the The Coast and "Best Pizza 2016" by The Chronicle Herald.

#4. SICILIAN: (5245 Blowers Street, 6302 Quinpool Road and 28 Titus Street, Halifax) Chances are if you've ever been to Halifax you've heard of Pizza Corner, and when you think Pizza Corner you think Sicilian. It's the "Home of the Big Slice" and it's been voted Halifax's BEST Pizza Slice six years in a row! Whether it's a late-night slice with the squad or a quick lunch for one, Sicilian has got you covered.

#5. EURO PIZZA: (31 St. Margaret's Bay Road, Halifax) I grew up near St. Margaret's Bay Road so this pizza place is near and dear to my heart. They import their olive oils from Greece and even make homemade tzatziki. You must try dipping your pizza in their homemade tzatziki — *IT IS SO GOOD*. Besides their delicious pizza, their roasted garlic fingers are *NEXT LEVEL* and a must-try in Halifax.

#6. KENNY'S PIZZA: (1038 Cole Harbour Road, Dartmouth) Originating in Sydney in 1989, Kenny's Pizza is a widely popular pizza chain not only in Cape Breton, but also in Antigonish and now finally in Dartmouth. You can always count on the Kenny's special (a slice and a pop for just $5). Their pizza is always piping hot with the freshest toppings.

#7. NAPOLI PIZZERIA: (465 Charlotte Street, Sydney and 1798 Kings Road, Sydney River) Established in 1962, if you've ever been to Sydney, Cape Breton there's a really good chance you've had Napoli. It's a family-owned business that has been voted the Best Pizza in Sydney by readers of the Cape Breton Post. They even offer take-and-bake pizzas so you can purchase it pre-made and cook it at home on your own schedule!

#8. SALVATORE'S PIZZAIOLO TRATTORIA: (5541 Young Street, Halifax) Located in the Hydrostone Market, this place is all about simplicity. On their menu you'll find their "original pizza," where a customer can add a total of three toppings (including homemade meatballs — *YOWZA!*) to any style crust. Their pizza crust can come with either sesame or poppy seeds, which adds a nice little bonus at the end of your cheese. Salvatore's is also a great spot for vegetarian/vegan customers because you can choose pizza toppings like vegan ricotta and veggie portobello sausage.

#9. PICTOU COUNTY PIZZA: (814 Abercrombie Road, New Glasgow) The secret is in the sauce! The Pictou County Pizza family recipe has been handed down through the generations. The Bonvie family was the first to produce the famous brown-sauce-style pizza in the 1960s. It has become very popular over the years. And if you're craving it, you don't even have to drive to New Glasgow to buy it. Due to high demand, you can now find the brown sauce and the pizza for sale at your local Sobeys.

#10. FREEMAN'S LITTLE NEW YORK: (6092 Quinpool Road, 1726 Grafton Street, 3671 Dutch Village Road [all located in Halifax] and 552 Sackville Drive, Lower 552 Lower Sackville) Freeman's opened their first set of doors in 1956 at their original Quinpool Road location. Freeman's has always been known as a late-night staple. The original location stays open 24 hours a day, seven days a week. Grafton Street is open until 5 a.m. and the other two locations until 2 a.m. Freeman's is the only place I know where you can get pizza after 4 a.m.! *#LateNightZa*

Dana Thompson, born and raised in Halifax, has always loved pizza. Today, she is known as the Pizza Queen. She first realized how deep her pizza obsession was when she watched the movie Home Alone *for the first time back in the early 90s. She instantly fell in love with young actor Macaulay Culkin, whose character was in love with plain cheese pizza. She grew up trying many different kinds of pizzas, but plain cheese has always had a special place in her heart. After graduating from high school, Dana studied acting at Dalhousie University for four years, then studied Radio at NSCC for two years. She landed her first radio gig in Fredericton, New Brunswick, where she had to wear a pizza-slice costume for two weeks collecting enough food to fill the food bank shelves. You can now hear her weekday mornings on Hot Country 1035 in Halifax. For the record, she is probably eating pizza right now as you're reading this.*

Elisabeth Bailey's List of the Top 10 Seafood Chowders in Nova Scotia

These Ten 10 sources for chowder are in no particular order, with the exception of my personal favourite being first. There's nothing I'd rather have in any restaurant, anywhere, than Seaside Shanty's lobster and seafood chowder brimming with scallops, shrimp, mussels, clams and haddock — and, of course, lobster! Check out the excellent patio view and indoor "boat bar" while you're there. The other restaurants on the list represent a province-wide smattering of truly excellent chowders that showcase the very best our oceans have to offer. I chose restaurants with great reputations — both with tourists and locals — all across the province. Some are casual and modestly priced; some are more upscale. All will send you away happy.

#1. SEASIDE SHANTY: 5315 Highway 3, Chester Basin

#2. CHARLENE'S BAYSIDE CAFÉ: 9567 Highway 105, Whycocomagh

#3. ESQUIRE RESTAURANT: 772 Bedford Highway, Halifax

#4. SHORE LINE RESTAURANT: 78 Water St, Digby

#5. PICTOU LODGE: 172 Lodge Rd, Pictou

#6. LANE'S PRIVATEER INN: 27 Bristol Ave, Liverpool

#7. EVAN'S FRESH SEAFOODS: Alderney Landing, 2 Ochterloney St, Dartmouth

#8. MASSTOWN MARKET: 10622 Nova Scotia Trunk 2, Debert

#9. CABOT LINKS: 15933 Central Ave, Inverness

#10. YE OLDE ARGYLER LODGE: 52 Ye Olde Argyle Road, Lower Argyle

Elisabeth Bailey is a local food writer who lives, gardens and cooks up a storm in Lunenburg. She is also the author of two cookbooks, Taste of the Maritimes *and* Maritime Fresh, *both published by Nimbus. You can follow her on Facebook, Twitter, or Instagram.*

Elisabeth Bailey's List of the Top 10 Fish and Chip Joints in Nova Scotia

The most important qualities in a great plate of fish and chips include high-quality fish, excellent batter and good potatoes. They need to be prepared by kitchen staff with tough skins and quick feet! Above all, the fish has to be as fresh as possible.

I can't imagine eating fish and chips in, say, Alberta (well—I can, but it's not a happy thought). In my experience the best fish and chips come from places where the cook knows a guy with a boat and gets potatoes from our next-door neighbor — Potatoes Everywhere Island.

I tried not to go too heavy on South Shore restaurants in making this list, although I ultimately couldn't bear to leave out either The South Shore Fish Shack in Lunenburg or Oh My Cod! in Mahone Bay. Note that Shore Line Restaurant in Digby is the only restaurant to make both this list and the list of Top 10 Seafood Chowders (elsewhere in this section)… I know where I'm going the next time my travels take me past Digby!

#1. THE SOUTH SHORE FISH SHACK: 108 Montague St, Lunenburg

#2. SYDELLE'S FISH AND CHIPS: 733 Rocky Lake Dr, Bedford

#3. JOHN'S LUNCH: 352 Pleasant St, Dartmouth

#4. THE LOBSTER POUND AND MOORE: 161 Queen St, North Sydney

#5. THE RED SHED: 79 Water St, Yarmouth

#6. MURPHY'S FISH & CHIPS: 88 Esplanade St, Truro

#7. SHORE LINE RESTAURANT: 78 Water St, Digby

#8. THE PORT: 980 Terry's Creek Road, Port Williams

#9. OH MY COD: 567 Main St, Mahone Bay

#10. 10 FREDDIE'S FANTASTIC FISH HOUSE: 8 Oland Crescent, Halifax

Elisabeth Bailey is a local food writer who lives, gardens and cooks up a storm in Lunenburg. She is also the author of two cookbooks, Taste of the Maritimes *and* Maritime Fresh, *both published by Nimbus. You can follow her on Facebook, Twitter, or Instagram.*

The Bologna Lover's List of the Top 10 Ways Nova Scotians Eat Bologna

Is there anything more versatile — or delicious — than bologna? It has been a staple on Nova Scotian tables for generations. Served as a quick lunch or as the main component of a more complex dinner recipe, bologna has crossed the gastronomically imagined boundaries to even be considered "fine dining" in some homes. Here then, for your dining pleasure is my list of top 10 ways to eat bologna. Enjoy!

#1. THE CLASSIC BOLOGNA SANDWICH: Simple really. Take two slices of bread (the fresher, the better), spread mayonnaise on each slice and add a thick slice of delicious bologna. There you have it — the classic bologna sandwich. Have at it. Tastes great with a glass of cold milk to chase it down or in many homes, a tall glass of cold pop, preferably one of the colas.

#2. THE DELUXE VERSION OF THE CLASSIC BOLOGNA SANDWICH: Similar in every way to the classic sandwich mentioned in number 1, except if you're craving the deluxe, gourmet-style bologna sandwich, you must add lettuce and tomato, maybe even a slice of cheese.

#3. A VARIATION OF THE CLASSIC BOLOGNA SANDWICH: Start with two slices of bread and this time, instead of using mayonnaise, spread butter on each slice and add mustard on top of the butter. Now, add a big ole thick slice of bologna and you're ready to serve.

#4. THE FRIED BOLOGNA SANDWICH: For the more adventurous sandwich lover, I suggest you take a bite out of the fried bologna sandwich. It's pretty simple to make. Put some cooking oil in a frying pan with the heat on medium. Once the oil is heated, add a slice of bologna to the pan, but make sure you cut a slit from the middle to keep the slice from curling or bubbling up as you want it to remain flat for the neatest sandwich. Once you've browned both sides of the bologna, add cheese to the slice just before removing it from the heat. Now, put mustard on two slices of bread (some prefer the bread to be toasted but that is a matter of personal taste). All that remains is to eat the sandwich so go ahead and gobble it up. Is there anything better? I think not.

#5. FRIED BOLOGNA, FRIED POTATOES, FRIED ONIONS AND BEANS: So if sandwiches aren't your thing or if you're looking for something just a little more hearty, I suggest you try this old Nova Scotian favourite. Simple to prepare but worth the effort. Start by frying potatoes in a hot pan with melted butter or margarine, whichever you use. Raw potatoes will work but I find that pre-boiled potatoes work best for this recipe. Once the potatoes are starting to brown, throw in a handful of chopped onions and a healthy amount of cubed bologna. Fry until the onions are translucent and the bologna looks cooked. Remove from heat and serve with a side of beans (homemade is best, but canned will do as long as it's beans in tomato sauce and not molasses — a personal preference). The only thing that can improve this dish is a squirt of ketchup over the potatoes. Delicious!

#6. BOLOGNA SOUP (STEW): For the more discerning or refined pallet, you may want to sink your teeth into this traditional bologna soup, or stew as it's called in some homes. It is um-um good and real easy to make. Here's what you need — two slices of chopped bologna, half-cup chopped celery, half-cup chopped carrots, one chopped onion, two medium-sized diced potatoes, one-cup chopped cabbage, two chopped green peppers, one can of tomatoes and four cups of water. To start, cook the bologna in the water for about 30 minutes. Add all the vegetables and cook for an additional

30 to 40 minutes, or until the veggies are soft. Serve with fresh biscuits or rolls and you have a meal fit for royalty.

#7. BOLOGNA CASSEROLE: Here's another meal fit for a king or queen and, again, it's pretty simple to make. You will need two cups of green beans, two cups of carrots, two cups of diced bologna, two cups of tomatoes, two tablespoons of flour and two tablespoons of melted shortening. Mix the flour and shortening in a frying pan over medium heat. Continue stirring until bubbling. Then drain beans and carrots. Add to the pan. Add tomatoes and bologna. Stir all ingredients until heated thoroughly. Remove from heat add a dash of salt and pepper. Put in a casserole dish and set aside. Now you need to make the casserole topping. You will need a quarter-cup shortening, two cups of flour, one cup of milk and two slices of diced bologna. Add the flour, milk and diced bologna and stir. Mix in shortening and stir until it becomes doughy. Drop this mixture on top of the other mixture. Put in oven and bake at 350 degrees until topping is done (brown on top). It's now ready to serve to dig in.

#8. FRIED-BOLOGNA CASSEROLE: If you liked the previous casserole you will love this one. It's out-of-this-world delicious and so easy to make. To get started, you will need eight slices of bologna, three tablespoons of butter, one chopped onion, four cups of warm mashed potatoes, and one-and-a-half cups of shredded cheddar cheese. Preheat oven to 350 degrees F (175 degrees C). Grease a one-quart baking dish and heat frying pan over medium to high heat. Fry the bologna slices in the hot skillet until browned on both sides, which takes about one minute per side. Drain on a paper-towel-lined plate. Wipe excess grease from the skillet, reduce heat to medium and stir in the butter and onion. Cook and stir until the onion has softened and turned translucent, about five minutes. Stir the onions into the warm mashed potatoes. Spread half of the mashed potatoes into the prepared baking dish. Layer with half of the fried bologna and sprinkle with half of the cheese. Repeat with the remaining ingredients. Bake uncovered in the preheated oven until the cheese is bubbly and the center is hot. This will take about 30 minutes. Here's a little tip I've discovered from all my years of making this casserole: I've found that aluminum foil helps keep food moist, ensures it cooks evenly, keeps leftovers fresh and makes clean up easy.

#9. BOLOGNA SUNDAE: Don't let the name turn you off. It's actually very tasty and those who like bologna will love this. Place one slice of fried bologna in a bowl and put one scoop of mashed potatoes on top of that. Pour a ladle-ful of hot gravy over the potatoes. If you wish, you can finish with your favourite topping, like shredded cheddar cheese, peas or just ketchup. And there you have it — bologna sundae. It's mouthwatering and delicious, but only the real bologna connoisseur would consider this to be a dessert.

#10. THREE OTHER WAYS TO SERVE BOLOGNA: For this item, I have decided to present three of my favourite ways to serve bologna — baked (buy a large chunk of high-grade bologna, cut in cubes bake in a 350-degree oven for 10 to 15 minutes and serve with various dipping sauces); barbecued (cut your chunk of bologna into thick slices, place on the barbecue until both sides are browned, put ing a bun, top with your favourite condiments and enjoy); and on a pizza (yes on a pizza: cut your bologna into cubes, sprinkle over your pizza along with all your other favourite toppings, bake as usual and serve).

No matter how you slice it, bologna always tastes delicious in these or any other recipe, but the real bologna lover will be content going to the refrigerator, grabbing a slice and enjoying it right out of the package, in all its great nakedness and without any additives or bread. That's the true sign that someone is a bologna lover!

Authors note: The Bologna Lover is a real person, but he wishes to remain anonymous. However, we thank him for his contribution to the book with this list.

The Kilted Chef's List of the 10 Best Ways to Eat Lobster

One of the most sought-after food delicacies in the world is the Atlantic lobster, but do you know how to eat them? Here are my suggestions for the top 10 ways to best eat lobster:

#1. COLD, DIPPED IN HOT BUTTER: For the ultimate experience add one picnic table and 12 cold beers.

#2. IN A LOBSTER ROLL: Preferably on a buttered and grilled soft-sided hot dog bun. Available in Canada only; we're so very sorry for the rest of the world.

#3. IN A CHOWDER: Some recipes are so closely guarded that they go to the grave with the owner and there are so many recipes that it's possible to eat a different chowder every day that you're here!

#4. CREAMED LOBSTER ON TOAST: It's a South Shore thing and I'm willing to bet there isn't a fisherman in those parts that hasn't whipped up this delight between hauling trawls.

#5. LOBSTER CAKES: The uppity cousin of the salt cod cake but we just can't help but love him anyway!

#6. LOBSTER BENEDICT: Move over ham this version is beyond delicious. Go ahead fill y'er boots!

#7. IN A SEAFOOD BAKE: Extremely popular on Nova Scotia menus province wide. Lobster can be found sharing the spotlight with haddock, shrimp and scallops in this tasty dish.

#8. LOBSTER PASTA: A little pasta, a little cream sauce, a bit of cheese and a lot of lobster. Need we say more?

#9. LOBSTER BISQUE: Unlike in a chowder, lobster doesn't share the limelight here. The bodies are boiled and reduced to a dark, rich liquor, add cream and lobster. So simple, yet so sinfully good!

#10. LOBSTER RISOTTO: I had to include this because it's a personal favourite; rich creamy risotto, succulent lobster and a cold glass of Nova Scotia white. Holy mackerel, it's some good!

Alain Bossé, also known as the Kilted Chef, has travelled the world, from kitchens to convention centres, sharing his expertise and love for buying and eating local ingredients with people near and far. With his signature tartan kilt, proud Acadian heritage and undeniable flair for cooking with local, he has earned a reputation as Atlantic Canada's culinary ambassador. He firmly believes that if you live local, then you should buy local. For more than a decade, Alain has promoted local commodities such as lobster, mussels, apples and wild blueberries.

Virginia Lee's List of the Top 10 Food Items Grown or Made in Nova Scotia

My food-writing career began many years ago and was born from the spirit of my home-cooking heritage. A love of Nova Scotia's regional foodstuffs — bountiful fresh seafood from cold northern waters, meats both hunted and farmed, together with fruits and vegetables from our native soil — made writing about food an easy and enjoyable profession.

Our small province is truly varied in its landscape and one finds diverse regions producing what grows best in a particular area. The fertile Annapolis Valley showcases its fruits and vegetables and the barrens of Cumberland and Colchester counties produce world-class crops of blueberries. In early spring our maple-hardwood stands bless us with maple syrup and offshore rocky islands like Tancook Island on Nova Scotia's South Shore originally produced the cabbages that make our special sauerkraut.

International food products are readily available to all but, rest assured, our traditional Maritime cuisine is not dying; it is only being enhanced. Professional chefs and home cooks welcome the infusion of global food products that give a new twist to old favourites. You never know what may turn up in your chowder or apple dessert these days but rest assured it will be delicious. So it is with this old and new in mind that I have compiled my list of favourite food items from Nova Scotia. I love the traditional, welcome the new and present them in no particular order, other than ending with a dessert!

#1. LOBSTER: Fresh steamed with lemon butter or a lobster roll or chowder.

#2. SALT COD: Fish cakes, of course, with rhubarb relish.

#3. SCALLOPS: Barely cooked.

#4. BLUEBERRIES: Wild for their pungent flavour, highbush for convenience.

#5. APPLES: From the first crop in late summer to the autumn varieties, unbelievable flavour.

#6. BROWN BREAD: Straight from the oven and made from scratch with oats, flour and molasses.

#7. RHUBARB: The welcome first vegetable posing as a fruit in spring…rhubarb cream pie, wow!

#8. MAPLE SYRUP: Drizzled over buttermilk pancakes.

#9. SAUERKRAUT: Traditional food product from Nova Scotia's German heritage; comfort food on a cold winter's day.

#10. PIE: So Nova Scotian, be it fruit or my favourite, coconut cream with meringue.

Virginia Lee is a food writer who began writing newspaper and magazine articles and two regional cookbooks before venturing into Canada-wide publications with the Flavours Series of cookbooks. She and her sister Elaine Elliot have had the most amazing times in their 20-odd years of working together travelling, compiling, testing and writing their signature books. So much fun and so many laughs, plus their families and friends ate well during the testing of recipes! These days, Virginia divides her time between North Palm Beach, Florida and Lower Canard in the lovely Annapolis Valley during the summer.

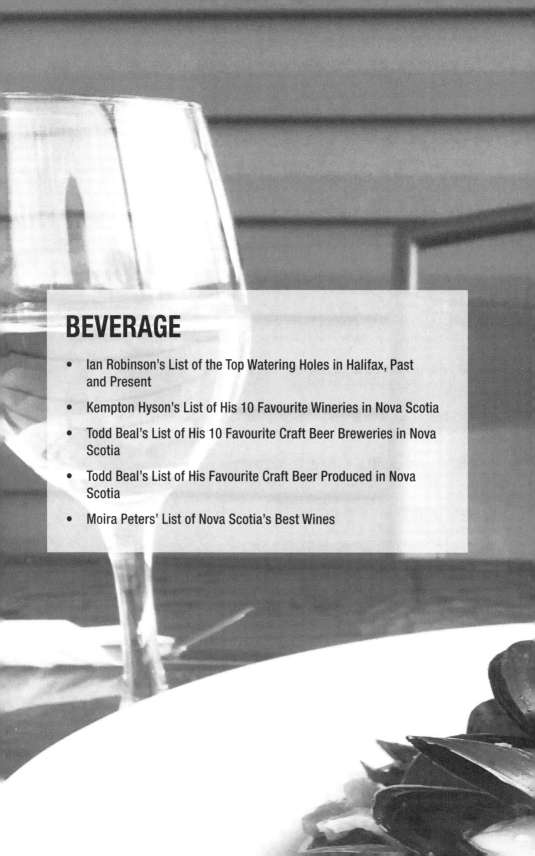

BEVERAGE

- Ian Robinson's List of the Top Watering Holes in Halifax, Past and Present
- Kempton Hyson's List of His 10 Favourite Wineries in Nova Scotia
- Todd Beal's List of His 10 Favourite Craft Beer Breweries in Nova Scotia
- Todd Beal's List of His Favourite Craft Beer Produced in Nova Scotia
- Moira Peters' List of Nova Scotia's Best Wines

Ian Robinson's List of the Top Watering Holes in Halifax, Past and Present

They say that Halifax has the most bars per capita in all of North America. Here's a list of the Top 10 Bars from yesterday and today!

Top 10 Bars from yesterday:

#1. MY APARTMENT ON ARGYLE: Such a cool name to confuse out-of-towners.

#2. LAWRENCE OF OREGANO'S ON ARGYLE: A part of the famous Liquor Dome, the garlic bread from the bread bar soaked up the trays of beers...

#3. SCOUNDREL'S ON GEORGE STREET: Saturday afternoons and $2 Long Island Iced Teas, need I say anymore? Hey Tarbender! I mean Bartender...

#4. THE THIRSTY DUCK ON SPRING GARDEN ROAD: It was a challenge to walk back down those stairs after a few pitchers.

#5. THACKERAY'S ON SPRING GARDEN ROAD: This was the media bar back in the day, a lot of radio and TV romances began there!

#6. ROSA'S CANTINA ON ARGYLE STREET: The last song played at 2 a.m. was "Margaritaville" by Jimmy Buffett; I know all the words by heart!

#7. THE MISTY MOON ON BARRINGTON: Classic Rock memories and stubby bottles.

#8. THE GRADUATE ON ARGYLE STREET: Mrs. Robinson's son spent a lot of time there, even graduated with a degree!

#9. THE PALACE ON BRUNSWICK STREET: Ended just a few nights there back in the day at dark-and-dirty o'clock.

#10. THE LIGHTHOUSE ON BARRINGTON STREET: Bachelor Party Paradise!

Top 10 Bars of Today:

#1. THE LION'S HEAD TAVERN ON ROBIE STREET: Affectionately called "Studio L" by us radio and TV types, many tall tales have been told with the ales there over the years!

#2. THE LOWER DECK ON UPPER WATER STREET: Is there any better place for s sing-a-long, if I don't know the words I just mumble them. Signal Hill at the Deck is the ultimate in the Halifax nightlife experience.

#3. THE OLD TRIANGLE ON PRINCE STREET: I had a pint or four or five there the night before Hurricane Juan.

#4. THE MIDTOWN ON GRAFTON: Both the old and new Midtowns are infamous for steak and fries. Years ago to get to the ladies washroom, women had to go through the kitchen.

#5. CHEERS ON GRAFTON STREET: I met Hockey Night in Canada's Bob Cole there the night of my Bachelor Party, at least my buddies tell me so… they bought him some B 52's!

#6. DURTY NELLIES ON ARGYLE: A great place for a few pops and a few durty jokes: A Caper, a Newfie and a chicken walk into a bar...

#7. THE ECONOMY SHOE SHOP ON ARGYLE STREET: Better known as "The Shoe" — I've been a "spilly talker" there a few times.

#8. THE SPLIT CROW ON GRANVILLE STREET: My bachelor party started there in 1991; I don't recall much after we left.

#9. BUBBA RAY'S SPORTS BARS: I'm a sucker for hockey jerseys and sports memorabilia, gimme a beer and I'm in heaven!

#10. YOUR FATHER'S MOUSTACHE ON SPRING GARDEN ROAD: Or if you're from Cape Breton it's "Your Fadder's Moustache B'ye!"

Ian Robinson has been in Halifax radio since 1987 and has been known to frequent a few watering holes over the years. He is currently the morning show host on Hot Country 1035 in Halifax with Dana Thompson and since 1997 has been the Public Address Announcer for the Halifax Mooseheads.

Kempton Hyson's List of His 10 Favourite Wineries in Nova Scotia

Ten years ago, it would have been very easy to compile a list of top ten wineries in

Nova Scotia. However, with the number of wineries now pushing close to 20 in number, the task becomes a somewhat daunting exercise.

The criteria I have used consist of history, friendliness of staff, quality and variety of wines produced, and overall ambience. There is no particular ranking order to this list.

#1. DOMAINE DE GRAND PRE`: After initially being opened by Roger Dial in the mid 1970s, Domaine de Grand Pre', following a four-year makeover, was reopened in 2000 by Hanspeter Stutz and his family. The current winery has set the benchmark for future wineries with their professionalism, friendliness, award-winning wines, winemaking museum, stunning gift shop and their outstanding restaurant, Le Caveau, under the guidance of daughter Beatrice Stutz and Chef Jason Lynch. The transformation was not an easy one. The family ripped out the old unkept vines, such as Severnyi and Michurnitz, and replaced them with winter-hardy grapes such as l'Acadie Blanc, New York Muscat, Seyval Blanc, Marechal Foch, Castel and Baco Noir, to mention a few. With Hanspeter's son Jurg as the winemaker the winery produces red, white, rose, sparkling and dessert wines. Tours are done regularly by an array of enthusiastic and knowledgeable staff. One can take in the impeccable view of Cape Blomidon and the Bay of Fundy. Their ability to cater functions in the beautiful courtyard has caused many a bride to book their wedding date two or three years ahead of time. The restaurant is one of the province's best, specialising in Swiss cuisine and game. Get there early to grab a spot under the pergola and sample some Muscat grapes just above your head. An annual icewine festival is held here in February on consecutive weekends with several wineries partaking, with food pairings included. Throw in a snowshoe tour of the vineyard and a warm bonfire to cuddle up to, and this is not an event to miss.

#2. LIGHTFOOT & WOLFVILLE: This winery officially opened its doors in mid-summer 2017 to the excitement of many a wine lover. Another family affair with Michael and Jocelyn Lightfoot at the helm, along with winemaker-daughter Rachel, the winery is proving that vinifera is alive and well and successfully being grown in their certified organic vineyard. Popular grapes such as Chardonnay, Pinot Noir and Riesling have rapidly shown that they can be successfully turned into marvellous wines. The winery has also shown success with Scheurebe and Chasselas. Winemaker Josh Horton is not only producing wild-yeast fermented table wines but also traditional method sparkling wines and icewine. The farmland has been in the family for four generations, with the emphasis now being to use only biodynamic practices and indigenous yeasts. The winery has quickly become a favourite for bus tours and anyone wanting to dine on the terrific pizza from the Patio Woodfired Oven & Bar. The marquee can sit 300 people for a plated dinner, during which patrons can take in the beautiful view of Cape Blomidon.

#3. BLOMIDON ESTATE WINERY: The first vines at Blomidon Estate were planted in 1986, when the winery was named Habitant Vineyards. The name was changed to

Blomidon Estate in 1997. With new ownership in 2007, the Ramey family was happy to bring Nova Scotian native winemaker Simon Rafuse back from Europe to take on the winemaking chores. Rafuse's love is Chardonnay and the opportunity to take this variety to another level in Nova Scotia sealed the deal. Rafuse produces both oaked and unoaked versions of Chardonnay and also has won many awards for his traditional-method sparklers. The reds include the very popular Baco Noir and the off-dry, rich blend named Blow me Down. Rafuse also finds time to teach part of the Sommelier program for the Canadian Association of Professional Sommeliers in Halifax. Found not far from Canning on the shore of the Minas Basin, the tasting room and retail shop at Blomidon Estate have been refurbished and the outside deck is a wonderful spot to enjoy a glass of wine and a cheese board while taking in the beautiful view of the Basin.

#4. GASPEREAU VINEYARDS: Just three km from downtown Wolfville, this cozy, boutique-style winery was established by Hans Christian Jost and later sold to Carl and Donna Sparkes. Led by Winemaker Gina Haverstock, the winery has always been known for its award-winning Rieslings. The cooler climate produces wines with higher acidity, providing a perfect match for the local seafood and shellfish. The reds perform magic with the local meats, cheeses, and charcuterie. Gina was happily enjoying her summer job at Jost Vineyards, saving money for medical school, when she fell in love with the wine trade and changed her September plans, instead enrolling at Brock University to begin her new dream. A few years down the road she was coaxed back to Nova Scotia and eventually found her way to Gaspereau Vineyards. Besides Riesling, the winery produces an array of terroir-driven wines such as the ever-popular New York Muscat, Tidal Bay and Luci Kuhlmann. Sparkling wines and dessert wines fill out the menu. The quaint gift shop and tasting room as well as educated staff make this a popular stop for many a wine lover. Add to this a newly constructed patio serving wines and light fare and it is a great point to rest before hopping into an innertube for a lazy trip down the Gaspereau River.

#5. L'ACADIE VINEYARDS: Bruce Ewert produces traditional- method sparklers and he does it very well. Ewert, after being head winemaker at British Columbia's Summerhill Pyramid Winery (Canada's largest organic Vineyard), packed up his family in 2004 and headed towards the next step in his career. His first goal was to have his vineyard be certified organic. He then wanted to use unique grape varietals for the production of his wines. Instead of using the classic champagne grapes — Pinot Noir, Pinot Meunier and Chardonnay — he chose varietals such as l'Acadie Blanc, Seyval Blanc and Marechal Foch. These grapes had already proven to ripen in this area and their higher acidity levels were ideal for sparkling wines. The star of the winery is the Prestige Brut Estate, aged an extended period of five years, producing a fine mousse and toasty flavours. And for the cider lovers, Ewart processes an organic cider. Ewert also makes an appassimento-style wine that he calls Passito, made with the Marechal Foch grape. During this process the grapes are dried, producing a rich, concentrated wine. Aged in American oak, this wine shows soft tannins and ripe berry fruit.

#6. SAINTE FAMILLE WINES: Overlooking the Avon River in Falmouth, Doug and Suzanne Corkum opened one of the original wineries in 1990, in one of the warmest regions in Nova Scotia. Starting out with Marechal Foch and Michurinetz (the latter now removed), the Corkums now grow 12 different varieties of grapes. These include some of their more popular grapes such as Muscat, Siegfried, Baco Noir and Luci Kuhlmann. Ste. Famille aims to produce affordable wines from 100 percent Nova Scotian grapes. Thrown into the mix of red and white wines are sparkling and dessert wines. The quaint tasting room and gift shop looks down on the cellar. And the outdoor patio gives a great view of the vineyard. The gazebo hosts many weddings and other events including the annual charity grape stomp in October. The latest buzz around the winery is the huge amount of blueberry wine that has just been shipped to Asia, with a second shipment on order.

#7. JOST VINEYARDS: Nova Scotia's largest winery was opened in 1983, just a few miles from the Northumberland Strait. Because of the warm waters of the Strait, this winery is the warmest and driest, enjoying the longest season in Nova Scotia. The winery has the largest portfolio of any other winery, enabling everyone to find the perfect wines for their palate. The wines are generally higher in acid and low in tannin, lively and aromatic, making a perfect pairing with Atlantic seafood and shellfish. The vineyard was opened by Hans Christian Jost and his parents in 1978, with the family growing grapes for family consumption. After sharing with the neighbours, pressure was put on the Josts to increase their production. In 1988, Hans Christian took over the winery after the death of his father. "H.C." quickly became the spokesman and unofficial leader of the Nova Scotian wine industry. The winery has since been sold to Carl and Donna Sparkes. The classy circular tasting bar resembles a large oak barrique that allows you to sample several of the wines. The boutique offers a splendid array of books, clothing, glassware, etc. Pick up a snack at the Seagrape Café and relax outside with a bottle of wine. Saturday afternoons brings music to the patio along with several festivals throughout the summer.

#8. BENJAMIN BRIDGE WINERY: Combine the vision of the McConnell family, consultants Peter Gamble and Raphael Brisbois, and inspired winemakers JB Deslauriers, Bastien Warskotte and Scott Savoy, and you have a recipe for success. With the focus on traditional-method sparklers produced from Chardonnay, Pinot Noir and Pinot Meunier, the accolades have been rolling in since day one. The winery began in 2000 with the vision to make the best sparkling wines in Canada. They have already reached that goal according to many wine tasters. Their fan favourite is their $25 Nova 7. But the winery also produces several table and dessert wines. The winery offers up the BB Club, a terrific opportunity to sample their small-lot wines. Tours and tastings are by appointment only in their sleek tasting room featuring local works of art. Two hundred meters down the hill, your inner-tube cruise begins.

#9. AVONDALE SKY: Located in Newport Landing, this winery is housed in St. Mathew's Church. The area has one of the warmest climates in Nova Scotia, just yards from the Avon River. Grapes had been grown here for decades but the question as to where a winery should be constructed remained unanswered. However, there was a lovely church some 42 km away in Walton. After careful planning, the church was put onto a barge and made its way to its new home, and the transformation to a full-fledged winery began. The church was rewarded the NS 2001 Heritage Built Award. The church is now the giftshop and tasting room. Owners Lorraine Vassalo and Stewart Crease along with the imaginative winemaker Ben Swetnam, focus generally on Germanic-style blends. The Geisenheim Grape rules in this vineyard, with the Bliss allotment often selling out within a week. Swetnam praises the gypsum subsoils, which contribute mineral notes to his grapes. Besides Bliss, Avondale Sky produces an array of wines including roses, reds, whites, sparklers and dessert wines. With the addition of their restaurant, D'vine Morsels, it is a wonderful stop for a small snack. The winery hosts a garlic festival in the late summer. This winery, albeit slightly off the beaten track, is the closest one to Halifax.

#10. LUCKETT VINEYARDS: Opened by Pete Luckett in 2010, planted predominantly with fruit, but then primarily with grapes in 2012, this winery has quickly become a hot spot for wine lovers. The winery produces a large amount of white, red, rose, sparkling and dessert wines. Winemaker Mike Mainguy and Vineyard Manager Marcel Kolb have had great success lately with a pair of big rich reds named Black Cab and Buried Red. The first wine recently won Best Red at the Lieutenant Governor's Award for best Nova Scotian red wine. The Buried Red is a wine where the barrels are buried underground. The beautiful patio is a great stop for small plates and a glass of wine, and the view is probably the best in Nova Scotia. Skip down to the red phone box in the middle of the vineyard and make a free phone call to any destination in North America. The winery can be rented throughout the year for weddings or private events. The large parking area allows room for many vehicles and tour buses, and Pete himself will often be the first one to meet you.

Kempton Hyson has spent 35 years working in the food and beverage industry in three different countries. He successfully graduated from the International Sommelier Guild in 2001 and is a member of the Canadian Association of Professional Sommeliers, have served as a board member, treasurer and cellar keeper. He has been Nova Scotia's representative judging the All Canadian Wine Championships since 2010 and has judged for the Canadian Amateur Wine Championships, the Atlantic Amateur Wine Championships, the Lieutenant Governor's Wine Awards and the Atlantic Wine Championships.

Todd Beal's List of His 10 Favourite Craft Beer Breweries in Nova Scotia

The craft-beer scene in Nova Scotia has exploded over the last few years, expanding the number of breweries to levels not seen for over 100 years. The breweries operating now are varied in what they offer. Here are my favourites currently producing in the province:

#1. BAD APPLE BREWHOUSE: (515 Parker Condon Road, Berwick) Jeff Saunders has been brewing beer that he loves to drink with no compromises and no apologies. Brewed on his property, you can currently only get this beer to go and usually only in growlers. The trip to the source is always worth it, though. Look for his IPAs and DIPAs.

#2. UNFILTERED BREWING: (6041 North Street, Halifax) Unapologetic, foul mouthed and brewing great beer. Greg Nash brews his style of hop-forward beers, which have attracted a loyal following. They have their regular beers on tap next door at Charm School all the time and other releases periodically. My favourite is Double Orange Ale Double IPA.

#3. BIG SPRUCE BREWING: (64 Yankee Line Road, Baddeck) Brewing organic beer on their farm overlooking the Bras d'Or Lake, Big Spruce is truly a beautiful spot. Owner Jeremy White must balance growth with sustainability as he must manage water usage and disposal carefully. Drinking a flight on his property is a very special experience.

#4. 2 CROWS BREWING: (1932 Brunswick Street, Halifax) The newcomer started by husband and wife Mark and Kelly Huizink and brewer Jeremy Taylor is brewing modern beer. The taproom is cool to visit, combining an industrial operation with art. A lot of the beer utilizes interesting yeasts and aging in foeders. There are new beers on tap all the time but their Promiseland DIPA is a favourite of mine.

#5. NORTH BREWING: (2576 Agricola Street, Halifax or 62 Ochterloney Street, Dartmouth) Devoted to Belgian-inspired beer, the brewery has tried to grow sustainably by minimizing its carbon footprint. Its Dartmouth location is attached to Battery Park, which they are partners in, and you can find a wide selection of Nova Scotia beers. Try any of their year-round beers or many seasonals, or one offs that come out regularly.

#6. TATAMAGOUCHE BREWING: (235 Main Street, Tatamagouche) Nestled in this seaside paradise, the brewery is very proud of their community. Owned by the Jost family, who are famous for wine, they have built their brewery in the heart of the town but made sure to stay within the look of the town. They brew a lot of ale and gained many fans in Nova Scotia. Grab a Deception IPA while you visit or one of the many special seasonals they brew throughout the year.

#7. BOXING ROCK BREWING: (78 Ohio Road, Shelburne) The brewery was founded by a couple of engineers with a passion for craft beer and a desire to live in a beautiful place. Boxing Rock is a shoal off Hartz Point in Shelburne Harbour that's exposed only at low tide. According to local folklore, it had a special purpose for the sea captains of our past. The rock was used to drop off bickering sailors to "work out" their differences.

#8. BRETON BREWING: (364 Keltic Drive, Sydney) Breton's passion for beer shows in the products they produce. A local gathering place almost since opening, they are also a great community supporter. When you go, look for their top selling Black Angus IPA or Stirling Hefeweizen, chosen the 2017 Atlantic Canada Beer Awards Beer of the Year.

#9. GOOD ROBOT BREWING: (2736 Robie Street, Halifax) The self-proclaimed "most questionable brewery in Halifax" has endeared itself to Halifax. Throughout the year you may find anything from glitter parties to baby goats to movies showing on the "gastroturf." The theme at their brewery in acceptance and inclusion no matter who you are. Their beers are always interesting and changing. Check out the Goseface Killah Gose, the Tom Waits For No One Stout, or the Damn Fine Coffee & Cherry Pie Pale Ale.

#10. ROOF HOUND BREWING: (2580 Ridge Road, Hillgrove) Co-owner Les Barr had a few careers prior to opening Roof Hound (and appearing on Master Chef Canada). Roof Hound opened atop the highest point in Digby County, affording a great view and making interesting beers as well as a great food-and-music venue. The brewery name pays homage to the family hound dog that got drunk after eating raisins left over from Barr's grandfather's homebrew. You can't really go wrong with any beer, but look for the Big Stink IPA, Big Brown Roof Hound, or one of his cocktail series.

Todd Beal has been closely following the craft-beer scene in Nova Scotia since 2013 through his blog the Maritime Beer Report. He's frequently asked to comment on television, radio, newspapers and magazines for his craft-beer knowledge. He also likes to travel to beer destinations when he can.

Todd Beal's List of His Favourite Craft Beer Produced in Nova Scotia

As the craft breweries grow here, quadrupling in numbers over the past five years, so does the selection. The beer we make here is as good as you will find anywhere. Here are my Top 10 picks for beer in Nova Scotia. Fair warning: I am a stout and IPA kind of guy.

#1. BAD APPLE BREWHOUSE BOXCUTTER IPA: Brewing in the Annapolis Valley, Bad Apple has made outstanding beer. This beer, named for how many boxes need to be opened to brew it, is a classic American IPA. Boxcutter has a complex aroma of citrus, hop resin and caramel. It can be found only on tap where Bad Apple is served.

#2. UNFILTERED BREWING DOUBLE ORANGE ALE: This single malt and single hop (SMaSH) double IPA is brewed using 2-row malt and citra hops only and "checks all the boxes" for me. Very citrusy with a slight sweetness. Ever since its arrival a couple of years ago, I watch social media and head to their taproom, Charm School, to grab a pint whenever they brew it.

#3. NORTH BREWING MIDNIGHT GLENORA BARREL-AGED STRONG DARK BELGIAN: North puts their beer in a Glenora barrel and lets magic take over. This awesome beer is warming and has cherry, raisins, chocolate, vanilla and whisky in the taste. It is as good as it sounds. Look for this one at the shops a couple of time a year.

#4. BOXING ROCK BREWING VICAR'S CROSS DOUBLE IPA: This offering took Nova Scotia by storm on its release. Definitely not extreme by today's craft standards, Vicar's is a little boozy and bitter, like a Double IPA should be, but well balanced with strong malt bill. This is available almost everywhere in Nova Scotia.

#5. GOOD ROBOT BREWING DAMN FINE COFFEE AND CHERRY PIE PALE ALE: Brewed as an homage to the Twin Peaks television series, I at first had my doubts about this beer. It has become a favourite of mine with each iteration of the brew. You will most likely have to visit the brewery to enjoy a pint of this one.

#6. TATAMAGOUCHE BREWING TWO RIVERS BALTIC PORTER: Named for the two rivers that dominate Tatamagouche, Nova Scotia, this hometown proud brewery has a lot to be proud of for this beer. The multi-award winning beer is a delicious dark treat with a lot of dark-chocolate flavour.

#7. BIG SPRUCE BREWING CEREAL KILLER OATMEAL STOUT: One of the brewers' original offerings and still one of their most popular. The rich stout is quite dry, with chocolate and coffee flavours. Who says beer isn't for breakfast?

#8. 2 CROWS BREWING WILD NORTHEAST IPA: This brewery offers a new take on beers and this beer is no exception. Brewed with wild yeast, this Northeast style IPA is hazy with a tropical and juicy flavour. Look for this one everywhere.

#9. PROPELLER BREWING REVOLUTION RUSSIAN IMPERIAL STOUT: This strong dark brew, with its roasty notes and dark fruit, was my "awakening" to craft beer. Look for this one in the fall.

#10. UNCLE LEO'S BREWERY SMOKED PORTER: Nova Scotia has a few unique beers but this one is a favourite. It gets its smokey flavour and aroma from using Beechwood smoked malt. The smoke is not over the top, giving the dark, full-bodied a nice flavour combined with dark-chocolate notes.

Todd Beal has been closely following the craft beer scene in Nova Scotia since 2013 through his blog the Maritime Beer Report. He's frequently asked to comment on television, radio, newspapers and magazines for his craft-beer knowledge. He also likes to travel to beer destinations when he can.

Moira Peters' List of Nova Scotia's Best Wines

What makes wine good is subjective. Balance, distinctiveness, value-for-money and importance to a given place and time are all factors that could determine good wine. To build a list of the best wines in Nova Scotia, I wanted to consider all these things, so I put together a set of criteria.

My criteria centre on accessibility. I did not want to make a list of expensive bottles; I did not want to write about wines that you can only taste if you are part of a wine club; I didn't want to highlight small-lot one-offs that are often very special but hard to anticipate.

This is not, however, a list of the best-loved or most popular wines in Nova Scotia. In fact, the wines below may challenge your palate. But they are affordable ($40 and under), reasonably consistent from year to year and available in liquor stores around Nova Scotia. And, aside from being great wine, each has a story that makes it interesting and important: deserving to be on a list of the best wines in Nova Scotia.

#1. L'ACADIE VINEYARDS VINTAGE CUVÉE ROSÉ: ($30) Do not let the awards, medals or accolades this wine claims, or its gorgeous pink hue, distract you from the simple fact that this is probably the best bang for your buck in Nova Scotia, and has been for years. The first organic winery in Atlantic Canada, L'Acadie Vineyards has been showing by example that the best wines come from healthy vines. L'Acadie Vineyards produces traditional-method sparklers that consistently show well in competition and blind tastings. Of note is the winery's commitment to grapes built for Nova Scotia's climate and soils; the payoff being that bubbly made from l'Acadie Blanc and Marechal Foch (the contents of Vintage Cuvée Rosé) scores just as well and better in competition than wines made from traditional European varieties. This wine is a party favourite: dry with grapefruit and red fruit lacing the tongue and a long, creamy finish.

#2. BENJAMIN BRIDGE NV: ($28) From the producers who laid much of the groundwork for Nova Scotia to become a traditional-method (Champagne-style) sparkling-wine region comes a wine that embodies the genesis of the style in Nova Scotia. Benjamin Bridge invested in much soil, subsoil, temperature, grape varietal and viticulture experimentation beginning in 2000, and in 2002 it made its first vintage of bubbly base wine. NV, or non-vintage, is the winery's first attempt at the Champagne tradition of blending wines from multiple vintages to create a wine that will be the signature style of the house, consistent from year to year. NV contains wine dating back to Benjamin Bridge's first vintage, 2002, and includes classic grape varieties like Chardonnay and Pinot Noir, and also Nova Scotia hybrids like Vidal Blanc and l'Acadie Blanc. The wine available in 2017 is the second "batch" of NV, and shows sophistication over its first release. This wine is toasty and fresh, shows depth and is fun to drink and, true descendent of Nova Scotia's first bubbly, is clearly here to stay.

#3. LIGHTFOOT & WOLFVILLE ANCIENNE CHARDONNAY: ($40) The first biodynamic winery in Atlantic Canada burst onto the wine scene only a few years ago with its release of Ancienne Chardonnay and Pinot Noir. These wild fermented, oak-aged wines showed national wine critics and local-wine lovers the potential for classy Chard and Pinot that maintains the critical stamp of Nova Scotian freshness. The Chardonnay in particular has gained much acclaim as a wine that could be Burgundy but is also clearly Nova Scotian. With plenty of lemon, apple and vanilla aromatics, this wine's balance of fruit, mineral and oak influences is carried long into the night and through the crowd by its backbone of structured acidity.

#4. GASPEREAU VINEYARDS MUSCAT: ($20) When people ask me what Nova Scotia wine they should share with a friend from away, I want a wine that will make them sit up and take notice. That wine is single-varietal Muscat, and Gaspereau Vineyards does a solid job every time. The intense bouquet of Muscat grape varieties — roses! pineapple! lychee! apricot! — clearly demonstrates the potential our long, cool growing season has to fully ripen grapes in a way that maintains their aromatics. The dry finish of this wine feels like a slight of hand (shouldn't this wine taste like a gummy bear?) and the freshness keeps you sipping, while the slight orange colour piques the imagination. This wine is, obviously, a personal favorite.

#5. DOMAINE DE GRAND PRÉ VINTNER'S RESERVE RIESLING: ($20) Riesling was the first vitis vinifera (classic European grape species) wine to show great promise in Nova Scotia, and today several local wineries produce a single varietal Riesling. Domaine de Grand Pré, built on the site of the first commercial winery in the province, makes some of the best stuff right now, with classic Riesling aromas of lime, lanolin and apple. A touch of satisfying bitterness adds complexity to its refreshing acidity.

#6. JOST VINEYARDS TIDAL BAY: ($20) Nova Scotia's appellation (regional quality standard) wine is a recent innovation rooted in the French appellation tradition and it's been a huge success. Tidal Bay refers to the Bay of Fundy, whose size and dramatic tides define a swath of Nova Scotia wine country. At the same time, Tidal Bay guarantees a particular style and quality to the wine it names. Twelve wineries currently make Tidal Bay and Jost Vineyards, the largest, longest-running and probably most important winery in Nova Scotia, always makes a classic. When you open a bottle of Tidal Bay you can expect an off-dry, low-alcohol, semi-aromatic white wine made from a blend of grapes all grown in Nova Scotia, designed to be a delicious accompaniment to seafood. I also recommend pairing Tidal Bay with ramen, curry and the spiciest veg burrito you dare.

#7. AVONDALE SKY WINERY LEON MILLOT ROSÉ: ($17) In the early years of Nova Scotia's wine scene, sweetish red wines found favour with locals (and they are still in high demand). Recent years have seen a surge in popularity of white wines but wineries still need to use the province's abundance of red grapes that were planted in the early days—vineyards are a huge and long-term investment and one would hate to see healthy local grapes go to waste. Rosé is an alternative use of red grapes and, aside from being versatile and delicious, it is often the most affordable wine style on the market. Avondale Sky has been making a variety of rosés from Leon Millot grapes for a long time and this one is my favourite—a light, dry wine that shows off the beautiful dark red fruit aromas of Leon Millot. It is the perfect food wine, pairing particularly well with lunchtime sandwiches.

#8. PLANTER'S RIDGE L'ACADIE BLANC: ($20) L'Acadie Blanc should never have made it. The grape, bred in Ontario, was declared a failure when Niagara's nurseries couldn't make good wine out of it. It was too late though: the grape had been planted and propagated all over Nova Scotia by Roger Dial, the grandfather of Nova Scotia wine, who named the grape after the French settlers to the area. L'Acadie Blanc, which is a pleasure in the vineyard because of its hardiness and consistency in yield, and which makes lovely wine, figures prominently in Tidal Bay. Some wineries reserve enough l'Acadie Blanc to make a single-varietal wine, to the relief and delight of local fans. Planter's Ridge, a relatively new winery to Nova Scotia, does a lovely job with our flagship grape, cleanly drawing out the lemon-pineapple-herb character we love in a delicately balanced dry Nova Scotian table wine.

#9. PETITE RIVIÈRE VINEYARDS ITALY CROSS: ($27) Rolling drumlin hills shaped by retreating glaciers tens of thousands of years ago define Nova Scotia's South Shore wine country. The combination of slopes, proximity to ocean and geological composition has created unique terroir, and Petite Rivière has been committed to expressing that terroir through red wines of complexity, depth and balance. Italy Cross is a superior example, using a bang-on blend of Leon Millot's lean, clean, red fruit character and Lucie Kuhlmann's smoky, meaty body. Aged 12 months in French oak, the wine fills the mouth with fruit and spice, and maintains that uncanny Nova Scotian dichotomy of richness and freshness.

#10. LUCKETT VINEYARDS BURIED RED: ($38) Stories sell wine and that is probably part of why Luckett sells out of its Buried wines every year. This winery literally takes a barrel (or two) of wine and buries it in the vineyard for a year. Wine may be the result of a natural process of yeast eating sugar but it is not normal to leave wine for an extended period of time without checking up on it, making sure it's doing alright, adjusting anything that needs adjusting. Luckett leaves all the adjusting to soil and time, unearthing the wine mid-summer, hoping it turned out alright. And it always does. Better than alright, in fact, and that's the other reason Buried wines sell out. Buried Red in particular gains balance, richness and a nuanced earthiness in its time underground. What's going on down there? It's hard to know, because it's impossible to measure. Luckett likes it like that: leaving a little extra mystique around wine gives us a little more space to just lean back and enjoy it, along with the quiet wonders of nature.

Now that you have my list of wines that a regular person can reasonably get most of the time, here are my top three Nova Scotian wines based on quality alone. They are all traditional-method sparkling wines, a style in which our region excels. This is because of our long, cool growing season, which fully ripens the right kind of grapes without bumping their sugar content too high or letting go of their all-important acidity.

Moira Peters' Top Three

#1. BENJAMIN BRIDGE BRUT RESERVE: ($75) I remember my first taste of Brut Reserve. It was the 2004 vintage, poured alongside a $200 Champagne wine in a blind tasting in 2012. It was unmistakably methode champenoise, and all the toasty, bready, creamy mouthfeel of a Champagne-style wine, but with a crisp, rhubarb burst that was also unmistakably Nova Scotia. Benjamin Bridge's Brut Reserve changes from vintage to vintage but its quality and character are consistently top-notch.

#2. BLOMIDON ESTATE WINERY LATE-PICK CHARDONNAY: ($45) Blomidon's Chardonnay program is second-to-none, making wine of every style from the grape that grows so well in its vineyards right on the Minas Basin. Its bubbly program is also exceptional, and the Late-Pick Chard is a traditional-method sparkling wine that is my choice for the New Year's Eve toast. Something about it is exciting and reliable

— a hint of exotic fruit like pineapple and blood orange, and the perfect balance and liveliness that I expect from good Nova Scotia bubbly.

#3. L'ACADIE VINEYARDS PRESTIGE BRUT ESTATE: ($48) This wine is nearly perfect nearly all the time. Made from 100 percent l'Acadie Blanc grapes grown on estate, this organic wine meets all the criteria for traditional method bubbly: it fills your mouth with apple and brioche before it melts away, leaving a soft hum of bubbles and residual acidity. It's an honour to pop this cork, and feels totally natural to drain the bottle.

Let's not forget Dessert Wines

As after a good meal, no discussion about Nova Scotia wine is over till we talk about dessert. Our dessert wines are the best in the country; our Icewine in particular excels because the acidity of our grapes offsets the sugar content of a dessert wine, giving us a sweet, refreshing treat. You rarely need any more than one, so here it is.

#1. BLOMIDON ESTATE WINERY VIDAL ICEWINE: ($29) I love Icewine; I like Blomidon's best because it is slightly oxidized. Exposure to oxygen gives it a caramel dimension and a little more texture on top of the apples and apricot from the Vidal grapes and the sweet-and-sour nature of Icewine. The perfect finish to a home-cooked meal.

Moira Peters is a New York-certified sommelier who runs Unwined, a wine education and tasting party business in Nova Scotia, and who co-authored The Wine Lover's Guide to Atlantic Canada *with Craig Pinhey. Originally from Margaree, she now lives and farms with her family in Maitland, on the Bay of Fundy.*

HISTORY AND HERITAGE

- A List of 30 Canadian or World Firsts that Happened in Nova Scotia
- A List of 36 Canadian, North American and World Records that Can Be Claimed by Nova Scotia
- John Boileau's List of the 10 Most Important Moments in Nova Scotia History
- Dr. Melissa Grey's List of the Five Most Important Fossil Finds from Joggins
- John Boileau's List of the Top 10 Heroes from Nova Scotia's History
- A List of 14 Mi'kmaw Place Names in Nova Scotia and Their Meanings
- A List of Black Milestones in Nova Scotia
- A List of 21 Things You May Not Have Known About Nova Scotia
- A List of 24 Things That Were Invented in Nova Scotia
- John G. Leefe's List of the 10 Most Famous Privateers in Nova Scotia History
- Dan Conlin's List of the Top 10 Pirates in Nova Scotia History
- Brian Tennyson's List of 10 Important Things to Know About Nova Scotia's Involvement in the First World War
- Mr. Know-It-All's List of Top 10 Little-known Nova Scotia Breakthroughs
- A List of 12 Interesting Things You Should Know About Nova Scotia Cemeteries
- A List of 11 Facts You Should Know About the History of Automobiles and Driving in Nova Scotia
- A List of 10 Important Sites and Locations That Have a Special Place in the Annals of Nova Scotian History

A List of 35 Canadian or World Firsts that Happened in Nova Scotia

#1. The first European settlement north of Florida was in Nova Scotia. Joao Fagudes was granted permission to claim new territories for Portugal by the king in 1519. In 1520 he sailed northeast and landed on the Northern shores of Cape Breton Island. He set up a small settlement here, which the king funded, but in 1523 he abandoned the colony because of bad relations with the Mi'kmaq. This marked the end of Portuguese interest in "the north." This was the first European settlement in North America after that of the Vikings 500 years before.

#2. The second European settlement in North America was by the French at Port Royal in 1605, where North America's first apple trees, grains and dandelions were planted.

#3. The Order of Good Cheer was established by Samuel de Champlain in Port Royal (then known as Acadie) in the winter of 1606-07. It was the first gastronomic society or social club in North America. The Order of Good Cheer provided good food and good times for the men to improve their health and morale during the long winter. Although it lasted only one winter, the society was a great success. Every few days, supper became a feast where, on a rotating basis, everyone at the table was designated Chief Steward. The Chief Steward had the duty of taking care that all around the table were well and honourably provided for. The members of the Order of Good Cheer were likely prominent men in the colony. Each day, a settler would gather local game, fish, fruits and plants, with the help of the Mi'kmaq, to produce that night's supper. There was music and great celebration as members of the tiny settlement enjoyed each other's company and a pleasant meal.

#4. The first Protestant service held in Canada was solemnized at the chapel of St. Anne, Port Royal in October 1710. Rev. John Harrison read the service and a sermon was preached by Rev. Samuel Hesker.

#5. The first regular Roman Catholic priest at Port Royal was Rev. Jesse Flesche, who accompanied Poutrincourt from France in February 1610. He performed the first baptism in Canada on St. John's Day, June 24, 1610.

#6. The first school in Acadia (Nova Scotia) was a seminary at Port Royal that opened in 1633 by pioneer schoolmasters who were members of the Capuchin Order of Missionaries. They came to Acadia with Governor Issac de Razilly to educate First Nations children and converts. It is also believed to be the first school in North America.

#7. North America's first Boy Scout Troop was established in Port Morien in 1908.

#8. *SATCOM* earth station started operations near Mill Village, Queens County, on October 24, 1966. It was Canada's first satellite communications earth station.

#9. The first tidal power plant in North America opened on Hogg Island, in the Annapolis River in 1984, making it the world's first outside of France.

#10. Fort Anne in Annapolis Royal became Canada's first National Historic Park in October 1917. Fort Anne is the oldest National Historic site in Canada. The key to Fort Anne, which had been taken to Boston in 1710, was finally returned to its original home in August 1922.

#11. Edward Cornwallis granted the first divorce in British North America in 1750 in Nova Scotia, 100 before the British House of Commons passed divorce legislation for England.

#12. Some Mi'kmaq from what is now Nova Scotia were the first Indigenous people of "North America" to receive a European education. The attended French schools from 1633-1653. A Mi'kmaq was the first Indigenous person from North America to return from Europe as a teacher.

#13. On April 10, 1984, Parrsboro resident Eldon George located the world's smallest dinosaur footprints at Wasson Bluff, a series of cliffs to the east of Parrsboro Harbour. The prints are now on display at the Parrsboro Rock and Mineral Shop and Museum, owned by George.

#14. A Nova Scotia Government Telegraph on November 15, 1849, carried the first European cable dispatches to and from the United States and Newfoundland.

#15. William Hall won the Victoria Cross on November 16, 1857, for his bravery at the Relief of Lucknow, becoming the first Canadian sailor, first Black Canadian and first Nova Scotian to be awarded the VC.

#16. Canada's first permanent covered skating rink opened in Halifax on January 3, 1863, as a private club — the Halifax Skating Rink.

#17. Canada's first naval college opened in the Halifax Dockyard on January 11, 1910.

#18. Duncan Gillis, who was born January 3, 1883, in Cape Breton, was a Canadian athlete who competed in the 1912 Summer Olympics held in Stockholm, Sweden, where he became the first to serve as Canada's flag bearer during the Olympic opening ceremonies. During the games he competed in the hammer throw, where he won the silver medal. He also participated in the discus throw and finished 14th. Gillis died in North Vancouver, British Columbia on May 2, 1963.

#19. North America's first all-electric paper-mill town was at Electric City in 1895. Electric City, otherwise known as New France, was the site of a settlement located in Digby County. It was located in the woods about 17 miles behind Weymouth beside the Silver River and the Langford Lake. It was founded in 1892 by the Stehelin family of France and abandoned following the First World War. On February 3, 2010, the Nova Scotia Department of Natural Resources announced that it had acquired the property from J.D. Irving Limited.

#20. Canada's first post office opened in Halifax on December 9, 1755, with subsidized direct mail to Britain.

#21. *The Halifax Gazette*, Canada's first newspaper, was established on March 23, 1752, in Halifax and was published weekly by John Bushell. He was carrying on a project that had been initiated by his partner, Bartholomew Green Jr. There is only one copy remaining of the Halifax Gazette printed by Bushell. The Massachusetts Historical Society in Boston holds that document, which flags the beginning of print culture in Canada.

#22. During the early days of settlement, the province's Annapolis Basin region served as the cradle for both French and English-language theatre of Canada. Théatre de Neptune was the first European theatre production in North America.

#23. English theatre in Canada also started at Annapolis Royal. The tradition at Fort Anne was to produce a play in honour of the Prince of Wales's birthday. The first play, George Farquhar's *The Recruiting Officer*, was produced on January 20, 1733, by the officers of the garrison to mark the Prince's birthday. Paul Mascarene translated Molière's *La Misanthrope* and then staged at least two productions of the work during the winter of 1743-1744. The second performance on January 20, 1744, had also coincided with celebrations in the colony to mark the birthday of Frederick, Prince of Wales. Four years after the Mascarene production, on January 20, 1748, Major Phillips and Captain Floyer also produced a play in honour of the Prince's birthday.

#24. Nova Scotia possesses an enduring movie heritage, which dates from the earliest years of film production in Canada. During the early years of filmmaking, the entrepreneurial possibilities and entertainment potential of cinema caught the imagination of enterprising Canadians. Long before Hollywood existed and dominated the North American film industry, film companies were incorporated across Canada. Most of these companies existed for only brief periods, but the optimism and excitement engendered by such ventures remained part of the Canadian economic and cultural scene well into the twentieth century.

Nova Scotia shared in the enthusiasm and adventure, though prior to 1912 moving pictures of Nova Scotia were created primarily by American and European companies. These films tended to be scenics and newsreels. Canadian railway companies also captured Nova Scotia on film for their promotional campaigns, aimed primarily at British and European audiences.

Nova Scotia's indigenous film history can be traced back to 1912 with the formation of the Canadian Bioscope Company of Halifax, followed in 1920 by the Maritime Motion Picture Company of Sydney. Both companies were greeted with enthusiasm as Nova Scotians looked forward to seeing their own stories, told by Nova Scotians, on the silver screen.Founded by British-born Captain H.H.B. Holland, Canadian Bioscope established offices in Halifax and New York City. A pioneer in the Canadian film industry (it was only the second such company established in Canada), this Maritime-based firm, employing both Nova Scotians and Americans, sought to develop an international distribution network from the outset, in order to ensure economic longevity and provide Nova Scotian films to the world.

Canadian Bioscope's signature piece, *Evangeline*, filmed in 1913, was the company's first project. It was the first commercially produced, full-length motion picture made in Canada. Based on Longfellow's poem by the same name and adapted by Marguerite Marquis, it told the tragic story of the 1755 expulsion of the Acadians from Nova Scotia, framed within the love story of Evangeline and Gabriel. Shot on historically relevant sites at Grand Pré, Annapolis Royal, Cow Bay and Eastern Passage, *Evangeline* achieved further authenticity through period costume. The leads were played by American actors, but local actors held supporting roles. *Evangeline* opened in February 1914 in Halifax to rave reviews. Popular and critical acclaim was also abundant from audiences across Canada and in the United States. The movie's success enabled Canadian Bioscope in 1914 to produce three more shorter dramas and three one-reel comedies. When the First World War broke out, the company was disbanded and its films were auctioned.

Today, the fate of Canada's first motion-picture feature is a mystery. Reportedly, a copy of *Evangeline* was last seen leaving Halifax with some of Canadian Bioscope's American production crew, but what became of it is unknown. All that remains in Canada of the film are a few stills of the production and the advertisements and newspaper reviews.

#25. Nova Scotia became the first province in British North America to win responsible government — a giant first step toward democracy — mainly because of Joseph Howe, a larger-than-life newspaperman, orator and politician. Howe, who was born December 13, 1804, in Halifax, was a journalist, politician and public servant. He is one of Nova Scotia's greatest and best-loved politicians. His considerable skills as a journalist and writer have made him a Nova Scotia legend. The son of John Howe and Mary Edes, he inherited from his loyalist father an undying love for Great Britain and the Empire. At age 23, the self-taught but widely read Howe purchased the Nova Scotian, soon making it into a popular and influential newspaper. He reported extensively on debates in the Nova Scotia House of Assembly and travelled to every part of the province, writing about its geography and people.

In 1835, Howe was charged with seditious libel, a serious criminal offence, after the Nova Scotian published a letter attacking Halifax politicians and police for pocketing public money. Howe addressed the jury for more than six hours, citing example after example of civic corruption. The judge called for Howe's conviction but, swayed by his passionate address, jurors acquitted him in what is considered a landmark case in the struggle for a free press in Canada. The next year, Howe was elected to the assembly as a liberal reformer, beginning a long and eventful public career. He was instrumental in helping Nova Scotia become the first British colony to win responsible government in 1848. He served as premier of Nova Scotia from 1860 to 1863 and led the unsuccessful fight against Canadian Confederation. Having failed to persuade the British to repeal Confederation, Howe joined the federal cabinet of John A. Macdonald in 1869 and played a major role in bringing Manitoba into the union. Howe became the third Lieutenant Governor of Nova Scotia in 1873, but died on June 1, 1873 after only three weeks in office.

#26. Kentville instituted the first system of home fire inspections in Canada in 1935.

#27. Kings College in Annapolis Valley was first colonial university in the British Commonwealth.

#28. The first dyke in North America was built in 1710 in Annapolis.

#29. On October 2, 1758, Nova Scotia's first legislative assembly met in Halifax and Canadian Parliamentary government was born. The 20 members of the assembly had been elected the previous July by the votes of Protestant, British males, over 21, owning freehold land, a franchise that seems remarkably restrictive to us, but was, in fact, liberal for that era.

#30. Dr. Eleonore Bergmann-Porter, a native of West Germany, moved to Nova Scotia in 1961. Dr. Bergmann-Porter was the first female doctor to practice at the Yarmouth hospital, and became an honorary member of the Canadian College of Family Physicians and a member of the Canadian Medical Association. In 1982 she had the distinction of being the first woman to be conferred the rank of senior member in the Medical Society of Nova Scotia.

#31. Ice hurley started in Windsor and developed into ice hockey before 1800. There is documented evidence that wooden hockey pucks were used for the first time in Nova Scotia in 1860. (By contrast, they were first used in Montreal in 1875 as ice hockey was introduced to the city by J.G.A. Creighton of Halifax). Hand-carved by Nova Scotia's Mi'kmaq, the first ice hockey sticks were used in 1860. In 1866, the first hockey skates were introduced by Starr Manufacturing Co., Ltd. of Dartmouth. The company patented their self-fastening "Hockey Skates," designed with rocker-shaped wider blades, rounded in back and front for easy turns and skating backwards, all necessary for maneuverability in playing ice hockey. The hockey skates were a modification of their 1863 patented, world-famous Acme Club Skates, which were held to boots by a cleverly designed self-fastening spring mechanism. Between 1872 and 75, the first hockey rules are developed. Known as the "Halifax Hockey Club Rules," they were used by J.G.A. Creighton of Halifax to teach Montreal athletes to play the Nova Scotia game when they first played in public Victoria Skating Rink. The Montreal Rules of 1877 were fashioned after the Halifax Rules. Around 1920 the National Hockey League was formed in Canada. It grew and rules evolved until today. Hockey is now played around the world.

#32. The Silver Dart (or Aerodrome #4) was a derivative of an early aircraft built by a Canadian-U.S. team, which after many successful flights in Hammondsport, New York, earlier in 1909, was dismantled and shipped to Baddeck on Cape Breton Island. It was flown off the ice of Baddeck Bay (Bras d'Or Lake) on February 23, 1909, making it the first controlled powered flight in Canada. The aircraft was piloted by one of its designers, John McCurdy. The original Silver Dart was designed and built by the Aerial Experiment Association the (AEA), formed under the guidance of Dr. Alexander Graham Bell. From 1891, Bell had begun experiments at Baddeck and Hammondsport to develop motor-powered heavier-than-air aircraft. By 1908, the success of the AEA was seen in a series of groundbreaking designs, culminating in the Silver Dart. By the time the Silver Dart was constructed in late 1908, it was the Aerial Experiment Association's fourth flying machine. One of its precursors, the June Buy, had already broken records. It won the Scientific American Trophy for making the first official one-mile flight in North America. The frame and structure of the Silver Dart were made of steel tube, bamboo, friction tape, wire and wood. The wings were covered with rubberized, silvery balloon cloth provided by Capt. Thomas Scott Baldwin of Hammondsport, New York; hence the name the "Silver Dart." Its Kirkham engine was a reliable V-8 that developed 35 horsepower (26 kW) at 1,000 rpm. The propeller was carved from a solid block of wood. The aircraft had what is now called a canard or an "elevator in front" design. Like most aircraft of its day, the Silver Dart had poor control characteristics. Likewise, it had no brakes.

#33. The world's first flooded mines to produce thermal energy was in Springhill in 1987 (their depth of 3.2 km. heats water to 20-23 deg C).

#34. The first Canadian sighting of a Supernova was at St. Mary's University, Halifax, in 1995.

#35. Situated on one of the cooler climate limits for vines, Nova Scotia has had a long and rich tradition for growing grapes for wine dating back to the early 1600s. It's actually quite possible this was one of the first areas to cultivate grapes in North America. The history of growing grapes in Nova Scotia goes back to 1611. That's when French settler Louis Herbert first planted a small vineyard in Bear River. Nova Scotia's first commercial vintage started in 1980 and years later, a Nova Scotia wine, Jost's 1999 Vidal Ice Wine, took home Canada's Wine of the Year Award.

Other Canadian Firsts that Occurred in Nova Scotia:

PROTESTANT CHURCH AND CATHEDRAL: 1750

PRINTED BOOK: 1752

REPRESENTATIVE GOVERNMENT: 1758

UNIVERSITY: KINGS COLLEGE: 1789

GOVERNMENT HOUSE: 1800

SUNDAY SCHOOL FOR BLACKS: 1813

LEGISLATURE (PROVINCE HOUSE): 1819

DECORATED ENGLISH CHRISTMAS TREE: 1846

FOUNDING OF THE HALIFAX BANKING COMPANY: (Now Imperial Bank Of Commerce) 1825

FOUNDING OF THE ROYAL BANK OF CANADA: (Formerly Merchant Bank) 1864

FOUNDING OF THE BANK OF NOVA SCOTIA: 1832

PUBLIC GARDENS: The finest Victorian in North America, 1836

SCIENCE INSTITUTE: 1862

LAW SCHOOL: 1884

LAWN TENNIS GAME: 1876

A List of 36 Canadian, North American and World Records that Can Be Claimed by Nova Scotia

#1. The Halifax-Dartmouth Ferry is the **OLDEST SALTWATER FERRY** in North America and the second oldest in the world after the Mersey Ferry that links Liverpool and Birkenhead, England. Today the service is operated by Halifax Transit and links downtown Halifax with two Dartmouth locations — Alderney Landing and Woodside. Today, the harbour ferry service and its recognizable ferry vessels are a distinctive feature of the historic Halifax Harbour. The three ferries constantly crisscross the second largest harbour in the world. The ferry service also provides an important symbolic link with the city's past as it is the oldest continuous saltwater passenger ferry service in North America. The Dartmouth Ferry, as it was originally known, began operation in 1752 and served as a vital link for the community of Dartmouth, which was settled a year after the larger British Military Garrison was established in Halifax. With vast farmland, woods and freshwater lakes, the Dartmouth settlers provided the Halifax garrison town with food products and ice for the many icehouses, which were used to keep food fresh. The Dartmouth ferry continued to serve as the only quick way of travelling across the harbour to Halifax until 1955, when the Angus L. Macdonald Bridge was first opened.

#2. The Bay of Fundy has the **HIGHEST TIDES** in the world and those enormous tides alone make it one of the world's greatest natural wonders. In fact, the highest tides on the planet occur near Wolfville in the Minas Basin. The water level at high tide can be as much as 52.5 feet higher than at low tide. The greatest difference between high and low tide ever recorded was at Burntcoat Head at 53.38 feet in the Bay of Fundy's Minas Basin on September 12, 1775. Fundy's twice-daily tidal change is equal to the daily discharge of all the world's rivers combined — 100-km cubed of water. It makes sense then, that Nova Scotia has North America's only tidal power plant.

#3. Government House in Halifax is the official residence of Nova Scotia's lieutenant governor and is the **OLDEST VICE-REGAL HOUSE** in Canada. Built for Sir John Wentworth, the former Loyalist governor of New Hampshire and his wife, Lady Frances, between 1799 and 1805, it is North America's oldest consecutively occupied government residence. Government House is truly a Nova Scotian creation with building materials from around the province used extensively, including stone from Lunenburg and Lockeport on the South Shore as well as Pictou, Antigonish, Cape Breton, Antigonish, Bedford Basin and the Northwest Arm. Sand was brought in from Shelburne, Eastern Passage and McNamara's Island. The bricks were from Dartmouth. Pine was from the Annapolis Valley, Tatamagouche and Cornwallis.

#4. The largest **CHAIN PICKEREL** ever recorded in Canada was caught in Doctor's Lake, Yarmouth County in 1989. It weighed 2.44 kg (5.38 lbs).

#5. The Old Meeting House Museum in Barrington, built in 1765, is the **OLDEST NONCONFORMIST CHURCH** in Canada.

#6. The French-speaking communities of West Pubnico, Middle West Pubnico and Lower West Pubnico were settled 1653 by Acadians. The villages make up the **OLDEST ACADIAN SETTLEMENT** in the world.

#7. Goat Island Baptist Church in Nova Scotia is the **OLDEST BAPTIST CHURCH** building in Canada being built in 1810.

#8. On April 18,1856, Abraham Hebb was deeded a plot of land in the community of Hebb Mills (near Bridgewater). It was a gift to him from his father, Johan George. The area was referred to as Indian Garden Lot and, over time, Abraham established a productive, bountiful agricultural operation, cultivating apples, peaches, grapes and other fruits. Today, five generations later, the land remains in the hands of the Hebb family descendants. After decades of work establishing Indian Garden Farms as a local producer, Abraham passed the property along to his son, William A. Hebb, who continued the farming tradition. In addition to having an excellent orchard, which produced more than 550 barrels of apples in the 1892 season, William was also responsible for pioneering the Hebb cranberry marsh.

After the turn of the century, the Hebb farm became a significant local exporter through the Hebbville Fruit Company, an association of local farmers. The major exports, apples, were shipped to England, but following the First World War, the Hebb focus returned again to the local Nova Scotia market. In the early 20th century, Fletcher Hebb took over the farm from William. Fletcher was an astute recordkeeper who understood the science of good growing. It was also under Fletcher's watch that the Hebb cranberries began to reach a bigger market, with major shipments made to Montreal. Following Fletcher's time, Indian Garden Farms continued to grow under the guidance of Gerald Hebb through the latter half of the 20th century. After seeing the farm market through a number of expansions, Gerald retired and Glen Hebb and his wife, Marilyn, took over the operation in 1995. In 1998, the Hebb cranberry marsh was recognized as being the **OLDEST CONTINUALLY OPERATED CRANBERRY MARSH** in Canada.

#9. On September 3, 1825, businessman Enos Collins founded the Halifax Banking Company with Samuel Cunard and five others. It was called the Collins Bank. However, the first chartered bank in Nova Scotia opened on August 29, 1832 when the first branch of The Bank of Nova Scotia opened for business in Halifax at the corner of Granville and Duke Streets. The bank's second branch opened seven years later in Yarmouth, but its real claim to fame is that it is said to have been the site of the **FIRST RECORDED BANK ROBBERY** in North America in 1861.

#10. Located at the Nova Scotia Brewery, which is actually the **OLDEST WORKING BREWERY** in North America, is Alexander Keith's. Alexander Keith's brewery was founded in 1820, making it one of the oldest commercial breweries not only in Canada, but in all of North America. As the name implies, it was founded by Alexander Keith, who emigrated from Scotland in 1817. Today, the brewery is under the control of Labatt Brewing Company, a subsidiary of Anheuser-Bush InBev.

#11. On August 31, 1922, The Berwick Register reported a three-pound Rome Beauty apple, the **LARGEST APPLE EVER GROWN** on record.

#12. Born in Yarmouth on May 18, 1806, Ezra Churchill was a 19th-century industrialist, investing in shipbuilding, land, timber for domestic and foreign markets, gypsum quarries, insurance companies and hotels among other of his interests. As a politician he held positions in the Nova Scotia Legislature and was appointed to the Canadian Senate as a representative for the Province of Nova Scotia. Churchill was also a Baptist lay preacher. In 1824, Churchill married Ann Davidson and subsequently, after Ann's death, married Rachel Burgess. His move to the eastern end of the Annapolis Valley came with the purchase of a 66-acre lot at Hantsport in 1841. He enlarged his landholdings in the area and over the years sold lots to workmen and their families, who were moving to Hantsport for the jobs being created by the shipbuilding boom. Although Hantsport and area had been the location of a number of shipbuilding ventures, Churchill was the catalyst who transformed a small gathering of farms along the confluence of the Halfway and Avon Rivers into a major shipbuilding port. Nearly 200 vessels were built in the Hantsport-area shipyards. Churchill became one of the largest shipbuilders and ship investors in Nova Scotia, launching dozens of large sailing vessels from his yards at Hantsport. Amongst his many vessels was Hamburg was the **LARGEST THREE-MASTED SAILING BARQUE** ever built in Canada.

#13. The 1,280 m Canso Causeway, linking Cape Breton Island to Nova Scotia mainland, opened on December 10, 1954. It is the **DEEPEST CAUSEWAY** in the world.

#14. The Theatre Arts Guild (TAG) of Halifax is Canada's **OLDEST CONTINUOUSLY OPERATED COMMUNITY THEATRE.** In 1931, the Little Theatre Movement and the Halifax Dramatic and Musical Club merged to found the TAG. The guild's mandate is "to promote the study, practice and knowledge of the dramatic and musical arts in the city of Halifax and the neighbourhood." The group's first production in May 1931 was A.A. Milne's *The Dover Road* at the Garrick Theatre, known today as the Neptune Theatre. During the Second World War, rather than plays, the focus was concert parties for the troops before their deployment overseas.

#15. Built in 1902 as part of the historic Town Hall, the theatre was known as the Liverpool Opera House. Its stage hosted touring and local shows until 1917, when silent films were introduced. Gradually the film presentation gained in frequency and popularity. In 1930, talking pictures were shown for the first time. At the same time the name was changed to the Astor Theatre after a theatre in New York. Today, the Astor is the **OLDEST OPERATING MOVIE THEATRE** in Canada. Until 2014, when it converted to a digital video and audio system, it used 35-millimetre film reels.

#16. Nova Scotia is home to nine universities and seven colleges, and Canada's oldest university — the University of King's College, which was initially established in 1788 as King's College in Windsor — is located in Halifax. It holds the title of the **OLDEST CHARTERED UNIVERSITY** and is perhaps the first college to be granted the university privileges in British-ruled North America. It is a small liberal arts university and primarily offers undergraduate programs.

#17. The Bridgewater Firemen's Band is the **OLDEST FIRE DEPARTMENT BAND** in Canada. The first brass band in Bridgewater was formed in 1868. For many years, the 22-member Bridgewater Brass Band was attached to the 68th King's County Regiment, being recognized as one of the best military bands in Nova Scotia. In 1952, at the disbanding of the Citizens Band, the Bridgewater Fire Department took over the former band's assets and organized a firemen's band, becoming the Bridgewater Firemen's Band. The near century old instruments were sold to the Caledonia Band along with the military-style uniforms. Since 1952 the band had 16 bandmasters and music directors. Today, the Bridgewater Firemen's Band membership consists of adults and youth.

#18. The Hants County Exhibition, held over two weekends in September in Windsor, is not only the **OLDEST AGRICULTURAL FAIR** in Nova Scotia, but it's the oldest in Canada and, in fact, North America. The fair was first held on the grounds of Fort Edward beginning in 1765 and the modern incarnation has been running continuously since 1815. Today, the fair is held at the Hants Exhibition Arena and exhibition grounds.

#19. Religion has played a major role in the history of the Nova Scotia and as such several milestones are worthy of note. For starters, on September 2, 1750, William Tutty founded St. Paul's Church in Halifax, making it the **OLDEST ANGLICAN CHURCH** in North America. Located in downtown Halifax, at the end of Grand Parade facing City Hall, the Georgian-style church is also the oldest building in Halifax. In 1749, upon the founding of Halifax, the location for St. Paul's was identified by town planners in the centre of the town plot. The following summer the cornerstone was laid by the Governor of Nova Scotia, Edward Cornwallis. While services began in the church several months later, it took nearly 10 years for the interior to be completed. Since that time the church has undergone numerous changes; however, the original oak-and-pine frame, which was precut and shipped from Boston, continues to support the main part of the building.

#20. Another religious cornerstone is the Zion Evangelical Lutheran Church in Lunenburg. Described as the "Rock of Lutheranism," it is the home of Canada's **OLDEST LUTHERAN CONGREGATION**. When German Lutheran settlers first arrived in 1753, they held services in the open air and later at St. John's Anglican Church. The first church on this site was built in 1772 and replaced in 1841. The only remains of the first Lutheran church are the key to the building and the Saint Antoine-Marie bell that had formerly hung in the Fortress of Louisbourg (a French fort located on Cape Breton Island), and had been purchased by the congregation in 1776. The present building dates from 1890. The large hall to the rear of the church was added in 1946 and serves as a meeting place and Sunday school.

#21. Another noteworthy development in the province's religious heritage was the emergence of St. Andrew's Presbyterian Church in Lunenburg. It is the home of the **OLDEST PRESBYTERIAN CONGREGATION** in Canada. Built in 1828, the current structure replaced an earlier church that was built on the same site. The church was substantially renovated in 1879.

#22. The Argyle Church in Yarmouth County is a one-storey wooden building located on a hill at Frost Corner, Argyle. The Argyle Historic Church and Cemetery is valued due to its associations with early settlers in Argyle Township. The history of this site goes back to the settlement of the area by New England Planters in the early 1760s. But the site is also notable for its association with Reverend John Frost, the **FIRST PROTESTANT MINISTER** ordained in Canada. He served here and is buried in the adjoining cemetery. Established in the 1760s and in use until 1891, the burial ground is one of the earliest and longest used graveyards in the area.

#23. Église Sainte-Marie is a Catholic church in Church Point and is the **LARGEST AND TALLEST WOODEN CHURCH** in North America. Built in the form of a cross, the church nave measures 58 metres (190 feet) in length, with transepts that are 41 metres (135 feet) across. The church spire rises 56 metres (184 feet) from floor to steeple, with its cross adding another 1.67 meters (5.5 feet). Originally 15 feet taller, the church steeple was struck by lightning in 1914, requiring part of the spire to be rebuilt.

#24. Ever wonder who were the oldest Nova Scotians on record? Well, wonder no more. Sister Anne Samson, born February 27, 1891, in River Bourgeois, Cape Breton; died November 29, 2004, in Moncton, New Brunswick. She lived a total of 113 years and 276 days. At the time of her death, it was believed she was **OLDEST NUN** ever recorded. Gertrude Marshall, who was born on October 16, 1902, in Caledonia and died on October 25, 2013, in Coquitlam, British Columbia, lived a total of 111 years and seven days.

#25. Ross-Thomson House Museum in Shelburne is the **OLDEST EXISTING STORE** in Nova Scotia and the **OLDEST RESTORED STORE** in North America. Its exterior and interior, which reflect the building's original uses as a store and residence since its construction in 1787, are virtually unaltered. Ross-Thomson House is also valued for its association with Shelburne's Loyalist history. It was built between 1785 and 1786 by brothers George and Robert Ross, who came to Shelburne to escape the American Revolution, as did many of Shelburne's earliest settlers. The brothers operated an international trading business, ran a small store for local residents and lived in the residential rear section of the building. In 1815 the building was sold to the brothers' former clerk Robert Thomson, whose son Robert Ross Thomson continued to operate the store until his death in 1880. Robert Ross Thomson served for a time as Shelburne's postmaster and the post office was located in the store. He was also a lieutenant colonel of the local militia in the late 1860s, during the Fenian raids, and the room above the store was used at that time as the militia room. The building is currently operated as a museum.

#26. The world's **BIGGEST ATLANTIC BLUEFIN TUNA** ever recorded was caught by Ken

Fraser in Aulds Cove, Nova Scotia on October 26, 1979. He landed the 1,496-pound (679 kilograms) fish in an impressive 45 minutes. The Atlantic bluefin tuna is one of the largest, fastest and most gorgeously coloured of all the world's fishes. Their torpedo-shaped, streamlined bodies are built for speed and endurance. Their colouring — metallic blue on top and shimmering silver-white on the bottom — helps camouflage them from above and below. And their voracious appetite and varied diet pushes their average size to a whopping 6.5 feet (two meters) in length and 550 pounds (250 kilograms), although much larger specimens are not uncommon. Atlantic bluefins are warm-blooded, a rare trait among fish, and are comfortable in the cold waters off Newfoundland and Iceland, as well as in the tropical waters of the Gulf of Mexico and the Mediterranean Sea, where they go each year to spawn. They are among the most ambitiously migratory of all fish and some tagged specimens have been tracked swimming from North American to European waters several times a year. They are prized among sport fishers for their fight and speed, shooting through the water with their powerful, crescent-shaped tails up to 43 miles (70 kilometers) per hour. They can retract their dorsal and pectoral fins into slots to reduce drag. And some scientists think the series of "finlets" on their tails may even serve to reduce water turbulence. Bluefins attain their enormous size by gorging themselves almost constantly on smaller fish, crustaceans, squid, and eels. They will also filter feed on zooplankton and other small organisms and have even been observed eating kelp.

#27. In August 2004, while Jamie Doucette was participating in the annual shark derby in the waters off the coast of Yarmouth, he ended up making a catch that was one for the record books. Fishing with a rod and reel, using a 200-pound test line and a hook baited with mackerel, and chumming 48 miles out of Yarmouth, it wasn't long until he felt the bite. He knew right away it was a big one. He worked it for 30 minutes before he saw the fin, rising a good foot from the water about 150 yards out. It was a short-fin mako shark. A regular visitor to Maritime waters, the sharks are often reported chasing mackerel with the Gulf Stream into the Bay of Fundy. When they finally got it on the official scale, lifted into place by a forklift to keep the scale from tipping, the shark weighed in at an astonishing 1,082 pounds — a Canadian record and one of the **LARGEST SHORT-FIN MAKO SHARK** ever caught. The female shark measured 10 feet, 11 inches in length and was estimated to be about 25 years old.

#28. North American lobsters are measured by the length of their shell, also known as the carapace. An average caught lobster is in the 1.5 pounds to two pounds range. According to the Guinness Book of Records, the **BIGGEST LOBSTER** ever recorded weighed an amazing 20-kilograms (44 pounds) and was caught near Nova Scotia in 1977. Its carapace was over 27 cm long. From the tip of its tail to the tip of its claws it measured more than 110 cm.

#29. Born in the small community of Alma, New Brunswick on February 23, 1916, Myrtle "Molly" Kool was North America's **FIRST REGISTERED FEMALE SEA CAPTAIN** or shipmaster. She was the daughter of Myrtle Anderson and Paul Kool, a Dutch sailor. She grew up sailing, eventually becoming captain of the Jean K, a 21-metre scow owned by her father. At 21, she joined the Merchant Marine School in Saint John, New Brunswick. She was the only woman to do so. Two years later she graduated and received her Master Mariner's papers from the Merchant Marine Institution in Yarmouth. As a result, a line in the Canadian Shipping Act had to be amended to read "he or she."

#30. Nova Scotia has one of the world's most amazing paleontological records that spans many geological time periods — including the world's **FIRST REPTILE**, the world's **FIRST LAND SNAIL**, the world's first evidence of herding behaviour/social behaviour in vertebrate animals, the world's **SMALLEST DINOSAUR FOOTPRINTS** and Canada's **OLDEST DINOSAURS**.

#31. The Halifax Common, or the Commons as most people call the area, is Canada's **OLDEST URBAN PARK**, with the North Common and the Central Common still in use as a public park area. The Common was created by surveyors following the settling of Halifax in 1749 to serve three purposes. The first was to provide pasturage for horses and livestock, both by the military garrison and the citizens of Halifax. The second was to create a large area in which regiments stationed and in transit through Halifax could set up camps. The third was to provide clear fields of fire for the garrison of the Halifax Citadel, so that invading forces would have no cover in the event of an assault on the fort.

#32. The Argyle Township Court House is Canada's **OLDEST STANDING COURTHOUSE**. Built in Tusket, Yarmouth County in 1805, it operated from 1805 until 1944. The offices of the Municipality of Argyle were located there from 1945 until 1976. Construction started in 1801 and was completed in 1805. The first session was held on October 29, 1805. In 1982-83 a partial restoration of the building took place and it was reopened in 1983 as a museum and community archive, marking it the first municipal archives established in Nova Scotia in the 1980s. The building was declared a National Historic Site in 2005.

NOTE: The Annapolis County Court House, built in 1837, is valued for its continuing function as a courthouse and jail, the oldest such building in Nova Scotia and one of the oldest in Canada. It is also associated with popular accounts of public hangings and floggings on the Court grounds.

#34. The **LARGEST SINGLE MIGRATION OF ENGLISH-SPEAKING PEOPLE** was in 1783, with the evacuation of 10,000 New York City Loyalists to Shelburne, then North America's fourth-largest city.

#35. The first North American **DOCUMENTED SIGHTING OF A UFO** was on October 12, 1786 at New Minas.

#36. The Killam Brothers' Shipping Office located on Water Street in Yarmouth established in the 19th century is Canada's **OLDEST SHIPPING OFFICE** and reflects the town's golden "Age of Sail."

John Boileau's List of the 10 Most Important Moments in Nova Scotia History

How long is a moment? Normally it is considered to be a very short period of time, but what does short mean, for example, in geological time, which spans eons? Similarly, even human historical time covers centuries. Sometimes an important moment can take place in an instant — such as the assassination of a head of state — but certain historical "moments" take much longer, such as some of the entries below, which are shown in chronological order.

#1. The end of the last ice age about 12,500 years ago gave Nova Scotia its current geography and geology, which in turn opened the way for the arrival of the first humans approximately 11,000 years ago.

#2. The founding of Port Royal in the summer of 1605 led to an influx of traders, soldiers and settlers and the creation of the new French colony of Acadia — the beginnings of the permanent European occupation of Nova Scotia.

#3. The fall of Port Royal to the British on October 12, 1710, and the subsequent Treaty of Utrecht, signed on April 11, 1713, resulted in a change of ownership of peninsular Nova Scotia and its occupation by the British.

#4. The founding of Halifax on June 21, 1749, was the first major British undertaking in establishing a large, permanent civilian presence in the colony.

#5. The Expulsion of the Acadians (1755-64), coupled with the fall of Louisbourg on July 26, 1758, drastically changed the demographic make up of the colony and resulted in uniting the mainland with Cape Breton Island.

#6. After several years of warfare, the Burying the Hatchet Ceremony at Halifax on June 25, 1761, ended several years of conflict and marked the start of permanent peace between the British and the Mi'kmaq.

#7. The arrival of the New England Planters (1759-68) to occupy vacated Acadian lands, and the later arrival of the Loyalists (1775-83), dramatically increased the British population of the colony.

#8. The establishment of responsible government on February 2, 1848, was the first for any colony in the British Empire and a major step on the path to self-governance for the province and later the country.

#9. The Confederation of four British North American colonies on July 1, 1867, eventually led to the Canada we know today of 10 provinces and three territories.

#10. The granting of women's suffrage on April 26, 1918, was the first major milestone in the women's rights movement.

If there were more than ten moments, an eleventh would be the Halifax Explosion of December 6, 1917, at 9:04:35 a.m., which in an instant killed 1,600 people and injured another 9,000, destroyed or severely damaged 1,630 structures (with lesser damage to another 5,000 buildings) and led to at least 400 more deaths in the coming days — the results of the largest, man-made, non-nuclear explosion in human history.

Retired army colonel John Boileau is the author of more than a dozen books of historical non-fiction, as well as more than 500 magazine and newspaper articles on a variety of subjects, book reviews, op-ed columns, travelogues and encyclopedia entries.

Dr. Melissa Grey's List of the Five Most Important Fossil Finds from Joggins

In 1985 the largest fossil find ever in North America was unearthed on the north shore of the Minas Basin near Parrsboro. More than 100,000 fossil specimens, some more than 200-million years old were found, including penny-sized footprints. In 1984, collector Eldon George found the world's smallest dinosaur tracks at Wasson's Bluff. The following is a list of the five the most important fossil from Joggins.

#1. HYLONOMUS LYELLI: The first reptile in the fossil record and Nova Scotia's Provincial Fossil! *Hylonomus* represents a branch of the evolutionary tree where tetrapods (vertebrates with four limbs) were able to live their lives solely on land without having to return to the water to reproduce (as amphibians do).

#2. STANDING LYCOPOD TREES: Lycopods are club mosses that could grow to tremendous sizes (over 30 m tall!). It is fairly rare to find them in situ (in their growth position — upright in the cliffs) and it's in these fossilized trees that *Hylonomus* was found.

#3. ARTHROPLEURA: The largest-known land invertebrate of all time! A relative of the millipedes, this critter could reach lengths of over 2 m. At Joggins, the trackways left by *Arthropleura* are abundant, but we've yet to find a body fossil.

#4. DENDROPUPA: Oldest land snail in the fossil record.

#5. "REX" – YET TO BE OFFICIALLY NAMED: The top predator at Joggins during the Carboniferous — a very large amphibian! Mostly trackways and footprints preserved — no fully intact skeletons found (yet!). Largest footprint size is about 12 cm across.

Dr. Melissa Grey, PhD is Curator of Palaeontology at Joggins Fossil Institute. The Joggins Fossil Institute is a not-for-profit, charitable organization that is dedicated to research, education and protection of the Joggins Fossil Cliffs UNESCO World Heritage Site.

John Boileau's List of the Top 10 Heroes from Nova Scotia's History

It may come as a surprise to many that the word "hero," a term usually associated with manly qualities, was originally the name of a beautiful Greek priestess. In despair over seeing her lover Leander drown in the Dardanelles (the Turkish strait separating Europe from Asia), Hero threw herself into the sea and also drowned. Eventually, hero came to mean a person distinguished by courage or noble deeds.

Today, perhaps no word is more overused in the English language than "hero," usually referring to those who have made notable achievements in sports, business or some other human endeavour. But they are not real heroes. The true heroes below are shown in chronological order of their deeds, as there is no greater or lesser degree of heroism among them.

Four of the 10 are recipients of the Victoria Cross (VC), the highest award for gallantry in the British and now the Canadian honours system. The rigorous standards applied to the award of a VC ensure that anyone who is awarded the medal is a hero.

#1. JEAN-BAPTISTE COPE (Kopit in Mi'kmaq, meaning beaver) (1698-1758/60) was born at Port Royal and was a Mi'kmaq chief in the Shubenacadie area. Sometimes known as Major Cope, he became a hero to his people for leading Mi'kmaq warriors and Acadians in guerilla warfare against the British occupation of Nova Scotia during Father Le Loutre's War (1749-55). In 1752, he was involved in negotiating a peace treaty with Governor Peregrine Hopson, which he burned the next year due to an unprovoked British attack on the Mi'kmaq. He then worked with Le Loutre to convince Acadians to leave peninsular Nova Scotia.

#2. JOSEPH BROSSARD (also known as Beausoleil) (1702-65) was born at Port Royal and was an Acadian leader who organized his people and Mi'kmaq warriors in several wars against the British occupation of Nova Scotia. During the Expulsion of the Acadians (1755-64) he was a leader of the armed resistance against the deportation. He was captured in 1762, released in 1764 and deported to Haiti with several other Acadians, but could not adapt to the climate and led his group to Louisiana. He is regarded as a hero by both the Acadians of the Maritimes and the Cajuns of Louisiana.

#3. JOE CRACKER (1784-?) was a 13-year-old boy when the frigate HMS Tribune was blown onto the rocks just outside Herring Cove by a fierce gale on November 23, 1797. Some sailors made it ashore in a rowboat, but few of the more than 100 who climbed into the rigging survived the night. Heavy surf discouraged rescue until late in the morning, when a lone local lad rowed a dory out to the wreck and was able to rescue eight survivors. Known to history only as Joe Cracker, his real name remains unknown.

#4. MAJOR-GENERAL (LATER GENERAL SIR) WILLIAM FENWICK WILLIAMS (1800-83) from Annapolis Royal was attached to the Turkish army during the Crimean War (1853-56) and successfully defended the mountain fortress of Kars against several Russian assaults for three months until forced to surrender. The Russians took Williams prisoner, but released him at the end of the war. In Britain, he was acclaimed the "Hero of Kars," knighted and made a baronet. In 1865, he returned to Nova Scotia to become its first native-born lieutenant-governor.

#5. LIEUTENANT COLONEL (LATER MAJOR GENERAL SIR) JOHN EARDLEY INGLIS (1814-62) of Halifax attained the status of Victorian hero in the summer of 1857 for successfully defending a fortified compound of 1,720 soldiers, civilians and non-combatant women and children against native troops at the Siege of Lucknow during the Indian Mutiny (1857-58). Although a first relief column was too small to drive the rebels back, a later force finally relieved Lucknow after bloody hand-to-hand fighting. In recognition of his heroic defence, Inglis was promoted major-general and knighted.

#6. ABLE SEAMAN (LATER QUARTERMASTER) WILLIAM NEILSON HALL (1829-1904) of Horton Bluff, King's County, was the first Black, first Nova Scotian and third Canadian to earn the VC. On November 16, 1857, at the second relief of Lucknow during the Indian Mutiny, he served one of two heavy naval cannons ordered forward to breach the stonewalls of the heavily-defended Shah Nujjiff Mosque. Even after the crew of the other gun were killed and only he and an officer remained on his, he continued to fire at the rebels at point-blank range, all the while under heavy fire.

#7. ELIZABETH (BESSIE) PRITCHARD HALL (1849-1930) from Granville Beach, Annapolis County, first joined her captain father at sea when she was 17 and quickly learned navigation and ship handling. In 1870, her father's 1,310-tonne ship departed New Orleans with a cargo of cotton two months late and short-handed. After her father and another crewman soon collapsed with smallpox, the remaining crew chose her to command the ship to Liverpool, England. She safely navigated the ship through several storms to England, where she was hailed as a hero.

#8. PRIVATE JOHN CHIPMAN "CHIP" KERR (1887-1963) from Fox River, Cumberland County, was a member of the 49th (Edmonton) Battalion and the leading soldier of twelve in a bombing (grenade) attack on a German trench near Courcelette on September 16, 1916, during the Battle of the Somme. Despite losing part of his right forefinger to an enemy bomb, he ran along the top of the trench and opened fire at point-blank range on the Germans who, believing they were surrounded, surrendered. Sixty-two prisoners and 230 metres of trench were captured.

#9. SECOND LIEUTENANT (TEMPORARY LIEUTENANT-COLONEL) PHILIP ERIC BENT (1891-1917) of Halifax was commanding a British infantry unit, the 9th Battalion, Leicestershire Regiment (nicknamed "The Tigers"), during the First World War. At Polygon Wood during the Battle of Third Ypres on October 1, 1917, when his battalion was being overrun and pushed back by the Germans, he quickly gathered a small reserve and personally led a successful counterattack with the rallying cry of "Come on The Tigers!", but was killed in the effort. As his body was never found, he is commemorated on the memorial wall in nearby Tyne Cot Cemetery.

#10. PRIVATE JAMES PETER ROBERTSON (1883-1917) from Albion Mines (now Stellarton) was serving in the 27th (City of Winnipeg) Battalion during the Battle of Passchendaele in the First World War. As his platoon approached the village of Passchendaele on November 6, 1917, he single-handedly attacked and captured a German machine-gun post. Later that day, he immediately went to the aid of two badly wounded Canadians in no man's land under intense fire. He was killed as he brought in the second one when a shell exploded nearby. Robertson is buried nearby in Tyne Cot Cemetery.

Note 1: One other VC recipient, Private John Bernard Croak, is usually classified as a Nova Scotian, but because he was born in Newfoundland and Labrador and moved to Nova Scotia at an early age, he is not included in this list.

Note 2: There are other individuals who performed heroic acts in Nova Scotia, such as Sub-Lieutenant (Nursing Sister) Margaret Brooke — or lived in the province after their heroic act, such as Sub-Lieutenant (later Rear Admiral) Robert Timbrell — but who are not included in this list because they were not born in Nova Scotia.

Retired army colonel John Boileau is the author of more than a dozen books of historical non-fiction, as well as more than 500 magazine and newspaper articles on a variety of subjects, book reviews, op-ed columns, travelogues and encyclopedia entries.

A List of 14 Mi'kmaw Place Names in Nova Scotia and Their Meanings

The Mi'kmaq are the First People of Nova Scotia. Mi'kmaw territory, known as Mi'kma'ki, includes all of Nova Scotia and Prince Edward Island, the Gaspé Peninsula, and parts of New Brunswick (north of the Saint John River), Newfoundland and the State of Maine. The word Mi'kmaq means "my friends." The Mi'kmaq originally identified themselves as L'nu'k, "the people." The word Mi'kmaw is the adjective form of Mi'kmaq. Throughout the province you'll find places that have Mi'kmaw names. Here are 14 of those places:

#1. ANTIGONISH: "where branches are torn off" [perhaps a reference to a location where bears would come to eat beechnuts or hazelnuts]

#2. CHEZZETCOOK: "flowing rapidly in many channels"

#3. ESKASONI: "green boughs"

#4. JOGGINS: "a place of fish weirs"

#5. KEJIMKUJIK (LAKE): "attempting to escape," or it may also mean "swelled private parts," a reference to the physical toll of an eight-km paddle across the lake

#6. (LAKE) BANOOK: "first lake in a chain"

#7. MALAGASH: "place of games"

#8. MERIGOMISH: "a place of merry-making"

#9. MUSQUODOBOIT: "suddenly widening out after a narrow entrance at its mouth"

#10. PICTOU: "an explosion"

#11. SHUBENACADIE: "place where ground nuts occur"

#12. TANCOOK (ISLAND): "out to sea"

#13. TIDNISH: "paddle"

#14. TUSKET: "a great forked tidal river"

A List of Black Milestones in Nova Scotia

The first recorded instance of a Black presence in Canada was that of Mathieu de Costa. He arrived in Nova Scotia sometime between 1603 and 1608 as a translator for the French explorer Sieur DeMonts. This expedition founded Port Royal. The following is a list of Black milestones throughout Nova Scotia's history:

1774: Born March 13, 1774, into slavery in the British Colony of Virginia, Rose Fortune, came to Annapolis Royal with the Black Loyalists when she was 10 years old. She went on to become a successful businesswoman and the first female police officer not only in Canada, but in all of North America.

1859: William Hall of Horton's Bluff becomes the first Canadian to be awarded the Victoria Cross.

1890: George Dixon of Halifax wins the World Bantamweight boxing title. This is the first time a Black man has won a world boxing title in any weight class.

1898: Nova Scotia's first African Nova Scotian lawyer, James Robinson Johnston, was called to the Bar.

1949: Nova Scotian William Andrew (Bill) White, III, was born February 7, 1915, in Truro. He was a well-known composer, educator and social activist, but he earns his place in history for being the first Black Canadian to run for federal office in Canada. He stood as the Cooperative Commonwealth Federation candidate in the Toronto electoral district of Spadina in the 1949 election, although he was not elected.

1960: Rev. W.P. Oliver is chosen to serve as president of the United Baptist Convention of the Maritimes — the first Black to be so honoured.

1967: Isaac Phils of Sydney becomes the first Black person appointed to the Order of Canada.

1984: Daurene Lewis is elected mayor of the town of Annapolis Royal. This is the first time in Canadian history that a Black woman is elected mayor of a town in Canada.

1992: George Boyd becomes the first Black anchor of a national news show, when he becomes an anchor on CBC Newsworld. He was born and raised in Halifax.

1993: Born 1943 in Halifax, Wayne Adams was first elected to the Halifax Municipal Council in 1979 and was re-elected five times. He was Deputy Mayor from 1982 to 1983. A Nova Scotia Liberal, he was elected in the 1993 Nova Scotia general election in the riding of Preston. He was the Minister of the Environment, Minister responsible for the Emergency Measures Act, and the Minister responsible for the Nova Scotia Boxing Authority in the governments of first John Savage (1993–1997) and then Russell MacLellan (1997–1998). Adams was Nova Scotia's first Black MLA and cabinet minister. He was defeated in 1998 by the NDP candidate, Yvonne Attwell.

1998: Born in 1943 in East Preston, Yvonne Atwell was Nova Scotia's first Black woman MLA. In 1996 she ran unsuccessfully for the leadership of the Nova Scotia New Democratic Party. She won a seat for the NDP in the Nova Scotia House of Assembly in 1998 for the riding of Preston, becoming the first black woman MLA in the province. She lost her seat in the 1999 provincial election.

2001: George Elliot Clarke wins the Governor General's Award for Poetry. He is the first Black Canadian writer to win this prestigious award.

A List of 21 Things You May Not Have Known About Nova Scotia

So you've lived in Nova Scotia for a long time and you think you know everything there is to know about the province, but did you know that …

#1. Nova Scotia was once a part of the county of Edinburgh, Scotland? In 1621, Sir William Alexander, wanting to claim the province as part of his territory, declared it part of his barony of Edinburgh.

#2. The first reported quintuplets in Canada were born at Little Egypt, Pictou County in 1880? The three girls and two boys, but they all died within two days of their birth.

#3. The average age of first marriage in Nova Scotia is 29.0 for brides and 30.9 years of age for grooms? Compare that to 30 years ago, when the ages were 21.1 years for women and 23.1 years for men.

#4. Nova Scotia was the sixth province/territory in Canada and the first in Atlantic Canada to legalize same-sex marriage?

#5. The highest number of Nova Scotian births in one year occurred in 1961, when 19,624 children were born?

#6. Inventor Alexander Graham Bell is buried near Baddeck in Cape Breton?

#7. There are more than 300 species of seaweed around Nova Scotia coasts? Seaweed growth occurs most abundantly on the rocky shores of the Atlantic coast. The main seaweeds attaching to rocks are the kelps and rockweeds. Eelgrass prefers the soft bottoms of protected inlets and bays, especially in the Northumberland Strait.

#8. When Nova Scotia joined Confederation in 1867, it was the wealthiest province in Canada?

#9. Canada's first coal mine opened in Cape Breton in 1720?

#10. Nova Scotia is home to an estimated three billion tonnes of coal?

#11. Nova Scotia is the world's largest exporter of lobsters, Christmas trees, gypsum, carrots and strawberry plants?

#12. More than 2,500 people grow Christmas trees in Nova Scotia, farming 10,000 hectares of land? Each year, nearly two million trees are sent to market, generating $30 million. Eighty percent of the trees are exported to the U.S.

#13. The Balsam Fir reigns as king of Nova Scotia's Christmas-tree industry, covering 99 percent of the total market?

#14. Nova Scotia was home to Canada's first decorated Christmas tree in 1846?

#15. In 1901, Nova Scotia became the first province in Canada to manufacture cars?

#16. Scotia issued its first liquor license in 1749 to John Shippey's tavern, the Spread Eagle? The tavern still exists today, but is now known as the Split Crow.

#17. Life for Nova Scotians was revolutionized in 1884 when electricity was first introduced in the province? The first to benefit were Haligonians, when 75 street-lights and 50 stores "went electric."

#18. In 1896, electric streetcars were introduced to the province?

#19. In 1919, the provincial Nova Scotia Power Commission was created?

#20. In 1890, Halifax-born George Dixon won the world bantam-weight boxing title, becoming the first Black person ever to win a boxing title?

#21. Remains of mammoths, mastodons, walruses and whales have been found on Sable Island, Sable Island Bank and Georges Bank?

A List of 24 Things That Were Invented in Nova Scotia

The old adage that necessity is the mother of invention appears to have held water for early Nova Scotians. Ingenuity and creativity have become the hallmark of the hardworking and resilient residents of Nova Scotia. That can certainly be said of these individuals whose efforts left an indelible and lasting impact on future generations:

#1. THE TELEPHONE: Today, most people take their telephones for granted, but did you know this game-changing invention traces its roots back to Nova Scotia and the great mind of Alexander Graham Bell? The Scottish-born Bell obtained the patent for a multiple telegraph unit in 1875, and by 1876, when Bell was 29, the telephone was born. A year after that, the Bell Telephone Company formed. Following his successful invention of the telephone and being relatively wealthy, Bell acquired land near Baddeck on Cape Breton Island in 1885, largely due to surroundings reminiscent of his early years in Scotland. He established a summer estate complete with research laboratories, working with deaf people — including Helen Keller — and continued to invent. Baddeck was the site of his experiments with hydrofoil technologies as well as the Aerial Experiment Association, financed by his wife, which saw the first powered flight in Canada and the entire British Empire when the AEA Silver Dart took off from the ice-covered waters of Bras d'Or Lake in 1909. Bell also built the forerunner to the iron lung and experimented with breeding sheep. Over his lifetime, Bell patented 18 inventions of his own, as well as 12 more with colleagues.

The Bell Family vacation home at Beinn Bhreagh was located near Baddeck on Cape Breton Island and eventually became Bell's final resting place. He died there on August 2, 1922. Bell's Nova Scotia connection remains alive and well in the province today. The Alexander Graham Bell National Historic Site in Baddeck houses exhibits of his first inventions including the Silver Dart, advanced recording technology, giant kites and, of course, the telephone.

#2. KEROSENE: The first flickers of the oil industry begin with kerosene and a Nova Scotia-born physician-turned-geologist named Abraham Pineo Gesner. Born in Cornwallis in May 2, 1797, Gesner was studying medicine in London when he pursued his lifelong interest in geology, later publishing a study on the mineralogy of Nova Scotia in 1836. It was in 1846 that Gesner developed a process to refine liquid fuel from coal, bitumen and oil shale. He named this clean-burning, affordable by-product kerosene and four years later founded the Kerosene Gaslight Company and began installing light posts in Halifax. Gesner took out Nova Scotia patent No. 108 in 1865 for kerosene. Gesner's contribution to the early petroleum industry continued. In 1861, he published a research paper called "A Practical Treatise on Coal, Petroleum and Other Distilled Oils." He died in Halifax on April 29, 1864.

#3. PAPER: Modern newspapers we read today have Nova Scotian-born Charles Fenerty to thank for their existence. He was born in January 1821 in Upper Sackville. The tale goes that in 1844, wasps chewing wood fibres to make nests inspired Fenerty to develop the process of making paper from groundwood pulp instead of rags. Fenerty himself never took out a patent on his process, but he did share his newly invented paper with the owners of the Halifax newspaper, the Acadian Recorder. The German F.G. Keller is most often credited as the original inventor, as Keller filed for a patent in 1845. North American paper mills adopted the process and Fenerty lived to see the first wood-pulp paper mill in operation near Sackville. Fenerty was recognized by Canada Post in 1987 on a set of four stamps commemorating Canadian inventors. He died June 10, 1892, in Lower Sackville.

#4. PROPELLER: Yarmouth-area sailor and fisherman Captain John Patch invented the ship propeller in 1833. One day, while watching a small boat being maneuvered with a single oar, he came up with the idea for a device which would allow steamships to travel without need of large, inefficient paddlewheels or wind-dependent sails. It would be 30 years before he would see his idea become reality. Born in Yarmouth in 1781, Patch tested his invention, a two-bladed, fan-shaped propeller in 1832 and demonstrated it to the public in 1833 by propelling a rowboat across Yarmouth Harbour. His invention came four years before a similar patent was filed in the United Kingdom, but Patch lacked the funds to travel across the Atlantic. Without American citizenship, he didn't qualify for a U.S. patent. It wasn't until 1849, when American laws changed, that Patch received his American patent. By this time, however, there were multiple competing versions on the market. There are several versions of the story of how Patch lost the rights to his invention, but the end result was that he was never recognized for it and never made any money. In 1858, more than 100 citizens of Yarmouth signed a petition asking the government to provide Patch with a pension as thanks for his work. The petition was presented to the Nova Scotia legislature but was eventually rejected and in 1861, Patch died penniless in a Yarmouth poorhouse.

#5. HIGH-SPEED AUTOMATIC PRINTING TELEGRAPH: The people of Mill Village and Canso have a brief history with Frederick Creed. But it's what he discovered while working in Canso, where he was a self-taught student of cable and landline telegraphy, that led him to his invention. Creed was born in Mill Village in 1871, moved to Canso in 1878 and then to Chile in 1888. In Chile, while Creed worked at a telegraph and cable company, he, out of boredom, created a typewriter-style machine to generate Morse code signals on paper tape. Creed left Chile for Scotland in 1897 to perfect his invention and soon after, his high-speed automatic telegraph could transmit 200 words per minute. This communications breakthrough led to the manufacture of the Creed Telegraph Printer, which by 1913 was the routine system used to transmit London newspapers to major centres in Europe. In 1923, Creed's system was used in ship-to-shore communications and seen as a valuable life-saving system for ships in distress. He died at his home in Croydon in 1957 at the age of 86.

#6. ODOMETER: The grandfather of the modern odometer was a Nova Scotian by the name of Samuel McKeen who was born April 17, 1777, in Truro. During the industrial revolution, countries the world over were developing their own modern ways to improve the economy. Other versions were popping up throughout the world, but it was McKeen who gave Canadians the early version of the odometer we know today. McKeen attached his device to the side of a carriage and measured the miles with the turning of the wheels. He died in 1845 when he fell from his horse while riding home on horseback.

#7. TIME ZONES: Nova Scotia may have been the second home of Sir Sandford Fleming, but his local legacy lives on. The Scottish-born engineer and inventor influenced the world's adoption of a single 24-hour clock not linked to a surface meridian and to be used the world over. Fleming, one of the founding owners of the Nova Scotia Cotton Manufacturing Company, retired in Halifax and, upon his death in 1915, left a proud legacy to the city, donating his house and surrounding 95 acres of land, which is now known as Sir Sandford Fleming Park or Dingle Park.

#8. TWO-CYCLE BOAT ENGINES: Some say that Forman Hawboldt was to the marine industry what Henry Ford was to automobiles. Hawboldt Industries was established in 1906 by Forman Hawboldt and Harry Evans, his brother-in-law, who later left the company. The primary function of the company, which operated from the family's barn for the first two years, was to build two-cycle boat engines. Hawboldt's invention changed the face of the fishing/marine industry and made way for the replacement of wind-powered sails and rowing. History tells a tale that after Hawboldt used one of his engines to propel a boat around the Chester harbour, onlookers carried him shoulder high from the wharf. The villagers, accustomed to using sails or oars, had seen the future of the fishing industry. A century later, the Hawboldt name continues to play a role in the future of the marine industry. Hawboldt, a natural-born mechanic who was never formally educated in engineering and mechanics, retired in 1946. Twenty years later the company was sold by the family.

#9. R-THETA COMPUTER: Jerry Wright, who was born in Liverpool on August 31, 1917, studied to become a pharmaceutical clerk and worked in a drugstore before joining the Royal Canadian Air Force (RCAF) in 1940. Wright was a sergeant by the time he was shipped to Greenock, Scotland, where he was placed as a navigator of one of the flying boats that flew across the ocean on missions lasting up to 32 hours. Later, he was moved to Madras, Spain, and promoted to flight lieutenant. In 1944, Wright worked with eight other experts on a review of navigational systems. This led to his invention and design of the R-Theta computer; a device that fit in fighter plane cockpits and continuously displayed the plane's distance and location from home base. As a result, pilots no longer had to rely on ground radio. The R-Theta remained an air-navigation standard until the 1970s, when it was replaced by gyroscopic technology and later by satellite systems. Wright holds 30 patents in navigation tools and he was inducted into Canada's Aviation Hall of Fame in 1973.

#10. OILSKINS: Located in Barrington, Shelburne County, the MacMullen Oilskin Factory played an important role in Nova Scotia's industrial history, notably for its manufacture of oilskins. Built between 1880 and 1890 by its owner and operator James F. MacMullen, the oilskin factory became the biggest of its kind in all of Shelburne County. Prior to the advent of rubberized clothing, oilskins were used by fisherman and sailors to stay dry while working at sea. Oilskins were created by immersing cotton clothing in linseed oil. The line of clothing that the MacMullen factory produced included aprons, sou'westers, children's jackets and overalls, and were sold directly to individuals, wholesalers and fishing outfitters as well as to major fish and lobster packing plants. Three generations of the MacMullen family worked in the oilskin factory that operated until the 1930s when it could no longer compete with new products offered by larger clothing manufacturers.

#11. DONAIRS: The traditional donair has origins in Greece but the Halifax donair, complete with its trademark sweet sauce, was, as the legend goes, introduced in Halifax in the early 1970s. King of Donair founder, John Kamoulakos, claims he developed the Maritime donair—a variation on the traditional Middle Eastern doner kebab—and first served up the now-popular meal at his restaurant on Quinpool Road in 1973. Maritime donairs are characterized by their distinctive sauce, a sweeter version of a traditional garlic sauce, made from evaporated milk, sugar, garlic or garlic powder and white vinegar. Traditional garlic sauce is usually made with yogurt or mayonnaise instead of evaporated milk and vinegar, and lemon juice rather than sugar. However, neither the meat nor the sauce were patented, leaving the donair's true origins up for debate.

#12. GRAPE-NUT ICE CREAM: Grape-Nut ice cream is a popular regional dish in the Maritimes and throughout New England. One origin story suggests that it was created by Chef Hannah Young at The Palms restaurant in Wolfville in 1919. The legend goes that she created the favourite flavour when she ran out of fresh fruit to add to ice cream and decided to throw in some cereal. It proved popular at the restaurant and the Scotsburn Dairy Company began mass producing the ice-cream variety, and it sold across the region. Variations of ice cream with Grape-Nuts sold beyond the Maritimes are also called brown-bread ice.

#13. THE ICE CREAM SODA: James William Black from Berwick invented the ice cream soda in 1886 when he created and bottled a syrup made from whipped egg whites, sugar, water, lime juice or citric acid, flavouring extract and bicarbonate of soda. When ice water was stirred into a small ladle of the mixture it produced a delicious, foam-topped drink.

#14. MACHINE ROLLERS: An innovation that has become invaluable to modern machine design was invented in 1879 at Bear River, Nova Scotia. George Welton Thomas wanted to eliminate or reduce the friction of moving parts against stationary ones such as a wheel revolving on an axle. Thomas achieved this with rollers in a cage, a design that continues to be used today in milling and factory machinery and just about everything that runs on wheels

#15. DRIED-FRUIT CEREAL: Do you enjoy your Raisin Bran or Apple Crisp flakes? If you do, you can thank George F. Humphrey of Bridgetown who, in 1924 and 1927 patented hot and cold breakfast foods infused with real fruit.

#16. GUM RUBBER SHOES: Charles L. Grant of Grand Pré invented the gum rubber shoe in 1920. His innovation was a rubber-coated tongue fastened to the shoe, making it waterproof. His invention is now standard practice in shoe manufacturing.

#17. TEAPOT PLUNGER: In 1909, James Rooney invented a tea and coffee pot design still in use today. It's a perforated receptacle with a plunger, which fits inside a tea or coffee pot letting leaves or grounds be easily removed after infusion.

#18. BACKUP LIGHTS: James A. Ross of Halifax is responsible for the backup lights on your automobile. Back in 1919 Ross realized the importance of such a device and connected the light to a switch on the gearshift lever and by doing so, lit the way for all future drivers.

#19. QUICK-RELEASE BUCKLE: Each time you buckle up your seatbelt or snap closed a carry case, thank inventor Arthur Davy of New Glasgow that releasing the belt will only require a flick of your thumb. Seatbelts weren't what Davy had in mind when he invented the quick-release buckle in 1911, when he came up with the idea to simplify attaching and detaching the reins from a horse.

#20. REPLACEABLE POOL-CUE TIP: The replaceable pool-cue tip was patented in 1920 by George W. Leadbetter of Springhill. His metal sleeve has now been replaced by plastic and the tip is glued on, but Leadbetter's invention is credited with forever changing the construction of pool and billiard cues.

#21. LONG JOHNS: What came to be known as "long johns" were invented in Truro in 1915 and were originally called "underwear combinations." It was long underwear in two pieces that could be adjusted to fit different body lengths. Frank Stanfield came up with the idea. In 1898 he and his brother John had developed "Stanfield's Unshrinkable Underwear."

#22. DEET: In 1959, Charles Coll of Truro invented the mosquito repellent Muskol. Its magical ingredient is the chemical DEET.

#23. FROZEN FISH FILLET: The frozen fish fillet was invented in Halifax in 1926 by Walter H. Boutilier and Frank W. Bryce. Sometime around 1940 they patented a process that allowed them to impregnate raw fish with a flavouring substance before freezing it.

#24. HOCKEY: The town of Windsor has long been a popular and important destination in the province, but it is its status as the birthplace of hockey that has put this Annapolis Valley town on the world map. Long before it was known as Windsor, the area around the junction of the Avon and St. Croix rivers was known by the Mi'kmaq as Pisiguit, appropriately meaning "Junction of Waters." The rivers empty into the nearby Minas Basin, which allowed ships to sail from the Atlantic Ocean, up the Bay of Fundy and down into the heart of the province. The fertile headlands around these rivers made for ideal farming and Acadian settlers to the area did just that, erecting mills along the rivers to harness their power. With the French and English battling over North America, the Acadian settlers became caught in the middle of the conflict. Shortly after settling Halifax in 1749, the British moved into the Pisiguit area and built Fort Edward to watch over the Acadians and discourage further development. Fearing for the safety and resenting the fort's ominous presence, most Acadians left the area for other parts of the province. In 1764, the township was settled by New England Planters who claimed the former Acadian farms and built their own homes and businesses. The town of Windsor also became an important stop for anyone travelling between Halifax and the Annapolis Valley.

Following the American Revolution and withdrawal of the British in 1783, King's College, New York, was renamed Columbia College and later Columbia University. United Empire Loyalists who left America and settled in Nova Scotia established a new King's College in 1788 in Windsor, making it Canada's first college. Professors from England, Scotland and Ireland introduced their particular national field games to the students from all over the British Empire who attended King's College. Students thus came to play the Irish field game of hurley and, in winter, developed it into an ice game by playing hurley-on-ice on their favourite skating ponds. It was a simple game with skates that strapped onto boots, rocks for goal posts, hand-made wooden hurley sticks and wooden pucks. King's College school boys began adapting the Irish field game of Hurley to the ice as early as 1800, and probably before. They came from all over the British Empire to attend Canada's first college (1788) at Windsor. King's College offered degrees in Arts, Law and Theology. One of the earliest King's students was Thomas Chandler Haliburton, who was born in Windsor in 1796. He later recorded that the boys at the school, circa 1800, played "… hurley on the long pond on the ice…" which went on to develop into ice hockey, thus making them the earliest to play it in Canada. This is the basis to Windsor's claim as the birthplace of ice hockey. Soon after the boys of King's College School adapted Hurley to the ice, the soldiers at Fort Edward, in Windsor, took up the new game. They carried the game to Halifax, where it gained impetus as it was played on the many and beautiful Dartmouth Lakes, and frozen inlets of Halifax Harbour and the rest is, as they say, history.

John G. Leefe's List of the 10 Most Famous Privateers in Nova Scotia History

Privateering is the licensing of privately owned vessels by government and authorizing attack and capture of an enemy ship during times of war. To enter into this activity without government approval constituted piracy. The practice of privateering was handed down from antiquity, but was ended by international agreement in 1856 excepting by the United States, which refused to sign. In the British Empire it essentially terminated with the end of the Napoleonic Wars in 1815.

When Britain declared war, vessels of many types, large and small, were converted from merchant to war ships. Owners would determine a cruise, apply to the governor of the colony for a licence or Letter of Marque, get outfitted with all the materials of war from cannons to cutlasses, pikes, powder and ammunition, and recruit a crew, usually at local taverns.

Nova Scotia privateers were active from the time of the Seven Years War to the War of 1812, ranging from the Atlantic Coast south through the Gulf of Maine to Cape Cod and on to the Caribbean and the famed Spanish Maine. Shipboard life was modelled on that of the Royal Navy with gun crews training regularly, many having marines on board.

Any vessel belonging to a belligerent nation was fair game. Once captured it was necessary to ensure that not only the vessel, but also the cargo, belonged to an enemy state. A crewmember from the prize, called a "davy" or "affidavit man," was retained. A prize crew was put on board and the vessel was sailed to the privateer's home port. Privateering was a heavily regulated business and the prize would have to be taken to the Court of Vice-Admiralty to determine whether ir belonged to the enemy. If so, the vessel would be sold and the proceeds distributed among the Crown, the crew and the owners. If it was found the prize belonged to a non-belligerent, it had to be returned to the legitimate owner.

During the Wars of the French Republic, Napoleonic Wars and the War of 1812, anywhere from 25 to 64 percent of Nova Scotia's privateers called Liverpool home port. Following is a brief description of some of our Nova Scotia's better-known privateers.

Seven Years War: 1756-1763

#1. The sloop *Yorke* was owned and commanded by Sylvanus Cobb, a native of Plymouth, Massachusetts. She weighed 80 tons, carried six carriage and four swivel guns and had a crew of 40 men. Yorke often sailed on government business, seeking out smugglers, fighting against the French and Mi'kmaq and generally making himself a nuisance to Britain's enemies as far distant as Cuba. Cobb served at Fort Anne with a company of Rangers, ferried troops and supplies from Halifax to the Bay of Fundy and Minas Basin and was present at the founding of Halifax. He was involved in an abortive attempt to capture the priest and French government agent, Abbé Le Loutre, missionary to the Shubenacadie Mi'kmaq. He played cat and mouse with the French Commander Sieur de Boishébert and his Wolastoqiyik (Maliseet) allies, at the mouth of the St. John River and assisted in the expulsion of Acadians from the Petitcodiac and St. John River settlements.

Cobb captured a few vessels that were auctioned in Halifax after being condemned by the Court of Vice-Admiralty. He was at the second siege of Louisbourg where it is said he took General Wolfe on a daring reconnoitre of the entrance to the harbour. In 1759-60 he joined John Doggett and others in the settlement of Liverpool at the mouth of the Mersey River. He left his new home in 1761 to participate in the successful siege of Havana, where he died of yellow jack. His very substantial home in Liverpool was destroyed by fire during the Second World War, a great loss to the human and architectural history of Nova Scotia.

American Revolution: 1776-1783

#2. In 1779, the schooner *Lucy* was purchased specifically to be outfitted as a Liverpool privateer. This was in response to the frustration of the town's population at being abused by American rebel privateers that were attacking the town's shipping, stealing vessels from the town's wharves and robbing captives, and occasionally holding them ransom. Her Liverpool investors included Captain Collins, Captain Howard of the King's Orange Rangers, Mr. Tinkham, Captain William Freeman, Captain Bartlett Bradford and Simeon Perkins. In December they met at Mrs. Snow's Sloop Tavern to iron out details. A few days later a rendezvous was convened at Mrs. Snow's and 14 officers and men signed on under command of Captain Bradford. She cruised from 1779 to 1781, capturing some 10 prizes, one of which, the *New Moddle*, was outfitted as the privateer *Delight*. Despite successes, early privateering was a poor investment; Simeon Perkins entered in his diary that he had lost £35 in the bargain: "a Great Looser [sic] on the whole".

War with the French Republic and Napoleonic War: 1792-1815

Increased privateering in what are now the Atlantic Provinces was conducted during the period 1798 to 1806 when Britain was at war with France and her allies. Saint John, Annapolis Royal, Windsor, Pictou, Halifax, Shelburne and St. John's all spawned privateers, but Liverpool was by far the most active centre.

#3. The full-rigged ship *Charles Mary Wentworth*, 16 guns, four and six pounders and a crew of 80 was built in Liverpool, specifically for privateering. One of her ship's logs has survived and is in the Nova Scotia Archives. Like most of the privateers of this period, she spent much time in the Caribbean, especially along the Spanish Main of modern Venezuela. In several cruises, she captured a number of prizes, four on her first trip. Almost all were brought to Liverpool to be sold at auction after condemnation by the Court of Vice-Admiralty. Two of her Spanish prizes were converted into privateers.

#4. The *Duke of Kent*, 194 tons, was the renamed Spanish brig *Nostra Seignora del Carmen* that had been captured by the *Wentworth*. She was converted to a full-rigged ship carrying nine and four-pound cannons and manned by a crew of 90 men and boys. During her career, she captured eight prizes tying the more famous *Rover* for the second most successful of Nova Scotia's privateers during this period. All prizes were brought to Liverpool to be condemned and sold. A prize of the *Duke of Kent*, the Danish schooner *Lady Hammond*, was renamed *Lord Spencer* and outfitted as a privateer. *Wentworth*, *Kent* and *Spencer* occasionally cruised as a squadron in the Caribbean.

#5. The 100-ton brig *Rover* was built in Herring Cove, now Brooklyn, across the bay from Liverpool. She was armed with 14 four-pound guns and a crew of 55 men and boys. Her most famous exploit took place on the Spanish Main on September 10, 1800, where she defeated a squadron of three Spanish naval vessels, the schooner *Santa Rita* and two gunboats. The *Santa Rita* with a crew of 125 men was armed with ten six-pound long guns and two English 12-pound carronades. Despite very unfavourable odds, superior leadership and training made for a hard-won victory for this Liverpool privateer. After an hour and a half slug match, the Spaniards struck their colours with 71 wounded and taken prisoner and 54 dead. This contrasts to not a man or ship's boy being even slightly injured on the *Rover*. So outstanding was this victory that Alexander Godfrey, *Rover*'s captain, was offered a commission in the Royal Navy, which, however, he gracefully declined.

#6. The privateer brigantine *Nelson*, 140 tons, mustered a crew of 80 men and carried 16 guns. Hailing from Shelburne, her shareholders included local luminaries George Gracie, James Cox and Jacob Van Buskirk among others. While Liverpool privateer shareholders were almost all of New England stock, those in Shelburne were largely Loyalists. The captain of the *Nelson* was Ephraim Deane of Liverpool. She had significant success in the Caribbean often sailing in company with Liverpool's

Charles Mary Wentworth, Duke of Kent and *Lord Spencer.* On December 24, 1799, she encountered a French privateer of 16 guns and was badly mauled, having to go to Barbados for extensive repairs. In the spring of 1800 she was captured by the French and shortly thereafter, recaptured by HMS Cambria. Re-acquired by her Shelburne owners, she captured the brig Austria, a valuable prize bound from New York to Havana. All told, Nelson successfully sent 12 prizes to be condemned by the Court of Vice-Admiralty. In this she was certainly one of Nova Scotia's best privateers.

#7. In September 1800, Simeon Perkins, Hallett Collins, Bartlett Bradford and others purchased the brig *Nymph*, converting her into a privateer carrying 18 guns and mustering a crew of 100. The owners invited Joseph Freeman to serve as captain, but he declared he would only accept if a guarantee could be gained providing immunity from impressment. Failing to acquire such protection, Lieutenant Governor Wentworth gave permission for up to 100 members of the Queens County Militia to serve on board Liverpool privateers. Perkins was the militia's Colonel. After a £1600 refit, *Nymph* left for a cruise on November 25. Within a week she had taken *Fabius*. Although an American-owned vessel, she was carrying a cargo of sugar, cocoa and logwood, the produce of an enemy country, Spain. Upon arrival in Liverpool, Perkins determined *Fabius* was not a legitimate prize and she was restored to her owners.

In the winter of 1801, Nymph cruised the Caribbean with some success, arriving in Liverpool on March 25 with prize goods valued at £1,500. On May 6, *Nymph* embarked on another cruise, sending in the schooner *Maria*. It was not a clean prize as she had previously been captured from the British. Adjudicating a compromise, the vessel and the part of the cargo comprised of sugar and cotton were returned to the Jamaica owners while a valuable load of Campeachy logwood, from which a purple textile dye is made, went to *Nymph*. With the approach of autumn and news that peace was at hand, the owners of several privateers decided to sell their vessels. *Rover* was the first to go to the auction block, followed on September 30 by *Duke of Kent* and then *Nymph*. Snow Parker of Liverpool was the successful bidder. Thus ended the career of the privateer *Nymph*.

Dan Conlin, an expert on Nova Scotia privateering, states that during the period 1793 to 1805, there were 12 privateers commissioned in Nova Scotia. Twenty-five percent were based in Liverpool yet, by prizes taken, Liverpool accounted for almost sixty percent.

War with America: 1812-1815

#8. The privateer *Liverpool Packet* was a sleek topsail schooner that had been tendered to a slaver. She was only 53-feet long with a beam of 18 feet, 11 inches. She mounted five guns, one six-pound and four 12-pound. She mustered a crew of 45. Her career was effectively separated into three parts. The first lasted from the beginning of the War of 1812 to her capture by the American privateer Thomas out of Portsmouth, New Hampshire on June 11, 1813. This was the period of her greatest success under her most famous captain, Joseph Barss Jr. The second phase found her as an American privateer at first retaining her name and owned at one point by the former captain of the *Teazer* of Mahone Bay fame. Renamed *Portsmouth Packet*, she was captured by *HMS Fantome* off Mount Desert Island, now the home of Maine's Acadia National Park.

In November she was auctioned in Halifax to original Nova Scotia owner Enos Collins. Formerly of Liverpool, Collins had removed his business interests to Halifax where he was a founder of what became CIBC, one of Canada's six major banks. She regained her old name and returned to Liverpool as a privateer. The final phase of the *Liverpool Packet*'s career continued to provide success for her crews and her owners first under Caleb Seely, a Saint John privateer captain who moved to Liverpool, buying Perkins House from Perkins' widow and finally by Lewis Knaut, who had come to Liverpool from Lunenburg. During her career, *Liverpool Packet* ranged from the Scotian Shelf across the Gulf of Maine as far south as Narragansett Bay. She is said to have captured more than 100 vessels, releasing those that were of little value. Forty-four prizes were brought to Nova Scotia where they were condemned and sold. She was noted in the American newspapers as "the bane of New England." According to historian C.H.J. Snider, the total value of her prizes was in the vicinity of $1,000,000.

#9. The topsail schooner *Retaliation* was a prize of war. Captured from the Americans as the *Revenge*, she was purchased at auction in Halifax and renamed by Thomas Freeman and Snow Parker of Liverpool. Freeman had been the first captain of the *Liverpool Packet* who had many years of privateering experience from Nova Scotia to the Spanish Main. She did well in the early years of 1813, bringing in some $30,000 in prize money. Freeman's health required his retirement and he was succeeded by Benjamin Ellenwood of Liverpool who continued the string of success initiated by Freeman. She cruised from Nova Scotia to the New England coast. Ellenwood was succeeded by Captain Harris Harrington of Herring Cove. *Retaliation*'s luck ran out in the fall of 1814. Her crew had been reduced as a result of many of them being pressed on *HMS Superb*. Instead of exercising prudence, she continued to cruise Cape Cod, where she was captured after a series of attacks by local New Englanders.

#10. The schooner *Rolla*, captained by Joseph Bartlett, weighed 132 tons and was 79 feet in length. Her armament consisted of five guns, a long 18 pounder and four 12-pound carronades with a crew of 60. She was originally an American privateer that had been captured on December 10, 1813 by *HMS Loire*. Her owners were Joseph Freeman, John and James Barss, James DeWolfe, Enos Collins, all of Liverpool, and Joseph Allison of Halifax. She began cruising in June 1814, especially in the waters from Cape Anne to Long Island Sound, taking seven prizes, two of them in company with *Liverpool Packet*. In early January 1815 she embarked on a cruise that began auspiciously when, on the 13th, she took the schooner *Comet* of

New Bedford, Massachusetts off Martha's Vineyard. A prize crew of John Darrow, Eli Page and Robert Slocomb took *Comet* back to Liverpool. A winter gale raged through the night of January 15 to 16 and *Rolla* foundered with the loss of all hands.

Five years later a storm-cast, seaweed-covered hulk was driven ashore on a beach in Essex County, Massachusetts. Her stern board showed name ROLL, with half of the letter "A" missing. The loss of *Rolla* was devastating, for her crew included no fewer than 20 well-known and respected Liverpool sea captains. Many were the grieving widows and families of this privateering town.

During the War of 1812, the majority of Nova Scotia privateers were based and largely owned in Liverpool. The crews were drawn not only from many Nova Scotia communities, but included foreigners as well. Following are the names and number of prizes captured and sold after being condemned in the Court of Vice-Admiralty: *Liverpool Packet* (48), *Sir John Sherbrooke* (18), *Retaliation* (17), *Shannon* (16), *Wolverine* (12), *Lively* (10) and *Rolla* (8). During the course of the War of 1812, 129 prizes were brought home by Liverpool privateers; that's 64 percent of all prizes condemned by the Court of Vice-Admiralty in Nova Scotia.While many Maritime ports can claim some history of privateering, by every measure, Liverpool is pre-eminent. As noted, in the period from the American Revolution to the termination of the War of 1812, Liverpool privateers comprised the majority of vessels carrying Letters of Marque. Historians estimate that at any one time, Liverpool privateers could account for 25 to 50 percent of Letter-of-Marque vessels. Some were converted fishing and trading vessels, others were built specifically for the business of privateering and others yet were prizes that were converted into Maritime privateers. They were of many sizes and types, running the gamut from sloops to fully rigged ships. Time and again the same local investors showed up as shareholders, Simeon Perkins, Joseph Barss and Snow Parker among them. Most recruitment was carried out in Liverpool taverns of which at least two survive as private homes. While the officers were almost always drawn from the Liverpool area, crews included men and boys from near and far, Perkins at one point referring to a number of men from different countries.

Today, privateering heritage of Liverpool is evident in the names of streets, sport teams, businesses and, in one of the largest community festivals, Privateer Days. It has been celebrated in literature, theatre and on television and is a focal point of the Queens County Museum. Much of Liverpool's architectural heritage has links with privateering, not the least of which are the homes of Joseph Barss, Simeon Perkins, Joseph Freeman, Bartlett Bradford and the 18th-century Dexter and West taverns. Older cemeteries are the final resting places of many privateers and the owners of the vessels, which they manned and cruised. As a Canadian phenomenon privateering, though fascinating, is not well known, even in Nova Scotia. Its story however, is still a work in progress.

Hon. John G. Leefe DCL is a Liverpool-based historian, author, retired teacher and former politician, having served as Queens County MLA from 1978 to 1999 and Mayor of the Region of Queens from 2000 to 2012. He was appointed Honorary Colonel of the West Nova Scotia Regiment in February 2012. His writings on privateers include: "A Bluenose Privateer of 1812," Nova Scotia Historical Quarterly, *Vol.3, No. 1, 1973;* "The Bounty Hunter," Nova Scotia Historical Quarterly, Vol.3, *No. 4 1973 and* The Atlantic Privateers: Their Story, *Petheric Press 1978.*

Dan Conlin's List of the Top 10 Pirates in Nova Scotia History

Piracy is violent robbery at sea and has a long history in Nova Scotia. Pirates differed from privateers, the legal sea warriors, who were regulated and operated only in wartime. Pirates attacked anyone in peace or war. They were in their own words, "enemies of all mankind." Their crimes peaked in the 1720s, the so-called Golden Age of Piracy, when some of the biggest and deadliest pirates came to Nova Scotia.

Piracy declined in Nova Scotia after the 18th century and became relegated to rare, once-a-generation incidents in our waters. However, piracy remains a deadly problem in other parts of the world today. Folklore and bogus treasure myths have romanticized and distorted the deeds of pirates to the point where every island and cove has its pirate legend. The reality was uglier and usually a story of greed and betrayal.

#1. BARTHOLOMEW ROBERTS, THE PIRATE KING, 1720: Roberts captured more ships than Blackbeard and Captain Kydd put together. Flamboyant and defiant, but not especially bloodthirsty, Roberts attracted hundreds of recruits and took more than 400 ships. He arrived off Cape Breton in 1722, raiding French fishing vessels before going on to capture and occupy Trepassey, Newfoundland. His rampage continued for another two years before he was killed in battle with Britain's Royal Navy in 1722.

#2. NED LOW, THE WORST OF THE WORST, 1722: Low was the cruellest and most violent pirate of his age, known for fiendish torture and random murders. He also spent more time in Nova Scotia than any other pirate, including a spectacular raid on Port Roseway (today's Shelburne) in 1722. He returned in 1723, robbing ships and murdering captains off Canso and Cape Breton. His own men eventually turned on him and he was cast away to his death in 1724.

#3. JOHN PHILLIPS, CARPENTER TURNED PIRATE, 1723: Phillips was a ship's carpenter who turned to piracy when his ship was captured in 1721. He briefly went straight and worked in the Newfoundland fishery before he succumbed to the temptation to steal a boat, recruit a crew and turn pirate again. A favoured hunting ground was around Cape Sable, Nova Scotia. But his luck ran out when a captured crew turned the tables. Killed with an axe, his head was mounted on the ship's bowsprit as the victors returned to Boston.

#4. SUSANNAH BUCKLER, AKA MRS. MATHEWS, 1736: A thief and prostitute from Dublin, Mathews helped lead a bloody mutiny aboard the convict ship *Baltimore*. Abandoned by her fellow convicts near Yarmouth, she posed as Susannah Buckler, wife of the murdered captain of Baltimore, and bamboozled the governor in Nova Scotia with her tale of woe. Given money and free passage to Boston, Mrs. Mathews vanished and is believed to have returned to Ireland.

#5. PETER BARNES, WRECKER, 1796: Many tales are told of wreckers, pirates who lured ships to their doom to rob bodies and murder survivors. In December 1796, a schooner was wrecked at Peter's Point, now known as Margaretsville, Nova Scotia. Six died and several of the bodies were mutilated and robbed. Suspicion fell on Peter Barnes, the only local settler, but nothing was proved. Barnes is believed to have died in a snowstorm years later at the very site of the schooner wreck.

#6. EDWARD JORDAN, THE LAST GIBBET, 1809: A fisherman deep in debt, Jordan's fishing schooner was seized for debts in 1809. He and his wife murdered the repossession crew off Canso, but one man jumped overboard and was rescued by a passing ship. A navy schooner from Halifax caught Jordan trying to sail to Ireland. He was executed in Halifax, near the present-day site of Pier 21. Jordan's body was placed in a gibbet, a chained iron cage, which was hung at Point Pleasant Park as a warning to other would-be pirates.

#7. WILLIAM CARR AND THE SALADIN PIRATES, 1844: William Carr was a young sailor aboard the barque *Saladin* sailing from Peru. A rich cargo of silver tempted half of the crew to murder the other half in two bloody mutinies. The six survivors were shipwrecked near Country Harbour, Nova Scotia. Tried in Halifax, four were convicted and hanged near the current site of the Victoria General Hospital, while two convinced the court that they had been forced to join the killings. One of them was Carr. He settled in Digby County and lived quietly, except once a year on the anniversary of the killings when he would get roaring drunk.

#8. JOHN C. BRAIN, CONFEDERATE PIRATE, 1863: A Confederate schemer during the American Civil War, Brain led an attack on the Portland-to-New York steamer *Chesapeake*, killing one of the ship's engineers. The pirates were caught near Ketch Harbour and faced trial in Halifax. Brain had a fake privateer license and claimed the ship as a capture of war, but the American government pushed for his crew to be hanged as pirates. The ship was returned to its owners. The pirates were freed by a mob attack outside court, orchestrated by some wealthy Haligonians who were sympathetic to the Confederacy.

#9. JOHN DOUGLAS, RACIST MUTINEER, 1865: Douglas led a mutiny aboard the brigantine *Zero* near Liverpool, Nova Scotia in 1865. The captain was killed. The mutineers' attempts to hide the crime failed and they were rounded up. Douglas managed to pin the blame for the murder on Henry Dowsey, the African-Nova Scotian cook aboard. Despite a provincial protest, Dowsey was hanged while Douglas got a life sentence.

#10. BRUCE MOORE, THE ONE-MAN PIRATE CREW, 1967: A fisherman who was unhappy with his employer in Lockeport, Bruce Moore stole the trawler *Cape Spry* on St. Patrick's Day 1967, after a night of drinking. He single-handedly led Canadian and American patrol ships and aircraft on a chase out into the Atlantic for three days. Eventually captured, he was tried under the piracy section of the Criminal Code, facing a possible life sentence, but the charges were reduced to theft and he went to jail for two years, one of the last to face the law for piracy in Canada.

Dan Conlin is a historian and curator at the Canadian Museum of Immigration at Pier 21. He is the author of Pirates of the Atlantic: Robbery, Murder and Mayhem off the Canadian East Coast, *wherein you can discover the lives of these and other pirates. He has more recently written about wartime photography in his book* War Through the Lens: The Canadian Army Film and Photo Unit, 1941-1934.

Brian Tennyson's List of 10 Important Things to Know About Nova Scotia's Involvement in the First World War

Having spent the last three years examining Nova Scotia's participation in the First World War and its profound impact on the province, I have prepared this list to suggest briefly the most important things to know.

It is not organized in order of importance but is loosely chronological. It is also somewhat opinionated because it reflects what I have learned and the conclusions that I have drawn. I expect that many people may be surprised at some of this information and some may well disagree with some of it. But that's a good thing, because the First World War is a huge and controversial subject.

#1. NOVA SCOTIA 100 YEARS AGO: Perhaps the first and most dramatic thing to know is how different the province was 100 years ago. The population was about half of what it is today and it was more widely distributed among many towns and villages. In other words, Halifax didn't dominate the province as it does today because it was home to only about 10 percent of the population. But the province's population was growing at an impressive rate despite the fact that people were, then as now, leaving in search of greener pastures in New England or the Canadian west. However, the tired cliché about the province's collapse into poverty after Confederation is simply not true. It is also not true that Nova Scotians failed to make the transition from the "old" economy of wood, wind and sail to the "new" industrial economy of steel and steam. Even a casual look at the towns and villages shows that there were all kinds of factories, mills and other enterprises that were integrated into the still strong traditional fishing, forestry, mining and agriculture industries. Even in places like Yarmouth, what we traditionally think of as a coastal communities devoted to fishing, shipbuilding and shipping had a wide range of industrial enterprises. But the major industrial growth was in the northeastern region of Cumberland, Pictou and Cape Breton countries, where coal mining and steel manufacturing had made Nova Scotia the industrial centre of eastern Canada.

When the war broke out, the Nova Scotia Steel and Coal Company's manager, Thomas Cantley, quickly proved that his mills could produce shell casings that met the British army's very high standards. The result was that Nova Scotia Steel was awarded massive orders and smaller foundries and steel fabricators throughout Nova Scotia received sub-contracts. Similarly, the Dominion Steel and Coal Company in Sydney was the only mill whose steelmaking process produced a waste product that, when processed, produced trinitrotoluol, which is TNT. Dominion quickly became the Canadian supplier, enabling Canada to produce not just shell casings but their explosive contents as well.

#2. ENLISTMENTS: More than 35,000 Nova Scotians, about 31 percent of the men of military age, served in the armed forces during the First World War. Actually, the number was higher because recruits were listed according to the province in which they enlisted, not their home province, and many young men had gone west in the years before the war broke out. As well, the records don't list men who served in the British, American or other forces, and we know that about 300 recent immigrants from France and Belgium returned home to serve. The figure given above does, however, include the more than 300 Nova Scotian women who served as nurses in military hospitals overseas or at home.

#3. NOVA SCOTIA'S MILITARY UNITS: Ten infantry battalions — the 17th, 25th, 40th, 85th, 106th, 113th, 185th, 193rd, 219th and 246th — were recruited, and three others — the 165th (Acadian), the 6th Canadian Mounted Rifles and the Royal Canadian Regiment — were partially recruited in Nova Scotia. Only two of the ten infantry battalions recruited in Nova Scotia, the 25th and 85th, plus the 6th Canadian Mounted Rifles and the Royal Canadian Regiment, actually served in the field. Nova Scotia also provided three artillery batteries, two overseas military hospitals, a casualty clearing station and No. 2 Construction Battalion. Hundreds of Nova Scotians served in many units not based in Nova Scotia as well.

#4. THE HIGHLAND BRIGADE: The 85th Battalion's success in filling its ranks in less than a month, no doubt because it was the first Nova Scotian battalion to be designated a Highland unit, prompted the government to form the Nova Scotia Highland Brigade. This required raising four more battalions — the 185th, 193rd, 219th and 246th — but with the exception of the 246th this was easily achieved because the idea clearly had great appeal to Nova Scotians. More than 10,000 people flocked to Camp Aldershot to see the new battalions receive their colours and be reviewed by the Governor General, the Duke of Connaught and Prime Minister Robert Borden before they went overseas. To the great shock, disappointment and outrage of Nova Scotians, all but the 85th were broken up in England to provide reinforcements for other battalions. The Brigade lives on, at least symbolically, in the Nova Scotia Highlanders and the Cape Breton Highlanders.

#5. VALOUR IN THE FIELD: Nova Scotia's two infantry battalions distinguished themselves in battle. At the Somme, the largest and bloodiest Allied offensive of the entire war, the only success was the capture of Courcelette in September 1916. Nova Scotia's 25th Battalion played a major role in this brutal battle, after which its commanding officer, Lieutenant Colonel Edward Hilliam, declared: "I have the honour of commanding the best body of men I have ever seen" and asked Premier George Murray to "let Nova Scotians know that all [of the] Canadian Corps is proud of [the] Nova Scotian Battalion's magnificent work." But that work was costly: 304 casualties, including 36 killed. As Howard Johnstone of Sydney said, it was "hard to know which of two feelings is upper most in my mind, pride in the glorious achievement of the regiment or sorrow at the loss of so many old comrades."

Nova Scotia's two infantry battalions played a major role in the capture of Vimy Ridge in April 1917. While the 25th participated in the preliminary assault, led by Major J.A. De Lancey of Middleton, two companies of the 85th led by Major Percy Anderson of Baddeck completed the victory by capturing Hill 145, the highest and most important point on the ridge. Vimy Ridge was the first major Allied victory on the Western Front since 1914. About 10 percent of the more than 14,000 casualties were Nova Scotians. Among the many heroes of the battle were Steven Toney, a Mi'kmaq from Pictou Landing who served as a sniper and reportedly killed 14 Germans at Vimy Ridge, and Jeremiah Jones, an African Nova Scotian from Truro who, despite being wounded, single-handedly destroyed a German machine-gun post and captured several prisoners.

Six months later the Nova Scotian battalions participated in the infamous battle of Passchendaele. Arthur Currie, who commanded the Canadian Corps, thought it was both ill-conceived and unnecessary and would involve heavy casualties. As usual, he was right. The battle was fought in heavy rain in swamp-like conditions, and the Germans used mustard gas for the first time. Even so, the Canadians captured

Passchendaele but, as usual, the cost was high: nearly 16,000 casualties, among them almost 500 men from the 85th Battalion, including its entire pipe band, whose members had gone in as stretcher bearers, and more than 200 men from the 25th Battalion.

#6. NO. 2 CONSTRUCTION BATTALION: Until 1916 African Canadians were not welcome in the army. A few were accepted, however, including Roy Fells of Yarmouth, who enlisted in the 25th Battalion in November 1914. But when the government became desperate for more men in 1916 it agreed to accept African Canadians but only in a segregated labour battalion. All of No. 2 Construction Battalion's officers were white, however, with the exception of the Reverend William White, a Baptist minister in Truro, who was appointed chaplain with the honorary rank of captain. When the battalion went overseas with only 19 officers and 605 men — almost all of them from Nova Scotia — it was seriously under strength and therefore not viable, so it was reduced to company status and was attached to the Canadian Forestry Corps. Lieutenant Colonel Daniel Sutherland, to his credit, accepted a reduction in rank to major so that he could serve with his men.

The men of No. 2 worked alongside white soldiers in their forestry work, but their accommodations and recreation facilities were segregated and if they were injured or fell they were placed in a segregated area of the local hospital. The white soldiers even refused to accept White as their chaplain and a white chaplain had to be brought in for them. What is really curious about the creation of No. 2 Construction Battalion is that at the very time it was created, the Militia Department began ordering the commanding officers of combat battalions to accept African Canadian volunteers, a dramatic change of policy that really did signify progress. Why the government created a segregated labour battalion while finally allowing African Canadian men to serve in combat battalions remains a mystery. But when conscription was introduced in 1917 it applied to all men regardless of race.

#7. NOVA SCOTIA'S VCS: Of the 71 Victoria Crosses — Great Britain's highest decoration for exceptional bravery in wartime — awarded to Canadians in the war, four went to Nova Scotians. Three of them were honoured posthumously and two of them were coal miners. John Chipman Kerr of Fox River, who served in the 49th Battalion because he was living in northern Alberta when he enlisted, earned his at Courcelette on September16, 1916 for single-handedly attacking an enemy trench, leading to the capture of 62 prisoners. Eric Bent, who was born in Halifax but had moved to Scotland as a child with his parents before the war, received his posthumously for his exceptional bravery while leading the 9th Battalion of the Leicestershire Regiment as temporary lieutenant colonel at Polygon Wood while leading on October 1, 1917. A month later, James Peter Robertson posthumously received the VC for rushing a German machine-gun emplacement at Passchendaele on November 6, 1917, killing four of its crew, then turned the gun on the others, enabling his platoon to continue its advance. Later, when two of his unit's men were wounded in front of their trench, he went out and carried one of them in while under fire, then returned to bring in the other man as well, but was killed by a bursting shell. Robertson was a miner from Stellarton who had moved to Medicine Hat, Alberta, and served overseas in the 27th Battalion. Finally, John Bernard Croak, a 26-year-old coal miner from New Aberdeen, was posthumously awarded the VC for his actions during the battle for Amiens on August 8, 1918. He not only captured a machine gun and its crew but also led his platoon, despite being wounded, in the capture of three more machine guns and an entire garrison. He died of his wounds later that day.

#8. FIRST AND LAST TO DIE: It is a curious coincidence that both the first and last Canadian servicemen to die in the war were Nova Scotians. The first was Anatole Descamps, a French coal miner from Lille who had immigrated to New Waterford about 1911. When the war broke out he returned home to serve in the French army and was killed on September 25, 1914. The Sydney Daily Post rightly described him as "one of Cape Breton's heroes" and "the first to fall in the field in the defence of his country." Better remembered are the four young midshipmen, recent graduates of the Canadian Naval College in Halifax, who joined Admiral Sir Christopher Cradock's Royal Navy squadron in August 1914. Malcolm Cann, John Hatheway, William Palmer and Arthur Silver died together on November 1, 1914, along with the entire crew of HMS Good Hope when it was sunk by a German naval squadron in the Battle of Coronel. The last Canadian to die before the armistice was George Price, a native of Falmouth, who was shot by a sniper near Mons just minutes before 11:00 a.m. on November 11th. He was also the last soldier from the British Empire to be killed in the war. Curiously, the last Royal Air Force pilot to be killed was also a Nova Scotian. Alexander "Billy" McHardy of McLellan's Mountain, Pictou County, died in an air battle over nearby Charleroi on the 10th.

#9. WHEN THE WAR CAME TO NOVA SCOTIA: In the summer of 1918 Germany launched a submarine offensive against commercial vessels sailing in Nova Scotian and New England coastal waters. This brought the war very close to home. It began in June when the crew of the *Dwinsk*, an American troop transport, arrived at Shelburne after it had been sunk off the coast of New England. Six weeks later Captain Archibald Publicover brought into LaHave on his schooner the 87-man crew of a Japanese freighter that had been sunk. A freighter, the *Dornfontein*, was sunk off Brier Island and the *Luz Blanca*, a tanker that had just left Halifax for Tampico, was sunk on the August 18th. Most of the ships sunk were fishing vessels, however, because the U-boats had great difficulty finding better targets. Twenty-one were sunk in the Gulf of Maine in August, while the Halifax-based steam trawler *Triumph* was captured near Canso and was used to sink eight schooners before running out of fuel and being scuttled. Some feared that German sympathizers were aiding the submarines by sending signals at night or providing information in some way. The awkward truth was that the U-boat captains had lived in Maine before the war, working with the US Fisheries Service or fishing out of Gloucester, so they knew the coastal waters well and even knew men who fished out of Lunenburg. The U-boat offensive failed to achieve anything meaningful other than alarming people in coastal communities and discouraging fishing vessels from going to sea. And the war was effectively over by August 1918, when the Allied armies, now increasingly reinforced by American troops, began pushing the German army back in what became known as the Hundred Days.

#10. HALIFAX EXPLOSION: All Nova Scotians are at least somewhat familiar with the explosion caused by the collision of two ships in the harbour that devastated Halifax on December 6, 1917. Curiously, this tragic event is portrayed as a bolt of lightning that appeared out of a clear blue sky, but that was not the case. There had been two ship collisions in the harbour just months earlier. *HMCS Deliverance*, a Canadian patrol vessel collided with the incoming Norwegian barque *Regin* off Chebucto Head on the morning of June 14th and just six weeks later the *Letitia*, a hospital ship that sailed regularly between Liverpool, England and Halifax ran aground while being guided into the harbour in thick fog in the same area. One might have thought that two accidents within six weeks would have suggested that the harbour pilotage system was not working well. But nothing was done to improve it, so the collision between the *Imo* and the *Mont-Blanc* a few months later should not have come as a complete surprise. What was surprising was that the port examining officer had not been informed that the *Mont-Blanc* was carrying explosives but had no special instructions for dealing with ships carrying dangerous cargoes anyway. Nor did the federal government's Public Traffic Regulations contain any guidance for munitions ships, despite the fact that the country had been at war for three years.

There very nearly was a second explosion in the harbour on December 6th. The British freighter *Picton* had earlier run aground, damaging its rudder, and was moored at the Acadia Sugar Company's wharf that morning. Its cargo of foodstuffs and 1,500 fused shells was being removed by longshoremen in preparation for repair work when the *Mont-Blanc* exploded only about 30 metres away. Sixty-nine of the longshoremen were killed and the *Picton* was set on fire. Fearing a second explosion, James Harrison, the *Picton*'s captain, after extinguishing the fire, commandeered three tugboats to move the vessel further from shore. When he attempted to beach it in the Eastern Passage two days later, it burst into flames again and was towed further out into the stream. On January 29th, when it was moved to the Ocean Terminal pier and was being unloaded it caught fire again. Luckily, the small blaze was speedily extinguished and the ammunition was unloaded without further incident.

In the subsequent investigation of the cause of the Halifax explosion, officials, both civilian and military, sought a scapegoat to take the blame. Because the *Mont-Blanc*'s captain and pilot, who had caused the collision, were both dead, their actions were not questioned and all blame was placed on Frederick Wyatt, the port's chief examining officer, Aimé Le Médec, the *Imo*'s captain, and Francis Mackey, its pilot. They were charged with manslaughter and negligence but the Nova Scotia Supreme Court declared that it lacked jurisdiction so no one was ever found responsible for the disaster, making Mackey — the least influential person involved — the scapegoat. He lost his pilot's license and was unemployed until a new federal government reviewed the case and reinstated him. One good thing that came out of the fiasco was that the federal government took over control of the port and tightened up its policies and management.

Brian Tennyson is Emeritus Professor of History at Cape Breton and the author of 17 books, most of them on aspects of Nova Scotian history and Canada's involvement in the First World War. His latest book, Nova Scotia at War 1914-1919, *was published in the fall of 2017. Since 2003 he has lived in Bridgewater and has served as chair of the Bridgewater Museum Commission and vice chair of the town's Heritage Advisory Committee.*

Mr. Know-It-All's List of Top 10 Little-known Nova Scotia Breakthroughs

You know, it's interesting. Every week for a decade I investigated a new slice of Nova Scotia's past for CBC Radio. Tracking tips and digging up new bits of the old. And it taught me something. Nova Scotia's history is a mystery. Its many twists and unusual connections make this place special. There's something here, something distinct.

Jutting out into the busy trade routes of world history, our province seems to have bumped up against more than its fair share of fascinating flotsam. Links to remarkable discoveries, world-famous events and iconic turning points seem to abound along our sea-bound coast. It's been great fun for a historical beachcomber.So, from my storied collection, here's an eclectic list of Nova Scotia's top 10 little-known links to big breakthroughs in the realms of science, the arts, entertainment and, well ... tartan. Enjoy.

#1. *Moby Dick*, the novel by Herman Melville, published in 1851, was a little-known book with few readers and all but lost to obscurity when Archibald MacMechan, a professor of literature at Dalhousie University in Halifax, discovered it, fell in love with it, wrote about it, promoted it to scholars at Harvard and in the United Kingdom and helped to make *Moby Dick* a household word and a must-read for students of literature everywhere. MacMechan revived Melville's novel. By the 1920s it was being taught in schools. "The Best Sea Story Ever Written" was the title of MacMechan's learned journal article trumpeting the big-whale tale. Melville's cordial reply to MacMechan's interest, written in his own hand and worth thousands today, is stored in the Dalhousie archives. Herman Melville's nautical novel was all but sunk and off the literary chart until this Nova Scotia teacher and collector of sea faring stories had rescued it, blew wind in its sails, and set it on course to become a literary classic. Call me interested.

#2. One of the earliest Superman comic books, published in 1939, told a story of mine-rescue drama straight from the pages of Nova Scotia history. Inspired by Nova Scotia's 1936 Moose River Gold Mine disaster story, a widely told true drama of men trapped beneath the earth until saved by mine-rescue workers called Draegermen, the comic-book makers had Clark Kent teach mean mine managers a lesson. In that comic book's storyline, the mine managers are too cheap to provide proper safety maintenance below ground, so Kent — AKA Superman — traps the managers in their own mine by causing a rock fall. They are scared and running out of oxygen. Then, using his superpowers, Kent removes the fallen rock, letting the Draegermen rescue the managers, who then see the error of their risky ways and vow to make their mine safer for the miners who work in them. Pow! Nova Scotia packs a punch in Superman comic-book history.

#3. Nova Scotia produced an actor who won two Oscars for the same role — his first acting role ever — in a Hollywood motion picture. Harold Russell of North Sydney was a double amputee war veteran with no hands when he was cast in the role and won best supporting actor in *The Best Years of Our Life*, which swept the Academy Awards in 1946. He won a second Oscar for "bringing hope and courage to fellow veterans." Later, he acted in a few other films and in TV roles, and he chose to sell one of his golden Oscar statues for $62,000 to help pay his ailing wife's medical bills. Now that's a class act.

#4. Simon Newcomb, a genius astronomer born in 1835 in tiny Wallace Bridge, Cumberland County, created a mathematical standard in calculating planetary movement that was used until the computer's invention. He headed up the American Astronomical Society, edited the *American Journal of Mathematics* and was recognized as one of the greatest astronomers of the 19th century. Newcomb's four-dimensional geometry is referenced in H.G. Wells' classic, *The Time Machine*, and his calculation of an anomaly in Mercury's orbit was pounced on by Albert Einstein as crucial proof supporting his famous General Theory of Relativity. Newcomb was born in Nova Scotia but his mind was out of this world.

#5. Deoxyribonucleic Acid, or DNA, was discovered as the stuff of all living things, the genetic blueprint for life, by a Nova Scotian born on Moran Street, close to the Halifax Armouries. Dr. Oswald Avery was the son of Joseph Avery, a Halifax preacher, and Elizabeth Crowdy, who came to Halifax from Norfolk, England in 1873. They raised the future geneticist in Halifax until age 10. Years later, Avery joined the Hospital of the Rockefeller Institute for Medical Research in New York where, in 1944, he isolated DNA as the central building block of life, later famously substantiated by Watson and Crick, who discovered the *structure* of the genetic material, proving Avery's work a historic scientific landmark. From NS to DNA!

#6. Photographs and film of Nova Scotia deer leaping down a wooded trail in Shelburne County, captured by a tripwire camera in the 1930s by a young Jack Loré, found their way to Walt Disney studios in California, where animators relied on the images to render deer in the 1942 classic, *Bambi*. Loré's father, a Manhattan physician, brought the family up to summer in Nova Scotia every year. He put his son's deer photos on his office wall in New York where Jack Oakie, an Oscar-nominated comic actor, saw them and borrowed them to bring to the Disney animators to help them capture the way deer move. They also received young Loré's film of a tame deer nurtured by Loré's Nova Scotia pal, Laddie. So, Bambi was a Bluenoser!

#7. Pieces of the United Kingdom's historic Stone of Scone, the coronation stone upon which Scotland once crowned its kings — and which is said to have served as the mythical Jacob's pillow in biblical times in the Holy Land — and known as the Stone of Destiny, once found its way to Nova Scotia's South Shore. Captured in 1296 by the English and stowed under the throne in Westminster Abbey, which was used for English coronations, the great stone was stolen back and smuggled into Scotland in 1950 by Scottish university students. The big rock was accidentally broken during the journey and was repaired by a stonemason. But rock remnants remained, meaning the bulk of the rock could not be returned to its full, original heft. A royal stone gathers no mass. So, the treasured leftover bits — specks really, much like ground pepper — were handed on until Nova Scotian jewellery artist Orland Larson received them as a gift in a small vial while working in Canada's arctic in the 1960s. Years later, in his Nova Scotia jewellery studio in Indian Harbour, he had planned to create an artistic jewellery-design installation featuring the historic stone bits. Talk about Crown jewels.

#8. The young man who wrote our nation's first French-Canadian novel fled for his life after planting a "stink bomb" in the Quebec House of Assembly, then died, destitute, in Halifax, and was buried in the old Poor House burial site on Spring Garden Road. Philipe-Joseph Aubert de Gaspé lived a tumultuous life, writing his novel *L'Influence d'un Livre*, or *The Influence of a Book*, the first novel to be published in French Canada, while hiding out in 1837 due to a warrant for his arrest. The rebellious, brilliant newspaper reporter had had a skirmish with a Quebec politician who had accused him of false reporting and he landed in jail for a month. Later, he fled to Nova Scotia to teach at the Poor House and report on our own House of Assembly. In 2003, the chair of the society named after this great pioneer of Canadian literature flew to Halifax to bring a plaque to city officials to mark the author's burial place. The location? Beneath the grounds of the former Halifax Memorial Library. For years, de Gaspé was buried beneath the books. Well, irony is a literary device.

#9. The dawn of Canada's moviemaking, the first feature-length film made in our country, was shot in 1913 in Nova Scotia, based on a timeless Nova Scotian tale of romance and tragedy, but it remains the Holy Grail of motion-picture history. The film tells the story of Longfellow's 1847 poem, "Evangeline," but movie buffs are still searching for a surviving print of the historic film. It's lost in time. Only a few cast photos and newspaper ads of the movie exist as evidence. But numerous Nova Scotian references still remain in old films, thanks to Prime Minister Mackenzie King's brainstorm to boost tourism through a marketing agreement with Hollywood moviemakers to drop Canadian place names into their films. Elizabeth Taylor sobs bitterly in the 1950 version of *Father of the Bride*, weeping openly to her father (Spencer Tracy) about her groom's proposed honeymoon plans: "Nova Scotia for a honeymoon," she wails, "it can't be Nova Scotia ... so he can fish some horrible salmon or something. I told him I wanted to go someplace romantic, but he said there was nothing as romantic as a fishing shack in Nova Scotia! (sniff!)" Hollywood? Holy mackerel!

#10. Nova Scotia's beautiful blue tartan once made it all the way to the fashion runways of Paris despite being a legally controlled substance that has been illegally produced and distributed for decades. Yes, our famous tartan has a checkered past. Back in the 1990s, it rode a designer trend toward plaid all the way to fashion's highest heights. But it was a much humbler scene way back when our tartan was startin'. Created by Nova Scotian crafter Bessie Baily Murray in 1953 for a rural exhibition mural, the blue, green, white, yellow and red plaid design was granted official tartan status under Premier Angus L. Macdonald and is controlled under the Nova Scotia Tartan Act, a law still on the books requiring all manufacturers of the wondrous weave to apply for a legal permit to produce it. Yarmouth-based Bonda was the first company to purchase a tartan licence — licence number NS1-double O-1. A licence to kilt. But that was decades ago and since then Nova Scotia's pretty plaid has been woven by companies in Mexico, the U.S.A., Germany, Ireland, Scotland and many Asian countries; none with a proper plaid permit. The illegal tartan traffickers have been dealing in Celtic contraband and getting off... ahem ... *Scot free.*

Born and raised in Antigonish, the son of the local radio station founder and his secretary, Bruce Nunn went on to tell stories of Nova Scotia history and heritage on CBC Radio and Television for about a decade as "Mr. Nova Scotia Know-It-All." Known for its research detail and unique narrative style, his eclectic story collection spun into three best-selling volumes — History with A Twist, More History with a Twist, *and* 59 Stories; *as well as four children's books, including* Buddy, The Blue Nose Reindeer *and* A Bluenose Twelve Days of Christmas.

A List of 12 Interesting Things You Should Know About Nova Scotia Cemeteries

#1. THE GARRISON CEMETERY is located on the grounds of Fort Anne in Annapolis Royal, next to the old Court House at the intersection of George St. and Nova Scotia Highway 1. Initially used as a burial ground for French military forces, it has since been used by Acadians, the British military and the parish of St. Lukes. The earliest remaining tombstone is from 1720, that of Bethiah Douglass, who died October 1, 1720 in her 37th year. Incidentally, the Douglass marker is the oldest English gravestone in Canada.

#2. THE GARRISON CEMETERY is also noteworthy as the final resting place of Rose Fortune (1774-1864), a Black Loyalist who has the distinction of being the first female police officer in what we now know as Canada. Rose Fortune was born into slavery in Philadelphia, PA, March 13, 1774, her family subsequently being relocated to Virginia by the Devones family. Escaping slavery during the American Revolution, the family was relocated to Annapolis Royal as part of the Black Loyalist migration when Rose was 10 years old. In 1825, she started her own business, carting luggage between the ferry docks and nearby homes and hotels. She became entrusted with safeguarding property and maintaining order on the wharves and warehouses of Annapolis Royal, acting as the town's waterfront police officer. Fortune died on February 20, 1864, in the small house she owned at the engineer's lot near Fort Anne. The business she founded was continued by her grandson-in-law Albert Lewis as the Lewis Transfer Company and continued for several generations, remaining in business until 1980. Rose Fortune was buried in Annapolis Royal in the historic Garrison Cemetery. Her grave is unmarked but a plaque in the Petite Parc on the Annapolis Royal waterfront commemorates her life and contribution to Nova Scotian history.

#3. THE OLD BURYING GROUND, founded in 1749, the same year as the settlement, is the oldest cemetery in Halifax. It was originally non-denominational and for several decades was the only burial place for all Haligonians. The burial ground was also used by St. Matthew's United Church in Halifax and in 1793 it was turned over to the Anglicans of St. Paul's Church. The cemetery was closed in 1844. The site steadily declined until the 1980s, when it was restored and refurbished by the Old Burying Ground Foundation, which now maintains the site and employs tour guides to interpret the site in the summer. Ongoing restoration of the rare 18th-century grave markers continues. Over the decades some 12,000 people were interred in the Old Burial Ground. Today there are roughly 1,200 headstones, some having been lost. Many people were also buried with no headstone. The Old Burying Ground was designated a National Historic Site of Canada in 1991. It had already been designated a Provincially Registered Property in 1988.

#4. HALIFAX' OLD BURYING GROUND is also historically important because Robert Ross is interred there. Born in 1766, Ross was a British Army officer who is best known for the Burning of Washington, which included the destruction of the White House and United States Capitol in August 1814, as retaliation for the destructive American raids into Canada, most notably the Americans' burning of York (Toronto) earlier in 1813. After a very distinguished career in the Napoleonic Wars, Major-General Robert Ross was given command of the British troops that were sent to America in 1814 after Napoleon's default to relieve the military pressure on Canada in the War of 1812. His troops were met by the American Army at Bladensburg, fives miles north of Washington, and Ross used Congreve rockets, which the Americans had never seen before. The British won the battle and marched in Washington, where they set fire to a number of public buildings, including the president's mansion. The building was so badly stained with smoke that it had to be painted — white. The following month the British attempted to land at Baltimore but they were defeated. According to legend, a young lawyer named Francis Scott Key, after watching Ross' "rocket's red glare," was moved to compose "a national anthem for his country to celebrate the sight of the Stars and Stripes flying bravely in the dawn's early light to signal British defeat." General Ross was killed at the Battle of North Point near Baltimore before the infamous Bombardment of Fort McHenry. His body was brought back to Halifax, where it was buried in the Old Burying Ground on September 19, 1814 with full military honours. His grave is marked with a very formal, high, flat tombstone.

#5. The last erected and most prominent structure in **HALIFAX'S OLD BURYING GROUND** is the famed Welsford-Parker Monument, a triumphal arch standing at the entrance, commemorating British victory in the Crimean War. This is the second oldest war monument in Canada and the only monument to the Crimean War in North America. The arch was built in 1860, 16 years after the cemetery had officially closed. The arch was built by George Lang and is named after two Haligonians — Major Augustus Frederick Welsford and Captain William Buck Carthew Augustus Parker. Both Nova Scotians died the Battle of the Great Redan during the Siege of Sevastopol (1854-55). This monument was the last grave marker in the cemetery.

#6. The **ZION UNITED CHURCH CEMETERY** on Main Street in Liverpool deserves to be on this list as it is the final resting place of settler and famed Nova Scotian diarist, Colonel Simeon Perkins. Recovered in 1897, the Perkins' diary is considered one of Canada's most valuable historic documents as it is essentially a 40-year testimonial to colonial life in Liverpool through his eyes and from his hand. A native of Connecticut, Perkins immigrated to Nova Scotia in 1762, during the Planter migration, participated in privateering and soon became one of Liverpool's leading citizens. He established himself as a successful businessman active in West Indian trade and the fisheries. Perkins was involved in many areas of local and colonial government, conducting business and entertaining royal governors, naval officers, private captains and wandering preachers in his home. From 1767 until his death in 1812 at age 78, Perkins recorded in his diary the experiences and events of everyday colonial life in Liverpool. Copies of the diary can be seen at the Queens County Museum, located next to the Perkins' House Museum. Simeon Perkins is buried in the cemetery located behind the present Zion United Church of Main Street, Liverpool. A beautifully carved and inscribed stone has been erected in his memory by Queens County Historical Society. As for his former home, Perkins House was restored to its pre-1812 state from descriptions in the diary. It is the oldest house in the Nova Scotia Museum collection. This Cape Cod was built in 1766 for Perkins.

#7. MOUNT OLIVET CEMETERY in Halifax is famous as the final resting place of Patrick "Vincent" Coleman. Born March 13, 1872, Coleman was a train dispatcher for the Canadian Government Railways (CGR) who was killed in the Halifax Explosion. Today, he is remembered as one of the heroic figures from the disaster. On the morning of December 6, 1917, the 45-year-old Coleman and Chief Clerk William Lovett were working in the depot station near the foot of Richmond Street, only a few hundred feet from Pier 6. From there, trains were controlled on the mainline into Halifax. The line ran along the western shore of Bedford Basin from Rockingham Station to the city's passenger terminal at the North Street Station, located at the corner of Barrington and North Streets.

At approximately 8:45 a.m., there was a collision between *SS Mont-Blanc*, a French munitions ship carrying a deadly cargo of high explosives, and a Norwegian vessel, *SS Imo*. As the Mont-Blanc caught fire and quickly spread, the crew abandoned ship. The vessel drifted from near the mid-channel over to the pier on the slack tide in a matter of minutes and beached herself. A sailor, believed to have been sent ashore by a naval officer, warned Coleman and Lovett of the ship's deadly cargo of high explosives. The overnight express train No. 10 from Saint John, New Brunswick, carrying nearly 300 passengers, was due to arrive at 8:55 a.m. Before leaving the office, Lovett called CGR terminal agent Henry Dustan to warn him of a burning ship laden with explosives that was heading for the pier. After sending his initial message, Coleman and Lovett were said to have left the CGR depot. However, the dispatcher returned to the telegraph office and continued sending warning messages along the rail line as far as Truro to stop trains inbound for Halifax. An accepted version of Coleman's Morse code message reads as follows: "*Hold up the train. Ammunition ship afire in harbour making for Pier 6 and will explode. Guess this will be my last message. Good-bye boys.*" The telegraphed warnings were apparently heeded, as the No. 10 passenger train was stopped just before the explosion occurred. The train was halted at Rockingham Station, on the western shore of Bedford Basin, approximately 6.4 kms (4.0 mi) from the downtown terminal.

After the explosion, Coleman's message, followed by other messages later sent by railway officials who made their way to Rockingham, passed word of the disaster to the rest of Canada. The railway quickly mobilized aid, sending a dozen relief trains with fire and medical help from towns in Nova Scotia and New Brunswick on the day of the disaster, followed two days later by help from other parts of Canada and from the United States, most notably Boston. (This is the reason Nova Scotia sends a Christmas tree to Boston every year as a way to thank the city for its aide during the disaster.) Even though Lovett had left the station, both he and Coleman were killed in the explosion. Vince Coleman was the subject of a Canadian Heritage Minute and a prominent character in the CBC miniseries Shattered City: The Halifax Explosion. Coleman's telegraph key, watch and pen are on display in the Halifax Explosion exhibit at Halifax's Maritime Museum of the Atlantic. Coleman is buried at Mount Olivet Cemetery in Halifax and a street is named after him in the Clayton Park neighbourhood of Halifax. In 2007, a section of Albert Street near his old home was renamed Vincent Street while a condominium near Mount Olivet Cemetery on Bayer's Road is named The Vincent Coleman, also in his honour.

#8. Considered one of the greatest marine disasters in recorded history, the story of *RMS Titanic* begins in Southampton, England on April 10, 1912, when the vessel left on her maiden voyage. For some of those who lost their lives aboard the ill-fated ship, Halifax is where the story ended. On Sunday, April 14 at 11:40 p.m., *Titanic* struck a giant iceberg and by 2:20 a.m. on April 15, the "unsinkable ship" was gone.

The first vessel to arrive at the scene of the disaster was the Cunard Liner *RMS Carpathia* and she was able to rescue more than 700 survivors. On Wednesday, April 17, the day before the *Carpathia* arrived in New York, the White Star Line dispatched the first of four Canadian vessels to look for bodies in the area of the sinking. On April 17, the Halifax-based Cable Steamer *Mackay-Bennett* set sail with a minister and an undertaker as well as a cargo of ice, coffins and canvas bags. She arrived at the site on April 20 and spent five days carrying out her grim task. Her crew was able to recover 306 bodies, 116 of which had to be buried at sea. On April 26, the *Mackay-Bennett* left for Halifax with 190 bodies. She was relieved by the *Minia*, also a Halifax-based cable ship. The *Minia* had been at sea when *Titanic* sank, but returned to Halifax in order to collect the necessary supplies before sailing from the Central Wharf on April 22 for the scene of the disaster. After eight days of searching, the Minia was only able to find 17 bodies, two of which were buried at sea. On May 6, the Canadian government vessel *CGS Montmagny* left Halifax and recovered four bodies, one of which was buried at sea. The remaining three victims were brought from Louisbourg to Halifax by rail. The fourth and final ship in the recovery effort was the *SS Algerine*, which sailed from St. John's, Newfoundland and Labrador on May 16. The crew of the *Algerine* found one body, which was shipped to Halifax on the *SS Florizel*.

The majority of the bodies were unloaded at the Coal or Flagship Wharf on the Halifax waterfront and horse-drawn hearses brought the victims to the temporary morgue in the Mayflower Curling Rink. Only 59 of the bodies placed in the morgue were shipped out by train to their families. The remaining victims of *Titanic* were buried in three Halifax cemeteries between May 3 and June 12. Religious services were held at St. Paul's Church and at the Synagogue on Starr Street. Burial services were held at St. Mary's Cathedral, Brunswick Street Methodist Church, St. George's Church and All Saint's Cathedral. Various individuals and businesses expressed their sympathy by donating flowers and wreaths. The coffins of the unidentified victims were adorned with bouquets of lilies. Most of the gravestones, erected in the fall of 1912 and paid for by the White Star Line, are plain granite blocks. In some cases, however, families, friends or other groups chose to commission a larger and more elaborate gravestone. All of these more personalized graves, including the striking Celtic cross and the beautiful monument to the Unknown Child (who has since been identified), are located at **FAIRVIEW LAWN CEMETERY**. The three Halifax cemeteries where *Titanic* victims are buried are **FAIRVIEW LAWN** (121 graves), **MOUNT OLIVET** (19 graves) and **BARON DE HIRSCH** (10 graves). Each cemetery has informational panels indicating the location of the gravesites.

#9. BROOKSIDE CEMETERY in Bridgewater is the unlikely final resting place for American Civil War hero, Capt. Lee Nutting. Capt. Nutting was born in New York in 1837. He enlisted as a private in Company H of the 61st New York Infantry in October of 1861, after the outbreak of the Civil War. By 1863, Nutting had been promoted to captain and he fought in several notable battles, including Second Bull Run, Antietam and Fredericksburg. Capt. Nutting was wounded on May 8, 1864 at the Battle of Todd's Tavern in Virginia. Miraculously, he survived the battle when a small Bible that he kept in the left breast pocket of his jacket deflected the potentially deadly shot. Had it not been for that Bible, his wounds would surely have been fatal and although Capt. Nutting survived, he was sufficiently wounded to receive a discharge and a pension from the military. In 1893, Capt. Nutting was awarded the Congressional Medal of Honor for leading his regiment in a charge at a critical moment. Capt. Nutting's oldest surviving daughter, Grace, was married to a man named Philip Moore and his involvement with a company called the MicMac Mines brought him to Bridgewater. Subsequently, Capt. Nutting and his wife, Arrietta, came to Bridgewater to be with their daughter. Both Arrietta and Lee Nutting spent their summers in Bridgewater for the remainder of their lives. Mrs. Nutting was killed in an accident near the MicMac Mines, located in the Hebbville area, in 1907, when two wagons collided. Mrs. Nutting died when the one in which she was seated overturned. Capt. Nutting died the following year on the front lawn of what was then Clark's Hotel in Bridgewater. He was 71 years old.

The Maritime Civil War Living History Association estimates that as many as 9,500 Maritimers served in the Union forces during the Civil War. According to known records, there are only three Congressional Medal honorees buried in Nova Scotia — two in Halifax and Capt. Nutting in Bridgewater.

#10. BAYVIEW CEMETERY is situated on a hillside above Edgewater Street at the head of the harbour in Mahone Bay. Some grave markers date from the late 1700s, including several rare Germanic gravestones. Bayview Cemetery is located close to seven other heritage properties on the main route leading into the town from the east. Municipal heritage designation applies to the land at the corner of Main Street and Clearland Road. Bayview Cemetery is valued for its tangible associations with the early history of Mahone Bay; for its particular association with the "foreign

Protestant" settlers and their rare Germanic gravemarkers; and for its continuous use as a community burial ground since the late 1700s. The historic value of Bayview Cemetery is evident in its late 18th and early 19th-century gravestones. Several of the earliest stones mark graves of foreign Protestants, mainly German-speaking Europeans, who immigrated as part of the British initiative to colonize the area. Initially based in nearby Lunenburg, they began claiming their farmland grants at Mahone Bay in 1754. Burials took place in Lunenburg until 1774, by which time the settlers had established a burial ground at Mahone Bay. The "burying ground at Mush-a-Mush," so-called after the nearby river, eventually became Bayview Cemetery. The early gravestones at Bayview Cemetery are valued as an expression of the austere life of the settlers and as testament to their faith and fortitude. The primitive quality of the earliest markers and the use of Germanic symbols and language evoke a sense of the settlers' isolation within the colony. Bayview Cemetery is also valued for its rare early Germanic gravestones marking the graves of foreign Protestant settlers. Lunenburg County's oldest surviving German inscription — that of Ana Catherina Zwicker (d. 1780) — is here. Her stone is roughly crafted of soft local slate with touchingly awkward and uneven block letters in German. Other hand-carved stones have Gothic script. Some depict traditional Germanic images — a tulip on the 1805 Eisenhauer marker, a heart on an infant's stone. By 1872, when the community was well-established, the burial ground was named Bayview Cemetery. The Bayview Cemetery Company, whose volunteers managed ongoing operations, was incorporated in 1925. When the Company disbanded in 2007, operations were assumed by the Town of Mahone Bay.

#11. CAMP HILL CEMETERY is the final resting place of Joseph Howe, journalist, politician and writer who is largely considered the father of the free press. Howe is often ranked as one of Nova Scotia's most admired politicians and his considerable skills as a journalist and writer have made him provincial legend. He was born in Halifax, the son of John Howe and Mary Edes. He inherited an undying love for Great Britain and her Empire from his loyalist father. At age 23, the self-taught but widely read Howe purchased the Novascotian, soon making it into a popular and influential newspaper. He reported extensively on debates in the Nova Scotia House of Assembly and travelled to every part of the province writing about its geography and people. In 1835, Howe was charged with seditious libel, a serious criminal offence, after the Novascotian published a letter attacking Halifax politicians and police for pocketing public money. Howe addressed the jury for more than six hours, citing example after example of civic corruption. The judge called for Howe's conviction but, swayed by his passionate address, jurors acquitted him in what is considered a landmark case in the struggle for a free press in Canada. The next year, Howe was elected to the assembly as a liberal reformer, beginning a long and eventful public career. He was instrumental in helping Nova Scotia become the first British colony to win responsible government in 1848. He served as premier of Nova Scotia from 1860 to 1863 and led the unsuccessful fight against Canadian Confederation from 1866 to 1868. Having failed to persuade the British to repeal Confederation, Howe joined the federal cabinet of John A. Macdonald in 1869 and played a major role in bringing Manitoba into the union. He resigned his Cabinet post to become the third Lieutenant Governor of Nova Scotia post Confederation in 1873. He died June 1, 1873 at aged 68, only three weeks after his appointment. He is buried in Camp Hill Cemetery.

#12. THE ROYAL NAVY BURYING GROUND is part of the Naval Museum of Halifax and was the Naval Hospital cemetery for the North America and West Indies Station Halifax. It is the oldest military burial ground in Canada. The cemetery has grave markers for those who died while serving at Halifax and were treated at the naval medical facility or who died at sea. Often shipmates and officers had the grave markers erected to mark the deaths of the crewmembers who died while in the port of Halifax. The number of burials that took place there is estimated at more than 400; however, there are only 89 stone markers remaining. There was a register of deaths established in 1860 for the burial ground. As well, surgeons of a ship registered the deaths of crew members, including how the person died and where they were buried. These reports were entered in the official register, with a detailed account sent quarterly to the medical director-general, Admiralty in England. There is no local record of who is buried. The four most common causes of death for those buried there are, in order: disease, falling from the topmast, drowning and naval battle. Along with two monuments that commemorate casualties of the War of 1812, the most prominent markers are for the crew that died on the flagships of the North American and West Indies Station — *HMS Winchester* (1841), *HMS Wellesley* (1850), *HMS Cumberland* (1852), *HMS Indus* (1859), *HMS Nile* (1861), *HMS Duncan* (1866) and *HMS Royal Alfred* (1869). There were many buried during the wars of the 18th century (American Revolution, French Revolutionary War and Napoleonic Wars) that do not have grave markers.

A List of 11 Facts You Should Know About the History of Automobiles and Driving in Nova Scotia

#1. The first road in Nova Scotia was opened between Port Royal and Minas in 1701. Located in the western part of the province and connecting Bedford with Yarmouth via the Annapolis Valley the road — known officially as Trunk 1 — is the oldest major road in the province and was known for many years as The Post Road because of its use for mail delivery and stage-coach service. In the early years, it was nothing more than a trail connecting Acadian communities, but it was expanded by the British as a link between the garrison of Annapolis Royal and the provincial capital of Halifax. It was upgraded to a road and became known in the 19th century as The Great Western Road connecting Halifax to its westward hinterland. But the name

The Post Road persists in some circles. Today, the road is more commonly nicknamed "the old number one" in contrast to the newer Highway 101. Old Windsor Highway and Rural Route 4 (R.R.4) are also previous designations. The highway is 323 km (201 miles) in length.

#2. The first gasoline-powered automobile brought to Canada arrived on April 12, 1898, when John Moodie imported a Winton automobile to Hamilton, Ontario. However, the first automobile ever seen in Nova Scotia didn't appear until September 11, 1899, when it arrived on the Allan liner *Siberian* from Liverpool, England. It was described as a gasoline horseless carriage and owned by William Exshaw, son-in-law of Sir Sanford Fleming. It was built in France and the propelling motor was operated by gasoline.

#3. In the spring of 1904, Archie Pelton along with Mr. Porter of Kentville, a successful businessman, went to the first automobile show in New York City, where they bought two Curved Dash Oldsmobiles and had them shipped to Nova Scotia. These were the first two cars brought into the province for resale. By 1904 there were 15 other cars in the province for sale, but these had been bought by their owners in the United States.

#4. Nova Scotia's Motor Vehicle Law went into effect April 28, 1907, providing for the registration of motor vehicles, the licencing of mechanics and employee-drivers as chauffeurs, and the registration of auto dealers. The one-time fee for auto registration was five dollars. The Motor Vehicle Law also provided for the issuance of a numbered vehicle-registration certificate to the owner of each vehicle and a four-inch-diameter metal disc bearing the registration number. The disc was supposedly affixed to the dashboard of an auto. It was the responsibility of each vehicle owner to have his license plates made and such plates were generally made by a local sign-maker or blacksmith. The plates were generally made of flat metal with the numbers painted on (typically black on white), or with metal house numbers riveted onto a leather base-plate (typically silver numbers on black). The province abbreviation "NS" was often added as a vertical suffix. Registration numbers for these homemade plates were assigned sequentially on a permanent basis from 1907 through the year 1917. In 1918, the provincial government began issuing license plates directly to motorists on an annual basis. All plates in use from 1907 to 1917 were now considered invalid.

#5. Plate #1 — the first ever in Nova Scotia — was issued May 8, 1907, to William Black of Wolfville for an Oldsmobile Touring Car, while #62 was the last number issued that year. Adhering to old superstition, #13 was not issued that year.

#6. The first pavement laid in Nova Scotia on July 2, 1907, was put down on Halifax streets by Barber Asphalt Company of New York, represented in Nova Scotia by Robert Low. The total job was valued at $75,000.

#7. The Town of Digby became the first jurisdiction in Nova Scotia to impose a speeding limit when, on July 29, 1910, it was decreed that, "No automobile shall be driven through the streets of the Town of Digby at a speed exceeding six miles per hour [10 km/h] and the drivers of automobiles shall keep the horn sounding while approaching and passing any person driving, walking or standing upon the streets. The penalty for a violation is $30.00 or sixty days in jail."

#8. At 2 a.m. on Sunday, April 15, 1923, the "rule of the road" changed in Nova Scotia. After that date, all traffic moved to the right-hand side of the road. Previously, automobiles, streetcars, horses, bicyclists and all other vehicles and travellers adhered to the left-hand side of the road. Since December 1, 1922, there had been a problem for automobile drivers who crossed the border between Nova Scotia and New Brunswick — on that date New Brunswick had switched to driving on the right-hand side of the road, while Nova Scotia remained with the left-side rule. For four-and-a-half months, drivers crossing the border in both directions had to remember to change to the other side of the road, and even with the relatively low traffic levels of that day there were some near-misses resulting from this conflict.

#9. The Cabot Trail is a highway and scenic roadway located in northern Victoria County and Inverness County on Cape Breton Island. The route measures 298 km (185 miles) in length and completes a loop around the northern tip of the island, passing along and through the scenic Cape Breton Highlands. It is named after the explorer John Cabot, who landed in Atlantic Canada in 1497, although most historians agree his landfall likely took place in Newfoundland and not Cape Breton Island. (Premier Angus L. MacDonald attempted to re-brand Nova Scotia for tourism purposes as primarily Scottish and, as part of this effort, created both the names Cape Breton Highlands and Cabot Trail.) Construction of the initial route was completed in 1932. In 1932 Reverend R.L. MacDonald become the first person to drive the Cabot Trail — over 10 hours to travel from Cheticamp to Cape North, approximately 80 kilometers (50 miles). The Cabot Trail is the only trunk secondary highway in Nova Scotiathat does not have a signed route designation. Road signs along the route instead have a unique mountain logo. The entire route is open year-round.

#10. One of Canada's first automobiles was manufactured at Hopewell, Nova Scotia in 1898. Named "The Victorian," the car was a two-passenger buggy with iron tires, chain drive and tiller steering. Hopewell is a small community located in Pictou County.

#11. In 1868, a group of Kentville businessmen formed the Nova Scotia Carriage Company, which was incorporated in 1889. This business was located on Cornwallis Street near the bridge where the library and police station are now located. Its purpose was to manufacture horse-drawn carriages, sleighs and slovens of all sizes and varieties. In 1908, Jack and Dan McKay from Prince Edward Island were living in Kentville. They rented the facilities of the Nova Scotia Carriage Company to carry on the carriage trade but they were also interested in the possibilities of the automobile trade, which was beginning in the United States. They were able to get financial backing for the project but needed a man with some knowledge of the automobile. They found such a man in Archie Pelton. Pelton was a Berwick man who had gone to the New England States to work for a company that manufactured machinery for the weaving trade. New England was the centre of the textile industry and Pelton's job was to install the machinery for the companies. Before the turn of the century he had joined the International Harvester Company and returned to Nova Scotia as its service manager for some of their farm machinery. These machines were equipped with one-cylinder gasoline engines and Pelton learned the principle of the internal-combustion engine. In 1904, Pelton and a partner from Kentville went to New York to attend the first automobile show. While in New York they purchased two Curved Dash Oldsmobiles and had them shipped to Kentville. These were the first cars in the province for resale. Pelton had never driven a car but when they arrived in Kentville he drove one into a barn and completely dismantled it. As he put it back together he learned what made it go. Both these cars were later sold in Halifax. This marked the first car dealership in the province. It was not until 1910 that the McKay brothers seriously began to consider manufacturing automobiles. Pelton, having no engineering background, went to Detroit and contacted E. T. Birdsall, president of the American Association of Automobile Engineers. On his advice Pelton bought engines, rear ends and other parts to make up the chassis of a car. He bought enough for 25 cars. Pelton's brother Roy and a man named Young, both cabinet makers, were in charge of building the wooden bodies for the cars. Another McKay brother who was a blacksmith, also joined the staff.

In the first four years more horse-drawn vehicles were made than cars but progress was being made. However, in 1912 a group of businessmen from Amherst interested the McKay brothers in relocating to Amherst. A new company was formed, the Nova Scotia Carriage and Motor Car Co. Ltd., and construction of a large building was begun. At first there were problems with the building but by 1913 all the equipment had been moved from Kentville. They planned to produce 1,000 cars a year at the Amherst plant. The car was successful but the company had financial problems and the company only lasted two years, closing in 1914. Before the company left Kentville, Dan McKay and Archie Pelton drove one of their 1911 production cars to Regina, a distance of 2,600 miles. Dealerships were planned along the way, from Port Elgin, New Brunswick, to Moose Jaw, Saskatchewan. Pelton recalled years later that they arrived in Regina with Kentville air still in the tires.

A List of 10 Important Sites and Locations That Have a Special Place in the Annals of Nova Scotian History

We've all heard of Port Royal, Fort Anne, the Halifax Citadel and Fortress of Louisbourg, but in a province like Nova Scotia that is filled with so much history, there are so many important sites that some of the lesser known sites and locations just fall through the cracks. Here is a list of 10 such places.

#1. THE BATTLE OF BLOODY CREEK (CARLTON CORNER): The Battle of Bloody Creek was fought December 8, 1757, during the French and Indian War. An Acadian and Mi'kmaq militia defeated a detachment of British of soldiers of the 43rd Regiment at Bloody Creek (formerly René Forêt River), which empties into the Annapolis River at what is the present-day Carleton Corner. The battle occurred at the same site as a battle in 1711 during Queen Anne's War.

#2. HALIFAX DOCKYARD (HALIFAX): Created in 1758 under the supervision of Captain James Cook, it was the earliest Royal Navy dockyard in North America and is still in use by the Royal Canadian Navy.

#3. KING'S COLLEGE (WINDSOR): The first university to be established in the Dominions of the British Empire; the original site of the oldest university in what was to become Canada (campus now located in Halifax).

#4. LITTLE DUTCH (DEUTSCH) CHURCH (HALIFAX): A small wooden church surrounded by an 18th-century burying ground and a stone wall, it is the oldest known surviving church in Canada associated with the German-Canadian community.

#5. MARCONI NATIONAL HISTORIC SITE (GLACE BAY): The isolated site where Guglielmo Marconi received the first transatlantic radio telegraph first message comprises the remains of two telegraph towers that once supported Marconi's antennae and the foundation walls of his receiving room and powerhouse.

#6. MARCONI WIRELESS STATION (CAPE BRETON REGIONAL MUNICIPALITY): A 350-hectare (860-acre) site containing the foundations of aerial towers and three abandoned buildings, this is the location of the wireless station, which, along with a sister station in Ireland, was the first to provide regular public intercontinental radio service commencing in 1908.

#7. OLD BARRINGTON MEETING HOUSE (BARRINGTON): This wood-frame building was erected by settlers from New England and is one of the oldest surviving buildings in English-speaking Canada, and a good example of a New England-style colonial meeting house.

#8. ST. PAUL'S ANGLICAN CHURCH (HALIFAX): A small wooden church with a gable roof and central steeple, this is the first building erected in Canada in the Palladian style and the first church outside Great Britain to be designated an Anglican cathedral.

#9. THINKERS' LODGE (PUGWASH): Here is the birthplace at the height of the Cold War of the Pugwash Movement, a transnational organization for nuclear disarmament and world peace.

#10. WOLFE'S LANDING (CAPE BRETON REGIONAL MUNICIPALITY): During the Seven Years' War, this was the site where British forces in James Wolfe's brigade launched their successful attack on the French forces at the Fortress of Louisbour.

ARTS AND ENTERTAINMENT

- Michael Melski's List of 10 Nova Scotia References in Popular Films and Television

- A List of 12 TV Series Filmed in Nova Scotia

- Hugh Creighton's List of His 10 Favourite Pipe Organs Located Throughout Nova Scotia

- Natalie MacMaster's Wish List of the Top 10 Nova Scotians She Would Like to Perform For

- Jimmy Rankin's List of His 10 Favourite Songs Performed By a Nova Scotia

- JC Douglas' List of the Top 10 Bands or Performers to Come Out of Nova Scotia

- The List of Nova Scotia's Connections to the Oscars

- Dan Soucoup's List of Nova Scotia's Best Books

Michael Melski's List of 10 Nova Scotia References in Popular Films and Television

We love making our own movies here in Nova Scotia, but it's always fun to see references to our beautiful province in mass media. From *The Simpsons* to *The West Wing* to *The Royal Tenenbaums*, you'll find Nova Scotia on the screenwriters' radar.

Here are a few of my favourites.

#1. JAWS (1975): This is one to stump your friends with, and more relevant than ever with visits from twitter-darling Hilton the Shark, who's made NS her summer home. In the movie, when Ellen Brody is looking through her husband's shark-research texts and arguing with her husband that their son is perfectly safe in his new sailboat tied up to the jetty, she turns a page to see a drawing of a great white biting through the hull of a dory. This portrait is the most famous representation of the Forchu Rammer, a great white shark attack on a boat off southern Cape Breton in 1955. Suddenly, Ellen no longer thinks her son is safe in his boat tied at the wharf.

#2. MY BLOODY VALENTINE (1981): George Mihalka's slasher classic is my favourite NS-shot horror film. While "the little town with a big heart" seems to be somewhere in the U.S., those shots of the cliffs and ocean make it unmistakeably Cape Breton.

#3. WORLD WAR Z (2013): The survivors of the zombie invasion in this Brad Pitt blockbuster take refuge in the last safe refuge — Nova Scotia. The final shot appears to have them in Peggy's Cove. ... Wait till they see what the summer tourist invasion is like.

#4. SOUTH PARK (2011): "The little mushroom people of Nova Scotia, screaming with horror ..." Need I say more?

#5. GOON (2011): The first stop for Sean William Scott's dim yet endearing enforcer is playing for the Halifax Highlanders in Canada's best homegrown hockey comedy. Extra points for the donair reference.

#6. THE DAILY SHOW "WEST BANK STORY" (2014): "Is the real Jewish Promised Land in Halifax, Nova Scotia?" suggests this hilarious fake news video on the sublime and awesome *Daily Show* with Jon Stewart. Correspondents John Oliver and Aasif Maandi duke it out with dueling pronunciations of "Halal-ifax."

#7. TRAITOR (2008): Not a great film, but a fun cheesy line as a jet lands at an airport, subtitled: Halifax, Nova Scotia — "You gotta be kidding me. The U.S. is going to be attacked today and we just arrived at the ass end of Canada!"

#8. HOW I MET YOUR MOTHER (2013): In which Geddy Lee of Rush declares that his first Tim Horton's donut was a Walnut Crunch eaten in Nova Scotia.

#9. THE DAY AFTER TOMORROW (2004): As major weather events lead to environmental and human disasters around the globe, and as the movie's heroes struggle to survive, a newscast is heard: "In Nova Scotia today, the ocean rose by 25 feet. What we have feared the last few days has indeed happened. The cold front moving down from the Arctic has created an enormous storm system, which incredible as it sounds, looks more like a tropical hurricane. If this system moves south, we could see a wind-driven storm surge that could threaten the entire eastern seaboard."

#10. THE SIMPSONS (2002): The episode in which Bart tells Lisa during social studies that the way to remember the four original Canadian provinces including Quebec, New Brunswick, Ontario and Nova Scotia, is to remember the acronym — "Quiet Nerds Only Burp Near Schools."

Michael Melski is a Halifax-based film director, writer and producer whose works include The Child Remains, Perfume War, Charlie Zone *and* Growing Op.

A List of 12 TV Series Filmed in Nova Scotia

The list of movies filmed in Nova Scotia over the years is long and extensive, including everything from big-budget and commercially successful Hollywood blockbusters to low-budget independent productions. But what about television series? Nova Scotia has been the backdrop to many high-profile series and the following is a list of 12 of the best-known television series that have been filmed in the province.

#1. BLACK HARBOUR (1996–1999): Katherine and Nick return to her childhood home in Nova Scotia after her mother becomes ill. Nick is a struggling screenwriter while Katherine is a partner in a successful Los Angeles eatery. Nick and Katherine decide to stay in Black Harbour with their two daughters and manage to buy a major share of the family boatyard, with the idea of building upscale boats for a rich clientele. But home holds many memories for Katherine, who ran away because she was constantly in conflict with her fellow townspeople. Black Harbour is still home to her first love, Paul, who works at the boatyard, but is also married and a father. Filmed mostly in the Hubbards and the Mill Cove areas on the South Shore, the series starred Canadian actors Rebecca Jenkins, Geraint Wyn Davies and Alex Carter.

#2 TRAILER PARK BOYS (2001–2018): *Trailer Park Boys* is a mockumentary created and directed by Mike Clattenburg. The show focuses on the misadventures of a group of trailer park residents, some of whom are ex-convicts, living in the fictional Sunnyvale Trailer Park in Dartmouth. The series, a continuation of Clattenburg's 1999 film of the same name, premiered on Showcase in 2001. The planned final season ended in 2007, and the planned series finale special premiered on Showcase on December 7, 2008, ending the initial run of the series. There have been three films released in the series. A few years later, the actors who portrayed Ricky, Julian and Bubbles (Robb Wells, John Paul Tremblay and Mike Smith) purchased the rights to the show from the original producers and created their own Internet streaming network called Swearnet. In March 2014, Swearnet began co-producing the show. Partnering with the streaming service Netflix, Seasons 8 and 9, as well as three new specials, were underway. Season 8 premiered on September 5, 2014, followed by Season 9, which aired on March 27, 2015. Later that year, the show received the green light for two more seasons and began production on Season 10. During that time, the Canadian government had granted the cast and crew money to help produce the new season and a new spinoff series. Season 10 aired to Netflix on March 28, 2016. A new eight-part series titled, *Trailer Park Boys: Out of the Park: Europe*, became available for streaming on Netflix on October 28, 2016. The new season, called *Trailer Park Boys: Out of the Park: USA*, became available on Netflix November 24, 2017. Season 11 was released on Netflix on March 31, 2017. On June 19, 2017, the cast confirmed that *Trailer Park Boy*s had been renewed for Season 12 and that filming for the season had begun. Filming had reportedly concluded by the end of August. John Dunsworth, who portrayed trailer park owner Jim Lahey, died on October 16, 2017 at the age of 71.

#3. HAVEN (2010–2015): H*aven* is an American-Canadian supernatural drama series loosely based on the Stephen King novel *The Colorado Kid*. The show, which deals with strange events in a fictional town in Maine called Haven, was filmed on the South Shore, mostly in and around Chester. It stars Emily Rose, Lucas Bryant, Nicholas Campbell and Eric Balfour, whose characters struggle to help townspeople with supernatural afflictions, and protect the town from the effects of those afflictions. The one-hour drama premiered on July 9, 2010, on Syfy in the US and on Showcase in Canada. It concluded on December 17, 2015. On January 28, 2014, the show was renewed for a split 26-episode fifth season. The first half aired in 2014, while the second half aired in the last quarter of 2015. In August 2015, Syfy cancelled the series after five seasons.

#4. THEODORE TUGBOAT (1993–2000): The beloved children's series, Theodore Tugboat, is about a tugboat named Theodore who lives in the Big Harbour with all of his friends. The show originated (and is set) in Halifax and was a co-production between the CBC and the now defunct Cochran Entertainment. It was filmed on a model set using radio-controlled tugboats, ships and machinery. Production of the show ended in 2001 and its distribution rights were later sold to Classic Media (now

DreamWorks Classics). The show premiered in Canada on CBC Television, then went to PBS in the US, and at one time had appeared in 80 different countries. The show deals with life learning issues portrayed by the tugs or other ships in the harbour. Most often, the tugs have a problem or get involved in a struggle with each other or another ship, but they always manage to help one another resolve these problems and see them through. Their main focus however, is to always make the Big Harbour the friendliest harbour in the world and to always do a good job with their work-related tasks. The Harbour Master was played by a Halifax native, the late Denny Doherty of the famed 1960s era pop group, The Mamas and The Papas.

#5. THIS HOUR HAS 22 MINUTES (1992 –): *This Hour Has 22 Minutes* (commonly shortened to *22 Minutes* since 2009) is a weekly comedy that airs on CBC. Launched in 1993 during Canada's 35th general election, the show focuses on Canadian politics with a combination of news parody, sketch comedy and satirical editorials. Original cast members included Cathy Jones, Rick Mercer, Greg Thomey and Mary Walsh. The series featured satirical sketches of the weekly news and Canadian political events. The show's format is a mock news program, intercut with comic sketches, parody commercials and humorous interviews of public figures. The on-location segments are frequently filmed with slanted camera angles. Recognized with 24 Gemini Awards and 11 Canadian Comedy Awards, 22 Minutes is taped before a live audience in Studio 1 at CBHT in Halifax. The series, which originally aired on Mondays for several seasons and later on Fridays, currently airs Tuesdays at 8:30 p.m. and remains one of CBC's most popular shows.

#6. LEXX (1997 TO 2002): *Lexx* is a science fiction series that follows the adventures of a group of mismatched individuals aboard the organic spacecraft known as Lexx. They travel through two universes and encounter planets, including a parody of Earth. The series was primarily filmed in Halifax and Berlin, with additional filming on location in Iceland, Bangkok, Nambia and London. It starred Brian Downey, Eva Habermann (season 1 – 2), Michael McManus, Xenia Seeberg (season 2 – 4), Jeffrey Hirschfield and Tom Gallant.

#7. BLACKFLY (2001 AND 2002): *Blackfly* was a Canadian sitcom, which ran on Global TV for two seasons in 2001 and 2002. Although shot single-camera like most Canadian comedies, this series was shot on videotape and contains a laugh track, rather than making use of the usual live audience, because most scenes take place outdoors. The show is set in 18th-century Canada back "in days when beaver fur was good as gold" and focuses on Benny "Blackfly" Broughton (Ron James), a Maritimes-born undersized but ambitious general jack-of-all-trades at the isolated Fort Simpson-Eaton on the colonial Canadian frontier. He is joined by the prissy by-the-book upper class British officer Corporal Entwhistle (Colin Mochrie) whom he is usually able to talk into his latest doomed-to-failure get-rich scheme. According to Ron James, the show was cancelled because the two seasons suffered low ratings. The show was produced by Salter Street Films and reruns began showing during the fall of 2009 on APTN.

#8. LIOCRACY (2001 AND 2002): *Liocracy* was a comedy series, which aired on The Comedy Network in 2001 and 2002. The show, a spoof of biographical documentary series such like *Biography* or *Life and Times*, starred Leslie Nielsen as host Terrence Brynne McKennie. Each episode presented a *Biography*-type profile of a fictional person loosely based on a real-life personality. For example, the first episode centred on *Fiendly Giant*, a *Friendly Giant*-like children's television host with a penchant for sadomasochism who became a pariah after being caught having sex with his rooster sidekick Rudy. Produced in Halifax, the show was created by Ian Johnston and Peter Hays, two former journalists for the Halifax Daily News. The show was titled *Liography* in its first season, but was changed to *Liocracy* in the second season after the A&E Network, the producers of the original Biography series, threatened a copyright infringement lawsuit. The second season premiered in November 2002 and ran for 13 episodes into early 2003. The series was not renewed for a third season.

#9. MR. D (2012 -): Qualified to teach gym class, Gerry Duncan is instead hired in the social studies department of the prestigious Xavier Academy, a private school for kids in Grades 5-12. Gerry struggles to stay ahead of his students as he fakes his way through each class, having decided that he knows enough to get by and he can just improvise everything else. A comedic take on the profession, *Mr. D* shows teaching from a teacher's perspective and reveals the truth — teachers just don't know everything. The series is based on Gerry Dee's life as a high-school teacher before he became a stand-up comic in 2003. The show is filmed on location at Citadel High School in Halifax. On April 6, 2017 Dee confirmed the show had been renewed for a seventh season.

#10. THE MIST: *The Mist* is an American science fiction-horror thriller television series developed for Spike TV. It is based on the horror novella of the same name by Stephen King. An unexplained mist slowly envelops the town of Bridgeville, Maine, creating an almost impenetrable barrier to visibility. The residents of the town soon learn the situation is even more precarious as hidden within the mist are numerous monsters of various sizes that attack and kill anything that moves, trapping several groups of people in a shopping mall, a church and a hospital. Eventually, people begin to see apparitions in the mist from their past, fears or guilty consciences that help or kill them, depending on how they react. In July 2016, the production company announced the series had been cast and gone into production in Halifax. The 10 episodes of the first season were reportedly produced on a budget of approximately $23 million, making it the biggest entertainment production ever to shoot in the province. The first season, consisting of 10 episodes, premiered on June 22, 2017. On September 27, 2017, Spike cancelled the series after one season.

#11. STREET CENTS (1989 – 2006): *Street Cents* was a teen-themed newsmagazine TV series that originally aired on CBC between 1989 and 2006. Produced in Halifax, it was one of a few shows focused on consumer and media awareness for young people. The series was created by producer John Nowlan and won several Gemini

Awards, and even an International Emmy for Best Youth Programming or Series. The series was lauded by critics for its efforts to be inclusive and representative of Canada's youth. The show aired without commercial interruption because the producers did not want the bias of advertising revenue to affect the potential criticism of the advertisers' products and/or services. The show promoted safety and ethics and action while empowering young people. Sponsor logos were briefly seen in the end credits of episodes in a manner akin to public television in the United States. In August 2006, CBC decided to cancel the series as viewership declined in its target demographic, teens and preteens. The last episode aired October 1, 2006.

#12. PIT PONY (1999): *Pit Pony* was a CBC series telling the story of small-town life in Glace Bay in 1904. The plot revolved around the lives of the families of the men and boys working in the Cape Breton coalmines. It was based on the award-winning 1997 TV movie, which was inspired by the Joyce Barkhouse novel of the same name. *Pit Pony* debuted on CBC on February 5, 1999 and ended on February 4, 2000. It ran for two seasons with 44 episodes. The Gemini-Award-winning series also aired in the United States on the Encore (TV network). In June 1999, production began for the second season. However, the series was subsequently cancelled on February 4, 2000.

Hugh Creighton's List of His 10 Favourite Pipe Organs Located Throughout Nova Scotia

What a difficult choice. There are very fine pipe organs throughout Nova Scotia and I realize I may have missed a few historic ones, such as Wedgeport and Arichat. These two places have older instruments I have not seen. This is a subjective list and others may not share my view!

#1. EGLISE ST. PIERRE DE CHETICAMP (CHETICAMP): The smallest organ on the list at one manual. It was built in 1905 and has mechanical action and fills the beautiful church with fine sound!

#2. ST. ANNE'S ROMAN CATHOLIC CHURCH (GLACE BAY): A beautiful, two-manual mechanical-action organ by the late Gerhard Brunzema. This is a fine organ with a wealth of useful stops. The acoustic is dry, an unexpected about which Mr. Brunzema was very sad.

#3. CHRIST CHURCH ANGLICAN (AMHERST): One of Casavant's early mechanical-action revival organs from the early 1960s. This was an important instrument in this period of rediscovery of mechanical action. It has two manuals.

#4. ST. NINIAN'S ROMAN CATHOLIC CATHEDRAL (ANTIGONISH): A small, two-manual, mechanical-action gem in a superb acoustic. This organ was built by the Hook and Hastings firm of Boston in the 19th century and lovingly restored by Casavant Freres, when Gerhard Brunzema was the tonal director.

#5. SAINT PATRICK'S ROMAN CATHOLIC CHURCH (HALIFAX): An 1898 three-manual Casavant voiced by Claver Casavant himself. One of the rare instruments to keep its original tubular pneumatic action. A splendid sounding organ in a fine acoustic. It is partly in the French romantic tradition and still has its original terraced console.

#6. CATHEDRAL CHURCH OF ALL SAINTS (HALIFAX): A 1910 Casavant of four manuals. A true cathedral instrument with much colour and éclat. There are plans to make some additions, which will make it a wonderful, versatile organ.

#7. ST. MICHAEL'S ROMAN CATHOLIC CHURCH (HALIFAX): A small and very flexible 14-stop, two-manual organ by Casavant in a cathedral-like acoustic. This fine instrument does far more than one would expect of a one this size.

#8. ATLANTIC SCHOOL OF THEOLOGY ST COLUMBA CHAPEL (HALIFAX): Another one-manual gem built by the late Hellmuth Wolff. This 11-stop jewel makes many beautiful sounds and shows what a small organ can do. The key action is a delight as built by Wolff.

#9. ACADIA UNIVERSITY MANNING MEMORIAL CHAPEL (WOLFVILLE): This mechanical-action organ followed Amherst and is a little larger and more refined. Another very versatile instrument! It was inaugurated with a concert by the late E. Power Biggs.

#10. ANGLICAN CHURCH OF THE HOLY TRINITY (YARMOUTH): The third in the trinity of one-manual organs, this one also by Brunzema. Another versatile instrument that was nearly lost to Nova Scotia. It was originally installed in the United Church in Wolfville and was saved by the music director of Holy Trinity, along with dedicated volunteers. Holy Trinity also has a fine Casavant three-manual organ, which is not being used at this time.

Other Notable Organs in Nova Scotia:

ARICHAT AND WEDGEPORT

ST. MATTHEW'S AND FORT MASSEY UNITED CHURCHES

ST. JAME'S ANGLICAN IN HALIFAX

TRINITY ST. STEPHENS UNITED CHURCH IN AMHERST

ST. JOHN'S ANGLICAN CHURCH IN LUNENBURG

Hugh Creighton was born in Halifax in 1950 and studied piano with Constance Hubley and Elaine Burns Ellis from age eight to 17. He studied organ for four years with Edward Norman from age 17 to 20; for two years with Clarence Ledbetter at Acadian as a private student; and with Lucienne l'Heureux-Arel and Gaston Arel as a private student for eight years. He has been interested in pipe organs since 1967. Some of his favourite organs are the great Cavaille-Coll organs in France. When he was 21, he heard the Notre Dame organ in Paris and has never forgotten those sounds. Spine tingling! In 1986, he got to briefly play the great St. Sulpice organ and the rear-gallery organ of St. Germain en Laye (Marie Claire Alain's church). He has heard the organs of Basilique Ste. Clotillde, eglise le la Madeleine, eglise Ste Eustache. He has also heard the great Silbermann organ of the Hofkirche (Cathedral) in Dresden, the great Mezler organ of Grossmunster, Zurich and some of the great cathedral organs of the UK and U.S.A. Hugh also has an interest in classical French organs and music, as well as the great Saxon organ builder Silbermann and the great German builder Schnitger.

Natalie MacMaster's Wish List of the Top 10 Nova Scotians She Would Like to Perform For

So, you're a world-class, award-winning fiddler. You've been given the opportunity to perform for any Nova Scotian (living or deceased). Who would you choose? If you're Natalie MacMaster, these would be your Top 10 picks:

#1. L'ARCHE: Well, this isn't just one individual but a small community. If you don't know about L'Arche communities, you must visit one. Founded in 1964 by Jean Vanier, they are dedicated to the creation and growth of homes and programs for people with learning disabilities. I used to play for L'Arche communities in Cape Breton 30 years ago. I learned early on in life that giving is just another way of receiving. Playing for the L'Arche community is a musical experience that leaves you appreciative of what you've been given, inspired by the dedicated people who work there and mostly, with a genuine recognition and respect for the dignity in all of God's creations. It is a joy to watch them receive the music!

#2. SIDNEY CROSBY: How can you not include this Cole Harbour boy in a list of anything for Nova Scotia? What dedication and talent! When people are really skilled at something, it always inspires me. Watching Sidney play is so beautiful that it sets my mind to greater things. I would love to bring him to my folks' place in Cape

Breton and have his family and a few trusted locals join us for a great night of fiddle tunes.

#3. THE TRAILER PARK BOYS: Well, this may come as a shocker, but I find those boys so sweet! Now imagine me sitting in Bubbles' trailer, fiddle in hand, hanging out with Ricky, Julien, and the gang. Wouldn't we have a riot? Music is also about light-hearted moments, just having fun and not having to think. I am pretty much guaranteed that quota from one good kitchen ceilidh with the Trailer Park Boys.

#4. DAN R. MAC DONALD: There are so many wonderful Cape Breton fiddlers who I grew up listening to but never met. Dan R. intrigues me the most because he was not only a delightful player, he was also an incredible composer. He wrote piles of tunes that are in my repertoire. But most appealing to me was his personality. I have a recording of an interview he did for CBC. He had such charm, wit and innocence, that I memorized every word and detail of the interview.

#5. MAGGIE ANN CAMERON: My grandmother! I played for her a lot before she died, when I was a child. Her character and appreciation of music was so grand that I would love to experience it again, as an adult. I would treasure the chance to be near her, to feel her love of the music so deeply. Not a more musical person have I met. Her musicality was not one of knowledge so much as feeling. And feeling music is most appealing to the soul — the eternity of music; the unity of music; the holiness of music!

#6. SARAH MCLACHLAN: With the limited experience I've had with Sarah, I know her to be a generous soul, appreciative of all good music and a bottomless pit of musical knowledge. To be in her company and to play for her would pull a new musicality out of me. I bet she'd be such a joy to share music with. And maybe after a bit she would join me on the piano.

#7. ALEXANDER GRAHAM BELL: One of Canada's most significant creative minds, Alexander was also a pianist. I feel that with his intellect, mental freedom and heart for music, he would receive the fiddle tunes in a unique and beautiful way. It would be such an honour to play my fiddle in his presence.

#8. RITA MACNEIL: It wasn't until after Rita died that I developed a deep appreciation for her and her music. There was an interview I read and another I watched where she told her life story. And she certainly wasn't one to dramatize things. In fact, I think she underplayed her suffering. But when I learned of her difficult child and young adulthood, her fame and her music became that much more beautiful. To rise above the horror around her, and to rise to such heights—it makes me love that lady, and feel that much more moved by her music. I did meet her a number of times and performed on her show, but I was too young to value it as it should have been valued. I would love to sit in her presence, to absorb her quiet beauty and have a cup of tea and a few tunes.

#9. DAVID AND MARGARET FOUNTAIN: Twenty years ago or so, I was invited to play at a house party for David and Margaret Fountain. Now, many's a house party I've played at over the years so I thought I knew what to expect. But, when I arrived at their home with fiddle in hand, it was a most unexpected and unforgettable experience. What a palace! The beauty of their home, the food, the guests … it was truly incredible. Before my performance, I had some time to tour this absolutely beautiful mansion, including watching a Barbara Streisand movie in their home theatre. But after this amazing night was over and just a memory, I discovered the generosity of that special couple. Their wealth was not just for them, but for the whole community to benefit from. They have donated so much over the years and most recently $3 million to NSCAD. I appreciate their spirit of giving and I hope that they will invite me back sometime to play some good old fiddle tunes for their fancy, kindred hearts!

#10. HUGHIE AND ALLAN: I remember them well. They used to do comedy acts at the various Cape Breton concerts I would attend as a little girl, but I grew to love them more as a young adult. Their brand of humour was so simple and sweet and their presence on stage so old fashioned (they wore overalls and plaid shirts) that I started recreating their performances in my own shows. Yes, I would dress up as an old man and tell their jokes, pretending to be one of them, or collaborating with Bruce Guthro as the duo. They still bring me much enjoyment even today. I think it would be so cool to have them around again, to hear their unique brand of humour and have them enjoy some fiddle tunes!

Natalie MacMaster is one of Cape Breton's most important exports and a superstar in the eclectic music world (though she's far too humble to admit it). Fiddler and step-dancer, Natalie MacMaster has built a sterling, multi-decade career on electrifying playing and must-see live performances. Her extensive discography showcases her both as a soloist and as a marquee collaborator, notably with husband and fellow fiddler Donnell Leahy. An Order of Canada is among many accolades the Ontario mother of six has received in recognition of her peerless artistic status.

Jimmy Rankin's List of His 10 Favourite Songs Performed by Nova Scotians

I cut my teeth playing at dances and weddings with my family band, The Rankins, in and around Inverness County in Cape Breton. Music was a constant at our house and friends would often stop in and we'd entertain them — it was just a part of life in Mabou.

Some of the artists on my Top 10 list were in heavy rotation in the Rankin Family household. Others were inspired by that musical tradition. In all honesty, there's so much musical talent in Nova Scotia — from singer-songwriter Ronnie MacEachern to international superstar Anne Murray — that for me, there's really no Top 10. But here are a few that come to mind — in no particular order ....

#1. ASHLEY MACISAAC AND MARY JANE LAMOND: "SLEEPY MAGGIE": This song was progressive for the time, beautifully marrying traditional Celtic with contemporary rhythms. Ashley's rock n' roll fiddle with Mary Jane's haunting Gaelic lyrics make this a classic.

#2. MOLLY RANKIN AND ALVVAYS: "ARCHIE, MARRY ME": I first heard Molly's songwriting when she was about 15 and to say that it was impressive beyond her years is a major understatement. Somewhere between then and now, she wrote "*Archie, Marry Me*." It became their breakout hit and now she's a rock star touring the world with her band, Alvvays.

#3. RITA MACNEIL: "WORKING MAN": Rita's Part of the *Mystery* album was a huge inspiration for me as a young songwriter because she wrote and sang with such honesty about her life and her roots. *Working Man* is one of my favourites as it exemplifies the strength of Rita's soulful writing and sound — a true Cape Breton anthem.

#4. JOEL PLASKETT: "ROLLIN', ROLLIN', ROLLIN'": I recently had the pleasure of working Joel when he produced my upcoming album, *Moving East*. He's an extremely talented and versatile singer-songwriter, musician and producer. I love how "Rollin's" modern-day kitchen party vibe effortlessly mixes with Joel's clever lyrics.

#5. RANKIN SISTERS: I might be slightly biased here but three of my favourite Nova Scotian singers happen to be my sisters: Heather, Cookie and Raylene. Together with The Rankin Family, their singular voices and harmonies helped bring East Coast music to the forefront of the national and international music scenes. Here are three songs that I think highlight their voices and remarkable talents. I consider these to be of equal ranking on my list:

HEATHER RANKIN: "NORTH COUNTRY": This song charted on Canadian and International Adult Contemporary radio and video, bringing stories from Nova Scotia to the world.

COOKIE RANKIN: "MO RUN G'EAL DILEAS (MY FAITHFUL FAIR ONE)": This was the opening track on the first Rankin Family album — an unusual way to start a record but it introduced many people to the beauty of Scotch Gaelic music and culture. I'll never forget Cookie's soaring vocals as we sang this song for HRM Queen Elizabeth II.

RAYLENE RANKIN: "RISE AGAIN": This was Raylene's signature song, written by Leon

Dubinsky. Still sends chills up my spine when I listen to Raylene's pure and clear voice — a Cape Breton classic.

#6. DUTCH MASON: "I GOT A WOMAN": I've always been a big fan of the blues and Dutch Mason is one of my favourites. I love the live version of *I Got a Woman*. Such a raw, a**kicking song.

#7. MATT MINGLEWOOD: "DAN WILLIE": When I was a kid, I used to sneak into adult dances just to hear Matt sing classics like *Dan Willie*. Matt was a town hero and rock star who made it big singing songs about home. So cool to see Matt still rockin' and sounding better than ever.

#8. JOHN ALLAN CAMERON: "BANKS OF SICILY": Growing up on Back Street in Mabou, we lived next door to John Allan's mother, Katie Ann. I remember John Allan delivering his very first record to our house. He was a musical pioneer — a great interpreter of songs and one of the first Cape Bretoners to bring Celtic music to the national stage. I've always loved his rendition of *Banks of Sicily*.

#9. STAN ROGERS: "DARK EYED MOLLY": Stan Rogers wrote about everyday folks and things I could relate to as a kid from rural Cape Breton. So many of his songs are classics but I particularly love his version of Archie Fisher's *Dark Eyed Molly* — a song I was listening to a lot when I wrote *Fare Thee Well Love*.

#10. DAVID MYLES: "CAPE BRETON": David is a New Brunswick-born, honourary Nova Scotian. "Come on pretty baby won't you come with me, let's go to Cape Breton and swim in the sea…" I love the playfulness of David's lyrics and his quirky, light-hearted delivery in this song about rekindling love.

Jimmy Rankin is an iconic Canadian solo artist and the lead singer, guitarist and songwriting lynchpin behind multi-platinum Celtic-Pop heroes, The Rankin Family, who achieved multi-platinum album sales, earned five Junos including the coveted Entertainer of the Year award and cemented their place in Canadian music history with Jimmy's gorgeous single, "Fare Thee Well Love" (Juno for Single of the Year and CBC's #1 East Coast Song of all Time). A renowned live performer with broad demographic appeal, Rankin's shows draw from an impressive catalog of hits, moving effortlessly between Roots, Country and AAA stylings.

JC Douglas' List of the Top 10 Bands or Performers to Come Out of Nova Scotia

Choosing Nova Scotia's Top 10 Musical Artists … piece o' cake!

Hmm… Canada's "father of country music," Wilf Carter, was born in Port Hilford, Nova Scotia, so he'd be a lock, right?! Well, unless — was he nudged out of contention by Hank Snow?

And in the 1960s, Nova Scotian country, folk and traditional music began to blur 'round the edges. The *Jubilee* gangs of Don Messer (neither Don, Charlie nor Marg were from Nova Scotia, so they're OUT) and that *Singalong* gang handed off to John Allen Cameron, whose TV fame paved the way for a national love affair with a family act from Mabou.

Oh, but the Barra MacNeils became national stars. Then Ashley MacIsaac and Buddy's girl, Natalie MacMaster, rewrote the book on Cape Breton fiddle tunes, leading a flurry of Capers who'd become some of the best-known Celtic artists on the planet. And of course, there's Bruce Guthro, who was making solo records in Canada while belting out European hits with Runrig.

And what to do with Stan Rogers? Well, he had family from Nova Scotia, but he was merely our most beloved Come From Away.

Hey, maybe the rock scene would be easier to choose from. Let's see … by 1964, The Beavers, in their Mohawk haircuts, had morphed into the kilt-clad The Great Scots, with future April Wine members begging to roadie for them. Under the guidance of manager Mike Duffy (yes, that Mike Duffy), the Scots were U.S.-bound for recording sessions in NYC and LA, resulting in a Top 10 Canadian hit and appearances on all the major pop television shows, including *Shindig!* and Dick Clark's *American Bandstand.*

By '66, they found themselves hangin' with Denny and the other Moms & Pops before their California dreams were shattered by Uncle Sam's Vietnam War effort and bassist Dave Isnor was drafted into the U.S. Army. The Great Scots would not make another public appearance until 2008 at the Seahorse in Halifax. In '68, Myles Goodwyn and Pam Marsh headed for the East Gate Sanctuary of Cape Breton, before Myles thumbed his way back to Halifax, where April Wine would ferment.

From Sydney, Moon-Minglewood & the Universal Power would launch the careers of two legends of live performance. And … on came the next generation of rockers, as an indie-Halifax sound took root in the 80s, with bands like the aptly named Grace

Babies, future film/TV exec Mike Clattenburg's The Spawning Grunions and Brett Ryan's The Little Ministers. John Wesley Chisholm's Black Pool's last bass player, Chris Murphy, would form Sloan.

Ahhhh, Halifax as "The Next Seattle." From the onslaught of releases on local labels, Cinnamon Toast Records and Chris Murphy's Murderecords, plus the heady signings of Jale, Eric's Trip and Hardship Post to Seattle's Sub Pop label. The birth of the Halifax Pop Explosion. Even Mike Smith, whom you know today as "Bubbles," had a national hit with "Curious," courtesy of New Glasgow's Sandbox ... the singer just happened to be Anne Murray's nephew, Paul Murray.

Then, as the East Meets West hype faded, out of the fog emerged a handful of gifted artists achieving success on a national scale: Matt Mays (from The Guthries), Yarmouth's Wintersleep, the raucous Celtic Punk of The Stanfields, and Joel Plaskett, whose Thrush Hermit had evolved into the Joel Plaskett Emergency. Whew!

Lunenburg's Dutch Mason ascended to the position of PM of the Blues, with protegees who continue to rock the blues today, like his son, Garrett, and fellow Truro boy, Charlie A'Court, as well as North Preston's Carson Downey.

Back to the pop/rock scene, oh my god! We follow the Bruce Wheaton thread from The Stitch In Thyme through Everyday People, where he hooked up with Pam Marsh from Ritchie Oakley's Soma, phasing into Molly Oliver with Bob Quinn and Tony Quinn. And Pepper Tree charted a few national hits then begat Ram, Molly Oliver, Horse and even future international West Coast hitmakers, Chilliwack! Frank MacKay, Doug MacKay, Kenny MacKay ... then Oakley would form his own band with Horse's Wayne Nicholson, and ... urgh!

Hello 80s, when Steps Around The House ruled the clubs while The Hopping Penguins segued into a Halifax hip hop scene. "Stinkin' Rich" Terfry became Buck 65, steering his "Tom Waits with a beatbox" style into national radio, while Classified proved that a location as unassuming as Enfield, Nova Scotia, could become a hotbed of hip hop.

Oh!! And that Holly Cole, the jazz singer ... man, she was cool.

Okay, so ... it wasn't easy. But you try it. Here we go ...

#1. ANNE MURRAY: A unique singing voice is rare. A voice as pure as young Anne Murray's was a gift. A natural wonder that replaced a mining disaster as Springhill's prime source of notoriety. Anne's rise to international fame coincided with that of Nova Scotia's most under-recognized music producer, Brian Ahern. He left CBC Halifax's *Singalong Jubilee* with Anne in 1968 to build a career producing 12 of her albums, 11 by his now ex-wife Emmylou Harris, and records by Johnny Cash, Glen Campbell, Linda Ronstadt, Willie Nelson, George Jones, Roy Orbison and more. In those early years together, Anne and Brian did not forget from where they had come, mining the catalogues of great Maritime songwriters like PEI's Gene MacLellan, New Brunswick's Ken Tobias and Halifax's Peter Pringle. Anne scored four Top 10 hits on *Billboard Magazine*'s U.S. Hot 100 pop chart, including a coveted #1 with *You Needed Me* in 1978.

#2. SARAH MCLACHLAN: Like Anne Murray, it doesn't take long to identify Sarah McLachlan's one-of-a-kind tones. Humble Halifax beginnings as a NSCAD student, singing with The October Game and selling hot dogs to Misty Moon patrons on Barrington Street led to international stardom. And Sarah remained true to her fans and her ideals. She launched the first ever female-focused festival tour, *Lilith Fair*. She put two singles into the Billboard top five in 1998, *Adia* and *Angel*. And Sarah won three Grammy Awards, one fewer than Anne Murray, who leads the way among Nova Scotian performers. (*Footnote*: Sarah performed at the very first East Coast Music Awards in 1989, shortly after moving to Vancouver. Yours truly hosted the event, establishing myself forever as an East Coast music trivia answer.)

#3. APRIL WINE: Myles Goodwyn was born in Woodstock, New Brunswick, but Nova Scotia was home for most of his youth: Dartmouth (Tuft's Cove) and Waverley, mostly. The first April Wine rehearsal took place in David and Ritchie Henman's basement in Lower Sackville in 1969. Within three years, the band had relocated to Montreal and had scored the first of their three Billboard Top 40 hits in the U.S. Over a 22-year chart run, April Wine would land 32 hits on the Canadian pop charts and seven in the States.

#4. DENNY DOHERTY: At his 2007 funeral, in the north-end Halifax neighbourhood Denny Doherty remained so proud of his entire life, family, friends and fans said goodbye. With the last surviving Mamas and Papas member, Michelle Phillips, looking on, Denny's sister, Frances, described how distances were tougher to bridge in the 1960s than with today's social media. It was 1966, and in order for his mom to hear her long lost boy's new chart-topper, the iconic *California Dreamin'*, Frances had to request the song from CJCH radio. When it finally hit the airwaves, they pulled their car over on Bedford Highway to crank the song for a celebratory first listen. From his early days with Zal Yanovsky (later of The Lovin' Spoonful) in The Halifax Three, through the meteoric success of The Mamas & The Papas, on through his national TV show in the 70s, his off-Broadway *Dream A Little Dream*, his Harbour Master character on the brilliant Theodore Tugboat and a recurring role on *Pit Pony*, there was never a dull moment for the well-loved Doherty. At their peak, between 1965 and 1967, The Mamas & The Papas put three straight albums into the U.S. top five (two went to #1), while scoring seven Top 10 singles on the Billboard Hot 100 during that same narrow window. The group won a Grammy for *Monday, Monday* in 1967, and was inducted into the Rock and Roll Hall of Fame in 1998.

#5. HANK SNOW: Canada had a musical trailblazer from Liverpool who revolutionized his genre long before Lennon & McCartney even met. For Hank Snow, it was a short drive down the Mersey River from his hometown of Brooklyn to Liverpool, Nova Scotia. And another couple of hours on to Halifax, where a teenaged Clarence Snow played in local theatres before the movies, and auditioned tirelessly to finally get his own program on CHNS radio in 1933. By the end of the Second World War, Hank "The Singing Ranger" was a Nashville star, penning timeless country classics like *I'm Moving On* in 1950, the first of seven international #1 country hits, and recording the definitive North American version of Geoff Mack's *I've Been Everywhere*. It was Snow who introduced a young Elvis Presley to the faithful at the Grand Ole Opry and to the man who would coordinate the rest of Elvis' life and career, while contributing to his early death, Colonel Tom Parker.

#6. THE TREWS: Bassist, Jack Syperek (son of Halifax artist/entrepreneur/restaurateur and one-time mayoral candidate, Victor Syperek) teamed up with the uber-talented MacDonald Brothers (singer, Colin; guitarist, John-Angus) in their hometown of Antigonish and launched the most consistent Canadian rock band of the 21st century. They're currently on a streak of five consecutive Top 10 albums in their home and native land. And in 2003, The Trews began a string of 17 Top 10s (including three chart-toppers) on the Canadian rock singles chart with the #1 smash, *Not Ready To Go*, a super-energized track custom made for opening montages on *Hockey Night In Canada*. With a big Trews fan, Ron MacLean, as HNIC host, it was only natural for them to recruit Colin MacDonald to record his own version of the *Hockey Tonight* pre-game theme in 2013.

#7. KEVIN MACMICHEAL: On a stormy winter day in the midst of Halifax's World Junior Hockey euphoria in 2003, I left the Metro Centre and trudged up the middle of Barrington Street toward St. Matthew's Church, to pay tribute to one of Nova Scotia's brightest musical lights, Kevin MacMichael. Lung cancer had taken Kevin at only 51. He had a stint with the much-loved local band, Spice, in which Kevin exercised his love of Beatlesque song structure and harmonies. In the early 80s, when Nick Van Eede was in town touring with The Drivers, he and Kevin decided to elevate their friendship to something professional — a new band, Cutting Crew. In 1987, they found the top of the charts worldwide with *(I Just) Died In Your Arms*. Kevin's next guitar challenge was to be as Robert Plant's sideman on his 1993 tour and album, *Fate of Nations*, for which came a Grammy nomination. One of my most cherished musical memories is jamming Beatles tunes with Kevin long into the night at the Red Fox in Bayers Road Shopping Centre, just over a year before his passing, as it would turn out. My team had just beat his team at Beatles trivia. True story.

#8. SLOAN: Halifax had its own labels, Cinnamon Toast and Murderecords, but it was the heady signings to the American Sub Pop label that signified the beginning of this city's era as the "Next Seattle." One Halifax pop band with real staying power would explode from a short-lived stay on the legendary Geffen Records. Sloan's indie/grungey debut EP *Peppermint* and its LP *Smeared* drew accolades as a cross between The Beatles and Sonic Youth. The band would come into conflict with Geffen for the DGC's lack of promotional effort and would remain a very self-directed band on singer/bassist Chris Murphy's own Murderecords. Eleven albums in, Sloan has consistently turned out ever-polished power pop, dripping in Lennon-McCartney harmonies and lean, raunchy, 70s classic-rock, riff-heavy guitars. Their debut single *Underwhelmed* was a surprise chart-topper on RPM's CanCon chart in 1992, and Sloan would land another three Top 10 singles plus nine Top 40 albums on the Canadian charts. The band toyed with breaking up about five years in but have managed to carve out careers as a Toronto-based unit, as well as separately fostering other pet projects such as Chris Murphy's critically-acclaimed 2016 album with TUNS, a collaboration with fellow Halifax buddies, Matt Murphy (The Superfriendz) and Mike O'Neill (The Inbreds).

#9. CLASSIFIED: Who could have predicted that Canada's most successful East Coast rapper would be a lanky white kid, fiercely proud to be from Enfield? And Classified (Luke Boyd) has never shied away from referencing his hometown and region in his music. A notoriously independent artist, Classified was 11 albums deep before signing with a major label deal. Three of his four major-label CDs have gone Top 10; his self-titled 2013 release shot to #1. In the same span, he landed 10 singles on the Canadian charts, all while steadfastly calling the shots. Brutal honesty is Luke's stock in trade. His lyrics openly share his personal life, his art, his career and the mistakes record execs have tried to railroad him into. (Check out *Heavy Head* from the Greatful CD. Has an artist ever stated his career manifesto so articulately?). This made me nervous: to introduce Luke to Christine Campbell, the versatile local singer-songwriter who recently opened for Bob Seger on his Maritime dates. But he was inspired by her writing and produced her second solo album, *Roller Coaster*. Luke loves finding cool Nova Scotian talent to work with and it's often the least predictable collaborations that have been the most exciting. The rapper in the "hoody and a ball cap" hooked up with the suit-clad folky jazzman, David Myles, to create the Juno-winning Rap Recording of the Year in 2013, *Inner Ninja*, a track which also hit the Top 40 in Ireland and New Zealand. This led to Halifax pop artist, Ria Mae, seeking out Luke to produce her 2016 album. *Clothes Off* would be nominated for the Single of the Year Juno Award. The Junos tapped Classified to co-host the Awards in 2013, another career highlight. Meanwhile, guest artists like Snoop Dogg, Maestro Fresh Wes and Jim Cuddy of Blue Rodeo have routinely dotted the recordings of Classified, paying testament to how well respected he is in the industry.

#10. THE RANKIN FAMILY: In the late 80s and 90s, The Rankins took up the mantle as champion of traditional East Coast folk/country music. And the pride of Mabou, Cape Breton, took their brand of Maritime music to new heights, with five Top 40 hits on the national charts and more than a dozen on each of the Country and Adult Contemporary Charts. Two albums have also topped the national Country chart. The group celebrated the cycle of life on their home island in iconic songs like Leon Dubinsky's *Rise Again*, Jimmy Rankin's *Orangedale Whistle* and Raylene Rankin's *Gillis Mountain*. Jimmy, John Morris, Cookie, Raylene and Heather were the second wave of Rankins to represent the family in musical form. They became darlings of stage and television throughout the 1990s, selling records and concert tickets in numbers that no traditional Nova Scotian artist had ever dreamed of. After a decade of success, the group announced they would split in order to pursue individual projects and solo careers. Four months later, John Morris Rankin would meet an untimely death in a car crash in Cape Breton. But by 2007, the four surviving members had reunited. Six Juno Awards including Group of the Year and Single of the Year for *Fare Thee Well Love* in 1994, three Canadian Country Music Awards and countless other accolades highlight the impact the Rankins had on the Canadian music scene of the 90s.

JC Douglas is a Grace Baby, born in Halifax, raised in Dartmouth ... "a child of the Stereo Twin Cities." Family roots in Southern Ontario led to JC spending his formative years there, but he hustled back at the age of 20 to seek a career in the white-hot spotlight of Nova Scotia show biz. An on-air stint at Bridgewater's CKBW in 1985 led to a gig at Q104 in Dartmouth/Halifax. JC eventually tested the TV waters as a co-host of Breakfast Television in 1998-99 before returning to the Q as program director in late '99. After interviewing his lifelong musical idol, Paul McCartney, and guiding the station into top spot in the Halifax market, JC figured he'd achieved his goals as a rock-radio programmer and went searching for new experiences. Eventually he returned to the air full-time, hosting the Afternoon Show at 89.9 The Wave and his current job, Mornings at C100 in Halifax, with Peter Harrison and Melody Rose.

The List of Nova Scotia's Connections to the Oscars

The Academy Awards, or the Oscars, are largely viewed as the greatest honour in the film industry. But did you know that three Nova Scotians have actually won an Oscar? That's right. Producer Michael Donovan won the golden statuette for the documentary *Bowling For Columbine* in 2003, choreographer Onna White won the award for 1968's *Oliver* and Cape Breton-born actor Harold Russell had a rare double win for 1946's *The Best Years Of Our Lives*.

Other Nova Scotians have been nominated for an Oscar, with Ellen Page being the most recent example for her role in *Juno*. In 2018, Dartmouth's Shane Vieau was the co-winner the Oscar for best production design for his work on the best picture winner, *The Shape of Water*. There is something about Nova Scotia that attracts Oscar to the province.

Following is a list of Academy Award winning actors, actresses and directors who have made movies in the province:

1976: Jodie Foster filmed *Echoes of Summer*. Won Best Actress Oscar in 1988 for The Accused and again in 1991 for *The Silence of the Lambs*.

1990: Charlton Heston filmed *The Little Kidnappers*. Won a Best Actor Oscar in 1960 for Ben-Hur.

1995: Kathy Bates filmed *Dolores Claiborne* and again in 2005 filmed *Ambulance Girl*. Won a Best Actress Oscar in for *Misery* in 1991.

1995: Robert Duvall filmed *The Scarlett Letter*. Won Best Actor Oscar in 1983 for *Tender Mercies*.
1996: Sandra Bullock filmed *Two If by Sea*. Won Best Actress Oscar in 2010 for *The Blind Side*.

1997: James Cameron filmed scenes from his 1997 blockbuster, 11-time Academy Award-winning film, *Titanic*, in Nova Scotia. With an initial worldwide gross of over $2 billion, *Titanic* was the first film to reach the billion-dollar mark and is the second-highest grossing film of all time.

2000: Sean Penn filmed *The Weight of Water*. Won Best Actor Oscar in 2004 for Mystic River and Best Actor Oscar in 2009 for *Milk*.

2000: Sissy Spacek filmed Songs in *Ordinary Times*. Won Best Actress Oscar in 1980 for *Coal Miner's Daughter*.

2000: The only woman to have won an Oscar for directing was Kathryn Bigelow in 2010 for *The Hurt Locker*. She directed two movies in Nova Scotia — *The Weight of Water* in 2000 and *K-19: The Widowmaker* in 2002.

2001: Kevin Spacey filmed *The Shipping News*. Won Best Supporting Actor Oscar in 1996 for *The Usual Suspects* and Best Actor Oscar in 2000 for *American Beauty*.

2001: Cate Blanchett filmed *The Shipping News*. Won Best Supporting Actress Oscar in 2005 for *The Aviator* and Best Actress Oscar in 2014 for *Blue Jasmine*.

2001: Judi Dench filmed *The Shipping News*. Won Best Supporting Actress Oscar in 1999 for *Shakespeare in Love*.

2001: Julianne Moore filmed *The Shipping News*. Won Best Actress Oscar in 2015 for *Still Alice*.

2009: Hilary Swank filmed *Amelia*. Won Best Actress Oscar in 2000 for *Boys Don't Cry* and again in 2005 for *Million Dollar Baby*.

2011: Olympia Dukakis filmed *Cloudburst*. Won Best Supporting Actress Oscar in 1987 for *Moonstruck*.

2011: Brenda Fricker filmed *Cloudburst*. Won Best Supporting Actress Oscar in 1990 for *My Left Foot: The Story of Christy Brown*.

2015: Louis Gossett Jr. filmed *The Book of Negroes*. Won Best Supporting Actor Oscar in 1983 for *An Officer and a Gentleman*.

2015: Cuba Gooding Jr. filmed *The Book of Negroes*. Won Best Supporting Actor in 1997 for *Jerry Maguire*.

For the record, although Kirk Douglas did not win a competitive Oscar during his legendary film career, he was given an honorary Academy Award in 1996 for 50 years as a creative and moral force in the motion-picture community. He filmed *The Secret* in Nova Scotia in 1992.

And in September 2017, the Academy of Motion Picture Arts and Sciences announced Donald Sutherland, the 82-year-old Canadian actor who grew up in Bridgewater, would receive an honorary golden statuette on November 11 in Los Angeles. Sutherland has had a six-decade career involving more than 140 films including *The Dirty Dozen*, *Cold Mountain*, *M*A*S*H*, *The Italian Job* and *The Hunger Games* series. He has also won two Golden Globes, an Emmy Award and is an officer of the Order of Canada distinction. The award honours extraordinary distinction in lifetime achievement, exceptional contributions to the state of motion picture arts and sciences, or for outstanding service to the Academy. Although Sutherland was born in Saint John, New Brunswick, his family moved to Bridgewater when he was young. Sutherland started his career at the age of 14 on the Bridgewater radio station, CKBW. Sutherland has five children who've pursued the craft, most notably Kiefer, star of *24* and *Designated Survivor*. Both starred in the 2015 film *Forsaken*, which marked the first time they shared the screen together. The last time Sutherland filmed in Nova Scotia was for the 2011 television miniseries, *Moby Dick*.

Dan Soucoup's List of Nova Scotia's 10 Best Books

Nova Scotia has a long and celebrated literary heritage — Canadian publishing began here — so attempting to select the 10 best Nova Scotia books is bound to create disagreements. Yet here it is, a list of 10 essential books along with a few honourable mentions. While not every author selected is strictly a Nova Scotian, all can lay claim to Nova Scotian roots and have made a significant contribution to the province's storytelling tradition.

#1. SAILING ALONE AROUND THE WORLD, JOSHUA SLOCUM: Joshua Slocum was born in 1844 on North Mountain, overlooking the Bay of Fundy. The Slocum farm was dirt poor and yet both sides of the family produced a number of mariners. Slocum's solo cruise circumnavigating the world by sail was a stunning achievement and Captain Slocum's historic adventure is a classic tale of man against the sea. When published in 1900, the book was immediately acclaimed a masterpiece and is still considered today, more than 100 years later, a highly readable and vivid story of his astonishing years alone at sea.

#2. FALL ON YOUR KNEES, ANN-MARIE MACDONALD: "There is no resisting this story," claimed the *Globe and Mail*. The novel narrates the saga of the Piper family, especially the four sisters, in Cape Breton during the latter years of the 19th century and early decades of the 1900s. The author exploits the dramatic Cape Breton landscape as well as the complex human relationships often found buried in family affairs. Almost instantly a Canadian bestseller when released in 1996, *Fall on Your Knees* became an international literary sensation after winning the Commonwealth Writers Prize for Best First Novel, as well as being named to Oprah Winfrey's Book Club. Translated into 17 languages, the book made playwright, actor and novelist Ann-Marie MacDonald one of Canada's most admired writers.

#3. THE MOUNTAIN AND THE VALLEY, ERNEST BUCKLER: Described by the celebrated Nova Scotia poet Alden Nowlan as "one of the great novels of the English language," *The Mountain and the Valley* was published in 1952 to widespread critical praise. Set in the Annapolis Valley where Buckler lived most of his life, this coming-of-age novel is regarded as one of the central works that help established Canada's modern literary movement.

#4. NO GREAT MISCHIEF, ALISTAIR MACLEOD: Perhaps the greatest novel to ever come out of Nova Scotia, MacLeod took 10 years to write the spelling-binding *No Great Mischief*, the mythic story of the MacDonald clan, first in the Scottish Highlands and then in Cape Breton. "A once-in-a-lifetime masterpiece" written by "the greatest living Canadian writer," declared the *Globe and Mail*. Alistair MacLeod began publishing short stories in the late 1960s and released two volumes to critical acclaim, *The Lost Salt Gift of Blood* (1976) and, 10 years later, *As Birds Bring Forth the Sun and Other Stories*. After mastering the craft of the short story, MacLeod published his most famous novel in 1999, winning literary awards in Canada and abroad, including the International IMPAC Dublin Literary Award.

#5. BLUENOSE GHOSTS, HELEN CREIGHTON: Sixty years after being released, *Bluenose Ghosts* is still a popular book recounting the supernatural in Nova Scotia. Folklorist Helen Creighton painstakingly collected these ghost stories involving haunted houses, forerunners, buried treasure, spook ships and other mysterious occurrences.

While a number of critics have questioned the picture Creighton creates of a historical Bluenose culture populated with superstition, *Bluenose Ghosts* remains a Nova Scotia classic, preserving and disseminating the original accounts of traditional Nova Scotian legends and beliefs.

#6. BAROMETER RISING, HUGH MACLENNAN: Winner of five Governor General's Literary Awards, Hugh MacLennan's first novel is set in Halifax during the Halifax Explosion, a tragic event that MacLennan had experienced first-hand. The classic novel (1941) weaves a compelling romance against the backdrop of war and disaster. While MacLennan's impressive strength as a writer is obvious from the outset, insisting on setting the story in a Canadian port city rather than a customary British or American location established his reputation as a distinctive Canadian novelist. This fact alone helped establish a modern Canadian literary identity.

#7. TIDAL LIFE, A NATURAL HISTORY OF THE BAY OF FUNDY, HARRY THURSTON AND STEPHEN HOMER: While *Tidal Life* (1990) is visually stunning, it is no ordinary coffee-table book. Writer Harry Thurston and photographer Stephen Homer have produced a powerful tribute to one of the most unique ecosystems on Earth. The book traces the natural and human history, from the mouth of the bay to its upper reaches, and presents the reader with a well-researched account of the delicate balance between the fishery, right whale migration and human activity. The call for conservation is as powerful today as when the book was published more than 25 years ago.

#8. WE WERE NOT THE SAVAGES: A MI'KMAQ PERSPECTIVE ON THE COLLISION BETWEEN EUROPEAN AND NATIVE AMERICAN CIVILIZATIONS, DANIEL PAUL: First published in 1993, *We Were Not the Savages* quickly became one of the most significant books published in Nova Scotia over the past 50 years. Author Daniel Paul argues passionately that a peaceful people were brought to the edge of extinction by a group of military men under the leadership of Edward Cornwallis, Charles Lawrence and other British officers. In writing the book, Paul forced Nova Scotians and all Canadians to confront the racist notion of the barbarians in need of civilizing. In challenging the conventional historical view of the Mi'kmaq, Paul also points out the systemic racism present today. This new perspective on the European-Indigenous divide has helped educate Nova Scotians on the work that lies ahead in order to rectify the situation.

#9. THE BIRTH HOUSE, AMI MCKAY: *The Birth House* was released in 2007 and, despite being Ami McKay's debut novel, became a #1 Canadian bestseller. It won three CBA Libris Awards and was nominated for the International IMPAC Dublin Literary Award. Set in a Nova Scotia village on the Fundy Shore in the early years of the 1900s, *The Birth House* is the story of Dora Rare, a young girl who learns traditional birthing methods and healing remedies as an apprentice to a local Acadian midwife. After the passing of the midwife and the arrival of modern medicine in the village, Dora struggles to maintain the traditional practises.

#10. THE NYMPH AND THE LAMP, THOMAS H. RADDALL: Thomas H. Raddall first made a name for himself as a short story and non-fiction writer, winning the Governor General's Award for *The Pied Piper of Dipper Creek* (1939) and *Halifax, Warden of the North* (1948). Yet he is best known today as a historical novelist and *The Nymph and the Lamp* (1950) is clearly his most renowned novel. Set in Nova Scotia during the 1920s, in Halifax, Annapolis Valley and Sable Island, Raddall depicts a traditional and patriarchal Bluenose society, yet manages to create a portrait of the heroine as a strong, independent woman, a rare occurrence in early Maritime literature. Raddall was able to write full time throughout his long and distinguished career, spanning six decades.

Five more essential Nova Scotian books:

THE CHANNEL SHORE, CHARLES BRUCE

ROCKBOUND, FRANCK PARKER DAY

UP HOME, SHAUNTAY GRANT AND SUSAN TOOKE

THE EDUCATION OF EVERETT RICHARDSON, SILVER DONALD CAMERON

DOWN THE COALTOWN ROAD, SHELDON CURRIE

Dan Soucoup worked as a bookseller and publisher for many years. He is the author of numerous books on the Maritimes, including A Short History of Halifax, Failures and Fiascos, *and* Maritime Firsts. *He lives in Dartmouth.*

LEISURE TIME

- Rick Howe's List of the Top 10 Tourist Attractions in Nova Scotia
- Pam Mood's List of the Top 10 Hidden Gems in Nova Scotia
- Sandra Phinney's List of the 10 Favourite Nova Scotian Coastal Getaways
- Jon Tattrie's List of 10 Ultimate Nova Scotian Daytrips
- Cruise's List of 10 Things that a Five-Year-Old Will Enjoy Doing in Nova Scotia

Rick Howe's List of the Top 10 Tourist Attractions in Nova Scotia

Wow. When I was asked if I would write down my top 10 Nova Scotia tourist attractions, I thought to myself, just 10? We live in a marvellous province full of scenic wonders, historical attractions and amazing people; anywhere in Nova Scotia is a great place to see.

I have lived here some 40 years and have spent many weekends and vacation days driving from Yarmouth to Cape Breton Island and here is my list of my favourite touristy things, in no particular order.

#1. Let's start with going for drives on Nova Scotia's back roads to see all the sights, sounds and attractions. Yes, the 100-series highways will get you from point A to point B faster but if you really want to see this province of ours take the back roads. A drive down the Number 3 highway from Tantallon to Liverpool is a wonderful drive with scenic ocean vistas and picturesque communities like Mahone Bay, Chester, Lunenburg and Liverpool. Be sure to bring a camera. Stop along the way to check out the whirleygig factory, have an ale at the Foc'sle or check out the many yard sales along the roadside. Head out the Number 7 highway to Musquodoboit Harbour and beyond and journey down the many side roads for some spectacular scenery. And of course, is there any prettier drive than along the Cabot Trail in Cape Breton. You'll find yourself in scenic heaven off the beaten path in any section of Nova Scotia.

#2. The Cabot Trail deserves its own spot on my top 10 list of best Nova Scotia places to visit. Spectacular does not begin to describe the beauty and ruggedness of the drive around and through Cape Breton's highlands. Each twist and turn will take your breath away. The narrow, curvy road is an adventure in itself. Take time to stop and gawk at the scenery, perhaps do some camping at Cape Breton Highlands National Park or take in a ceilidh in Mabou; the Cabot Trail is consistently a world-ranked must-see stop. If you have not yet driven around the trail, you're missing out.

#3. Next on my list, you cannot mention attractions without talking about our province's many beaches. My wife and I have a particular affection for the South Shore and the white sandy beaches at Beach Meadows, the mile long Summerville Beach, Carter's Beach, Cherry Hill Beach and on and on and on. Take in the warm waters of Melmerby Beach on the Northumberland shore or search for sea glass at Ingonish Beach in Cape Breton. Nova Scotia has more than 100 beaches, each with its unique attractions. Enjoy a day playing in the waves at Clam Harbour, watching the surfers ride the waves at the beach at Lawrencetown or simply relaxing while watching the kids have fun at Rainbow Haven just outside of Halifax.

#4. We went for a drive one Saturday through the Rawdon area and up to the Fundy Shore when we discovered a spectacular scenic area at Burncoat Head near Noel. The province says it is the home of the world's highest tides but the attraction is when the tide is out. You can walk on the ocean floor for miles. Think Fundy National Park in New Brunswick with its famous Hopewell Rocks, but on a smaller scale. You can hunt for fossils or shells, watch a spectacular sunset and visit the nearby lighthouse. A can't-miss stop.

#5. Up next, food. If you love food you'll love Nova Scotia. From the donair, Halifax's official food, to lobster to more exotic Thai or Indian foods, every food you can imagine can be found somewhere in Nova Scotia. Try the halibut at the Red Shoe in Mabou, owned by the Rankin sisters, a clubhouse at the MicMac Tavern in Dartmouth or the Seascape in Hunts Point where they claim to have the world's best clams. Halifax itself is a food connoisseur's delight where you can find great greasy fries at Bud the Spud's food truck, tender steak at Ryan Duffy's or tavern fare at the Split Crow. Halifax's growing diversity has also resulted in eateries specializing in food from countries around the world. Or try some of the many varieties of dishes offered by a growing food truck industry. But outside of Halifax, communities like Wolfville and Lunenburg offer dishes prepared by world-class chefs. And if you love fish, well I need not say more. Food is certainly one of my favourite tourist things to do.

#6. Nova Scotia's capital city is also a top 10 attraction. I first came to this city in 1978 and immediately fell in love with the place. And while it is becoming a modern 21st-century city, there's still a small-city feel about Halifax, where strangers will greet you with a hello in a hallway or neighbours gather for a weekend barbecue. Halifax has a thriving nightlife and many historical attractions for your daytime enjoyment including the Citadel, the old British fortress that protected the city back in the day. Walk along the waterfront boardwalk or take a quick trip across the harbour on a Halifax Transit ferry to Dartmouth and visit Sullivan's Pond or the Shubenacadie Canal system. Visit Halifax's downtown library, described as an architectural marvel, shop in the many boutiques that line Spring Garden Road or enjoy a scenic walk through the forest at Point Pleasant Park in the city's south end.

#7. Peggy's Cove outside of Halifax makes my list. It is perhaps the most visited tourist attraction in the province; it's the most photographed anyway. We'll occasionally take a drive out and sit on the rocks to watch the waves come crashing ashore. It's even more spectacular when there's a storm system off the coast, resulting in even higher waves hitting the rocks. We'll also at times remind a wandering tourist about the risks of getting too close to the water. The signs say stay off the black rocks for a reason. The village itself offers some nice scenes for camera buffs and the landscape outside of Peggy's Cove, with big rocks dotting the landscape, shows leftovers from the glacial ice age that are rugged and scenic.

#8. The province's many historic attractions and museums are also worthy of my top 10 list of favourite tourist spots. I love to wander through the Maritime Museum of the Atlantic and its display of Titanic memorabilia. The Army Museum at the Halifax Citadel is another spot to check out. Just outside the city, visit the Uniacke Estate in Mount Uniacke, the country estate of Richard John Uniacke, who served as attorney general in Nova Scotia in the 1800s. The grand country house is described as one of the finest examples of Georgian Architecture in all of Canada. The Navy museum at CFB Stadacona in Halifax offers a look at the navy's history in our city. Or check out the UFO museum in Shag Harbour, site of the October 1967 incident where witnesses claim a UFO crashed in the harbour waters. Fortress Louisburg outside of Sydney is a very popular attraction and recreates life back when the French dominated *Acadie*. General James Wolfe, who led the British forces at the Battle of the Plains of Abraham in Quebec, took part in the siege of Louisburg that ended French rule in Nova Scotia. There are fisheries museums in several communities and a Museum of Industry in Stellarton that at one time featured a display of a spectacular Nova Scotia business failure, the Clairtone debacle. And, as you travel some of the province's back roads, take time to read the historical markers that dot the roadsides.

#9. I can't say it was my favourite experience — due to seasickness — but before the nausea I enjoyed a couple of journeys out into the Bay of Fundy for some whale watching. We rented a cottage for a couple of days overlooking St. Mary's bay, itself a very relaxing experience, then journeyed down the road to Freeport on Digby Neck. The trip out to sea was enjoyable and seeing the huge humpbacks break water was a site I'll always remember. The nausea on the other hand, not so great. My advice for others in a similar boat — pardon the pun — is take some Gravol. We went out from Briar Island on a converted lobster boat with about 20 to 25 other people. The tour guides are great and very knowledgeable about the whales that journey into the Bay of Fundy in the spring and summer months hunting for food. The whale adventures can be hit and miss, but most times you do get to see these spectacular creatures.

There are whale-watching tours offered around the province and if you do venture out, keep an eye out for the great white sharks now visiting Nova Scotia's shores in increasing numbers.

#10. And Nova Scotia's scenery itself makes my top 10 list of favourite tourist spots. I like to take photos and have some fantastic sunset shots as I sit outside a cottage on the ocean shore and watch the waves come in. You can rent some pretty nice places all around Nova Scotia. A sleepy fishing village with its lobster boats moored on a foggy morning, the mix of colours in the rocks on a beach, a herd of deer grazing in an open field or the ruggedness and beauty of the highlands, this province is a camera buff's delight.The bottom line, no matter where you go, is that there's always something special to see or do. So get out of the house and enjoy this great province of ours.

Rick Howe has been in the radio business since 1972 with stops in Campbellton, Newcastle and Saint John, New Brunswick before moving to Halifax in October 1978. He has been a labour and police reporter, on-air anchor and news director before becoming a talk-show host in 1998. He currently hosts the Rick Howe Show on News

95.7 in Halifax. He lives in Fall River with his wife, Yvonne. He has three grown sons, Jason, Greg and David, and two granddaughters, Brihanna and Madeline.

Pam Mood's List of the Top 10 Hidden Gems in Nova Scotia

Oh, how many times I've heard folks say of Nova Scotia, "We are our own best kept secret!"

How true! Around every corner a hidden gem is found. For my list, I chose those that make me smile, cause me to breathe deeper in appreciation, take my breath away and are steeped in culture.

Nova Scotia, herself, is a hidden gem, and her people make it so.

#1. BIRCHDALE: Once home to monks and the Nova Nada Monastery, Birchdale is 56 acres of the most serene environment in all of Nova Scotia. Sixty km from Yarmouth and seven miles down a dirt road, you'll find a lodge and surrounding cabins, but you won't find electricity, internet or cell phones. It's home to writing, paddling and other retreats for those searching for peace for the soul.

#2. LE VILLAGE HISTORIQUE ACADIEN DE LA NOUVELLE-ECOSSE: Located in Lower West Pubnico, Le Village is a celebration of the language, culture and traditions of an Acadian Village in the early 1900s. As a special treat, savour home-cooked Acadian cuisine and gingerbread cookies straight out of the oven.

#3. COSBY'S CREATIONS: Step into a magical kingdom of bigger-than-life concrete sculptures created by Ivan Higgins. From dragons to athletes, to an enchanting castle, all are nestled among the most glorious flowers, trees and shrubs, all lending to the magical feel.

#4. Old train rails turned trails: Extending throughout most of the province, the old rail trails, looked after by locals are used for walking/running, horseback riding, bicycling and even ATVs.   Much of the way is tree canopied, inviting all to take time out of a busy day.

#5. COCOON SLEEPING: Look up; wayyyyy up and you'll see a cocoon suspended in the trees above Ingonish Beach, Cape Breton Island. Parks Canada has introduced this hidden gem of another calibre, enticing campers to snooze suspended among the trees. What fun!

#6. TUSKET ISLANDS: Steeped in history that includes everything from lobster fishing to Second World War spies to drug trafficking (yikes!), the Tusket Islands are an island-hopper's paradise. More than 200 islands are sprinkled with fishing shacks and camps and we're told nearly every one of them has a guitar or two and at least one large pot for boiling lobster! What a treat.

#7. BEAR RIVER: Tucked into one of Nova Scotia's valleys, this sleepy little village also known as little Switzerland, is a haven for artists and artisans celebrating their crafts. From roasted coffee to pottery, it all happens here and it's an experience simply meandering through the shops and studios.

#8. CARTER'S BEACH: Located in Port Mouton, Queens County, this white-sand beach is made up of three individual beaches that have something for everyone. Be ready to battle for a parking spot, though, as this hidden gem is a local favourite.

#9. FREAK LUNCH BOX: Not only is this fun, enticing, candy shop filled floor-to-ceiling with treats that remind us of our youth, but the mural painted on the side of the building on Barrington Street, Halifax, is a fun, colourful landmark that awakens the visual senses. You'll want to take in both! And while you're at it, step over a couple streets and walk the Argyle Pattern on Argyle Street.

#10. SWEENEY FISHERIES MUSEUM: Tucked into a working fish plant across from Yarmouth's Frost Park, the W. Laurence Sweeney Fisheries Museum is a step back in time. Created by Mr. Sweeney's children, every inch of the hands-on museum is rich with authentic gear celebrating the fishery in Southwestern Nova Scotia. A wonderful surprise for all ages!

BONUS HIDDEN GEM: Nova Scotia's people. We are always surprised and delighted to find a hidden gem in our travels, and when visitors take the time to chat with Nova Scotians, they discover what we locals have always known — our people are our best hidden gem. We are known the world over for our friendly, welcoming, "come in for tea!" personalities that ensure every person is treated like family, because in the end, we are one big happy family.

Pam Mood is a born and bred Nova Scotian, coming to us from what she describes as the "best piece of real estate on earth" — the seaside town of Yarmouth, Nova Scotia. As serving mayor of her community, she understands the beauty of the entire province and its diverse people. Of Lebanese descent, she appreciates all that is Nova Scotia and takes every opportunity to share the rich stories of our history and never misses a chance to talk about the potential of this amazing province. She is a proud Acadia graduate, leadership expert, professional speaker and loves nothing more than a good cup of tea, a great conversation and a good belly laugh.

Sandra Phinney's List of the 10 Favourite Nova Scotian Coastal Getaways

There's nothing like heading to the ocean for a few days. Salt air, beachcombing, coastal hikes, delicious sunrises and sunsets — they all help us to unwind — or rewind! One of my favourite places to hunker down is Inverness Beach Village on the west side of the Cabot Trail [*macleods.com/beach-village/inverness-beach-village.html*].

There are multiple reasons I love it here. For starters, the first sentence on their website reads, "Location is all or so it's said." I can attest to that! Every time my husband Barrie MacGregor and I attend the International Celtic Colours Festival, we make the "village" home base, as a multitude of concerts and events are within easy driving distance from here. It's also only a short distance from Mabou, famous for the Red Shoe Pub, Farmer's Market and Saturday night dances.

Of course, Inverness itself has buckets of charm. It's an old coal mining "company town" yet one of the world's top golf courses, Cabot Links, is next door to Beach Village. Bordering the community is a handsome boardwalk with views that money can't buy.

Then there's the hiking. Famed historian G. M. Trevelyan often said: "After a day's walk, everything has twice its usual value." That's how Barrie and I feel after hiking in this region where there's everything from challenging treks to gentle forests and spectacular coastlines. Get used to saying "wow" a lot. If you have your heart set on seeing a moose, head up to the Skyline Trail, which is part of Cape Breton Highlands National Park and is only an hour's drive north from Beach Village.

Speaking of views, the cottages are on a high bluff with easy access to two miles of beach. Bonus: owners Ivan and Anita MacLeod (brother and sister) know everything there is to know about Cape Breton. Want to know the best place to find oatcakes? Check. Where to find a ceilidh, homemade woollen mittens or Egypt Falls? Check, check and check! And be sure to ask Anita about the best place to find beach glass. She's an expert on the subject and there's some closer than you think.

One of the many things I love about Nova Scotia is that we are practically surrounded by the sea. Not only do we have 7,600 km of coastline, we are also spoiled for choice when it comes to choosing a coastal getaway — we have everything from five-star inns and resorts to more modest cabins and cottages, campgrounds and yurts. Take your pick!

BRIER ISLAND: This storied island is only two short ferry runs from mainland Nova Scotia at the end of Digby neck. It's really a gateway to another world. Although there's a fair amount of choice for accommodations on this little island, you'd best make reservations before going, as it is a well-known birder's paradise as well as the East Coast's premier place to go whale watching. Brier Island is also a photographer and painter's paradise [*brierisland.org*].

CAPE BRETON ISLAND NATIONAL PARK — Ingonish Beach: For a walk on the wild side, spend the night in the Cocoon Tree Bed, which overlooks the ocean at this campground. Another option is to rent an oTENTik, (think a solid tent but on a platform with a deck). It has built-in beds, a heater, indoor table and chairs. Leave your computer and cell phone behind [*pc.gc.ca/en/pn-np/ns/cbreton/activ/camping*].

CAPE D'OR: The Lighthouse at Cape d'OR is something else. For starters, you have to walk down a rather steep driveway to get there. So a backpack with bare necessities is recommended. But the stay in the lightkeeper's cottage (more than one room; common living room; shared bathrooms) is well worth the walk. Bonus: the owner is a fabulous cook. Although the selection at meals is limited, you can't go wrong [*capedor.ca*].

CLARE: The yurts in Le Petit Bois at University Saint Anne are situated on Baie Sainte Marie, adjacent to the university in Church Point. They are ideal for families or a group of friends. Within seconds you are at the shore, where you can also enjoy the new Church Point Lighthouse, a hike along the coastline or a stroll through "le petit bois," a series of paths that loop through remnants of an Acadian forest. [*lepetitbois.ca/en/yurts*].

HUNTINGTON POINT: This spot is on the Bay of Fundy (close to Hall's Harbour) and is home to some of the most unusual homes in Atlantic Canada. Referred to as "ferries houses" (or hobbit houses), they were built by Charles Macdonald — a genius who loved concrete — in the mid 1930s. They are colourful, whimsical and look like they could be homes for the seven dwarfs. The Blue Cottage is available to rent by the week and is a stone's throw away from the beach [*concretehouse.ca*].

LOCKEPORT: Situated on the Allendale Bay Peninsula, Lockeport is connected to the mainland by the Crescent Beach Causeway. It's a sleepy town but loaded with characters and interesting nooks and crannies to explore. If you want to hunker down in a cottage on Crescent Beach, consider Seaside Cottages at Ginger Hill [seasidecottages.ns.ca] or Ocean Mist Cottages [*oceanmistcottages.ca*]. The latter is open all year and is pet friendly.

OCEAN STONE RESORT: This inn, restaurant and cottages is a gem of a place outside of Halifax on the South Shore. Although it's small in the grand scheme of things, it consistently receives recognition by the Canada Wedding Industry and Elle Canada by wining awards and placing in the Top 5 Places in Canada to get married. But you don't have to get married there to enjoy an intimate get-away! Just go [*ocean stoneresort.com*].

WHITE POINT BEACH RESORT: On the outskirts of Liverpool, this place is more than just a resort. It's all about tradition, experiences and family. When you visit White Point you are treated like gold. It's the perfect place to cash in on relaxation and fun. You can be as busy as you please or as laid back as you want. The staff are experts in programming and keep coming up with ways and means to provide unforgettable experiences. [*whitepoint.com*].

YE OLD ARGYLER LODGE: Located Southwest Nova Scotia, it combines modern amenities with old-world Maritime charm. It has five rooms that are part of the lodge along with a full service restaurant. The owner, Jonathan Joseph is also a fine chef and turns out meals that both locals and visitors love. The lodge faces the famed Tusket Islands — kayaking heaven — and is close to numerous place of cultural and historical interest [*argyler.com*]

Sandra Phinney is an award-winning journalist who writes from her perch on the Tusket River in Canaan, Nova Scotia. Although she's travelled to several exotic places around the world, many of Sandra's fondest memories come from her own back yard — right here in Nova Scotia.

Jon Tattrie's List of 10 Ultimate Nova Scotian Daytrips

So, it's a weekend or you have a day off and you're bored. There's nothing to do; or so you think. But in fact, there's lots to do. Consider any one of these daytrips … you'll be glad you did. They're all just a short drive from anywhere in mainland Nova Scotia.

1. FISHERMAN'S COVE: A short, pleasant drive takes you to a community of working fishermen coming and going alongside colourful shops selling original art, souvenirs, books and more. There's also a great beach, several walks and the starting point for a bigger kayak or canoe adventure. Fisherman's Cove was once a cove worked by fishermen, but the decline of the industry reduced the port to a shadow. It was revived in the 1990s as a hybrid working village/tourist destination. Wander the two boardwalks of shops. A&M Sea Charters will take you whale watching — and if you don't see a whale, your next trip is free.

2. HOPE FOR WILDLIFE: It can take a leisurely couple of hours to explore Hope for

Wildlife (5909 highway 207). A bright red barn at the entrance houses an education centre and a few animals. Topaz, an elderly parrot, moved in when his owner died; Cornelius the corn snake turned up at a Halifax hotel; and there's also Danny California, the frog who snuck into a shipment of lettuce at Pete's Frootique. The centre also explains the work done by HFW and wider wildlife issues. The second red barn houses the rehab clinic and that's where you go to see baby squirrels being hand-fed. You may also see bald raccoons in cages. Beyond the two barns stretch a semi-wild area with enclosures housing birds (including some awe-inspiring eagles), deer, foxes, otters, owls and many other animals. All of them have been injured and are rehabbing — most will return to the wild. It is an active centre, so newly injured animals arrive regularly.

3. SHUBENACADIE WILDLIFE PARK: Stroll through a beautiful, 50-acre Nova Scotia forest populated by black bears, Sable Island horses, cougars, wolves, beavers and eagles, and you won't get eaten or trampled by any of them. Shubenacadie Provincial Wildlife Park (149 Creighton Road) has 26 different species of mammals and 65 types of birds in a serene 50-acre wildlife sanctuary. It's one of the most entertaining walks in the province. Many of the animals, like moose, black bears, beavers and bald eagles are native to Nova Scotia. It's easy to live your whole life here and never see them in the flesh. That's quickly corrected with an afternoon in the park. There are also different wolves, foxes, deer (including actual reindeer!), otters, hares, pheasants, turkeys and swans. The park is super fun for adults, but of course it caters to kids, too. Two km of the park are wheelchair-friendly.

4. JOGGINS: Gape in awe at one of the world's finest collections of fossils from the ancient past, most of which were hand-gathered by an elderly, self-taught local man. Where else can you stroll along a primeval beach and pick up a tiny ancestral dinosaur bones? Joggins is one of Nova Scotia's most globally important sites, which is why it is a UNESCO World Heritage Site. The Joggins Fossil Centre (100 Main Street) is a super-modern facility sitting on the reclaimed Old Joggins No. 7 Coal Mine. It has fantastic displays that explain the area's 300-million year history. The location is fitting. Most of the world-class collection was gathered by the late Don Reid, an amateur paleontologist who dropped out of school in Grade 6 when his father was injured in a Joggins coal mine. From boyhood to old age (Reid was 87 when he showed me around in 2009), he combed the ever-changing beach looking for fossils and carting them back to what was once his own private museum, which has now grown into the Joggins Fossil Centre. The displays show off the exceptional fossil collection from the Carboniferous Period, ranging from dinosaurs to other reptiles and plant forms. The remains of the lycopods, an ancient pre-tree plant, look more like crumbled Grecian columns than the ghosts of flora long departed. Interactive exhibits and videos round out the experience. The highlight of a trip to Joggins is a guided tour of the beach.

5. GRAND PRE: The Deportation of the Acadians was a seminal event in Nova Scotia history and this beautiful park/museum brings that past alive. The Grand Pre National

Historic Site of Canada commemorates the Acadian settlement in the area from 1682 to 1755. The Visitor Reception and Interpretation Centre offers a multi-media theatre, exhibit hall and gift shop to tell the story of the deportation from the perspectives of the Acadians, their allies, the Mi'kmaq and the British who ordered the expulsion.

6. BEAR RIVER: The village on stilts offers several layers of Nova Scotia. The quirky community took its modern identity from waves of hippies seeking a different way of life — some stayed, and now create the art and love of nature that defines the "Switzerland of Nova Scotia." Under that identity is a deeper one — the central gathering place for Mi'kmaq governments and people in pre-European Mi'kma'ki. A great trip to explore the many local shops and eat at a restaurant near the river.

7. MAHONE BAY: The three churches reflecting in the water of the bay are one of province's perma-beauty sites. In snow, in sunshine, for the first time or the 99th time, it's a picture of captivating beauty and the backbone of a relaxing day in rural Nova Scotia. As a bonus, the village gets more sunshine than anywhere else on the coast.

8. TANGIER: If you're into kayaking, this is the place. Paddle off the beaten path with a sublime kayak tour guided by a passionate marine biologist. Sign up for the day-long Eastern Shore Islands adventure, a half-day introduction to kayaking, or a multi-day journey along Nova Scotia's eastern shore at Coastal Adventures. This small company started when Dr. Scott Cunningham took a break from his career in science for a once-in-a-lifetime adventure. He paddled around the coast of Nova Scotia in a canoe. It changed his life. He left the science world and started his tour business; he was later joined by his partner, Gayle Wilson, who brings her artistic training to the rough beauty of the jagged coastline.

9. SHERBROOKE VILLAGE: Time travel to Nova Scotia's past in this living ghost town of lumbering, goldmining and shipbuilding in the 1800s. It's a long drive, but that's half the fun of this day trip. Marine Drive beyond Musquodoboit Harbour is spectacular. The road curves through the Head of Jeddore and Lake Charlotte, turning down a lightly travelled rural road past Tangier, Sheet Harbour before bringing you back inland to Sherbrooke. Lots of places to stop to take in the view, or for a leg-stretching stroll. Sherbrooke Village is about the same size as the modern village of Sherbrooke and is the reason most people come here. The attraction's 80 buildings recreate life between the 1860s and the start of the First World War through dusty streets, well-maintained homes, churches and workplaces, with costumed interpreters skipping along the squares or riding high and pretty on a penny-farthing bicycle. Twenty-five of the buildings are open to the public and most have costumed interpreters inside to guide you to the past.

10. MAITLAND: The highest tides in the world are amazing to behold; they are astounding to ride. Tidal bore rafting, mud bathing and swimming score 10 out of 10 for the amount of exhilarating fun you can have in Nova Scotia. The Bay of Fundy has the highest tides in the world and water comes into the bay with such force that it reverses rivers. You can watch it happen: the Shubie is flowing out, and then gets whacked back in. The whack part is where the tidal bores form, and where you get your ride. Local rafting companies offer short (two-hour) and long (four-hour) rides. The longer ones venture closer to the edge of the Bay of Fundy. It takes a while to putter out on the Zodiacs, but it's a fun, leisurely way to see the river. The tidal bore rafting itself feels like the most dangerous thing you've ever done, although if you look at other boats it appears tame. It's only when you're on the bore that you feel its power. If the weather is good, the boats often stop at a natural mudslide where you can have a wicked good time before taking a swim to rinse off.

Jon Tattrie is the author of seven books, including Dan Paul: Mi'kmaq Elder, Cornwallis: the Violent Birth of Halifax, *and the* Hermit of Africville. *He is also the author of* Day Trips from Halifax: The Ultimate Daytripper's Guide *(MacIntyre Purcell Publishing).*

Cruise's List of 10 Things that a Five-Year-Old Will Enjoy Doing in Nova Scotia

Parents often struggle with the same dilemma — how can I keep my children entertained? This is especially true during the summer months and holiday weekends. Well, here's my list of the 10 things that a five-year old (and anyone else) will enjoy doing in Nova Scotia.

#1: I missed this trip but my wife told me how much fun Jackson had exploring The Ovens in Riverport. There are plenty of hiking trails and really cool sights on the ocean-side trails. I've been here once before but I missed this family adventure, which only means we'll have to head back soon.

#2: Every Wednesday evening at the Discovery Centre in Halifax is free. So one night we decided to check it out. It was packed with kids burning off what seemed to be endless energy. Jackson really enjoyed seeing the dinosaurs, playing and learning. Definitely worth checking out what's happening here.

#3: On several occasions we've had spontaneous road trips to Peggy's Cove. Sometimes it's the whole family or sometimes it's just Jackson and myself. We've spent hours climbing the rocks, staring out at the ocean and having fun adventures pretending we are climbing mountains.

#4: Last summer we had a spontaneous trip to Cape Breton to visit family. We went cruising in the side-by-side and hit up my old stomping grounds at Rockdale Beach. Jackson had a blast, playing in the water and collecting shells. The water is always nice here. Back in the day, this beach was packed with people on a hot day; now it's pretty quiet. We saw only about 10 people there that day.

#5: One spot we frequent at Jackson's request is the "Pirate Playground," as he calls it. The ship-inspired grounds are located in DeWolfe Park, Bedford. There's nothing really spectacular about this playground, but he really enjoys it there. I guess you have to look at it through the eyes of a five-year old.

#6: This past summer we spent as much time as we could biking around Shubie Park in Dartmouth. Jackson is still a little small to be keeping up so we plop him in a toddler seat and he gets to enjoy the ride without any of the work. There's even a canteen to grab a drink and a breather before continuing on your adventure.

#7: When the snow flies and it's time to haul out the sleds there's a great spot, affectionately referred to as "The Pit." It's in the north end of Halifax and its official name is Merv Sullivan Park. Be warned though, this hill isn't for the faint of heart and you should probably wear a helmet.

#8: Another great day trip is heading to Victoria Park in Truro. You will want to pack a lunch for this spot. Spend the day checking out the various waterfalls and make your way up Jacob's Ladder a time or too. It's a good way to have the kids burn off energy.

#9: Jackson just loves being in the water. There are a few really fun water parks he likes to visit. The first is the one near Halifax Shopping Centre, Westmount School Splash Pad, at 6700 Edward Arab Ave. The other is in Sackville at 71 First Lake Drive. It's the largest water park in the municipality.

#10: The Shubenacadie Provincial Wildlife Park makes a great day trip from Halifax. I recommend packing a lunch and having a picnic on the grounds there. It's a great way to get some exercise and fresh air and to learn about wildlife. Jackson really loves watching the otters.

Cruise, a Cape Bretoner, migrated to Halifax in 2000 and worked about every job possible before landing a gig as afternoon drive host at Hot Country 103.5. He's married to a stellar lady and he's not sure how that happened, but they have three wonderful kids together. In his spare time, he likes to make his own beer, play guitar, do wood work and playing around with his home studio. And he likes video games too.

HEALTH

- Dr. Allan Marble's List of the Top 10 Milestones in Medicine in Nova Scotia History

- A List of Nova Scotian Home Remedies From A to Z

- Laurie Lacey's List of Five Common Nova Scotian Ingredients Used in Home Remedies

- Dr. Allan Marble's List of the Top 10 Physicians and Surgeons in the History of Nova Scotia

Dr. Allan Marble's List of the Top 10 Milestones in Medicine in Nova Scotia History (In Chronological Order)

1846: First use of ether anaesthesia in surgery by Dr. Daniel M. Parker in Halifax

1868: Establishment of the Dalhousie University Faculty of Medicine

1869: First use of carbolic acid antiseptic in a surgical operation in Nova Scotia

1888: First Public Health Act passed by the Nova Scotia Legislature

1892: First School of Nursing training in Nova Scotia established at the Victoria General Hospital

1917: Response of Nova Scotia Doctors and Nurses and the American Hospital Units to treat the injured from the Halifax Explosion

1918: Outstanding work of Doctors William H. Hattie, Norman E.MacKay and Arthur C. Hawkins in protecting Nova Scotians during the Spanish Influenza

1943: First use of Penicillin in Nova Scotia

1958: Passing of the Nova Scotia Hospital Insurance Commission Act by the Nova Scotia Legislature.

1960: First use of Chlorpromazine in Nova Scotia.

Dr. Allan Marble is chair of the Medical History Society of Nova Scotia.

A List of Nova Scotian Home Remedies from A to Z

In the 18th century, the treatment of illnesses, disorders and diseases was not based on scientific fact but rather on the healing powers of natural agents and other homemade concoctions.

At first glance, these remedies may appear strange, ridiculous and very crude by modern standards. But today's generations have reaped the benefits of centuries of exhaustive research in the medical profession. Hundreds of years earlier, though, it was typical of medical personnel to use natural cures and remedies to treat the sick and the ailing.

Here's a list of some of the more unusual home cures:

ACNE (PIMPLES): Potatoes are not only good for eating, but also for treating ACNE. Wash your face with water and leave it a bit damp. Grate one raw potato and rub the pulp and juice onto your face. Let it dry for about 30 minutes and rinse with warm water.

ALLERGIES AND SINUSES: Add some crushed mint leaves to a cup of tea and drink.

ARTHRITIS: Chew on a piece of willow bark to relieve joint pain, particularly in the knees, back, hips and neck.

ATHLETE'S FOOT (THE DEMON FUNGUS): Urinate on your feet when you are in the shower the fungus will go away. Do this one to two times a day for a week. Obviously a doctor is not going to tell you to urinate on yourself but according to folklore, it does work.

BEDWETTING: Stir one-half teaspoon of dry mustard-seed powder in a cup of warm milk and have your child drink it one hour before going to bed.

BLACK EYE: Dip a teabag in water then place it in the freezer. Once the tea bag has frozen, place it on the black eye.

BLEEDING: Crush half an onion and mix with honey. Apply to the cut and leave in place for one hour.

BLOOD CLOTS: Mix together spinach leaves and one bulb each of pepper, garlic and cloves and then drink the mixture to help dissolve the blood clot.

BOILS: Take a thick slice of onion and place it directly on the boil. Wrap the onion with a cloth so that the heat of the onion reaches inside the skin. Remove after an hour and repeat this process four times a day.

BUG BITES AND STINGS: Crush two or three pieces of used charcoal and mix with the powder with just enough water to form a paste. Apply to the affected area and leave for 30 minutes, then wipe off with a wet cloth.

BURNS: Use three or four teabags, two cups of fresh mint leaves and four cups of boiling water. Strain liquid into a jar and allow to cool before using. Dab the mixture on burned skin with a cotton ball or washcloth.

CHAPPED LIPS: Collect a handful of rose petals from your garden and wash thoroughly in cool water. Soak the petals in milk for a few hours, then mash them into a thick paste and apply to your dry lips two to three times a day and every night before going to bed.

CHARLEY HORSE (LEG MUSCLE CRAMPS): If you have a charley horse, quickly plant your feet on a cold surface to remove the cramps.

CHICKEN POX: Cook several cups of fresh green peas. Drain but keep the water. Crush the peas into a paste and apply the paste to the affected area. Allow it dry for about one hour, then wash using the water in which the peas were cooked.

CONSTIPATION: Mix two teaspoons of dried dandelion leaves into a cup of hot water. Cover and let steep for about 10 minutes, then drink the tea. Do this up to three times a day.

CORNS AND CALLUSES: Soak a cotton ball or piece of cloth in vinegar and tape it to your corn or callus. Leave it on overnight. In the morning, rub the area with a file or pumice stone.

COUGHS AND COLDS: Boil a whole onion and drink the water once it cools. You can add a little butter and salt if the taste is unbearable.

CRAMPS AND DIARRHEA: Mix gin and warm water with a little sugar.

DANDRUFF: Mix two teaspoons of vinegar in a cup of beet juice. Massage the mixture into your scalp and leave it sit for about an hour, then rinse. Do this daily until the dandruff clears up.

DRUNKENNESS: Eat several slices of plain bread with nothing on them.

DRY AND CRACKED HANDS: Wash and dry our hands thoroughly, then apply vinegar. Put on a pair of soft gloves and leave them on overnight.

EARACHES: Squeeze the juice from a fresh onion, heat gently and put a few drops into the ear.

FEVER: Before going to bed, tie an uncooked fish (preferably mackerel) to the bottom of both feet and cover them with a sheet. Keep in place over night. In the morning, remove the fish and the fever will be gone.

FLU: Mix one teaspoon of dried thyme leaves in one cup of boiling water. Let steep for five minutes while inhaling the steam. Strain the tea, sweeten with honey and slowly sip.

HAIR GROWTH: Rub cow manure on your head once a day for an entire week will encourage your hair to grow.

HEADACHES: Rub peppermint oil on your forehead, temples or back of the neck.

HEARTBURN AND INDIGESTION: Peel and eat a raw potato as you would an apple; your indigestion will go away.

HAEMORRHOIDS: Place a warm, moist teabag on the haemorrhoid.

HICCUPS: Mix some lemon juice with water and drink the mixture.

HIGH BLOOD PRESSURE: Mix one-half teaspoon each of onion juice and honey and take it twice a day for one to two weeks.

HOT FLASHES: When the hot flash hits, tie a piece of salt pork to each of your feet and cover with socks or wrap in a cloth. Keep your feet covered until the hot flash passes.

INFECTION: Mix the white of an egg with the powdered dust of seashells, dried and powdered seaweed, goose grease and mouldy bread. Apply the paste to the infection.

INGROWN NAILS: Soak the nail in lukewarm water mixed with either salt or vinegar for about 20 minutes.

INSOMNIA: Make a warm compress using grated raw potatoes and warm water. Place the paste in a cloth and secure it to your forehead before going to bed.

ITCHING: Pat some mud on the affected area.

JOINT PAIN AND STIFFNESS: Drink tea made from dandelion leaves or throw a handful of fresh dandelion leaves into a salad.

LICE: Rinse your hair using a equal mix of water and white vinegar.

MEASLES: Boil sheep droppings and drink the "tea."

MEMORY LOSS: Put a quarter of teaspoon sage, rosemary or basil in a cup of boiling water. Steep for five minutes and then drink the mixture.

MORNING SICKNESS: Cut or grate some ginger root and pour hot water over it, then drink as a tea.

MUMPS: Make a thick paste from dry ginger and water and apply it on to the swollen area around the ears.

NAUSEA AND VOMITING: Steep one tablespoon of dry mint leaves in one cup of hot water for 30 minutes, strain and drink.

NOSEBLEEDS: Mix salt and baking soda in warm water. Slowly rinse your nostrils.

OILY HAIR: Mix two ounces of alcohol with two cups of water, rinse through your hair and allow to set for several minutes before washing. Take note that they also say that vodka is the preferred choice.

OILY SKIN: Whip one egg white, add the juice from half a lemon and mix it well. Apply the mixture on your face, leave it on for 15 minutes and then rinse it off with warm water.

PINKEYE: Before going to bed soak a small piece of white bread in milk and place it over you closed eye. Secure it over each eye and leave on over night. Remove in the morning.

POISON IVY: Mix equal parts of apple cider vinegar and water. Dab on the affected skin areas and allow to dry.

RASH AND SKIN IRRITATIONS: Get some fresh bean leaves from the garden and mash them until they get mushy and juicy. Next, apply the mush to the rash, cover with a sterile cloth and leave in place.

RAZOR BURN: Apply creamy peanut butter to the affected area for 10 to 15 minutes then wipe clean and follow by rubbing lemons or lemon juice and sprinkle salt on it. Immediately rinse and pat dry. Repeat if necessary.

RINGWORM: Make a paste by mixing shortening with cigarette or pipe ash and then apply it to the affected area.

SHINGLES: Make a lotion by mixing cold tea, a drop of honey, a drop of lemon juice and a drop of vinegar and apply to the affected areas.

SNORING: Add one drop of peppermint oil to a glass of cold water and gargle with the mixture.

SORE EYES (STY): Place a piece of uncooked pork over it.

SORE FEET: Grind some mustard seeds and add them to half a bucket of warm water. Soak your feet in the water for 10 to 15 minutes.

SORE MOUTH: Wash your mouth with the dirty water from the blacksmith's forge to cure cold and canker sores.

SORE THROAT: Tie a piece of salt herring around your throat at bedtime and leave it there all night.

SPIDER BITES: Crush several chrysanthemum flowers and smear the mush over the bite to stop the itching and swelling and reduce the chance of infection.

SPLINTERS: Place a slice of raw potato on the splinter such that the fleshy part touches the splinter and press the potato slice downwards; if the sliver pierces the slice, it can be lifted off easily.

STIFFNESS: Crush several bulbs of fresh ginger and massage into the affected joints.

STOMACH ACHES: Crush some willow bark into a fine powder and mix with water; drink the mixture.

SUNBURNS: Mix raw eggs in warm water and apply the mixture to affected areas.

TICK REMOVAL: Alcohol-based fuels, like gasoline, are also effective against ticks. Pour two tablespoons of gasoline in a container. Now, dip a cotton ball in it and place it on tick. Let it rest for at least three minutes. With this, ticks will get suffocated and can be easily removed with the help of tweezers.

TOOTHACHES: Place a piece of tobacco on the tooth.

URINARY OR BLADDER INFECTIONS: Eat raw cabbage several times a day.

VARICOSE VEINS: Apply apple-cider vinegar, just as it comes from the bottle, directly to the varicose veins at night and in the morning, to help shrink the veins in a matter of days. In addition to applying the vinegar to the veins, two teaspoonfuls of apple-cider vinegar added to a glass of water are also recommended twice a day.

VIRILITY: Make a juice from celery, apples and ginger and drink at least once a day.

WARTS: Rub a piece of pork rind or raw potato over it, wrap it in a piece of cloth and burry it out back.

WEIGHT LOSS: Add a handful of fresh or dried rose petals to about two cups of water in a pot. Place the pot on the stove, put in the rose petals and cover with water. Cover the pot with a tight fitting lid and simmer for 15 to 20 minutes or until the petals lose most of their colour. Strain the liquid into a glass jar and keep in the refrigerator for up to six days. Drink about half a cup of the water every morning on an empty stomach.

Laurie Lacey's List of Five Common Nova Scotian Ingredients Used in Home Remedies

#1. SALT: Common table salt had many uses in Lunenburg County folklore. My mother would fill a sock with salt, sew it shut, heat it in the oven of the old wood stove and use it as a salt pack to treat tooth ache or a swollen jaw due to an infected tooth. We'd hold the heated sock against the side of our face or take it to bed with us, sleeping with our cheek against the heated sock.

#2. VINEGAR: Vinegar (mostly apple-cider or white vinegar, although any type would suffice) had many uses in local folk medicine. We put it on fried potatoes for its flavour or to prevent stomach gas or indigestion from the fatty potatoes. It worked every time!

#3. PLANTAIN: One important local remedy for bee or wasp stings was plantain (Plantago major), known locally as "Pigs Ears." The leaves were rubbed until moist and applied to the sting.

#4. RED SOIL: The red ground was packed on the sting and held in place until the pain subsided. It was said to draw the poison from the sting area. We would pack it on the painful sting for a minute or so and then replace it with a fresh packing of ground or soil. It was quite effective.

#5. BLACKSTRAP MOLASSES: Molasses was used as a spring blood tonic in Lunenburg County and in many other areas of the Maritimes. It's rich in iron and other minerals.

Laurie Lacey is a specialist in Mi'kmaw plant medicines and ethnobotany. He is a naturalist, author and speaker on traditional plant medicines and nature therapy.

Dr. Allan Marble's List of the Top 10 Physicians and Surgeons in the History of Nova Scotia (In No Particular Order)

#1. DANIEL MCNEILL PARKER

#2. °ALEXANDER PETER REID

#3. EDWARD FARRELL

#4. WILLIAM H. HATTIE

#5. JOHN STEWART

#6. JOHN G. MACDOUGALL

#7. AVERY DEWITT

#8. CHESTER STEWART

#9. C. EDWIN KINLEY

#10. THOMAS J. MURRAY

Dr. Allan Marble is chair of the Medical History Society of Nova Scotia.

SPORTS

- Philip Croucher's List of the Top 10 NHLers to Come from Nova Scotia

- Bill Spurr's List of the 18 Toughest Golf Holes in Nova Scotia

- Patrick Hirtle's List of the Top Nova Scotian Athletes

Philip Croucher's List of the Top 10 NHLers to Come from Nova Scotia

It is great time for Nova Scotia hockey. Three players are among the best in the NHL today and are ranked in my top 10 NHLers to come from Nova Scotia. The trickle-down effect is that the next Sidney Crosbys, Nathan MacKinnons and Brad Marchands are probably not too far off. We are developing great players like never before. This is due in large part to the Quebec Major Junior Hockey League having two teams in Nova Scotia for the past two decades.

The elite junior league is showing kids that if you have talent and you work hard you can maybe one day play for the Halifax Mooseheads, Cape Breton Screaming Eagles or another team in the QMJHL. And if you are very, very good, you also can walk up on that stage like a Crosby and or MacKinnon and be taken first overall in the NHL draft. Putting together my top-four for this list was easy. Numbers five through 10 were more difficult and there is no right answer. Remember, it's not all about points. It's about impact, skill-level, longevity and being a champion.

One final note. I didn't consider Bobby Smith. While born in North Sydney, he moved as a baby to the Ottawa region and played all of his minor hockey there.

#1. SIDNEY CROSBY: A no-brainer. The star forward for the Pittsburgh Penguins and Cole Harbour native has done it all. He is one of the best 10 players to ever play in the National Hockey League with a skillset and knowledge few can match. His resume is outstanding — three Stanley Cups, two Conn Smythe Awards, two Olympic gold medals, more than 1,000 NHL points. The list could go on and on. He's a great ambassador for Nova Scotia hockey.

#2. AL MACINNIS: He'll be joined soon by Sidney Crosby — maybe others — but for now the former blueliner and hockey legend from Port Hood remains the only Nova Scotia player to be inducted into the Hockey Hall of Fame. There's good reason. MacInnis is one of the best defenceman to play in the NHL, finishing with more than 1,200 points and a Stanley Cup ring. He's best remembered for his cannon slapshot, one that goalies feared and one he fired with incredible accuracy.

#3. BRAD MARCHAND: Some love him. Others hate him. But there's no denying how good he is. The Hammonds Plains forward has developed into an NHL superstar. If he can avoid injuries and suspensions for undisciplined play, he could win a Hart Trophy as league MVP and/or the Art Ross Trophy for top league scorer before his career is done. Marchand is now that good. He's also a lot of fun to watch. A true personality, which is rare in today's game.

#4. NATHAN MACKINNON: Another star from Cole Harbour taken first overall in the NHL draft, MacKinnon has developed into an elite top-line centre and league star. The sky is the limit for Nathan and the best is yet to come. His drive to be great was on display when he led the Halifax Mooseheads to the QMJHL title and then the Memorial Cup in 2013. I suspect one day you'll see him hoisting the Stanley Cup in Cole Harbour, like his good friend Sidney.

#5. MIKE MCPHEE: This first four were easy. Now it starts getting tough. I'm going next with McPhee, a River Bourgeois forward who enjoyed an 11-year NHL career with the Montreal Canadiens and Dallas Stars. He finished with 200 goals and 399 points in 744 games. McPhee was a solid, versatile and dependable two-way forward and a Stanley Cup champion. One of the best from our province to lace up the skates.

#6. LOWELL MACDONALD: For those who saw him play, it was magic on ice. The New Glasgow forward played in more than 500 NHL games and during four seasons with the Pittsburgh Penguins in the 1970s amassed an impressive 134 goals and 290 points. Several injury-plagued years prevented MacDonald from being higher on my list but there's no arguing his place on the top 10.

#7. GLEN MURRAY: A pure goal scorer, this power forward from Bridgewater played in more than 1,000 NHL games and finished with 337 goals and 651 points. His best year during his 15-year career came with the Boston Bruins during the 2002-03 season, when he found the back of the net a whopping 44 times. In fact, Murray scored at least 20 goals in a season seven times. He also hit the double-figure mark for goals 13 times.

#8. AL MACNEIL: Known for being a great coach as well, one can't forget the accomplishments on the ice for this Cape Breton hockey great. More than 500 NHL games as a defenceman during the 1950s and 1960s, a time when there were six teams, not 30. MacNeil finished with only 15 goals but was steady, dependable and could play very physically.

#9. NORM FERGUSON: He played in fewer than 300 NHL games, but this skilled forward from Sydney left an impression, scoring 34 goals and 20 assists as a rookie with the Oakland Seals. He went on to record double-digit goal totals the next three seasons, before deciding to leave the NHL for what was then the more lucrative World Hockey Association.

#10. COLIN WHITE: Tough, dependable and a character-type guy. He played in almost 800 NHL games, all but 54 of which with the New Jersey Devils, where he won two Stanley Cups. He never scored more than five goals in a season but he was there to make life tough on opposing forwards. There are few who did it better.

Philip Croucher lives in Bedford and is the author of the best-selling book Road to the NHL. *He's also worked as a journalist in Nova Scotia for the past 25 years and is the Halifax bureau chief of StarMetro.*

Bill Spurr's List of the 18 Toughest Golf Holes in Nova Scotia

When Leon Carter won the first of his four Nova Scotia amateur golf championships on a windy, hard-baked Hartlen Point track, he was asked just how challenging it had been. "I'm a member at Dundee," he said. "Not much is tough compared to that."

Carter was right that day in 2000, and he still is. Dundee is known for its rigour (as one of my playing partners said after we finished there, "not a level stance on the course"), but is by no means the only place where you need to bring your A game. The Links at Brunello is above-average difficult for any average golfer and I once played in a scramble at Granite Springs with a guy who bought 18 balls in the pro shop before his round, then got a dozen more at the turn.

In an effort to identify the 18 toughest holes in Nova Scotia, we canvassed golf-course employees across the province, staff and customers at Golf Central and the people we play with. One caveat: we chose one first hole, one second hole and so on. As soon as we started talking about this idea, there was instant debate about whether Northumberland Links or Clare had the toughest No. 5 and which par-three second hole — Digby's or Brightwood's — was most likely to result in a double bogey.

Hole No. 1

#1. AMHERST GOLF CLUB: From the club: "#1, also the #1 handicap hole, is a 568 yard double dog-leg par 5 which plays to a very narrow fairway with trees on both sides. It's aptly named Eye-Opener. The conservative player hits an iron off the tee. A long drive to the left will find a steep embankment and to the right are trees, tall grass and bushes. The fairway opens up after the second shot and plays down a slight incline to a bunkered green. The green has three tiers and if you are left or long, you have to chip back up the hill to get on the green."

#2. LEPORTAGE GOLF CLUB: "It's a good thing the view on the second hole is nice, almost makes you forget the first hole," says one nomination. Also receiving votes: Bluenose Golf Club, Highlands Links Golf Course

Hole No. 2

#1. DIGBY PINES GOLF RESORT: If you can accurately hit a high, softly landing draw to a small target with a mid-iron, this hole isn't that scary. But short is wet, long is on a steep bank of thick rough and double is common.

#2. ABERCROMBIE COUNTRY CLUB: "If you are lucky enough to have (an approach) into the slanted three-level green, you will have to challenge a large pond and another small but deep trap in front," a member says. Also receiving votes: Sherwood Golf and Country Club, Brightwood Golf and Country Club

Hole No. 3

#1. THE LINKS AT BRUNELLO: From the white tees, 572 yards, so a three-shot hole for anyone, especially considering the elevated green that adds a club or two to the approach. From the tee, the landing area is as narrow as it looks, and firm, with woods left and a marsh left. The second shot requires navigating traps on both sides of the fairway and a deep, massive bunker guards the front of a huge, undulating green. A brute of a par 5.

#2. BERWICK HEIGHTS GOLF COURSE: "From the right, where most tee shots end up, you have a blind shot over a bunker with trees and a hazard to the right. Most people bail out to the left on the hill, leaving a very difficult chip shot. Those that hit the green find it difficult to stay on because of the slope," says club president Dan Keddy. Also receiving votes: Oakfield Golf and Country Club

Hole No. 4

#1. OLD ASHBURN: "It's a very long 395 uphill, and the fairway slants so you don't get a good roll, it's almost always into the wind and it's got the toughest green on the course. Other than that, it's a walk in the park," says a 40-year Ashburn member who's a 10 handicapper. "I haven't parred it this year."

#2. THE LINKS AT BRUNELLO: "The toughest hole to make par on in the province," one regular says. Also receiving votes: Northumberland Links, Truro Golf and Country Club, Highlands Links Golf Course, River Oaks Golf Club

Hole No. 5

#1. NORTHUMBERLAND LINKS: Named the Grim Reaper to acknowledge the 18th-century cemetery adjacent to the fairway, and also because this par 5 is where promising rounds go to die. A creek runs the length of the right side, there are woods left and large mounds guard the front of a sloped green that is typically Northumberland hard.

#2. CLARE GOLF AND COUNTRY CLUB: Formerly a par 5 and now the "toughest par 4 I ever played," a member says of this uphill hole, with OB all the way up the left hand side, and a tee shot over water to a side hill stance for the approach to a long, narrow sloped green. "The cards says the hole plays 430 yards, but I think it's 455." Also receiving votes: The Lakes Golf Club, Brightwood

Hole No. 6

#1. GLEN ARBOUR GOLF COURSE: A former member describes the longest and hardest hole at Glen Arbour like this: "A bit of a dog leg right off the tee. Even if you hit a good drive you now are on a downhill lie, and must hit a long shot across a creek with scrub on both sides, before an approach uphill to a horseshoe-shaped green."

#2. THE LINKS AT PENN HILLS: Hard to choose a target area from the tee on this par 4 that has a creek crossing the fairway diagonally right where a good drive would come to rest. "A bad hole, but very tough," says one writer. Also receiving votes: Digby, The Lakes, Cabot Links

Hole No. 7

#1. HIGHLANDS LINKS: The runaway winner, getting more votes than any other hole in Nova Scotia. Sample comments: "If you are on the wrong side of the green, two putts will be almost impossible." "Bunkers all around as you approach the green. I have brought my bucket and shovel to each and every one of them." "If you par this hole, you have had five outstanding shots." "Not only does it take three remarkable shots to get on the green, but the green itself is tremendously tough. I play it as a par 6 and hope."

#2. PARRSBORO GOLF CLUB: How's this 209-yard par 3 sound? "Apple tree on right front of green surface means you can be on the green and still have an unplayable lie. Over the green slightly lands you in an (orchard) if you are lucky enough to stay in bounds. Slope of green, once you are actually on the green, makes putting no bargain, and three putts are common. Wind blows strongly off the Bay of Fundy constantly with the changing tides." Also receiving votes: Avon Valley Golf and Country Club

Hole No. 8

#1. AVON VALLEY GOLF AND COUNTRY CLUB: Commonly heard on the tee here: "I don't have this club." The 200-yard shot is both downhill and to an elevated green at the same time, with a mucky pond left and a slope right that funnels errant shots under a tree. At first glance, this hole doesn't look that hard, but it is.

#2. RIVER HILLS GOLF AND COUNTRY CLUB: If you hit a big enough drive on this 395-

yard par 4, you might get to the crest of the hill and have a view down to a tiny green. Also receiving votes: Cabot Links, Le Portage

Hole No. 9

#1. NEW ASHBURN: No problem here. Just bomb a drive straight down the middle about 290, crush a hybrid straight down the middle a couple of hundred more yards, then hit a nice soft wedge to a spot on the two-tier lightning quick green where you can lag one up to tap-in range.

#2. BRIGHTWOOD: The big trench in front of the tilted green comes after a drive that first has to elude thick and wide branches on both sides of the fairway, and a lengthy approach shot. Also receiving votes: Bluenose

Hole No. 10

#1. GLEN LOVAT: Downhill and not that long at 413 yards, this quirky par 4 gets its teeth from four ponds, including two in front of the green, to go with a pair of bunkers.

#2. CHESTER GOLF CLUB: If you can land a three-wood or hybrid approach on an elevated green and make it stop quickly, this hole gets much easier. Also receiving votes: Cabot Cliffs

Hole No. 11

#1. CHESTER GOLF CLUB: A visually confusing target area off the tee, along with soft earth and thick rough in front of an elevated green, combine to make par elusive here.

#2. MOUNTAIN GOLF CLUB: A long par 5 with a fairway starts wide and inviting. But a water hazard crosses the entire fairway where most players like to lay up. That leaves a long approach to a green protected by trees and a ravine. Also receiving votes: Dundee, Brightwood, Oakfield, Paragon, Hartlen Point Forces Golf Club, Highlands Links

Hole No. 12

#1. CABOT CLIFFS: "Maybe the toughest par 3 in the province," says a golfer who makes an annual pilgrimage. Any par 3 where you're hitting your driver off the tee is obviously difficult.

#2. THE LAKES: A par 4 into the prevailing wind with an uphill approach to a small, narrow green. Also receiving votes: Digby Pines, Osprey Ridge Golf Club

Hole No. 13

#1. FOX HOLLOW GOLF CLUB: If you're above this severely tilted green, you'll be very pleased with bogey. Or, as one member says, "you're done." To get there, a righthander has the ball below his feet for an approach shot with a wood or hybrid. It's 420 yards, usually into the wind, and there's water.

#2. BRIGHTWOOD: The hole's configuration keeps golfers on adjacent #14 alert for errant shots, and the second shot is a blind one to a shallow green. Also receiving votes: Clare, Bell Bay, Eden

Hole No. 14

#1. CABOT CLIFFS: The only golf course that appears twice on this list, appropriately because it was recently named the best course in Canada. Another par 3, most notable for the large rock hump that sits surrounded by bunkers. The rock was discovered while earth-moving was done and the designers decided to leave it there.

#2. HARTLEN POINT FORCES GOLF CLUB: Long and almost always into the wind coming off the ocean, with a water hazard the length of the hole on the left and a small green that's tough to hit in regulation. Also receiving votes: Penn Hills

Hole No. 15

#1. HARTLEN POINT FORCES GOLF CLUB: One member says, "I've seen full drivers and pitching wedges find the green. It's a bit windy. The entire left side is out of bounds and it happily accepts hooks, especially those accentuated by a headwind."

#2. NEW ASHBURN: One Ashburn member used to get home from a round to have his father ask him not what he shot, but what he had on 15. At 410 yards from the whites, a lot tougher on the course than it looks on the scorecard. Also receiving votes: Brookfield, Amherst

Hole No. 16

#1. KEN-WO: Greenwood and Northumberland also have exceedingly tough 16s, but most voters favoured the par 4 at Ken-Wo. A huge bank guarding the green makes par nearly impossible if you don't have a big sweeping draw in your arsenal.

#2. NORTHUMBERLAND LINKS: An ugly hazard in front of the green that swallows long approach shots makes double bogey common. The view of the water and PEI eases the pain. Also receiving votes: Cabot Cliffs

Hole No. 17

#1. PARAGON GOLF AND COUNTRY CLUB: Just average in length, 159 from the whites and 181 from the blues, but three strategically placed pot bunkers mean tee shots have to fly all the way to the green. The flag on this kidney-shaped green is often tucked behind the bunkers and on the other side a ridge funnels balls off the carpet.

#2. BELL BAY GOLF CLUB: "A tremendous test of nerve," reads one submission about this par 3. "All that stands between tee and green is a chasm. The hole grabs your attention, because short, left or right are quickly eaten up by Mother Nature." Also receiving votes: Glen Arbour, Glen Lovat Golf Club

Hole No. 18

#1. OAKFIELD GOLF AND COUNTRY CLUB: After one of the longer walks in the province, golfers often arrive at 18 fatigued, but there's no respite. Describing "this beast" of a hole, one of the club's best players says "It's tough, but fair. There's nothing quirky about it. Hit a good drive, and a good second, and you have a fair chance. Hit a poor shot, and you will certainly be penalized."

#2. SEAVIEW GOLF AND COUNTRY CLUB: Hopefully your swing is grooved by this point in your round, because there is little margin for error off the tee in either direction. Also receiving votes: Amherst, New Ashburn

Written by Bill Spurr and originally published in The Chronicle Herald *on September 8, 2017. Reprinted with permission.*

Patrick Hirtle's List of the Top Nova Scotian Athletes

The task of crafting a list of the top 10 of *anything* is challenging. Putting individuals or events in their proper context and then assigning them a number based upon their importance is, without question, a subjective task and one that is widely open to debate — indeed, that's why we do it and why we're so quick to read lists and gleefully pick them apart.

The challenge, when it comes to a list of the top 10 Nova Scotian athletes, then, is made all the more difficult by the fact that not all sporting accomplishments are created equal. Equally difficult to measure is the cultural impact of athletes and their endeavours across time and space. Success on the field or on the ice is one thing, but how do amateur athletes measure up against professionals? How does the significance of a great pugilist at the turn of the century compare to that of a dominant goal scorer or paddler 70 years later?

After weighing my own knowledge against the input of several colleagues familiar with the history of sport in Nova Scotia, I found myself staring at a list of 24 potential candidates — each worthy of consideration. Stripping the names away to get down to a final 10 was almost painful. So, in presenting this list, please understand that I expect you to disagree. After all, context for sporting success and cultural impact is all in the eye of the beholder.

#1. SIDNEY CROSBY: Before Sidney Crosby burst into the hockey consciousness of this country, sometime around 2005, you could've had a pretty spirited debate about just who, exactly, is the most successful athlete to come out of Nova Scotia. Now over the age of 30, Sid the Kid had grown up — he's become the pre-eminent hockey player of his generation, leading the NHL's Pittsburgh Penguins to four Stanley Cup Finals, including three titles in 2009, 2016 and 2017. Beyond that, Crosby has also won multiple gold medals representing Canada on the international stage, including "the golden goal" in Vancouver to win the 2010 Olympic hockey gold in a thrilling overtime win against the arch rivals of the era, Team USA. It's awe-inspiring to consider what Crosby might have done in his career had he not lost a significant amount of playing time to concussion-related injuries. Even with the time lost, Crosby's career performance has thrust him into consideration as one of the Top 5 greatest NHL players *of all time*.

#2. SAM LANGFORD: Samuel Langford hailed from tiny Weymouth Falls, but would come to make a name for himself boxing out of Boston in the early years of the 20th century. He was once described by American sports broadcasting leader ESPN as "the greatest boxer you've never heard of." Langford was the World Coloured Heavyweight Champion a total of five times. His career record was 180-29-39 and included an impressive 128 wins by knockout. Despite these successes, Langford never got a shot at the world heavyweight title. Racial discrimination was rampant in boxing during the era. Ironically, the heavyweight title-holder for much of the period was a black boxer, Jack Johnson, who preferred to fight white fighters because of the bigger purses. Langford and Johnson only ever fought head-to-head once, in 1906, for the World Coloured title, prior to Johnson claiming the World Heavyweight belt. The match went 15 rounds and ended in a decision for Johnson, despite many observers claiming that Langford should have been declared the winner. It's widely believed that Johnson refused to fight Langford again because he was the greatest threat to his title. Langford was enshrined in Canada's Sports Hall of Fame in 1955.

#3. SUE HOLLOWAY: Sue Holloway's athletic accomplishments extended well beyond the podium. She was a pioneer. In 1976, the Halifax native became not only the first Canadian, but also the first woman, to compete in two Olympic games in the same year, competing in canoe sprint in Montreal (where she finished fourth) and again in Innsbruck, Austria in cross-country skiing (her 4x5km relay team finished seventh). Holloway was also selected as the flag bearer for the Canadian contingent that was to attend the 1980 Games in Moscow, but was denied that opportunity because of the boycott by western nations. In 1984, Holloway would twice land on the podium, earning silver and bronze medals in the K2 and K4 canoe-kayak sprints. She was elected to the Canadian Olympic Hall of Fame in 1986.

#4. AL MACINNIS: For more than 20 years, with his booming slap shot and a Stanley Cup title, Port Hood's Al MacInnis terrorized goaltenders in the National Hockey League and was perennially among the top defenders in the game. A first- or second-team all-star seven times, MacInnis made two appearances in the Stanley Cup Finals with the Calgary Flames, winning the title and earning Conn Smythe Trophy honours as playoff MVP in 1989. MacInnis also twice represented Canada at the Winter Olympics, including having a role with the 2002 gold-medal-winning team in Salt Lake City, which ended Canada's 50-year Olympic hockey gold drought.

#5. COLLEEN JONES: Colleen Jones began her curling career at the age of 14 and, more than 40 years later, she's still at home on the sheets. In 1982, at just 22 years of age, she was the youngest skip in history to lead a team to a Canadian women's curling title. Between 1982 and 2004, she would win the Scotties Tournament of Hearts six times, losing in the gold-medal game on two other occasions. Internationally, while she never realized her dream of getting to represent Canada at the Olympics, Jones won world titles in 2001 in Lausanne and 2004 in Galve. Most recently, in 2017, she claimed gold at the 2017 World Senior Curling Championships in Lethbridge, Alberta.

#6. AILEEN MEAGHER: Born in Halifax in 1910, Aileen Meagher was a member of the Canadian Olympic women's 4x100 relay team that claimed bronze at the 1936 Berlin Olympics. Prior to that, she had extensively distinguished herself on the track in competition, winning a gold medal, three silvers and a bronze in races during the 1934 and 1938 British Empire Games. In 1935, she was presented with the Velma Springstead Trophy in recognition as Canada's outstanding female athlete. Meagher was inducted in the Canadian Olympic Hall of Fame in 1965.

#7. JOHNNY MILES: Johnny Miles was born in West Yorkshire, England, but before he turned 11 he found himself in Sydney Mines, Nova Scotia, working in the coalmines to help support his family. As a teenager, it became clear that Miles had a talent for running, winning several local races. According to legend, he trained by running behind a horse and wagon while making grocery deliveries throughout the countryside. Miles' athletic career came to be defined by his accomplishments at the Boston Marathon, where he twice won the event in 1926 and again in 1929. What made the first victory all the more impressive was that he had never before run a race greater than 10 miles. Miles also subsequently represented Canada at the 1928 and 1932 Olympics.

#8. ROCKY JOHNSON (WAYDE DOUGLAS BOWLES): The case for Rocky Johnson is as large as the man himself. The Amherst native, in subsequent years, has become more widely known as the link that connects his famous wrestler-turned-movie-star son, Dwayne "The Rock" Johnson, to Nova Scotia. But, being much more than merely the man who lit the flame for The Rock, Rocky Johnson himself was a professional wrestler of distinction, who was in the industry for more than 27 years. He was one-half of the first Black wrestling tag team (along with partner Tony Atlas) to be crowned World Wrestling Federation champions in November of 1983.

#9. ANGUS WALTERS: There are those who will argue that Angus Walters does not belong on this list because he was not, in the true sense of the word, an athlete. However, I would counter that Walters' role as captain of *Bluenose* during the heady days of the International Fishermen's Race in the 1920s demanded unmatched skill and command. Moreover, Walters had to task and lead his crew in decisive victories over American counterparts, which, ultimately, became the stuff of legend and has had a profound cultural impact on Canada, the ripples of which still linger and cruise along coastal Nova Scotia in the summer months.

#10. NANCY GARAPICK: Halifax native Nancy Garapick was a swimming phenom. At just 13 years of age, she set a world record in the 200 m backstroke, clocking in at 2:16:33. One year later, she would represent Canada at the 1976 Summer Olympics in Montreal, where she claimed bronze medals in both the 100-metre and 200-metre backstroke events. She was inducted in the Canada Sports Hall of Fame in 2008.

Patrick Hirtle is a communications professional with a passion for writing, research and the history of Atlantic Canada. He holds a Master's degree in history from the University of New Brunswick and for a decade he wrote a regular sports column while working as a reporter/photographer at the weekly Bridgewater Bulletin. *Patrick later traversed the gulf between print and radio by serving as an on-air co-host of a weekly sports-talk show on CKBW for five years.*

POLITICS

MAN OF THE PEOPLE

Michael de Adder's List of the Top Nova Scotians that a Political Cartoonist Likes to Draw

An editorial cartoon, also known as a political cartoon, is a drawing containing a commentary expressing the artist's opinion. Obviously, then, an artist who writes and draws such images is known as an editorial cartoonist. They typically combine artistic skill and satire in order to question authority and draw attention to the issues of the day.

Nova Scotia is blessed to boast several talented and well-respected political cartoonists. One of the province's best working today is the award-winning Michael de Adder. Following is de Adder's list of his favourite top 10 political figures he has drawn over the years and why, specifically what characteristics stand out about them.

#1. HALIFAX MAYOR WALTER FITZGERALD: I made a name for myself drawing this mayor. His whole character made him a caricature on his own.

#2. PREMIER JOHN BUCHANAN: Great comb over, old-time pork-barrel premier.

#3. RODNEY MACDONALD: Not the most politically astute premier we've had.

#4. RUSSELL MACLELLAN: Big nose, at least to cartoonists.

#5. GERALD REGAN: He was kind of creepy. (I only drew him as a defendant.)

#6. DARRELL DEXTER: Chubby cheeks.

#7. JOHN HAMM: Tall, old country doctor.

#8. STEPHEN MCNEIL: Angry eyebrows.

#9. DON CAMERON: White bowl-cut hair.

#10. JOHN SAVAGE: White hair, large glasses, big smile.

Michael de Adder has won the American Association for Editorial Cartooning Golden Spike Award and has been nominated for a Reuben. In addition to The Chronicle Herald, *de Adder draws for the* Toronto Star *and is the cartoonist of record for* The (Parliament) Hill Times. *His work has appeared in the* Chicago Tribune, Vanity Fair, The Guardian *and* The New York Times, *among many others. He is the author of four bestselling books including* You Might Be From Nova Scotia If ... *and* You Might Be From Canada If ....

Graham Steele's List of the Top 10 Nova Scotian Provincial Politicians Since 1945

#1. ROBERT L. STANFIELD: MLA 1949-67, premier 1956–1967. Progressive Conservative icon. As premier, increased his party's majority in every election.

#2. ANGUS L. MACDONALD: MLA and premier 1933–1940, 1945–54. Liberal icon. His time as premier was broken only by wartime service as MP and federal cabinet minister.

#3. ALEXA MCDONOUGH: MLA 1981-1995, provincial NDP leader 1980-1995. NDP icon. Feisty trailblazer.

#4. JOHN BUCHANAN: MLA 1967-1990, premier 1978-1990. The consummate Main Street politician. Led PCs to four consecutive majorities. Legacy tarnished by financial woes.

#5. JOHN HAMM: MLA 1993-2006, premier 1999-2006. Let the PCs believe in themselves again after the crushing defeat of 1993. Might be higher if he had not retired as premier after only six years.

#6. PETER M. NICHOLSON: MLA 1956-1978, finance minister 1970-78. Set the gold standard for ministers. Smart, respected.

#7. PAUL MACEWAN: MLA 1970-2003. Eccentric, iconoclastic, but a fighter for his constituents, and his constituents loved him for it. Elected nine straight times.

#8. BILL GILLIS: MLA 1970-1998, cabinet minister 1970-78 and 1993-98. Held tough portfolios in Savage government. Respected by colleagues, loved by constituents.

#9. MAUREEN MACDONALD: MLA 1998-2016, cabinet minister 2009-2013, interim NDP leader 2013-16. Held senior portfolios in Dexter government. Did every part of an MLA's job well.

#10. GUY BROWN: MLA 1974-1998, cabinet minister 1976-78 and 1993-96. The epitome of the constituency politician. Big heart.

Graham Steele's List of the Top 10 Federal Politicians from Nova Scotia since 1945

#1. ALLAN J. MACEACHEN: MP 1953-58, 1962-84, cabinet minister 1963-1979, 1980-1984. Shrewd political sense. Valued adviser to succession of Liberal prime ministers.

#2. ROBERT L. STANFIELD: MP 1967-1979, federal PC leader 1967-1976. Frequently referred to as "the greatest Prime Minister Canada never had." Highly respected, but couldn't beat Pierre Trudeau.

#3. JAMES LORIMER ILSLEY: MP 1926-1948, cabinet minister 1935-1948. Federal finance minister during most of the Second World War. Later chief justice of Nova Scotia.

#4. PETER MACKAY: MP 1997-2015, leader of the federal PC party 2003, cabinet minister 2006-15. Led the federal PCs into merger with Reform Party to create the Conservative Party. Held senior cabinet posts in Harper government.

#5. FLORA MACDONALD: MP 1972-88, federal cabinet minister 1979-80, 1984-88. Consummate political organizer. Represented Kingston in the House of Commons, but makes this list for being born and raised in Nova Scotia.

#6. ALEXA MCDONOUGH: MP 1997-2008, federal NDP leader 1995-2003. One of the few Nova Scotians to serve as a federal party leader in the modern era. Never lost the fire.

#7. GEORGE NOWLAN: MP 1948-1965, federal cabinet minister 1957-1963. Also MLA (1926-33). Known as a hard worker and good constituency MP. Succeeded in office by son Pat Nowlan (MP 1965-1993).

#8. ROBERT (BOB) WINTERS: MP 1945-57, 1965-68, federal cabinet minister 1948-57, 1965-68. Almost became prime minister in 1968, but finished second to Pierre Trudeau in Liberal leadership contest.

#9. BILL CASEY: MP 1988-1993, 1997-2009, 2015- . Best known for taking a stand for Nova Scotia against his own government in 2007. In the 2008 federal election, he achieved the rare feat of being elected in a landslide as an Independent.

#10. CLARRIE GILLIS: MP 1940-1957. While representing Cape Breton South for the CCF, Gillis was a passionate, colourful champion of labour and social rights.

These lists were compiled by Graham Steele, MLA 2001-13, provincial cabinet minister 2009-13 and author of What I Learned About Politics *(2014) and* The Effective Citizen *(2017).*

NATURE AND THE ENVIRONMENT

- Lowell R. DeMond's List of the 10 Most Popular Sports Fish Found in Nova Scotia

- Andrew Hebda's List of the 10 Most Unusual or Rare Zoological Discoveries Made in Nova Scotia

- Environment Canada's List of the Top 12 Weather Events in Recent Nova Scotia History

- Donna Barnett's List of the Top 10 Beaches in Nova Scotia

- Allan Billard's List of the Top 10 Waterfalls in Nova Scotia

- Sandra Phinney's List of 10 Favourite Natural Spaces in Nova Scotia

- David Currie's List of the Top 10 Birds that You are Likely to Find in Nova Scotia

- Laurie Lacey's List of 10 Favourite Berry Plants Native to Nova Scotia

Lowell R. DeMond's List of the 10 Most Popular Sports Fish Found in Nova Scotia

First, a word of caution. If you have never fished, you should carefully consider whether or not it is wise for you to start. There is a genuine belief that once you start, you are addicted, and there is no known cure! Nova Scotia is a great place to fish. It has 7,600 km of saltwater coastline, 6,700 lakes and 100 rivers, which offer a wide variety of sport fishing for both beginners and experienced anglers. As the air and water temperatures warm up, spring and summer are the best and most productive seasons to fish. In Nova Scotia, it is also possible to fish in the fall and winter.

Sport fishing can be enjoyed by everyone and it is an important industry for the province. In 2016 it generated more than $58 million. There are many sports fishing items to spend money on, some of which include a license, rod, reel, line, rubber boots, raincoat, gloves, black fly and mosquito repellant, lunch kit... the list goes on. Once you become addicted you might want to move up to a higher class of angler and buy a fishing vest, fish with flies instead of bait, waders (to replace the rubber boots), graphite rod (to replace your alder pole) and a hardier reel. Now that you are now ready for the big leagues, you can buy a canoe, or a boat with a motor, and a trailer to transport them. Oh, I almost forgot to tell you. It's also possible to fish with the minimum: an alder pole, a short piece of line, a hook, a tin can to carry your worms and a camera to photograph your prize!

What can you fish for in Nova Scotia? There are at least 17 different fish available in the freshwater lakes and rivers. Below are a list of nine of the most angled for and a few lines about each. I have included one ocean fish, which can be angled from Nova Scotia`s coast.

#1. ATLANTIC SALMON: This fish was a major food source for the Mi'kmaq dating back thousands of years. The first European anglers who settled here fished for the Atlantic salmon as early as the 1600s. Although there are still a few rivers in Nova Scotia where the Atlantic salmon can be angled, it is only a hook-and-release season. The only legal way a salmon can be fished is with a single barbless artificial fly. This fish spends part of its life in the Atlantic Ocean and the rest in the river, where it spawns. It is labelled a cold-water fish and is considered an endangered species. A special license is required to angle for the Atlantic salmon. Changes are made frequently to the seasons and rivers where it can be fished. This information is obtainable from the Department of Fisheries and Oceans. If you hook an Atlantic salmon, you will have no doubt that you've had a bite. Once hooked, it's like a silver bullet. You will need a good reel and plenty of line to land it.

#2. SPECKLED TROUT: The speckled trout is Nova Scotia's provincial fish. They are found in small ponds, brooks, lakes and rivers and in salt-water estuaries. These fish feed on a variety of insects, leeches, small fish (often called minnows) and amphibians. The speckled trout is a very colourful fish, green or a dark brown with a black back. They also have light-coloured worm-like markings on their backs. On their sides are red spots, surrounded by blue circles and many light yellow spots.

After spending the winter at the bottom of a lake or a still water brook they emerge to the running water of brooks and rivers to gorge. During this time they are easy to catch with bait or a lure. When the water temperature rises and the wing flies begin to hatch on the water, trout become very active and visible and almost appear to be playing a game by jumping for flies (stone, caddis and may flies). This period lasts about two weeks and the skilled fly fisher has a field day. At around the end of June, when the water becomes warmer, the trout leave the running water and migrate to a cool spring at the bottom of a lake. There they will remain until almost spawning time in October. A license is required to fish for speckled trout, and the bag limit is five fish a day. Speckled trout can't be kept from in September.

#3. RAINBOW TROUT: The rainbow trout, also known as the steelhead trout, is native of Canada's west coast and was introduced to Nova Scotia around 1930. Almost all of the rainbow trout angled in Nova Scotia are reared in hatcheries. The Nova Scotia government provides data on where stocking takes place. It is easy to identify a rainbow trout. Their backs range from dark-brown to a dark-blue. Below this they have pinkish bands running the length of their bodies. There are black spots on their back fins and tails. A license is required to fish for them. Special management areas have special regulations and these are spelled out in the angler's handbook. There are some lakes in Nova Scotia where winter fishing for rainbow trout is permitted.

#4. BROWN TROUT: Brown trout are another species that was introduced in Nova Scotia, during the late 1920s. It was believed to be a hardier fish than our speckled trout that would survive the high water temperatures of our deforested streams. Although this appeared to be true, there were instances when brown trout were introduced into lakes containing speckled trout. The latter species gradually declined in numbers and in some cases disappeared. Brown trout range in colour. Some are largely silver with relatively few spots on the belly; some have medium-sized spots surrounded by lighter halos; and some brown trout have red spots. Brown trout can be difficult to catch. They like cover and are easily spooked. There are some waters in Nova Scotia where brown trout can be fished at night.

#5. WHITE PERCH: Open season for white perch coincides with an open season for sport fish, trout or smallmouth bass. They have silver bodies, a dark grayish back and a white belly. The dorsal fin has spines and it can be difficult to take off a hook. They are good to eat and fun to catch.

#6. AMERICAN SHAD: This fish has sharp scales on its stomach and its chest is like a saw. Its body is thin from side to side. Their backs are shiny blue and their bellies are white. They live in the ocean but spawn in freshwater rivers and lakes. On the average, they weigh about 2.5 kg. Females are three times larger than males and can weigh up to 5.4 kg. They too are good to eat and fun to catch. A good rod and reel with ample line is required.

#7. YELLOW PERCH: The yellow perch has a yellow body with dark black vertical stripes on its sides. The open season for fishing is the same as listed above for white perch. As well, it has a bag limit of 25 fish. It is easy to catch and generally likes bait, worms, corn or other meat scrap, and small lures. In Nova Scotia they rarely grow larger than 12 inches, (30 cm). Yellow perch are good to eat and make excellent fish chowder.

#8. SMALL MOUTH BASS: Small mouth bass were introduced for sport fishing to Yarmouth County in 1942 by the Nova Scotia government. At first they were introduced to only a small number of lakes. With small mouth bass angling programs being shown regularly on TV, illegal introduction escalated to enhance sport fishing and by 2008 they were reported found in 188 lakes.

Today, it is illegal to introduce any live fish into the waters of the province. The small mouth bass is a sandy-yellow colour and has red eyes; the body has dark-brown vertical bands. It differs from white perch in that it lacks the long horizontal band on its side. This fish is easy to catch with bait, lures and streamer artificial flies. It is powerful and puts up a real fight once hooked. It can be found in both rivers and lakes. The small mouth bass is considered an invasive species. Its introduction has raised a red flag because of its insatiable desire to eat the native fish. To address this difficulty the Nova Scotia government, angling groups and the Mi'kmaq community are collaboratively attempting to develop effective management strategies.

#9. CHAIN PICKEREL: The chain pickerel is an invasive species that was illegally introduced in Nova Scotia around 1945. Now, in 2018, with illegal introductions, it is found in almost all counties of Nova Scotia. This fish likes shallow warm water, cover and in winter months is active in deeper water. It eats other fish, rodents and amphibians. It will sometimes resort to cannibalism. Chain pickerel rely on their sight and explosive speed to attack and kill with their large, sharp teeth. Their narrow bodies are about 40-50-cm long. Their snouts are long and their dorsal fins are just slightly ahead of their v-shaped tails. The name chain pickerel comes from a chain-like pattern found on their sides. They are bright green in colour but black on their backs and fins. They have long, flat heads with small, hook-like teeth in the roof of their mouths, and long canine teeth at the sides of their mouths. They are easy to catch and will attack almost any bait, streamer flies or lures. Anglers should only attempt to remove a hook using pliers. Never put a finger in a chain pickerel's mouth. The Nova Scotia Anglers Handbook states: "Chain pickerel negatively impact native fish communities through direct predation and altering food webs. It is illegal to introduce chain pickerel in provincial waters or possess them live." They are, however, edible.

#10. OCEAN MACKEREL: The ocean mackerel is a fun fish to catch along the ocean shores of Nova Scotia. The best angling times are late summer and autumn. This fish has a blue-green colour with wavy black bars on its back. The lower part of its body is white. It grows to about 17 inches (42 cm) and weighs about two pounds. It has a streamlined body that narrows toward the tail, which is v-shaped. A good place to angle for this fish is off of fishing wharfs and breakwaters but it can also be fished along the shore from a boat. Angling gear to fish for mackerel includes a spinning rod and reel, red feathers and lures. It has an oily, rich flavour, great for smoking and barbecuing.

Lowell R. DeMond was born in 1936 and raised on a small farm in South Brookfield. In 1956, after completing training as a meteorological technician in Toronto, he was employed by the Canadian government for a two-year tour of duty at Eureka Weather station, 600 miles from the North Pole. He attended Acadia University and the University of New Brunswick, where he received a Bachelor of Arts and a Bachelor of Education respectively. For the next 15 years, he worked as an educator in New Brunswick and Nova Scotia. He then received a Master's of Education at Dalhousie University and retired in 1994 as principal of Bridgewater high school. Since his youth, DeMond has been an enthusiastic sports fisherman. He is a lifelong member of The LaHave River Salmon Association and for his long-time conservation efforts to help the Atlantic salmon survive he was presented with the Atlantic Salmon Federation Roll of Honour award. He self-published, Hooked! Angling Sport or Madness, *selling all 2,000 copies. He recently published* Where Did the Nickel Go? *He also runs an 80-acre tree farm, where he has planted 50,000 trees over the years.*

Andrew Hebda's List of the 10 Most Unusual or Rare Zoological Discoveries Made in Nova Scotia

How do we choose the 10 most unusual or rare zoological discoveries made in Nova Scotia? For some discoveries we have the words of raconteurs who had the time, resources or the courage to record unusual discoveries. Many times, little remains of those discoveries other than their words. For other rarities we have the persistence in the endeavours of naturalists. In either case, our lands and waters have given us some species that have very interesting stories to tell.

On the water

A **MERMAN** was encountered and described by the crew of the Captain Pierre Rouleau in Canso Harbour in 1656. The account of the event and description of the beast was recorded by Nicolas Denys, governor of the whole coast of the Bay of St. Lawrence and the isles adjacent, from Cape Canso to Cape Rosiers. Denys, in his masterful work *Description géographique et historique des costes de l'Amérique septentrionale avec l'histoire naturelle du païs*, published in 1672, provided the first extensive description of the flora, fauna, geography and inhabitants of Nova Scotia. His detailed descriptions were generally ignored until they were translated into English by W.F. Gagnon in 1908. The merman was described in the following manner: *His hands, whereof the fingers (if indeed the things were fingers that stood in the place of fingers) were firmly bound to each other with membranes just as those of swan's feet or geese feet, he brushed out of his eyes his mossy hair, with which he also seemed to be covered over the whole body as far as it was seen above the water, in some places more, in some places less.* What the crew probably encountered was a ringed seal, a northern species that would have inhabited our waters at that time, a prolonged era of cold climate. Unlike most other seal species, the ringed seal has a cat-like face, rounded with a somewhat foreshortened rostrum (snout), as opposed to the more common species with the dog-like face of a harbor seal or even the horse-head-like appearance of the gray seal with which many of us are more familiar. What makes this sighting unusual is that in modern times it has rarely been encountered south of the 55th parallel of latitude (mid Labrador coast).

The two sailors

It has long been said that "it's an ill wind that blows no good." However, on a very few occasions, it was that very wind that has brought two remarkable and unusual travelers to our shores. These are both animals lacking the ability to propel themselves through the water and thus relying almost entirely on the wind to move them on the surface of the sea. Yet, these are both sea creatures that may only appear on our shores. It is sometimes 50 to 100 years between sightings.

The first is the tropical Octopus called the **PAPER NAUTILUS**, *Argonauta argo,* an unusual species that does not live on the bottom of the sea, but rather near the surface of the water. Using glands on two of their modified tentacles, the females secrete a paper-thin spiral shell that looks very much like the fossil ammonites. These spiral shells capture a bubble of air, which allows them to float on the surface of the water, allowing the wind to carry them as it wishes. The females will take shelter in these brood chambers. This is one of the many species of marine organisms where the female may be quite large, as much as 10 times the size of the male.'What makes them unusual in our waters is that they are, indeed, tropical animals. So their appearance in our waters is indicative of a significant event in the Atlantic, allowing for the movement of a large mass of warm water to approach our shores (aside from the normal machinations of the Gulf Stream). This has occurred (according to museum records) only three times since the beginning of the last century, with two of those reports from the Shelburne-Yarmouth area and one from just south of Halifax, from the remembrances of a museum visitor who recalled seeing them as a boy when he visited his grandmother in Prospect Village in the mid-1920s. These beautiful and delicate shells readily conjure up visions of the tropics, warm waters and sunny climes.

The second "sailor" is the dreaded **PORTUGUESE MAN O' WAR**, *Physalia physalis*, often called the "Floating Terror." The species is an unusual group of colonial organisms comprising specialized cells of the same species that cannot survive by themselves. Some of the cells create the "sail," others create the hanging tentacles (up to 30 metres in length) with their stinging cells used to immobilize prey, others create the feeding polyps, while yet other cells specialize in reproduction. It's a true example of collaboration for the greater good. As with the paper nautilus, these are tropical organisms that are moved by the wind against the gas-filled bladder or sail. There have been only a handful of occurrences on our shores, according to museum records, and they've been primarily on the Eastern Shore. However, a persistent period of winds from the southeast in the summer of 2017 resulted in at least five confirmed reports of their presence from the South Shore to the Eastern Shore. Is it a sign of change in climatic conditions? Their occurrence in our waters is, indeed, rare.

By the sea

In February of 1940, a 7.7-m, porpoise-like sea monster was trapped under a wharf owned by Richard Crooks of Peggy's Cove. It looked like a small whale but had two horns sticking out above the top of its head. Crooks sold it to Lester Hubley of Seabright, who travelled the province charging people to see the "Horned Marvel." Its identity was a mystery until its true nature was revealed by Professor Henry Raven of the American Museum of Natural History in New York. Raven had purchased it from Mr. Hubley. The animal turned out to be a rare specimen of a beaked whale, called the **BLAINVILLE'S BEAKED WHALE** (*Mesoplodon densirostris*). What makes this species unusual is that it has only two teeth, in the strongly curved mandibles. The tips of the teeth stick up above the top of the head, giving the appearance of horns. This was only the ninth specimen of this species ever seen to that point. This is a member of the family of beaked whales that have frequented deep waters associated with the edge of the continental shelf, deep marine canyons known as "The Gully." They are rarely encountered on the coast.

Under the sea

As the storms of winter pass over the province, it is difficult to imagine that our ice-filled coves and inlets support populations of tropical marine fishes during the summer and fall months, even though we can find up to 75 such species present in coastal waters from July to November. It is, however, even more astounding to find three warm-water or tropical residents here year round.

The first is an unusual **TROPICAL SPONGE**, whose common name has reflected the machinations of geopolitical attitudes over the last 130 years. This is the hexactinellid (glass) sponge, *Vazella pourtalesi*, which was first described by provincial museum curator Reverend David Honeyman in 1889 as a **"CAP OF LIBERTY"** sponge, also referred to as the **"RUSSIAN HAT"** or **"COSSACK SPONGE"** until the time of the Russian revolution, when the name **"LIBERTY CAP"** sponge came back into vogue. It is now, again, called the **RUSSIAN HAT** sponge. 'What makes this sponge so unusual is that until these discoveries on Shelburne Bank, and at an undescribed location on the "fishing banks" 60 kilometers south of Sambro, these sponges were recorded no farther norther than the Carolinas, from waters substantially warmer than we may expect, year round, off our coasts. They are a group of sponges that has now raised considerable interest within the scientific community.

The second tropical animal is a year-round resident that enjoys the warm coastal habitats of the eastern Atlantic Ocean, from Senegal to Port Elizabeth (South Africa), and in the western Atlantic Ocean from the west coast of Brazil (south of the sharp bend at about eight degrees south latitude) then as far north as Massachussetts and the southern tip of Maine. Travelling more than 500 kms to the north in a few spots in the Minas Basin and Cobequid Bay, we find the **FALLEN ANGEL-WING CLAM**, sometimes called the **ATLANTIC MUD PIDDOCK** (*Barnea truncata*). This small, delicate boring clam makes its home in fine beds of soft, Triassic-age mudstones in these waters, where it is protected from our harsh winters and the scour of ice pans by more resistant rock, or in the lee of large boulders or cobbles. Due to its very limited distribution, it is protected from harm under the Species at Risk Act.

The third warm-water resident is a fish species that is normally associated with the offshore climates of Florida and the Carolinas, and southern portions of the Boston states. One would not even think to associate it with the cold waters of the Bay of Fundy. Yet, in a small lake just south of Yarmouth, called Eel Brook Lake, one can find this warm-water fish year round. The **TAUTOG**, *Tautoga onitis* (one of the wrasses) lives in the deeper reaches of the lake. The lake receives salt-water input only at the highest of tides. The salt water, being denser, sinks to the bottom, and is then overlain by a band of fresh water from the adjacent watershed. It is this fresh water that freezes in the winter, isolating the warmed salt water from winter temperatures and storms, thus allowing this tropical fish to survive here, year-round, even in the harshest of winters.

Aside from these permanent-resident tropicals, we had an even more surprising discovery in 1994. A fisherman from Fox Point, Lunenburg County, encountered several very strange-looking fish in his mackerel traps, somewhat mackerel-shaped but with a silver-coloured body with bright orange tail. These turned out to be members of a species called the **RED-TAILED SCAD** or **ROUGH-CHEEKED SCAD** (*Decapterus tabl*). The fisherman had discovered a fish species in his trap, which is commonly found within a circum-equatorial distribution in the Gulf of Mexico, but rarely north of there. It is unusual to find these fish this far north, let alone so near the surface. Their preferred depth range is 50 to 80 fathoms, slightly deeper that the Fox Point locality.

In our rivers

Fish have long been a staple food for many Nova Scotians, from our Mi'kmaw predecessors to modern anglers. What is unusual about fish is their inability (for the most part) to tolerate sharp and sudden changes in the salinity of the water in which they live. There are only limited numbers of fish that can survive spending part of their time in salt water and the rest in fresh water. One is readily drawn to such migratory species as the Atlantic salmon, which will spawn in clear, cold, fresh waters, but as an adult will travel as far as the waters off Greenland to finish growing, before returning to those natal fresh waters to spawn. This mode of life is called anadromy. The fish are called anadromous.

Then there are those species that will spawn in marine waters, then come to fresh waters to mature and grow to adulthood. The Atlantic eel comes to mind, spawning in the mid-Atlantic, in the Sargasso Sea, then migrating up (in the Gulf Stream) to enter our rivers and streams in the spring. This is called catadromy. The fish are called catadromous. These changes in salinity are a challenge to the fish, physiologically, requiring radical changes in kidney function, so there are, consequently, many more species that will live in either one or the other, but few that can live in both.

In Nova Scotia, we have a species of fish that is both catadromous and anadromous in habit, something that is very unusual among fishes. That is the **STRIPED BASS** (*Morone saxatilis*) of the Shubenacadie River. Adult bass from this population can be found year round in both the Minas Basin/Cobequid Bay and Shubenacadie Grand Lake. In late May, the fish from the marine waters head up to the Shubenacadie River to the confluence of the Stewiacke River. Just below the town of Stewiacke, they turn left and spawn in an area near the highway and railroad bridges.

The water there is brackish — only slightly salty. To these fish, they have come into fresh water. They spawn there and the eggs sink through this brackish water to settle on top of the salt wedge caused by the tide. They then return to the marine waters of the bay. At the same time, fish that spend their lives in the lake come down the river and turn right at the Stewiacke River, entering brackish water, which to them would be considered salt water. They spawn, much like their cousins from the Bay, then return to the lake.

One species … two totally different lifestyles.

On the land

Hearkening back to the journals of Nicolas Denys, we encounter a rare and elusive animal that challenged his attempts at living the bucolic life of a gentleman farmer, at what is now called St Peter's at the base of the Bras d'Or lakes. He recounts how this creature, which he called **QUICAJOU**, at one time killed a three-year-old heifer by jumping on its back, grasping the neck and breaking it. Denys then went on to describe it as "cat-like with a long tail," and gave an account of how moose, which were very common in the area at the time, dealt with such attacks, drawing the beast, while still attached to the back of their necks, under the water, causing it to release its hold. The Enlish version of Denys' works translated the common name as wolverine, a species that has only been recorded twice in Nova Scotia. This was the first account of the presence of a **COUGAR** in the province. Although there have been many reports of it in the intervening 300-plus years, the description and details of its hunting habits provide much more insight into this elusive animal than most contemporary reports.

Andrew Hebda is the curator of zoology at the Nova Scotia Museum, a lecturer on many topics in natural history, and the author of more than 80 publications, including The Serpent Chronologies: Sea Serpents and other Marine Creatures from Nova Scotia's History, *The* Mi'kmaw Bestiary *and the* "List of Mammals of Nova Scotia with synonyms used in the literature." *He is often called upon in the media to help explain natural events in Nova Scotia and is a regular contributor to events in the wild kingdom on CBC Radio (Mainstreet).*

Environment Canada's List of the Top 12 Weather Events in Recent Nova Scotia History

Throughout its history, Nova Scotia has been rocked with many major weather events that have left death and destruction in their wakes. Following are 12 of the most powerful storms to blast the province since records have been kept. They are listed chronologically by date.

#1. SAXBY GALE (OCTOBER 4-5, 1869): A powerful post-tropical storm that coincided with a perigean spring tide (on a new moon) causing extensive flooding from storm surge in the Bay of Fundy. The isthmus between Nova Scotia and New Brunswick was almost completely under water. Hundreds of lives and farms were lost. A tropical cyclone hit the Bay of Fundy and the gale destroyed miles of the newly completed Windsor and Annapolis Railway along the Minas Basin near Horton and Wolfville.

#2. THE GREAT NOVA SCOTIA HURRICANE (AUGUST 1873): Some historical records indicate as many as 500 lives (mostly sailors), 1,200 boats and 900 homes were lost in Nova Scotia. An additional 100 lives were lost in Newfoundland, making it the second-deadliest hurricane in Canada with 600 dead. In total, records suggest some

1,200 ships were wrecked. This was arguably Nova Scotia's deadliest hurricane on record, with Halifax being hit by an eye-wall of hurricane (cat 2/3 storm, 167-185 km/hr). This would not to happen again until Juan in 2003.

#3. AUGUST GALE (AUGUST 8, 1926): On August 8, 1926 at 10:00 UTC, Storm #2 made landfall near Canso, Nova Scotia as a category-one hurricane with winds of 130 km/h (70 knots). An estimated 49-52 crew members aboard two ships, which ran aground on Sable Island, were lost. Five crew members aboard a Norwegian ship were lost and one other was injured. The storm did considerable damage to many other ships and fishing gear throughout Nova Scotia and Newfoundland.

#4. GREAT GALE (AUGUST 24-25, 1927): In late summer 1927, a hurricane swept through Atlantic Canada, washing out roads, filling basements and swamping boats. In Newfoundland, 56 people died at sea. Storm #1 made landfall late on August 24 as a category-two hurricane in Nova Scotia, northwest of Yarmouth, and crossed the province with winds reaching 166 km/h (90 knots). Nova Scotia reported 11 to 15 deaths. In Nova Scotia, New Brunswick and Prince Edward Island damage included power failures, flooding, structural damage, damage to crops and dozens of sunken vessels.

#5. HURRICANE BETH (AUGUST 15, 1971): Hurricane Beth brought punishing winds and up to 300 mm of rain, causing considerable crop damage and swamping highways and bridges, temporarily isolating communities on the eastern mainland of Nova Scotia. More rain fell during Beth than did during Hazel in 1954. Fresh-water supplies in Dartmouth were contaminated for days because of extensive runoff into Lake Antigonish. Making landfall on Copper Lake, Hurricane Beth continued over Cape Breton the following day. Maximum winds for this category-one hurricane were 120 km/h. A man was killed in a storm-induced automobile accident. Damage was estimated at more than $10 million.

#6. HURRICANE JUAN (SEPTEMBER 29, 2003): At 12:10 a.m. ADT, Monday, September 29, 2003, Hurricane Juan made landfall in Nova Scotia as one of most powerful and damaging hurricanes to ever affect Canada. Hurricane Juan made a direct hit on Halifax and forever changed the face of the city. Juan was the most damaging storm to hit Halifax in modern history. Losses across Nova Scotia and Prince Edward Island totalled over $100 million, with additional insurable losses of more than $82 million and counting. Even more tragic was the irreplaceable loss of 100-million trees, some of them more than a century old. In Halifax's popular Point Pleasant Park, the hurricane destroyed 70 percent of the park's 86,000 trees. Eight people died from the storm and its after-effects. At its peak, Juan left more than 300,000 homes without power in Nova Scotia and Prince Edward Island.

#7. WHITE JUAN (FEBRUARY 18, 2004): Blowing snow and high winds maintained blizzard conditions for a day or more and created monstrous drifts as tall as three metres. Halifax, Yarmouth and Charlottetown broke all-time 24-hour snowfall records, receiving almost a metre of snow. For Halifax, the 88.5 cm of snow on February 19 nearly doubled its previous record for a single day. The storm generated the greatest snowfall for Shearwater, 95.9 cm (period of record 1955 to 2004), fell in 6, 6-hr periods. It was also the second-greatest snow event for Greenwood with 63.1 cm. Its central pressure, one mark of a storm's intensity, plunged 57 mb in 42 hours, making it one of the most explosive weather bombs ever.

#8. NOR'EASTER (FEBRUARY 8-9, 2013): Nova Scotia got the worst winds, upward of 140 km/h, while east of Yarmouth at Woods Harbour and Cape Sable Island extreme gusts peaked at 164 km/h. A storm surge at Shelburne was the biggest since a major storm nearly 40 years earlier. The storm blew the roof off mobile homes and damaged the fronts of some retail stores. Many trees were toppled and power outages left thousands throughout the Maritimes in the dark. Snowfall amounts were highly variable, measuring as much as 66 cm at Debert and 50 cm in Greenwood with drifts metres deep, while Halifax received 26 cm and Sydney 31cm. The storm surge at high tide flooded roads, damaged docks and shore buildings, and lifted boats onto wharves on Cape Sable Island. The majority of flights at Halifax were cancelled and nearly all Marine Atlantic ferries stayed tethered to shore over the weekend. In places, chunks of floating ice and large rocks were pushed or tossed onshore landing on the front steps of homes and shops. Snowplows were used to clear highways of rocks and gravel.

#9. POWERFUL WINTER STORM (FEBRUARY 17, 2013): The powerful storm led to the drowning of five young fishermen off Nova Scotia on February 17. The deadly storm was the third in two weeks, but not the largest or most powerful. Still, it had the intensity of a category-one-to-two hurricane. Everywhere along the coast, winds were gusty and strong, approaching 160 km/h in western Cape Breton Island. Across the Maritimes thousands of customers lost power and inter-city bus services were cancelled. Numerous flights in and out of Halifax and Saint John airports were delayed or cancelled. Turbulent seas along the Nova Scotia coast created treacherous conditions with 10-metre waves and high winds. Sadly, in the midst of hurricane-force winds and zero visibility, the Miss Ally from Woods Harbour and her five-member crew of fishers went down in heavy seas.

#10. MARITIME'S VALENTINE STORM (FEBRUARY 14-17, 2015): A major storm system formed off the United States eastern coast and moved towards the North Atlantic. On February 15, the storm system hit Nova Scotia, bringing with it snow, ice and rain. In Halifax, the weather changed from snow to rain, creating flooding in the streets, which turned into an overnight flash freeze. Greenwood, Nova Scotia received 56 cm of snow, while on Cape Breton Island wind gusts were recorded of up to 176 km/h. A White Juan-a-be, this hard-hitting nor'easter forced the cancellation of everything from church services and festivals celebrating winter. By storm's end, parts of New Brunswick had received another 45 cm of snow. Prince Edward Island received 80 cm. Several Maritimers couldn't resist comparing the Valentine storm with the infamous White Juan blizzard 11 years earlier. By some accounts, the Valentine weekend storm was worse and certainly much longer.

#11. SUMMER DROUGHT (2016): From June 1 until September 18, 2016, the region received only 90 millimetres of rain, far less than the normal 315 mm. The drought was called an emergency and a disaster. In southwestern Nova Scotia, where wells were dried up, local municipal governments resorted to handing out bottled water. Municipal and provincial properties were open to the public for showers and as filling stations. Several wildfires burned throughout the region. Some areas of the region didn't report relief until well into October that fall.

#12. THANKSGIVING DAY ATLANTIC WEATHER BOMB (OCTOBER 9-11, 2016): Hurricane Matthew was the costliest tropical storm since Sandy and the first Atlantic category-five hurricane in nine years. On October 9, Matthew's core was about 320 km east of Cape Hatteras, North Carolina, yet its "atmospheric river" extended 1,600 km north to Atlantic Canada, where it interacted with an intense, slow-moving but rapidly strengthening storm. The hybrid system intensified and began lashing and soaking eastern Nova Scotia and later Newfoundland and Labrador. Cape Breton Island bore the brunt of the storm. Sydney received 225 mm of rain, which shattered the city's previous one-day rainfall of 129 mm. The J.A. Douglas McCurdy Sydney Airport was forced to close all runways. The storm also provided Nova Scotia's second-wettest day ever. The most severely impacted community was Eskasoni First Nation, where 100 homes were flooded and an undetermined number of people were evacuated due to high water levels. More than 140,000 Nova Scotians went without power, some for up to three days. Loss estimates from the Insurance Bureau of Canada totalled $103 million, with the vast majority of claims being made in Nova Scotia.

Bridget Thomas is a climate services meteorologist with Client Service Operations Atlantic/Meteorological Service Canada, Environment and Climate Change Canada.

Donna Barnett's List of the Top 10 Beaches in Nova Scotia

In my experience, everyone has a different reason to go to the beach, often changing from visit to visit. Sometimes, perfection is found through a contemplative stroll along the shores. Other times, one's soul is satisfied by exploring the plethora of ocean life found along the beach. And of course, there are those times when the beach is just the ideal place to play — in sand, water and sun.

I have chosen the following "best" beaches because each one satisfies a variety of moods and activities beach visitors pursue. In a province endowed with an exceptional number of world-class beaches, the ones on this list represent just a sample of the magical places to explore, whatever your yearning.

#1. BURNTCOAT HEAD: With the highest recorded tides in the world, this beach is a delight for the ardent beachcomber. Dramatic cliffs plunge to expansive tidal flats bathed in the hues of green sea grass and red mud and rock. Tidal pools dot the landscape, crawling with myriad sea creatures. It is almost impossible for the young and young at heart to resist the great pleasure of plunging into the soft, delightful muck. But beware the incoming tide, as it rises quickly and powerfully, occasionally catching the unwary at the base of the cliffs. One can watch the power of the incoming tide from a serene picnic park at the top of the cliffs.

#2. CABOTS LANDING ASPY BAY: Before even stepping foot on the sand at this beach, visitors make the mental and physical transition to beach mode by leaving their shoes on the shore and fording a narrow channel of water. This is a highly appropriate entrance to a place that inspires awe from every direction. The longest beach in the province, it is bounded by the hills of Cape Breton, making it as pleasing to gaze inland as it is to look offshore. The soft dark sand and long line of low dunes invite endless exploring, walking and just sitting and absorbing the exceptionally beautiful landscape.

#3. CRYSTAL CRESCENT BEACH: While its proximity to Halifax attracts many visitors, it is the beauty of the unique coastal-barren landscape that is the real draw. Oh yes, and the three pristine white-sand beaches. Hiking trails snake between, and well beyond, the beaches, offering scenic views over the ocean. This is truly a destination where something can be found for everyone, whether it is relaxing on the sand, hiking the shoreline or splashing in the waves.

#4. MARTINIQUE BEACH: The epitome of the classic white-sand beach, Martinique is the ideal place to find solitude amid the power of nature. It is a large beach, which easily absorbs visitors within its stretch of towering dunes, rolling surf and abundant shorebirds. The periodic fog that descends here only seems to enhance the experience. This is an ideal beach to go for a long, vigorous walk.

#5. MAVILLETTE BEACH: Situated on the foggy southern tip of the province, this beach is surrounded by substantial dunes, flocks of shorebirds and dramatic moodiness. Large tidal flats offer endless exploration, while high tide brings great surfing possibilities. A boardwalk and bird-viewing platform offer alternative activities when playing on the wide, soft sand of the beach gets stale. This truly is a destination where you could spend a full day and never get bored.

#6. MELMERBY BEACH: Melmerby is the perfect location for that classic day at the beach. Invitingly warm, calm waters lap gently at the magnificent two-kilometre long white-sand beach. Backed by low, marram-grass-covered dunes, the dense sand is perfect for building sand castles and lying in the sun to dry off after each dip in the ocean. Lugging beach paraphernalia is made easy by parking lots that are located just behind the dunes.

#7. RAINBOW HAVEN BEACH: This is a go-to beach for nearby city dwellers. But beyond its soft sand and proximity to the urban core, Rainbow Haven offers a number of enticing natural features. As a large salt marsh, bird life is teeming here, often easily in sight of the beach. The beach curves gently into the waters of the salt marsh, providing an arc of privacy for those who venture beyond the crowds congregated between the lifeguard patrol flags. Here is where real exploring can happen. Terns dive into the shore waters, fields of clams are revealed at low tide and flowers bloom among the dunes.

#8. SAND HILLS BEACH: At low tide, Sand Hills offers seemingly endless sand flats that are teeming with shorebirds and sea creatures. You can spend hours relaxing or exploring in the sand and sun-warmed shallows. But beware, as the tide comes in over the low flats, it moves exceptionally quickly and you can be left sprinting for the protection of the shore. The large dunes on the shoreline host a forest of loosely spaced mature trees. This makes a great spot for a wind-protected picnic during high tide.

#9. THE HAWK: A trip to this spectacular beach feels like a journey to the very remote edges of where the land meets the ocean. Everything is on a large scale here, from the wide and long stretch of white sand to the seemingly oversized sky itself. Masses of birds congregate, offering great birding opportunities. As if that weren't enough to fill a visit, at the south end of the beach low tides reveal an eerie "drowned forest", a remnant of ancient trees whose stumps have somehow managed to remain intact.

#10. WEST MABOU: This gorgeous beach is tucked away among the striking hills of the West Mabou Highlands. Large grassy dunes provide a picturesque and protective backdrop to the dark sand and warm, frothy waves. One is compelled to explore here, either along the winding coastal hiking path or on the warm sand. A variety of shorebirds gather in great numbers, adding to the remote, rugged feel of the beach.

Donna Barnett is a freelance photographer with a passion for outdoor and water-related subjects. She is the author/photographer of four books, including photo-graphing the recently released Beaches of Nova Scotia *and* Best Nova Scotia Beaches.

Allan Billard's List of the Top 10 Waterfalls in Nova Scotia

Nova Scotia has long been known for its spectacular seascapes and breathtaking vistas. They have attracted hundreds of thousands of visitors each season, particularly in the autumn when the foliage turns every imaginable shade. Most visitors to this province, however, never venture inland from the coast to experience the fairy-like charm of a woodland waterfall, cradled in the lap of a v-shaped gorge. The waterfall sites chosen as the best in the province share the overwhelming power of nature with the admiring hikers who stand in awe, water plunging with a roar at their feet. Some of these sites are hard to access but they are all worth the effort.

#1. NORTH RIVER FALLS (CAPE BRETON): North River Falls in Cape Breton stands like a reigning monarch. It is the highest waterfall in the province, and perhaps the most statuesque. It was this icon that convinced officials to create the North River Wilderness Area, protecting the upper reaches of the river, including the falls, along with the neighbouring backcountry areas. Knowing that this attractive enclave would someday be extremely popular as a wilderness-hiking destination, provincial officials moved in advance to protect the still-pristine environment from unsustainable development. In an attempt to reduce the impact of more and more hikers, they did establish a trail, but the simple amenities hikers might expect are few and far between. While the arduous, nine-kilometre walk into the site discourages many, gazing upon this hidden treasure is the reward for those who do make the journey. The broad, sunlit gorge presents a variety of photo opportunities. The trail leads right to the base of the falls, so there is no need to scramble down a loose-rock wall to get the best view. The rock formations offer many places to perch for a picnic and the cool waterfall pool provides a natural spa for the hot and tired hiker. There is a steep path to the top of the gorge, many hundreds of metres up, but the view it provides seems less awesome than the one from the base. Up there the roar of crashing water is lost in the wind, no spray covers your face and the connection with one of Cape Breton's natural wonders seems too faint.

#2. PIPER'S GLEN (MARGAREE VALLEY): Like so many places in Cape Breton, this lovely site near Scotsdale is referred to by many local names. With "Piper's Glen" being such a common name in Scotland, and in Canada as well, some call this site Egypt Falls, although it is not located on the nearby Egypt River. The waterfall is actually on Matheson Glen Brook, where a fault line separates the largely siltstone and sandstone formations. Like the whole of the Upper Margaree Valley, it is one of the prettiest natural sanctuaries on Cape Breton Island, regardless of what it is called. The meandering trail leads across rolling hills for most of the short journey in, winding between young hardwoods with a thick understory of new saplings and sprays of wildflowers. At the lip of the gorge, a rope is secured to the trees, placed to assist with both the descent and the return from the base of the falls. In the fall, the whole site is aflame with a brilliant display of leafy colour. When the falls are flush with water, in the spring and after a good rainfall, the broad rock face fills with a sheet of white water. At these times, it would be easy to forget the outside world and to contemplate staying right here, forever. Even in times of reduced flow, the rising mist at the base of the gorge, the leafy canopy and the pesky mosquitoes can still evoke visions of a lonely piper, striding along the trail then stopping at the brow of the cliff, serenading the sun as it slowly leaves the gorge in the twilight.

#3. INDIAN FALLS (LAHAVE RIVER): Anglers come to Indian Falls on the north branch of the LaHave River because it is one of those places where the fish gather and rest during their long journey upstream to spawn. They also come here for the same reason as hundreds of other visitors, to enjoy this open and airy site and to gaze upon this magnificent waterfall, which is flushed with tawny-brown water. As in all river systems, the spring rains really swell the LaHave. The broad, grey cliff that faces the afternoon sun becomes completely awash at this time of year. The falls project a powerful presence. It is a marvel that fish could ever navigate up the torrent of water. Late in the summer, there is much less flow and the falls are reduced to a shadow of the way they appeared just a few months earlier. The Lunenburg District Municipality has taken the site under its wing, noting its value as a tourism attraction, and built a new access road. They even carved out a large parking lot near the site. As word spreads that these formerly private lands are now easy to access, this lovely site will become a favourite family picnic destination. It is large enough for all to enjoy the grassy fields, the colourful wildflowers and the many species of migratory birds that are also attracted to waterfalls. To drive right up to the site, take Exit 11 north from Highway 103; follow that road through Cornwall to Newburne. The new road leads off to the left, just past the Veinotte Road. While all waterfall sites present a danger to hikers, particularly small children, who always seem to head straight for the edge of any cliff, the lands around Indian Falls are fairly safe to wander. A rough 10-metre descent to the base of the cliff offers access to a very pleasant gravel beach used by fly fishermen, and even better views of the site than from above.

#4. MOORES FALLS (KENTVILLE): Sometimes Nova Scotia hides her waterfalls deep in the wilderness. At other times, the enchantment of a pretty waterfall site is right next to a major highway. Just on the outskirts of Kentville, Route 101 passes through North Alton and crosses Moores Brook. It is here that the brook chooses to descend many metres in a rush. People stop at this busy highway's edge to take in the view for a few minutes because the sound of the falling water and the comforting image of a wall of water sliding down the rock face present such a nice alternative to the rushing of the traffic. The serenity of the upper falls, however, is completely overpowered by the majesty of the lower falls, just a few metres away on the other side of the highway. They can be located by following the gentle brook through the thicket of undergrowth to a precipice. The gentle brook becomes a graceful bridal veil as it drops 20 metres to the gravel riverbed below. Moores Falls is simply one of nature's wilderness tableaus. It stands as an example of how cascading water can hold onto a person's gaze and capture the human spirit, even with the rush of traffic just a few steps away.

#5. MARY ANN FALLS (INGONISH): This gorge was left behind as the glaciers receded, scouring the bedrock and carving out a rough channel in the granite and gneiss, which is a layered rock made up of mica, feldspar and quartz. It is rugged but still beautiful and very accessible, with a well-maintained road right up to the top of the gorge. The park management has also provided plenty of parking, washrooms and viewing platforms. With access to this pretty site being so easy, it is always fairly crowded. The more daring visitors swim and jump off the rocks, some from great heights, and everyone seems to enjoy the view. Each season there are many international visitors who put Mary Ann Falls on their itinerary. It is certainly not a match for Niagara Falls but it is a lovely, wide cascade offering great photo opportunities for travellers. It is a little like Niagara Falls in another way, as well; it claims to be the spot in Nova Scotia where the most wedding proposals are offered (and accepted). Early in the morning, before the human visitors arrive, moose are often seen here, munching away on the bushes beside the road. For the most part, they avoid the tourist times here, but a moose in this lovely part of Cape Breton has surprised many a foreign tourist. Niagara Falls can't offer that!

#6. UISGE BAHN (BADDECK): Uisge Bahn (yoosh-ghi ban) was the name given this delightful site by early Scottish settlers. Roughly translated, it means Whisky Falls, but the pioneers knew their water, and their whisky, a whole lot better than that. Locals will tell you that what was really meant was that the falls offer the water of life, flowing endlessly and serving countless generations of newcomers to this rocky land. They had the same feelings about their whisky, too.With its fetching name, its location on Falls Brook just a few kilometres north of Baddeck, and the splendidly moody gorge that surrounds it, this site has become a tourist mecca. Provincial officials have recognized that fact and promote it as one of the best ways to enjoy a hands-on visit to Cape Breton. They care well for the site, providing the needed trail amenities and protection for the surrounding natural habitat, ensuring that the abundant wildlife the water supports will endure as long as the falls themselves. The two-kilometre trail is quite suitable for most visitors. There are a few small hills but no steep slopes, and several rest stops are provided. Attractive footbridges have been located at a number of stream crossings, adding to the enjoyment of this wilderness adventure. A sudden narrowing of the valley and a floating mist forewarn of the final few steps to the falls. Then the roar of the five-storey cascade, as it drops into the pool below, almost drowns out conversation. Most hikers are tired and perspiring at this point and the idea of a quick dip in the dark water comes to mind. The water is too cold for swimming, however, even in summer, so most visitors settle for a drink. Somehow just one slurp from this mountain oasis seems to provide an immediate energy boost. It is a beautiful site, one that affords Nova Scotia bragging rights for having such a dramatic waterfall. Hikers who have completed the trip brag as well, about having tasted the magical "waters of life."

#7. CUTIE'S HOLLOW (ANTIGONISH): The origin of the name given to this falls is not recorded anywhere in the popular literature of Nova Scotia. It is a shame that nobody knows what lovely lass (or laddie) might have been the inspiration. Of course, this is an old province and many generations of settlers have come and gone from these lands, obscuring all but the very notable references, or the very royal. Still, the falls are "cute," in a beautiful and ageless way, showing the weight of eons of time. The broad bowl through which it now flows shows countless stress fractures. Tonnes of rock at the base give evidence to the fact that the face is slowly wearing away. The falls are hidden in the hills north of the Trans Canada Highway at Marshy Hope, where there is a small collection of hunting camps. Summer residents have marked the two-kilometre path as it follows an original pioneer cart track. It is well marked and bursting with local flora and fauna until it drops into a steep and dangerous gorge. While it does receive some minimum maintenance from the local nature club, it is also damp and rutted. While the falls can be seen from points along the path, through the understory of foliage, the final 20-storey drop into the gorge itself is really the only place to enjoy the cascade. Be warned, though, the descent is not for the faint of heart or muscle. It is steep, deep and the footing is very loose. Whatever the assault on the surrounding lands and whatever the future may bring, there is a timelessness of nature at this site. At the bottom of the hollow, time stands still for everybody. The events of the past are faint memories, the future is yet to be told, but Cutie's Hollow stands as she has through it all, with majesty.

#8. DAWSON BROOK FALLS (WINDSOR): The Dawson Brook waterfall remains as it must have appeared before Europeans came to these woodlands. The faint trail into the top of the gorge is overshadowed by old hemlock and pine and the forest floor is soft with deep layers of last year's foliage. The rays of the sunlight rarely break through the canopy, discouraging all but a few bunchberry and hearty blueberry plants. Huge tracts of this landscape are still under the control of long-time owners, who have cut and sold wood for generations here. Even though the surrounding hills have been cut over for their valuable stands of timber, the lumbermen bypassed many acres of commercial softwood at this jagged gorge. They are familiar with this site and are proud of how it stands as at least a small reminder of the respect that is owed to the environment. That faint trail just seems to disappear about the same time the gorge becomes visible. There is a choice of good perches offering a view right into the chasm, but no access down to the base. Dawson Brook has its headwaters just upstream from the falls, draining a marsh called Stillwater Station, and there is not enough water to offer a year-round supply for the only stream that leads away from it. When there is a good volume, Dawson Brook flows full for a few hundred metres and then splashes water everywhere dropping over a precipitous six-storey lip into the gorge below. At these times, the site is dramatic. During a long dry summer the gorge stands almost empty. Whatever the water conditions, the site is a sanctuary from the whir and rush of humanity. Even though a four-lane, high-speed highway passes just a few hundred metres to the east, the waterfall gorge on Dawson Brook is a reminder that life sometimes can stand still.

#9. ANNANDALE FALLS (WENTWORTH): Many of the waterfalls in Nova Scotia were created long ago when the surface layers of earth shifted. Those gorges are narrow, steep and extremely difficult to access. Other waterfalls resulted less dramatically when the rivers draining high plateaus simply carved their way through the earth's exterior all the way to the seacoast. However they were formed, there are some waterfalls in Nova Scotia that are just too difficult to approach safely. This falls site, just northeast of the Wentworth Valley, present one example of a site that nobody, even experienced rock climbers, should take for granted. The walls of the gorge next to the waterfall are 35 metres high and extremely steep where the east branch of Swan Brook comes roaring out of the Cobequid Mountain Range. Complicating the descent into this secluded canyon is the very loose footing and the lack of anything substantial to hold on to. All that having been stated, once down at the base of the falls, and putting the return ascent out of mind, the misty aura is captivating. It is actually overwhelming to be right up next to a giant bridal veil of white water that tumbles ceaselessly out of the solid grey rock face. The flush of water seems to fly down the 10-metre drop and, almost in an instant, become just another rocky brook at peace with its surroundings and ready to move along. In spite of the uneven landscape, a thick undergrowth and mixed hardwood overstory make up most of the vegetation in the gorge. Wildflowers almost carpet the forest floor, bringing many butterflies and other insects to the margins of the babbling stream. It's all a perfect lesson in the amazing variety which nature provides. Who knows how many small woodland creatures make this lush vegetation their home?

#10. WENTWORTH VALLEY FALLS: One of the best-kept secrets in Nova Scotia is this intimate waterfall site. Like several other hidden treasures, it can be accessed by anyone with a desire to discover a simple natural pleasure. But like all the falls in the well-known Wentworth valley, most remain largely ignored. When the Trans-Canada Highway used to pass through this popular skiing destination prior to 1997, upwards of ten thousand people a day would drive right past this lovely cascade, completely unaware that it stood just a few metres off to the west, behind a grove of spruce trees. The access road is unmarked, except for a simple iron post a few hundred metres south of an old motel. The track is rough and rutted, but the walk is short and the reward great. This is one of the true "bridal veil" falls in the province. When it is full of water there are few falls anywhere, which offer a more postcard perfect image. There is no deep gorge, no broad bowl, not even a deep, dark pool at the base, just a solid wall of white water spreading latterly from the apex. Unfortunately, the natural supply of water feeding these falls is only a small watershed atop a few local hills. Without a constant supply of water there is no guarantee that the flow will cover the wide rock face. There is always some water running here, however, and the wading pool at the base of the falls offers another simple pleasure; a perfect place for the kids to splash in the water. On some bright morning following a few days of rain, take the old highway through the Wentworth Valley and stop for a lunch at this special place. Let the rest of the world speed by as you enjoy the sun shining down onto the picnic tableau. Go ahead, take off your shoes and get your feet wet too.

Allan Billard had been a wildlife biologist for many years but only took up writing about the fascinating natural wonders of his home province in 1997. Besides waterfalls, he has published books on Nova Scotia's beaches, lighthouses, canals and canoeing.

Sandra Phinney's List of 10 Favourite Natural Spaces in Nova Scotia

It's a balmy August day. Four vehicles pull up at Mason Point in Tangiers, Nova Scotia, each carrying one canoe, two people and enough gear and grub to last four days. We're headed out to Baltee Island — part of the 100 Islands — where we'll set up camp.

Over the years, hundreds of kayaks have left these shores. That's not a big deal; what's unusual is that we intend to do this trip in canoes — a rare sight, as few venture out for a wilderness canoe trip over the briny deep. What's even more unusual is that we've never done this before. Sure, we've all paddled rivers and lakes in various parts of Atlantic Canada, but never the ocean. Do we have what it takes to camp and explore the 100 Wild Islands — Nova Scotia's largest coastal wilderness region — for four days? The weather forecast calls for everything from sun to rain, wind, fog and an electrical storm.

Nutshell: we not only survived, we thrived. Sure, the swells on the second day were a bit of a challenge (read: downright scary), but we took our time crossing to Carryover Cove, where the rocky cliffs and emerald lagoons were simply spectacular. That trip was so memorable, I returned last season with a group of women friends for a wilderness trip. There were five kayaks and two canoes with a total of nine women. This time, we set up our base camp on Shelter Cove, where we tucked our tents into the woods on the edge of a crescent beach and did day trips exploring the region.

When I think "Natural Spaces" in Nova Scotia, my mind zigzags around the province from one end to the other, not knowing exactly where to land, as there are so many choices! Narrowing a list down to a mere 10 is a gargantuan task. So I simply started my list with one that came to mind first: the 100 Wild Islands. The remaining nine I offer in alphabetical order–they really all deserve the #1 spot.

THE 100 WILD ISLANDS feature more than 250 kilometres of coastal habitats and 400 acres of wetlands. It includes everything from boreal forests, bogs and barrens that have remained isolated for more than 10,000 years, to hidden coves, islands galore and pristine sandy beaches. And we can thank the staff and volunteers at the Nova Scotia Nature Trust for acquiring — and preserving — this region. If kayaking (or canoeing) is your thing, this is nirvana. Don't have a boat? Sign up for a kayaking excursion with Coastal Adventures at Mason Point.

BAXTERS HARBOUR FALLS, located on the Bay of Fundy in Kings County (about 15 km from Kentville) is a little-known yet charming spot that's well worth exploring. It features a waterfall that you can walk right up to at low tide (and step behind it!) as well as stunning columnar basal formations all along the shore and cobble beds that are also visible at low tide. Great place both summer and winter; a photographer's delight.

CAPE SABLE ISLAND (not to be confused with Sable Island) is home to the famous Cape Island Boat or "Cape Islander." The island is located in the most southern part of Nova Scotia and is accessible by a causeway from Barrington Passage. Once on the island, head to The Hawk. Designated as an Important Bird Area, it is a destination for bird lovers the world over. At low tide it's also home to the 1,500-year-old "drowned forest" of exposed petrified tree stumps [*barrington municipality.com/cape-sable-island.html*].

JOGGINS FOSSIL CLIFFS is a UNESCO World Heritage site which just happens to be the world's most complete fossil record of life in the Coal Age, dating back 300 million years. Best appreciated by taking a scheduled tour of the cliffs with an interpreter from the centre, a hired guide from the village, or by walking down to the ocean floor and wandering around the base of the cliffs on your own [jogginsfossilcliffs.net].

KEJIMKUJIK NATIONAL PARK AND NATIONAL HISTORIC SITE offers a plethora of stunning natural spaces to explore. You could spend days here and never see or experience the same thing twice. Of particular interest: the "Hemlocks and Hardwoods" trail — a 5-km loop that will take you through a section of the forest featuring 300-year-old trees and a boardwalk [pc.gc.ca/en/pn-np/ns/kejimkujik].

MARTINIQUE BEACH is the longest sandy beach in the province. Situated in East Petpeswick on the Eastern Shore, it has lots of dunes and is home to the endangered Piping Plover as well as many migratory birds. This is a beachcomber's haven. Surfers also love this beach as it often has inviting waves. Bonus: Martinique Beach Provincial Park is located here [novascotia.com/see-do/outdoor-activities/martinique-beach-provincial-park/1745].

POLLETS COVE is considered nirvana for hikers. The trail is accessible from Gampo Abbey in Pleasant Bay, Cape Breton. It's an exhilarating 7-km hike in but when you reach the cove, you'll be privy to a fine-sand beach; wildflower-filled hillside pasture on one side and steep forested banks on the other. In the middle, blue-grey hills fold into each other as far as the eye can see. This is privately owned land but the owner is hiker-friendly.

SABLE ISLAND (not to be confused with Cape Sable Island) is a National Park Reserve located far out in the North Atlantic. This is home to the famous Sable Island wild horses, where they roam freely. It's also home to giant shifting sand dunes (the landscapes constantly changes), as well as the world's biggest breeding colony of grey seals and scores of plants, birds and bugs. The island's human history is rich, varied and ancient. Accessible only by sea or air [pc.gc.ca/en/pn-np/ns/sable].

TOBEATIC WILDERNESS AREA is the largest wilderness area in the Maritimes. It spans parts of five counties and encompasses 118,000 hectares. Referred to as "the Tobeatic," it features everything from old fire barrens to unique old-growth forests, giant erratics, expansive wetlands, long stillwaters, more than 100 lakes, the Heritage Shelburne River—and more. Of course it is also home to diverse flora and fauna. It's a provincial jewel [novascotia.ca/nse/protectedareas/wa_tobeatic.asp].

TUSKET ISLANDS. Local lore says there are 365 islands, one for every day of the year. That's a tad exaggerated but most agree that including islets and significant ledges, there are more than 200 islands, each with a distinct personality. As the crow flies, The Tusket Islands stretch about 20 miles from Robert's Island off of Yarmouth, to Seal Island off of Shag Harbour. To get a sense of the islands, their history and culture, sign up for Tusket Island Tours [tusketislandtours.com].

Sandra Phinney is an award-winning journalist who writes from her perch on the Tusket River in Canaan, Nova Scotia. Although she's travelled to several exotic places around the world, many of Sandra's fondest memories come from her own back yard — right here in Nova Scotia.

David Currie's List of the Top 10 Birds that You are Likely to Find in Nova Scotia

When thinking of the Top 10 birds that you are likely to find in Nova Scotia, these come to find. Most are common, but a few will be more difficult to locate. However, with a bit of effort in a few cases, these birds often leave an impression on anyone who encounters them, whether hard-core birders or novice outdoor types. There are other birds that people "could" find in Nova Scotia, but those would be more for the hard-core birder types, and the chances are low, so I decided to exclude those from this list.

#1. ATLANTIC PUFFIN: One of the most identifiable and endearing birds to both visitors and residents, with its formal appearance and massive and colourful bill, is the Atlantic Puffin. Several breeding colonies can be found offshore that can be visited with regularly scheduled boat trips making seeing one a certainty between May and August each year.

#2. COMMON EIDER: A spectacularly colourful sea duck that breeds all along our coastline, making it not only easy to locate but also likely to leave a lasting impression. Can be found in all months of the year and from almost any lookoff on the coast.

#3. COMMON LOON: These huge aquatic birds are synonymous with wilderness and northern boreal habitats of Canada. Common Loons can be found here all year but they are most often appreciated in full breeding plumage during summer, in almost any large freshwater lake in Nova Scotia.

#4. OSPREY: Our provincial bird, the "fish hawk" can be found here from April to September, often near its huge nests. Watch for it during summer, hovering in shallow bays and lakes as it hunts for its meal of fish.

#5. PIPING PLOVER: This critically endangered bird still uses a select number of sandy beaches in Nova Scotia. With only 100 or so birds left, seeing one is very significant but likely in suitably un-crowded beaches. Walking along the water's edge during summer and keeping pets on leash will help to reduce further mortality.

#6. ROSEATE TERN: Another critically endangered species, the result of habitat and food loss, this elegant tern is found only in the most southern coastal portions of this province. Once seen, it is worth any amount of effort.

#7. CHIMNEY SWIFT: These amazing aerial insectivores fly all day long catching insects before roosting in large numbers in various brick chimneys in the province from June to August. The Robie Tufts Centre in the town of Wolfville is monitored each evening just before dusk to count the birds entering the chimney there. People gather to watch the amazing spectacle of the funnelling in the chimney of sometimes hundreds of birds.

#8. BOREAL CHICKADEE: This uncommon chickadee of the Boreal Forest reaches its southern latitudes in Nova Scotia. Listen and watch for it in thick coniferous forests in Central, Eastern and Northern parts of the province. Unlike its cousin, the Black-capped Chickadee, this "Brown-capped" chickadee is far less abundant; it's secretive and quiet.

#9. HERMIT THRUSH: Found almost anywhere in the province just before and after dusk or early morning, this bird's lilting and melancholy voice fills you with the sounds that resonate in your soul. Add a shroud of fog and it becomes unforgettable.

#10. CANADA WARBLER: This stunningly beautiful wood warbler migrates to Nova Scotia to breed in specialized habitat. Due to habitat loss in both its winter and summer habitats, it has been added to Canada's Endangered Species List, but it can still be found along trails and within parks throughout much of the province.

David Currie has been president of the Nova Scotia Bird Society since November 2012.

Laurie Lacey's List of 10 Favourite Berry Plants Native to Nova Scotia

When Vernon approached me to do a top 10 list of my favourite plants, I realized it would be impossible, as I couldn't rank the plants in terms of favourites. I seem to enjoy all the plants and trees, equally well. I then considered doing an article featuring 10 plants, without ranking them in terms of favourites. However, this didn't seem the proper approach for Vernon's book. At the last moment, I realized that I did have favourite berries and could do a list of my 10 favourite berry plants, native to Nova Scotia.

In doing the list, I discovered that it was heavily influenced by my childhood experiences. This was a revelation to me. I had forgotten how much several of the native berry plants had influenced my early years, as I wandered about, playing and learning in the natural world. My years of involvement with plant medicines has also influenced the list. Together they have shaped my love and respect for the green world. I hope you enjoy the list below.

#1. WILD BLUEBERRY (*VACCINIUM ANGUSTIFOLIUM* AND OTHER NATIVE VARIETIES): This is my favourite berry plant. They are abundant in Nova Scotia. I enjoy them in pies, eaten straight from the bush, stewed and in many other ways. The berries and leaves are rich in antioxidants and have many medicinal uses, including for anti-inflammatory purposes.

#2. WILD STRAWBERRY (*FRAGARIA VIRGINIANA*): The wild strawberry holds a special place in my heart. In my childhood, I would wander about my parents' old farm fields in search of those delicious berries. What a thrill it was to discover a patch of strawberries! The leaves have much medicinal value in the treatment of stomach cramps and diarrhea.

#3. BLACKBERRY (*RUBUS ALLEGHENIENSIS* AND OTHER VARIETIES OF THIS TYPE):

There is no greater delight in nature than the discovery of a blackberry thicket loaded with large, juicy berries! The berries are well worth the scratches one might receive while picking them. Both the blackberry and raspberry offer medicinal benefits, similar to those mentioned for strawberry, above.

#4. RASPBERRY (*RUBUS STRIGOSUS* AND OTHER VARIETIES OF THIS TYPE): My fondest memory of raspberry occurred perhaps 40 years ago. While I was taking photographs for a plant medicine book, I came upon a large raspberry bush, full of berries. I took a photo, then on to the berries. What a treat! The medicinal value of raspberry is generally similar to the blackberry and strawberry, above.

#5. CRANBERRY (*VACCINIUM MACROCARPON*): This is one of my favourite berries to pick. I experience something akin to pure delight when picking cranberries along a lakeshore during the autumn season — a season free of black flies, mosquitoes and deer flies! And, of course, no Christmas dinner is complete in Nova Scotia without cranberry sauce. Medicinally, cranberry is excellent in treating infections of the urinary tract.

#6. BUNCHBERRY (*CORNUS CANADENSIS*): The bunchberry is a member of the dog-wood family. Its orange-red berries have a mild flavour and are a tasty treat to eat. The bunchberry is a traditional Mi'kmaw medicine plant with several uses. For example, the leaves were steeped in water and used to treat kidney ailments.

#7. HUCKLEBERRY (*GAYLUSSACIA BACCATA*): This is one of Nova Scotia's most common berry plants. They are more difficult to pick than blueberries. I learned this as a young boy, when my mother sent me to the lakeshore to pick huckleberries for a pie. It took me all afternoon! However, they did make a delicious pie. The huckleberry is high in anti-oxidants.

#8. WINTERGREENS (*GAULTHERIA PROCUMBENS* AND *G. HISPIDULA*): I've included both the teaberry (red berries) and the snowberry (white berries) under number eight. A delightful characteristic of these plants is that the leaves and berries remain over the winter months. The berries of both species are a tasty treat. The plants contain a type of aspirin — teaberry leaves, in particular, steeped in water, were used by the Mi'kmaq as a blood-thinning medication to treat and prevent blood clotting.

#9. PARTRIDGEBERRY (*MITCHELLA REPENS*): This plant trails low to the ground. Its berries have two eyes and look somewhat like the head of a snake. Hence, it is also known as "snakeberry." I always enjoy finding the plant in the forest, because of its strikingly distinctive leaves. The berries have a mild flavour. The plant should not be confused with the Newfoundland partridgeberry, which is a different species, belonging to the genus vaccinium, which includes blueberry, foxberry and cranberry.

#10. CROWBERRY (*EMPETRUM NIGRUM* AND *COREMA CONRADII*): I've included both the black crowberry and broom-crowberry under number 10 on my list. The inclusion of crowberry on the list, might surprise some people. However, I admire the uniqueness of the plants and the tenacity they display as they grow and form carpets over rocky landscapes. The berries are often scattered and you may search a while before finding one. They are surprisingly juicy and well worth the search.

There are many other berries that I could have listed here. For example, foxberry, cloudberry and bearberry. Any of them could become a favourite, on a whim. For instance, give me a bottle of delicious cloudberry jam, and it would likely make the list!

Laurie Lacey is a writer, painter, naturalist and medicine maker of mixed ancestry, including Mi'kmaq and Irish. He is the author of Mi'kmaq Medicines: Remedies and Recollections *and* Medicine Walk: Reconnecting to Mother Earth, *both available through Nimbus Publishing, Halifax, Nova Scotia. Connect with him on Facebook or visit his website at **wildworldofplants.com**.*

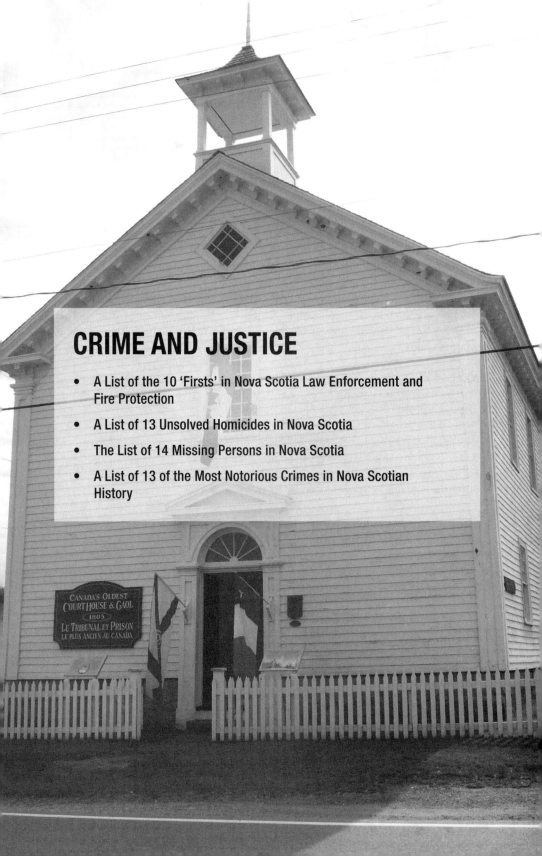

CRIME AND JUSTICE

- A List of the 10 'Firsts' in Nova Scotia Law Enforcement and Fire Protection

- A List of 13 Unsolved Homicides in Nova Scotia

- The List of 14 Missing Persons in Nova Scotia

- A List of 13 of the Most Notorious Crimes in Nova Scotian History

CANADA'S OLDEST
COURT HOUSE & GAOL
1805
LE TRIBUNAL ET PRISON
LE PLUS ANCIEN AU CANADA

A List of the 10 Firsts in Nova Scotia Law Enforcement and Fire Protection

Perhaps it's because of its age, but the province of Nova Scotia has the distinction of hosting a number of Canadian and North American firsts in law enforcement and fire protection, including:

#1. The first ever traffic violation in Canada was issued on October 7, 1793, to George Weiss of Halifax for "disorderly riding in the streets." He was given the option of paying a fine of 10 shillings, working on the highway for four days or being sent to the House of Correction to receive "10 stripes" then discharged.

#2. In 1862, Halifax Police received the first telegram to a police department that helped warn them of criminals headed their way. The telegram came from Horton, Nova Scotia and warned of two horse thieves heading to town. The two were arrested when they arrived. It's the first known case of using a telegram to combat crime.

#3. Halifax became the first city in Canada to introduce radio patrol cars to their fleet. The transmitter was set up October 6, and the first car went on patrol at 4 p.m. October 9, 1934.

#4. Halifax has the oldest fire department in Canada. It was initiated in 1754.

#5. The first all-Black fire department in Nova Scotia and Canada, which was upper Hammonds Plains, was formed in the 1960s.

#6. The Shelburne Fire Department was established in 1784. It has the distinction of using the first hand pumper in North America to fight fire. It acquired the hand pumper in 1786.

#7. Stewiacke is home to a volunteer fire brigade that was the first department in North America to use specialized foam as a fire suppression agent.

#8. Born March 13, 1774, into slavery in the British Colony of Virginia, Rose Fortune, came to Annapolis Royal with the Black Loyalists when she was 10 years old. She went on to become a successful businesswoman and the first female police officer not only in Canada, but in all of North America. Fortune died on February 20, 1864. She was buried in Annapolis Royal in the Garrison Cemetery. Her grave is unmarked, but a plaque in the Petite Parc on the Annapolis Royal waterfront commemorates her life and contribution to Nova Scotian history.

#9. Theresa McNeil from Upper Granville in the Annapolis Valley, who was left to raise her 17 children alone when her husband, Burt, died in 1973, still managed to find time to carve out an impressive career. In 1977, she went on to become the high sheriff of Annapolis County — the first woman to hold such a position in Canada. McNeil, who was named to the Order of Nova Scotia in 2005, died in March 2009 at the age of 81.

#10. The Argyle Township Court House is Canada's oldest standing courthouse. Built in Tusket, Yarmouth County in 1805, it operated from 1805 until 1944. The offices of the Municipality of Argyle were located there from 1945 until 1976. Construction started in 1801 and was completed in 1805. The first session was held on October 29, 1805. In 1982-83 a partial restoration of the building took place and it was reopened in 1983 as a museum and community archive, marking it the first municipal archives established in Nova Scotia in the 1980s. The building was declared a National Historic Site in 2005.

NOTE: The Annapolis County Court House, built in 1837, is valued for its continuing function as a courthouse and jail, the oldest such building in Nova Scotia and one of the oldest in Canada. It is also associated with popular accounts of public hangings and floggings on the Court grounds.

A List of 13 Unsolved Homicides in Nova Scotia

Homicide, the most serious of crimes, is defined by the Merriam-Webster dictionary as the killing of one human being by another. Following is a partial list of unsolved homicides that are cases currently listed on the Rewards for Major Unsolved Crimes Program administered by the Nova Scotia Department of Justice:

1. LORI KATHERINE JOLLIMORE (DOB: JUNE 23, 1958): On April 27, 2017, members of Halifax Regional Police responded to a report of a deceased female at an address on Farquharson Street, Dartmouth. When officers arrived, they located the victim, Lori Katherine Jollimore, inside the address. The investigation determined that Lori Jollimore was a victim of a homicide.

2. DONALD JERMAINE STEVENSON (DOB: MARCH 10, 1989): On October 16, 2010, members of the Halifax Regional Police responded to a report of a possible shooting at 39 Jarvis Lane, Halifax. When officers arrived, they located Donald Jermaine Stevenson at the noted address suffering from a gunshot wound, which was fatal.

3. LYNDA ANNE COMEAU (DOB: JANUARY 28, 1953): On September 1, 2016, at 3 p.m., the Digby RCMP received a call for assistance at a residence on Fort Point Road, Weymouth North. The body of Lynda Anne Comeau was discovered within the residence. It was determined that Ms. Comeau's death was as a result of an injury and the manner of the death was ruled a homicide.

4. EDWIN MICHAEL THOMAS FORGERON (DOB: OCTOBER 21, 1975): On March 9, 2007, at approximately 3 p.m., Edwin Michael Thomas Forgeron was located at 12 Convoy Avenue, Halifax, and was pronounced dead on the scene. Mr. Forgeron's death was ruled a homicide.

5. JOHN FULTON NEWCOMBE (DOB: APRIL 7, 1985): On June 1, 2012, at approximately 2:08 a.m., John Fulton Newcombe was shot outside of Winston's Pub located at 278 Lacewood Drive, Halifax, and pronounced dead on the scene.

6. JAUMAR CARVERY (DOB: JANUARY 23, 1987): On May 3, 2008, members of Halifax Regional Police responded to reports of shots fired in the area of Olympic Court and Sunrise Walk, Halifax. When officers arrived they located 21-year-old Jaumar Carvery unconscious and unresponsive suffering from a gunshot wound. Mr. Carvery was transported to the hospital by emergency workers where he was pronounced dead as the result of the gunshot wound he received.

7. ANGELA PATRICIA HALL (DOB: OCTOBER 6, 1971): On April 29, 2011, a 911 call was received that a woman was injured at 44 Primrose Street, Dartmouth. Police responded to the scene and Angela Patricia Hall was transported to hospital, where she was pronounced dead a short time later. An autopsy confirmed Ms. Hall's death was a homicide.

8. ELMER YUILL (DOB: JULY 30, 1914): In the early morning hours on October 26, 1991, one or more persons hid in the loft of Elmer Yuill's barn, in Beaverbrook, Colchester County, and shot Mr. Yuill two times as he tended to his cows. Mr. Yuill was discovered by an employee, face down on the barn floor.

9. RICKEY WALKER (DOB: JUNE 21, 1968): At approximately 2:50 a.m. on September 1, 2016, Rickey Walker was located in medical distress behind John McNeil Elementary School at 62 Leaman Drive, Dartmouth. He was subsequently transported to the hospital where he was pronounced deceased. An autopsy confirmed Mr. Walker's death as a homicide.

10. TERRENCE (TERRY) PATRICK IZZARD (DOB: FEBRUARY 17, 1958): On November 14, 2016, at 11:07, a 911 call was received of a gunshot in the area of Cragg Avenue, Halifax. Police responded to the area and located a male lying in front of a residence on Cragg Avenue. The male was later identified as Terrence (Terry) Patrick Izzard. An autopsy was completed and confirmed that Mr. Izzard's death was a gunshot homicide.

11. TYLER RONALD JOSEPH KEIZER (DOB: AUGUST 4, 1994): On November 21, 2016, shortly before 11 p.m., police and EHS responded to a weapons call in the area of Gottingen Street and Falkland Street in Halifax. Upon arrival, a male, later identified as Tyler Ronald Joseph Keizer, was located and transported to the QEII where he was later pronounced deceased. The investigation has determined that Tyler Keizer was the victim of a homicide.

12. STEVEN MICHAEL HALL (DOB: JUNE 16, 1974): Steven Michael Hall disappeared on Saturday, April 27, 1996. He left his parent's home in Seffernville, Lunenburg County, around 10:30 a.m. Mr. Hall paid a bill at the Ultramar in Chester Basin. While at the service station, Mr. Hall was seen having a brief conversation with a person in a vehicle at the gas pumps. He was last seen hitchhiking on Highway #3 towards Chester. Mr. Hall's body was discovered on November 23, 1996, in a wooded area on the Hogg Lot Road, which is off Highway #14, approximately 13 kms north of the Chester area. This was seven months after his disappearance. It was determined that he died of unnatural causes. An extensive investigation ensued. However, no criminal charges have been laid in the case. Although this investigation remains unsolved, it is still ongoing.

13. ANDREA LYNN KING (DOB: December 15, 1973): On January 1, 1992, the victim, Andrea Lynn King, flew from her home in New Westminister, British Columbia, to Halifax, intent on travelling and working in Nova Scotia for a period of time. Ms. King was last heard from on January 1, 1992, when she called a family member in British Columbia from the Halifax International Airport to advise them that she had arrived safely and that she would call them back the following day with an address where she would be staying. This was the last time that anyone heard from her. On January 4, 1992, Ms. King's family reported her missing and an extensive missing person investigation was conducted. On December 22, 1992, the skeletal remains of Andrea Lynn King were located in a wooded area approximately 200 feet from the end of a dead-end street in the Sackville Business Park. It was determined that she had been murdered.

Rewards for unsolved crimes

*The Nova Scotia Department of Justice is offering cash rewards of up to $150,000 for information leading to the arrest and conviction of person(s) responsible for these specified major unsolved crimes. Unsolved cases are submitted by the policing agency of jurisdiction to the Department of Justice for consideration and approval into the Rewards for Major Unsolved Crimes Program. As unsolved cases are accepted into the program they will be posted on this website: **novascotia.ca/ just/public_safety/rewards/.** If you have any information relating to these major unsolved crimes, call toll free **1-888-710-9090**. Callers must provide their name and contact information, and may be called to testify in court. All calls will be recorded. The amount of the award will be based on the investigative value of the information provided.*

A List of 14 Missing Persons in Nova Scotia

In one year alone — 2015 — police in Canada recorded more than 71,000 reports of missing persons across the country. Some 45,000 of these cases were children while another 26,000 were adults. Who are these people? Why did they go missing? How many have been found? What happens when these people are not found? If a missing person is never found, how do families cope without answers about whatever happened to loved ones? Truthfully, for some families, there is never any closure and answers are never forthcoming. Nova Scotia has its fair share of missing-persons cases.

Following are the 14 missing persons cases currently listed on the Rewards for Major Unsolved Crimes Program administered by the Nova Scotia Department of Justice:

#1. IAN MACKEIGAN (DOB: DECEMBER 12, 1962): Ian MacKeigan was reported missing on October 25, 1984, at 11 p.m. He was last seen by a family member leaving his residence on Manor Lane, Halifax, driving a red 1978 Plymouth Horizon TC3, hatchback. Mr. MacKeigan told his family member that he was going to meet some friends, possibly at the former Palace on Brunswick Street, Halifax, but has not been seen by family or friends since that time. Prior to Mr. MacKeigan's disappearance, he had graduated from a welding course in Sydney, Nova Scotia, and moved to Halifax in July 1984. He was employed in his trade for two weeks prior to his disappearance.

#2. DANIEL BAKER (DOB: APRIL 4, 1957): On December 12, 1997, at approximately 11 p.m., Daniel Baker left a residence on Preston Street, Halifax, and was going to walk to a local restaurant on Quinpool Road. It has not been confirmed if Baker made it to his destination and he has not been heard from since. Mr. Baker was 6' 1" tall and approximately 155 lbs with short dark blonde hair, blue eyes and a fair complexion. When last seen, he was wearing a dark blue, red and white dress shirt, blue jeans, black suede jacket, white Reebok sneakers and black leather gloves. He alternated his residency between Halifax and Bridgewater for many years before moving back to Halifax in July 1997.

#3. GREGORY SAMUEL BRUSHETT (DOB: JANUARY 20, 1964): On April 12, 1999, police received a report from Mrs. Brushett, mother of Gregory Samuel Brushett, that her son had not been seen since April 10, 1999. Gregory Brushett was residing at 11 Dawson Street, Dartmouth, at the time of his disappearance. The investigation revealed that Mr. Brushett was a former member of an outlaw motorcycle club in the Halifax area. He was last seen driving his vehicle, a maroon Honda Accord, on Tacoma Drive, Dartmouth, around 6 p.m. on April 10, 1999. He had been at a bar in Dartmouth earlier on the date of his disappearance. The circumstances of Mr.

Brushett's disappearance are suspicious and foul play is suspected. Police believe there are persons who have information that could result in an arrest and possible charges.

#4. TROY COOK (DOB: JULY 16, 1978): Troy Cook has been missing since June 12, 1998. At approximately 10 a.m. on June 11, 1998, he was dropped off near his apartment, 1 Victoria Street, Truro, by his father. At 10:30 a.m., Sharon Tucker, an employee at the Atlantic Superstore, received a call from a person claiming to be Troy Cook. She is certain that the caller was Mr. Cook, but recalled that he sounded different. Cook advised her that he would not be into work for his evening shift. Mr. Cook has not been heard from since his disappearance and there have been no confirmed sightings. He had not mentioned leaving town, his wallet and ID were located in his apartment and there have been no transactions on his bank account. It has also been established that Mr. Cook has no history of compulsive behaviour or mental illness.

#5. BRUCE ANDREW FORBES (DOB: JULY 13, 1964): On July 17, 2002, police received a report from Paula Forbes, wife of Bruce Forbes, that her husband had not been seen since July 16, 2002. Mr. Forbes was residing at 35 Lansdowne Drive, Halifax, at the time of his disappearance. The police investigation revealed the victim was last seen in Halifax on July 16, 2002, at a Regent Road residence. It is believed the victim had a large sum of money in his possession at the time of his disappearance. The victim suffered from a serious health condition and required medication on a daily basis. It is believed that he was not in possession of this medication at the time of his disappearance. The circumstances of Mr. Forbes' disappearance are suspicious and foul play is suspected. Police believe there are persons who have information that could result in an arrest and possible charges.

#6. LESLIE ANNE KATNICK (DOB: AUGUST 30, 1966): On November 4, 1991, Montreal Police received a complaint from Mr. Katnick, who reported that his daughter, Leslie Anne Katnick, was missing. Leslie Katnick had been residing at 3407 Rosedale Street, Montreal, Quebec, until November 1, 1991, which was the last time she was seen by either friends or family. The investigation revealed that Ms. Katnick registered into the Halifax YMCA on November 2, 1991, for several nights and returned the key on November 4, 1991. Her banking card was also used on November 2, 1991, in Halifax. No further information has surfaced with respect to the whereabouts of Ms. Katnick, the circumstances of her disappearance are suspicious and foul play may be involved. Police believe there are persons who have information that could result in an arrest and possible charges.

7. ALLAN "KENLEY" MATHESON (DOB: MAY 8, 1972): Allan "Kenley" Matheson was a student at Acadia University, Wolfville, in September 1992. He was in his first two weeks of university when he travelled with some new friends to Corkum's Island, Lunenburg County, for the weekend. He returned to Acadia for the upcoming week and on Saturday, September 19, 1992, he attended a party on campus. Mr. Matheson was seen by his sister and others at Crowell Tower (Acadia University) on September 20, 1992. On September 21, 1992, it is reported that he was seen by a friend walking on Main Street in Wolfville. This was the last time anyone has seen or heard from Allan "Kenley" Matheson. There has been no contact with any family members or friends and there has been no activity on his bank account since that date. Police believe there are persons who have information that could result in an arrest and possible charges.

#8. KIMBERLY ANN MCANDREW (DOB: JULY 17, 1970): Kimberly McAndrew has been missing since August 12, 1989. At 4:20 p.m. she left her place of employment, Canadian Tire Ltd. at 6203 Quinpool Road in Halifax, where she was employed as a cashier. There were unconfirmed reports that Ms. McAndrew was last seen at the Gardenia Flower Shop in Penhorn Mall in Dartmouth. She was identified by an employee at the flower shop as having bought a balloon and a rose. At the time of her disappearance, she was wearing pleated, ankle-length navy cotton slacks with slash pockets in front and one pocket in the back, a white, short-sleeved "Esprit" T-shirt with red and green squares, a navy cotton oversized cardigan, and jade green flat-heeled slip-on loafers.

#9. ARLENE MCLEAN (DOB: MAY 12, 1971): On September 8, 1999, at 8:30 p.m., Arlene McLean left her residence at 1 Melrose Place, Eastern Passage, in the family car, a 1993 four-door green Hyundai Elantra, bearing Nova Scotia plate CMG-691. When she left, she gave her common-law husband the impression that she would not be gone long; however, she has not been seen since and her vehicle has never been recovered. When Ms. McLean left her residence, she took only her purse and the clothes she was wearing. She left behind her eight-year-old son and her common-law husband. Arlene McLean is described as a Caucasian female, height: 157 cm. (5'2"), weight: 61 kg (135 lbs), brown hair and eyes and fair complexion. No further information has surfaced with respect to the whereabouts of Ms. McLean, the circumstances of her disappearance are suspicious and foul play may be involved.

#10. LYNN ADEL OLIVER (DOB: SEPTEMBER 10, 1956): On Saturday, August 25, 1979, at approximately 11:40 a.m., Lynn Adel Oliver left her place of work at Quality Cleaners, 141 Stellerton Road, New Glasgow, for lunch and did not return. She has not been seen or heard from since. Ms. Oliver had expressed concern for her physical safety and was described as nervous at work that day. She had previously given a friend and co-worker a note with instructions to call her mother immediately if she ever went missing. Additional information was within the note. Lynn Adel Oliver is a Caucasian female; height 5'5"; weight 105 lbs; green eyes and brown hair. She was 22 years old when she went missing and left behind a two-year-old son. There has been no activity in her bank account, MSI account or with her Social Insurance Number. Extensive inquiries across the country throughout the years have had negative results.

#11. LEONETTE MARIE PURCELL (DOB: DECEMBER 10, 1948): Leonette Marie Purcell, a 56-year-old homemaker, has not been seen or heard from since she disappeared on December 16, 2004, from her Grand Lake home situated near the Halifax International Airport. Items in the Purcells' home appeared out of place or disturbed contrary to normal routine. An extensive search in the area of Grand Lake failed to reveal her whereabouts. Her personal banking and communications devices have not been accessed since her disappearance. Investigators are interested in identifying two unidentified males who were seen on a security camera at the Enfield Irving Big Stop, one of whom the camera caught calling the Purcell home on the morning Purcell disappeared. Neither of these men have been identified. The investigation is ongoing and police are asking for the public's assistance.

#12. SHEN CHIU "ANDY" TSOU (DOB: AUGUST 11, 1975): On June 30, 2005, police received a complaint from the wife of Shen Chiu "Andy" Tsou, who reported that her husband had not been seen since June 26, 2005. Mr. Tsou was a resident of Richmond, British Columbia, and had travelled to the Halifax area for business. He had been staying at the Halifax Casino Hotel and other private residences prior to his disappearance. He was associated to numerous people in the metro Halifax area and elsewhere in Nova Scotia. The investigation revealed that Mr. Tsou was registered at the Halifax Casino Hotel for the night of June 26, 2005; however, he never arrived at the hotel. He has not been seen since June 26, 2005. Mr. Tsou was operating a 2005 white Pontiac Grand Prix rental car while in the Halifax area. This vehicle has never been located.

#13. RHONDA JOYCE LOUISE WILSON (DOB: JUNE 25, 1971): On August 10, 2002 Rhonda Joyce Louise Wilson's husband reported to New Minas RCMP that she left their Kentville home on August 7 at approximately 9:30 p.m. to go for a walk and did not return. Mrs. Wilson, a mother of three, was 31 years old at the time of her dis-appearance. During the course of the investigation there have been several possible sightings of Wilson; however, none were ever substantiated. To date, there has been no activity on her bank accounts.

#14. JAIME MOREY WYATT (DOB: AUGUST 24, 1934): On December 3, 1996, family members of Jaime Morey Wyatt made a report to the St. John's RCMP, that Jaime Wyatt had not been seen since November 12, 1996. He had been residing in Newfoundland; however, he left Newfoundland in September 1996 to seek employment in Nova Scotia. The investigation revealed that Mr. Wyatt had been staying at the Twin Elms Motel on Inglis Street, Halifax, where he was last seen on November 16, 1996, although he was paid up until November 17, 1996. On the evening of November 16, 1996, Mr. Wyatt informed staff at the Twin Elms that someone was going to be picking him up that evening to go out to a dinner party and other functions during the evening. He was never heard from again. The circumstances of Mr. Wyatt's disappearance are suspicious and foul play may be involved. Police believe there are persons who have information that could result in an arrest and possible charges.

Rewards for unsolved crimes

*The Nova Scotia Department of Justice is offering cash rewards of up to $150,000 for information leading to the arrest and conviction of person(s) responsible for these specified major unsolved crimes. Unsolved cases are submitted by the policing agency of jurisdiction to the Department of Justice for consideration and approval into the Rewards for Major Unsolved Crimes Program. As unsolved cases are accepted into the program they will be posted on this website **novascotia.ca/ just/public_safety/rewards/**. If you have any information relating to these major unsolved crimes, call toll free 1-888-710-9090. Callers must provide their name and contact information, and may be called to testify in court. All calls will be recorded. The amount of the award will be based on the investigative value of the information provided.*

The List of 13 of the Most Notorious Crimes in Nova Scotian History

By no means does the following list represent the most horrific or serious crimes ever committed in the province of Nova Scotia, nor does it reflect the full inventory of crimes that have occurred in this province over the centuries. Instead, this list of 13 of the most notable crimes in Nova Scotian history offers but a snapshot of the province's long varied record of criminal record.

#1. CANADA'S FIRST TRIAL FOR MURDER: Peter Cartcel has the dubious distinction of being the first Halifax murderer charged and tried for his crime. On August 26, 1749, Cartcel fatally stabbed Abraham Goodsides as the two fought on the streets of the infant city. Because Nova Scotia had no court system at the time, the murder required Gov. Edward Cornwallis to take immediate action. Empowered to establish courts for the fledgling city, Cornwallis named himself and six councillors to the city's first court. On August 31, five days after he committed the crime, Cartcel appeared without a lawyer before the hastily established court for Canada's first ever trial under British law. After hearing four witnesses, the court deliberated for just half an hour before they found the defendant guilty. Two days later, Cartcel was hanged.

#2. OUTLAWING LIQUOR: In the late 19th and early 20th centuries, the use and sale of alcohol was a political and social hot potato. Following a crusade that began in the early nineteenth century, pro-temperance Nova Scotians got their wish when Canada passed the 1878 Canada Temperance Act legislation that allowed all communities to vote on whether or not they would become "dry." Most Nova Scotian municipalities

— one exception being Halifax — voted to outlaw drinking. With the Temperance Act of 1910, Nova Scotians were legally allowed to buy alcohol only for "medicinal, sacramental, art, trade and manufacturing purposes." Again, Halifax was the exception. There, people continued to drink, entitled by law. In 1916, Nova Scotia abandoned the local-option approach to prohibition and went stone dry. Alcohol consumption was banned across the province, even in Halifax. For the next 14 years, Nova Scotians could not legally have a drink.

#3. (RUM) RUNNING FROM THE LAW: Out of prohibition sprung a new, lucrative and illegal rum trade. Former temperance inspector enforcement officer and New Glasgow native Clifford Rose recalls that his own sleepy Nova Scotia hamlet contained illegal rum dives that were "thick as bees." One of the most colourful characters in Rose's memoirs is Delores N., the feisty proprietor of a local watering hole and a woman with an "obscene and profane tongue," a disabled husband and several children to raise. In one raid on Delores' establishment, the businesswoman acquainted the back of Rose's head with a liquor bottle. Recognizing the pervasiveness of the illegal industry, the financial rewards that drove Nova Scotians like Delores to embrace it and the utter corruption of so-called enforcement officials, a cynical Rose celebrated the 1929 defeat of prohibition in his province.

#4. SMUGGLER'S PARADISE: Nova Scotia is still a haven for smuggling illicit substances, thanks to its sheltered coves and inlets and its isolated, unguarded coastline. In the late 1970s, heightened coastal protection in the United States, coupled with its geography, made Nova Scotia a favoured drop-off spot for drug smugglers. While the entire South Shore had seen a rapid rise in smuggling activity over the three decades of the 1970s, 80s and 90s, the remote coasts of Queens and Shelburne counties emerged as the biggest pipelines for illegal drug transactions.

In the 1970s, the Coastal Watch Program was initiated at RCMP request. Nova Scotians living near the coast are asked to report suspicious offshore activities. RCMP estimates at the time suggested that 10 percent of the cocaine and 50 percent of the cannabis imported into Canada arrived by water and a good deal of this comes via Nova Scotia's South Shore.

On May 27, 1990, the largest seizure of hashish in Canadian history went down in Ragged Harbour, Queens County. Thanks to reports furnished by a local lobster fisherman, police were tipped off to a smuggling operation of 25 tonnes of hashish, with an estimated street value of more than $400 million. In another historic case, in February 1994, Nova Scotian authorities made another huge bust off the rocky shore of Nova Scotia. Two years of RCMP investigations were rewarded with a massive drug seizure in Shelburne. The vessel, Lady Teri-Anne, was weighed down with 5,419 kilograms of cocaine, worth $1 billion.

#5. CONFESSIONS OF A KILLER: "I've done a terrible thing. I shot four people." This was the chilling confession that Aubrey Lutz made to officers at the Kentville, Nova

Scotia RCMP detachment on February 12, 1964. Lutz had recently married 18-year-old Rosalie Pudsey. But not long after the nuptials, Rosalie and Aubrey's marriage began to sour. Fearing for her safety, Rosalie took the couples' newborn baby, Kimberly, to live with her parents and two sisters. Rosalie's move enraged Aubrey and on that fateful day he loaded his gun and went to confront his wife and her family. At the house, Aubrey met and killed Rosalie's mother first. When Rosalie's younger sister, Audrey, sought refuge in the bathroom, Aubrey fired through the door, instantly killing the 15-year old. On hearing the commotion, Rosalie Lutz climbed the stairs from the basement and placed baby Kimberly on the living room couch. When she confronted her husband, he fired, striking her in the shoulder. Just as Aubrey was about to make his escape, Arthur Pudsey returned home to the awful scene. For the fourth time, Aubrey fired his gun, this time killing his father-in-law. Aubrey grabbed his unharmed baby and travelled to Kentville, where he confessed to police. Rosalie Lutz and her nine-year-old sister, who had been at school, were the sole surviving members of their family.

Deemed unfit to stand trial, Lutz was sent to the Nova Scotia Hospital. For almost 15 years he remained a volatile, dangerous man who was heavily medicated and received almost 500 shock treatments. In the late 1970s and 1980s, however, Lutz's demeanor improved and he was classified a voluntary patient, free to check himself out. On December 27, 1990, the murderer of three left the Nova Scotia Hospital a free man and returned to his Annapolis Valley home. Horrified, Rosalie called police. Lutz was again arrested, charged with three counts of murder and prepared for trial. In March 1991, the courts made a familiar ruling — Lutz was deemed unfit for trial and remanded into the custody of the Nova Scotia Hospital. Amazingly, Rosalie has forgiven Aubrey: "I believe everyone should leave him alone. I have forgiven my husband for what he has done."

#6. MUTINY AND MURDER: In May of 1844, the ship *Saladin* ran aground on Nova Scotia's eastern shore. The small crew of six claimed that the captain and other crew members had died at sea, which raised immediate suspicions. The crew members were placed under arrest and charged with killing their captain and five crewmates. As confessions were elicited, a grizzly story of mutiny and murder took shape. The ringleader, George Fielding (this former captain had been in prison prior to the journey, but made a deal with authorities to work the trip for free passage for himself and his 14-year-old son), had convinced four crewmen to help him carry out his dastardly deed. On April 14, 1844, they used axes and other tools on board to kill the captain and five mates. When his compatriots learned of Fielding's plans to sweeten his own share of the loot through further killings, they turned on him, throwing him and his son overboard. After only 15 minutes of deliberation, the jury returned guilty verdicts in three cases. Two of the men, tried separately, were acquitted. The convicted pirates were hanged on July 30, 1844. Hundreds of Haligonians brought their families to witness the event on the South Common, now the site of the Victoria General Hospital.

#7. THE MCDONALD'S MURDERS: In the early pre-dawn morning of May 7, 1992, three young Sydney-area men arrived at the city's McDonald's restaurant intending to commit robbery. Derek Wood, Darren Muise and Freeman MacNeil were sure that the restaurant's safe contained as much as $200,000. The robbery turned deadly when the three encountered the four staff members on the midnight shift. Armed with knives, a .22 caliber pistol and a shovel, the three robbers brutally murdered Donna Warren, Neil Borroughs and Jimmy Fagan, and lefT Arlene MacNeil badly wounded and near death. The horrific crime stunned and outraged the small city, and indeed the whole nation, as national media descended on Sydney.

The perpetrators denied their involvement but evidence against them mounted, and by the middle of May all had confessed their crime. They were variously charged with murder, robbery and the unlawful confinement of Donna Warren, who had been forced to open the safe before she, like the others, was shot in the head. Harsh punishment was meted out to the murderers. Darren Muise was sentenced to life in prison without parole for 20 years and Freeman MacNeil got life in prison with no parole for 25 years. Derek Wood was sentenced to two life terms in jail, and 10 years for robbery and unlawful confinement. In 2012, Darren Muise was granted full parole and in 2015, Derek Wood was denied day parole for his part in the murders.

#8. A DUBIOUS DISTINCTION: Everett Farmer, a Nova Scotian labourer charged with murdering his brother-in-law, has the dubious distinction of being the last person to be hanged in the province. As a poor, Black, Shelburne County man, Farmer had access to legal counsel of dubious quality. Farmer insisted that his crime had been one of self-defense, but without adequate representation it was hard for him to make his case. A lawyer was not assigned to his defence until just one week before the opening of his September 1937 trial.

As the first capital case to be heard in Shelburne County for a century, the Farmer trial became a media circus. Juried by 12 white men, the trial lasted just two days and ended in a murder conviction. Everett Farmer was sentenced to die. According to a newspaper account, at 5 a.m. on December 15, 1937, Farmer climbed the stairs of the hanging scaffold "with the same coolness that [had] characterized him since he [had] been in jail." As the hood was placed over his head, and as his spiritual advisor recited scripture, Farmer uttered his last words before the trap was sprung: "Good-bye, boys."

#9. GUILTY UNTIL PROVEN INNOCENT: On May 28, 1971, 16-year-old Donald Marshall Jr. was walking through a Sydney park when he met up with Sandy Seale, another youth from Sydney. The two teenagers then encountered Roy Ebsary, described as an "eccentric old man with a fetish for knives." Without warning, Ebsary brutally and fatally stabbed Seale. Police arrested and charged Marshall, a Mi'kmaq from Membertou, with Seale's death, and in November 1971 Marshall was sentenced to life in prison. For 11 years Marshall was incarcerated; for 11 years he maintained his innocence. In 1982, Marshall was released on bail as then Justice Minister, Jean

Chrétien, referred the case to the Nova Scotia Supreme Court for rehearing. In 1983, Donald Marshall Jr. was acquitted of all charges, but in a strange outcome the police who had wrongly charged him were absolved of all wrongdoing. In a now infamous statement, Chrétien reasoned that any miscarriage of justice was "more apparent than real." Roy Ebsary was eventually convicted of manslaughter in the death of Seale. For 11 lost years of his life, Donald Marshall accepted a lump-sum payment of $270,000 from the Nova Scotia government, but was required to pay his own legal bills. Marshall died in 2009.

#10. THE BUTTERBOX BABIES: This is one of the darkest chapters in Nova Scotian, if not Canadian, history. William and Lila Young operated the Ideal Maternity Home in East Chester from the late 1920s through the late 1940s. In 1928, Lila, a 29-year-old recent graduate of the National School of Obstetric and Midwifery, and her husband, a 30-old, un-ordained Seventh Day Adventist minister, missionary and licensed as a chiropractor, opened the Life and Health Sanitarium, which by the 1940s became known as the Ideal Maternity Home. The Home promised maternity care for married couples and discreet birthing and placement for the children of unwed mothers. In truth, it was a source of babies for an illegal trade in infants between Canada and the United States. At this time, U.S. laws prohibited adoption across religious backgrounds, which led to an acute shortage of babies available for Jewish couples to adopt. The home in East Chester would provide these desperate people with black-market adoptions, charging up to ten thousand dollars for a baby. In the 1940s, many of the babies ended up in Jewish homes in New Jersey. The Youngs also charged the new mothers 500 dollars for the services they received in the home, which were often performed in unsanitary, deplorable conditions. Since many of the mothers could not afford this amount, which in those days was a large sum, they were often forced to work at the home for up to 18 months to pay their bills.

Years later, it was discovered that the Youngs had purposely starved "unmarketable" babies to death by feeding them only molasses and water. On this diet, the infants would usually last only two weeks. Any deformity, serious illness, or "dark" colouration would seal a baby's fate. In some cases, married couples that had come to the home solely for birthing services were told that their baby had died shortly after birth. In truth, these babies were also sold to adoptive parents. The Youngs would also separate or create siblings to meet the desires of their customers by pretending unrelated babies were siblings.

It is estimated that between 400 and 600 babies died at the home, while at least another 1,000 survived and were adopted. Babies who died were disposed of in small wooden grocery boxes typically used for dairy products. That is how the term "Butterbox Babies" originated. The Butterbox Babies' bodies were buried on the Youngs' property, at sea, or adjacent to a nearby cemetery. Some were burned in the Home's furnace. By 1933, the Youngs' lucrative business had attracted the attention of the Nova Scotia child welfare director as well as the health minister. Health officials finally intervened in 1945 and won convictions against the couple for violating new adoption licensing laws.

New regulations were slowly introduced. A new amendment to the Maternity Boarding House Act of 1940 had broadened licensing requirements to apply to incorporated companies and the Youngs' licence application was swiftly rejected. The Ideal Maternity Home was ordered shut down in November 1945, but the Youngs' legal woes were mounting amid stories of illegal baby smuggling and medical malpractice. On June 5, 1946, the Youngs were convicted of illegally selling babies to four American couples and were fined $428.90. William was later convicted of perjury based on his testimony at the June trial, but babies were still being born at the Ideal Maternity Home in early 1947. The Youngs, bankrupt and debt-ridden by the end of 1947, sold off their property in East Chester and moved to Quebec. The Home, which was scheduled for conversion into a resort hotel, burned to the ground on September 23, 1962. William died of cancer before Christmas that year, and Lila died of leukemia in 1967. Following their deaths, the truth about the Ideal Maternity Home remained buried for many years. The full scope of this heinous story was not known until decades later, when a caretaker admitted to Halifax journalist Bette Cahill that he was paid to bury the babies in open graves and in butter boxes from the local LaHave Dairy. Cahill's 1992 book, Butterbox Babies, became an international bestseller, and was subsequently made into a movie under the same title.

#11. LIFE WITH BILLY: On March 11, 1982, Jane (Hurshman) Stafford killed her abusive common-law husband, Billy Stafford, as he slept drunkenly slumped behind the steering wheel of his pickup truck near their home in Bangs Falls, Queens County. She had no idea of the impact her actions would have on the Canadian legal system and the issue of domestic violence. Hurshman's first-degree murder trial at the historic Liverpool Court House, and the publicity that surrounded the sensational case, eventually helped to broaden the legal definition of self-defence in Canadian law. Hurshman was famously acquitted in the first trial. But, concerned with the legal precedent, the Crown later appealed, and in turn, Hurshman pled guilty to manslaughter. She received a six-month sentence and was released after two months. Following her release, she became an advocate for women's rights, conducted one-on-one counselling with other victims, and she led the charge against spousal abuse. The Stafford case spawned several books, including Life With Billy by Brian Vallee and a television movie of the same title; and it exposed the issues of wife battering and domestic violence for the crimes that they truly are.

On February 23, 1992, Jane Hurshman's body was found in a car on the Halifax waterfront, dead from a single gunshot wound. Autopsy results showed that she died from a bullet that hit her heart and right lung. The autopsy report said the bullet wound was consistent with suicide but that murder was also a possibility.

#12. RANDOM KILLINGS: On the evening of August 8, 1964, 11-year-old Gordon

Hartling had accompanied his sister to the corner store on Halifax's Tower Road located on Halifax's south end. He was waiting outside on the sidewalk while she went into the store to buy Popsicles, when a teenager on a bicycle rode up and shot him in the head with a pistol.

Gordon, one of three boys shot in the span of 40 minutes that day, died, as did James Squires. Twelve-year-old Michael Smith miraculously recovered. James and Michael were both 12 years old at the time of the shootings. It has never been determined what made Edward Thomas Boutilier shoot a boy standing on a sidewalk, another picking blueberries with his mother and another on his way home from the Waegwoltic Club. But for two days, until Boutilier gave himself up, Halifax lived behind locked doors, in fear. That night, 20 minutes before Gordon was gunned down, Michael Smith was walking home along the railway shortcut near Jubilee Road after sailing at the Waeg. He stepped out of the way of a cyclist and then, just after someone yelled a warning, felt what he thought must have been a boulder slam into the side of his head. In fact, he'd been shot just below the ear. "The next thing, everything was reddish liquid. I had a funny taste in my mouth," Smith, who has since died, told *The Chronicle Herald* in 1999. "I heard them scream, then just a bunch of confusion and then the ambulance came. The last thing I remember is going up in the elevator in what must have been the old Victoria General hospital."

Jimmy Squires was also near the railway tracks when he was shot at the Maplewood crossing. He had asked his mother that afternoon to take him blueberry picking. The two had just moved from one patch to another when Jimmy's mother saw Boutilier approaching on a bicycle. At first, she thought he was another blueberry picker. "He … let Jimmy walk about three steps ahead of him," Verna Squires told a reporter from the *Mail-Star* at the time of the shootings. "There was a terrible bang and, just then, Jimmy fell in a heap. I had to walk over to him to convince myself he had been shot and I saw blood gushing from his head."

As the streets emptied, 200 police officers, some carrying machine-guns, began to comb the city for a suspect for which they had just a vague description. Two days later, Boutilier turned himself in to police near Halifax Stanfield International Airport. By a pre-arranged signal, a police officer fired three shots into the air and Boutilier walked out of the woods and surrendered. Psychiatrists quickly diagnosed Boutilier, aged 18, as "grossly mentally disturbed" and "definitely certifiable." He was committed to the Nova Scotia Hospital for an indefinite period, where he spent 10 years before killing himself.

#13. UNDERCOVER SPY AND MURDERER: Notorious 19th-century criminal Alexander "Sandy" Keith, Jr. was born in 1827 in Caithness, Scotland, immigrating to Halifax when he was a small boy. The nephew of Alexander Keith, founder of the Alexander Keith's Brewery, the younger Keith worked for a time as a clerk in his uncle's brewery. Keith became a secret agent for the Confederate States of America during the American Civil War, acting mostly as a blockade-runner and courier. Keith assisted in helping Confederate sympathizers escape justice in the Chesapeake Affair. He was also involved with Luke Blackburn in an infamous plot to send clothes infected with yellow fever to northern cities in the United States.

In 1865, he swindled his associates-in-crime and fled to St. Louis, Missouri, settling finally on the prairie. There, he married Cecelia Paris, a milliner's daughter from St. Louis. Hunted down by one of his victims, Keith fled again with Cecelia to Germany, where they lived the high life hobnobbing with wealthy socialites and Saxon generals under the assumed name of "William King Thomas."

When the couple began to run out of money, Keith concocted a plot to blow up passenger ships and collect the insurance money. This led to a major catastrophe in Bremerhaven, on December 11, 1875, when a time bomb he had placed in a shipping barrel accidentally went off on the dock, killing 80 people, most of them aboard the steamship *Mosel*, a German emigrant ship. She was under the command of Captain Leist, replacement for the ailing captain Hermann Neynaber for a crossing to New York. The explosion happened when the passengers were on board and the final baggage was being loaded. With only a few large shipping crates on the pier, one of Keith's barrels slipped out the stevedores' hands while being loaded and struck the ground, exploding in a huge column of fire whose blast caused two ships at the quay to overturn. At the time, the deed was called the "crime of the century." Keith was aboard another ship in Bremerhaven at the time of the explosion and was thus aware of the premature detonation of his time bomb and the massive carnage that ensued. He went to his suite and shot himself. He died a week later.

After the tragedy was revealed as a murder/insurance scam on a large scale, the disappearance of other ships were looked into to see if Keith and his possible associates were involved. One was the disappearance of the *SS City of Boston*, which vanished in January 1870.

BUILT HERITAGE

- A List of 10 Must-See Nova Scotia Museums

- A List of 10 Must-See Nova Scotia Historical Museums

- A List of 10 Must-See Nova Scotia Historical Homes

- Chris Mills' List of the Top 10 Most Important Lighthouses in Nova Scotia

- A List of 10 Famous Ships Built in Nova Scotia

A List of 10 Must-See Nova Scotia Museums

There is a wealth of museums throughout Nova Scotia, but if you are looking to discover the unique history of the province, these 10 must-see museums will give you a fascinating snapshot:

#1. ALEXANDER GRAHAM BELL MUSEUM: The Alexander Graham Bell National Historic Site is a 25-acre property in Baddeck, Cape Breton overlooking the Bras d'Or Lakes. The site includes the Alexander Graham Bell Museum, a unit of Parks Canada, which is the only museum in the world containing the actual artifacts and documents from Bell's years of experimental work in Baddeck. This site was designated a National Historic Site in 1952.

#2. ATLANTIC CANADA AVIATION MUSEUM: The Atlantic Canada Aviation Museum (ACAM) is an aerospace museum located near the Halifax Stanfield International Airport. It is the only museum devoted to preserving all aspects of Atlantic Canada's aviation heritage.

#3. BLACK LOYALIST HERITAGE CENTRE: One of Canada's best kept secrets, this was the site of the largest free-Black settlement, in the 1780s, where people voted with their feet for freedom. This unique historic site is nestled in beautiful Birchtown Bay on the western shores of Shelburne Harbour, the third-largest natural harbour in the world. Explore the site and visit the historic buildings including the Old School House and Saint Paul's Church, where you can view the Bunce Island exhibit and movie. The National Historic Monument, situated on the shore, commemorates the 1783 Black Loyalist Landings in Nova Scotia. You can also walk the Heritage Trail and visit the Pit House.

#4. CANADIAN MUSEUM OF IMMIGRATION AT PIER 21: The Canadian Museum of Immigration at Pier 21, in Halifax, is Canada's national museum of immigration. The museum occupies part of Pier 21, the former ocean-liner terminal and immigration shed from 1928 to 1971. Pier 21 is Canada's last remaining ocean-immigration shed. The facility is often compared to Ellis Island (1892-1954) in terms of its importance to mid-20th-century immigration to Canada, an association it shares with 19th-century immigration history at Grosse Isle, Quebec (1832-1932) and Partridge Island in Saint John, New Brunswick (1785-1941). The museum began as an independent institution run by the Pier 21 Society in 1999. It became a national museum run by the federal government in 2011.

#5. FIREFIGHTERS MUSEUM OF NOVA SCOTIA: Discover the history of firefighting in this province at the Firefighter's Museum in Yarmouth. Imagine the clang of the fire bell, the smell of smoke and the feel of hot steam as firefighters of the past raced to save burning homes in communities across Nova Scotia. See the types of fire engines used from the 1800s to the 1930s. Marvel at antique hand-drawn and operated engines such as Canada's oldest horse-drawn steam engine, an 1863 Amoskeag Steamer. Take the wheel of a 1933 Chev Bickle pumper and see collections of antique toy fire engines, shoulder crests, patches and badges from fire departments around the world. Antique auto enthusiasts in particular will enjoy the important collection of vintage equipment: the pumpers, hose wagons, and ladder trucks. Even though these fire trucks had long service careers before being retired, they're all in excellent condition, which makes perfect sense. Given that firefighters routinely risk their lives as part of their job, they always make sure the equipment they depend on is in good running order.

#6. FISHERIES MUSEUM OF THE ATLANTIC: The Fisheries Museum of the Atlantic operates seasonally from mid-May through mid-October and is located in the UNESCO World Heritage Site of Lunenburg. The Fisheries Museum of the Atlantic commemorates the fishing heritage of the Atlantic coast of Canada. Housed in brightly painted red buildings, with floating vessels at wharfside, the museum offers a host of attractions, a maritime gift shop and restaurant. Retired fishermen and experienced heritage interpreters accentuate the experience of visiting the museum.

#7. JOGGINS FOSSIL CENTRE: Joggins is famous for its record of fossils from a rainforest ecosystem approximately 310 million years ago, dating to the Pennsylvanian "Coal Age" durin the early Carboniferous Period. The dramatic coastal exposure of the Coal Age rocks, known as the Joggins Fossil Cliffs, are continually hewn and freshly exposed by the actions of the tides in the Cumberland Basin. Geologists were first attracted to this locality in the late 1820s. However, the true fame of Joggins dates to the mid-nineteenth century and the visits in 1842 and 1852 Charles Lyell, the founder of modern geology and author. In his Elements of Geology (1871), Lyell proclaimed the Joggins exposure of Coal Age rocks and fossils to be "the finest example in the world." In 2007, a 14.7-km length of the coast constituting the Joggins Fossil Cliffs was nominated by Canada to UNESCO as a natural World Heritage Site. It was officially inscribed on the World Heritage List in on July 7, 2008.

#8. MARITIME MUSEUM OF THE ATLANTIC: The Maritime Museum of the Atlantic, located in Halifax, is a member of the Nova Scotia Museum system and is the oldest and largest maritime museum in Canada with a collection of more than 30,000 artifacts, including 70 small craft and a steamship — the *CSS Acadia* — a 180-foot, steam-powered hydrographic survey ship launched in 1913 and received by the museum in 1982. The museum was founded in 1948. It was first known as the Maritime Museum of Canada and located at the HMCS Dockyard, the naval base on Halifax Harbour. The museum moved through several locations over the next three decades before its current building was constructed in 1981 as part of a waterfront redevelopment program.

#9. NOVA SCOTIA MUSEUM OF NATURAL HISTORY: The Nova Scotia Museum of Natural History, part of the Nova Scotia Museum system, is located in Halifax. The museum includes collections and exhibits concerning the natural sciences as well as artifacts of cultural significance to Nova Scotia.

#10. SPRINGHILL MINERS' MUSEUM: Springhill Miners' Museum is located in Springhill (off Route 2) in the Fundy Shore and Annapolis Valley region. Tour the depths of a Springhill coalmine, famous in song and legend. Hear stories of the disaster of 1891, the 1916 subterranean fire, which raged through the galleries, the loss of 39 men in the 1956 explosion and the major "bump" in 1958, which killed 75 men. The Miners' Museum displays unique artifacts of the history of the town and its remarkable industrial heritage.

A List of 10 Must-See Nova Scotia Historical Museums

For a historical perspective of Nova Scotia, these are the 10 must-see historical museums in the province:

#1. ARGYLE TOWNSHIP COURT HOUSE AND GAOL: The Argyle Township Court House and Gaol is Canada's oldest standing courthouse, built in the village of Tusket in 1805. It operated as a working courthouse and jail from 1805 until 1944. The building served as the municipal offices for the Municipality of Argyle from 1945 until 1976. In 1982, the building was partially restored and reopened as a museum and historic site. In 2005, the building was declared a National Historic Site.

#2. FORT ANNE NATIONAL HISTORIC SITE: Fort Anne is a four-star fort built to protect the harbour of Annapolis Royal. The fort repelled all French attacks during the early stages of King George's War. The 1797 building that housed the officer's quarters was renovated in the 1930s and now houses the museum with exhibits about the fort's history and historic artifacts from the area. The fort is a National Historic Site and is managed by Parks Canada.

#3. FORTRESS OF LOUISBOURG: The Fortress of Louisbourg (*Forteresse de Louisbourg*) is a National Historic Site and the location of a one-quarter partial reconstruction of an 18th-century French fortress at Louisbourg. Its two sieges, especially that of 1758, were turning points in the Anglo-French struggle for what today is Canada. The original settlement was made in 1713 and initially called Havre à l'Anglois. Subsequently, the fishing port grew to become a major commercial port and a strongly defended fortress. The fortifications eventually surrounded the town.

The walls were constructed mainly between 1720 and 1740. By the mid-1740s Louisbourg was one of the most extensive (and expensive) European fortifications constructed in North America. It was supported by two smaller garrisons on Île Royale, located at present-day St. Peter's and Englishtown. It was captured by British colonists in 1745 and was a major bargaining chip in the negotiations leading to the 1748 treaty ending the War of the Austrian Succession. It was returned to the French in exchange for border towns in what is today Belgium. It was captured again 1758 by British forces in the Seven Years' War, after which its fortifications were systematically destroyed by British engineers. The British continued to have a garrison at Louisbourg until 1768. The fortress and town were partially reconstructed in the 1960s and 1970s, using some of the original stonework, which provided jobs for unemployed coal miners. The site is operated by Parks Canada as a living history museum. It stands as the largest reconstruction project in North America.

#4. HALIFAX CITADEL NATIONAL HISTORIC SITE: Although all four fortifications constructed on Citadel Hill since 1749 are variously referred to as Fort George, only the third fort (built between 1794 and 1800) was officially named Fort George, by General Orders of October 20, 1798, after Prince Edward's father, King George III. The first two and the fourth and current fort were simply called the Halifax Citadel. The Citadel is the fortified summit of Citadel Hill, a National Historic Site restored to the Victorian period. The hill was first fortified in 1749, the year the town of Halifax was founded. Those fortifications on the hill were successively rebuilt to defend the town from various enemies. A series of four different defensive fortifications have occupied the summit of Citadel Hill. Although never attacked, the Citadel was long the keystone to the defence of the strategically important Halifax Harbour and its Royal Navy Dockyard.

#5. HIGHLAND VILLAGE MUSEUM/AN CLACHAN GÀIDHEALACH: The Highland Village Museum/An Clachan Ghàidhealaich is a living history museum dedicated to Nova Scotia's Gaelic folk-life, culture, and language. Highland Village is located in Iona, on 43 acres of natural landscape overlooking the Bras d'Or Lake in Central Cape Breton. The roots of Gaelic Nova Scotia are found in the Highlands and Islands of Scotland where significant socio-economic changes in the 18th century disrupted a pastoral life-style. These changes prompted many to emigrate to Nova Scotia. Throughout the late 18th and early 19th centuries, thousands of Scots settled in eastern Nova Scotia. Through a pattern of chain emigration, settlers often chose to create new communities based on family connections, religious or political beliefs. The settlers faced new hardships such as a vastly different climate, however they persevered and began clearing land, building homes and outbuildings, cultivating their land and establishing new lives and communities.

#6. LE VILLAGE HISTORIQUE ACADIEN DE LA NOUVELLE-ÉCOSSE/ THE HISTORIC ACADIAN VILLAGE OF NOVA SCOTIA: The Acadian Villag, located in Lower West Pubnico on a breathtaking 17-acre point of land overlooking picturesque Pubnico Harbour, represents the unique Acadian culture of Nova Scotia. Le Village's mission of providing a greater understanding and appreciation of the Acadian culture, traditions, language and way of life is fulfilled by allowing visitors to take a step back in time and experience traditional Acadian culture and the lifestyle of bygone days. Le Village demonstrates many aspects of the life of the Acadian fishermen, including the building of boats, lobster-fishing traps, mending fishing nets and much more.

#7. MARCONI NATIONAL HISTORIC SITE: The Marconi National Historic Site and the Marconi Wireless Station National Historic Site are two National Historic Sites located on Cape Breton Island. Both sites commemorate the efforts of Guglielmo Marconi to transmit transatlantic radio signals between North America and Europe in the first decade of the 20th century. The two sites are located within approximately eight kilometres of one another and are connected by the Marconi Trail.

#8. PORT-ROYAL NATIONAL HISTORIC SITE: Port-Royal National Historic Site is located on the north bank of the Annapolis Basin in the community of Port Royal. The site is the location of the Habitation at Port-Royal, established by France in 1605 and was that nation's first settlement in North America. Port-Royal served as the capital of Acadia until its destruction by British military forces in 1613. France relocated the settlement and capital eight-km upstream and to the south bank of the Annapolis River, the site of the present-day town of Annapolis Royal. The relocated settlement kept the same name "Port-Royal" and served as the capital of Acadia for the majority of the 17th century until the British conquest of the colony in 1710, at which time the settlement was renamed Annapolis Royal.

#9. ROSS FARM MUSEUM: The Ross Farm Museum is an agricultural museum located in New Ross. The exhibits feature working artisans, live animals, historic buildings and antique implements and furnishings. The goal of the Ross Farm Museum is to give visitors an understanding of the importance of Nova Scotia's rural heritage. It includes a country store displaying the types of products available then, a working cooper shop, historic breeds of farm animals, a blacksmith, a working farm and a village schoolhouse. Costumed guides are on hand to explain life in that time period. Wagon rides are often available.

#10. SHERBROOKE VILLAGE MUSEUM: In the 1860s, timber, tall ships and gold brought prosperity to Sherbrooke's people. Today, you can explore this amazing village with its 25 original buildings, to experience life as it was along the St. Mary's River before the 1900s. The French were the first European visitors to Sherbrooke, arriving as early as 1655. By 1815 the settlement, which developed at the head of navigation, became known as Sherbrooke, in honour of Sir John Coape Sherbrooke, Lieutenant Governor of Nova Scotia. For years the community prospered, supported by farming, fishing and the timber trade. Busy mills produced deal, planks, laths, spars, ships' knees and shingles for the British and West Indian markets. Then in 1861, the cry of "Gold!" was heard and the town became a live and energetic mining camp. Nineteen mining companies had flocked to participate in the discovery by 1869 and

Sherbrooke boomed. The boom lasted approximately 20 years, a time which could be described as Sherbrooke's Golden Age. Lumbering continued as a major industry. The Sherbrooke Village Restoration area was established in 1969 to conserve a part of Sherbrooke as it was during the last half of the 1800s.

A List of 10 Must-See Nova Scotia Historical Homes

Nova Scotia is blessed to host a wealth of historical properties, many of which are open for public viewing. Here is a list of just 10 of the must-see historical homes in the province.

#1. BLAIR HOUSE MUSEUM: Located in Kentville, the Atlantic Food and Horticulture Research Centre is a branch of Agriculture and Agri-Food Canada's national network of 19 research centres stationed across the country. The Centre's programs address agricultural challenges throughout the Canadian horticultural and food network, but primarily focus on the regional requirements of Atlantic Canada. Two structures at the centre are officially recognized by the Canadian government as historical places: The Main Barn, built in 1912, is noted both for its historic and architectural value and was designated as a Federal Heritage Building in 1994. "Building 18" (also known as Blair House) was built in 1911 and served as the presiding superintendent's residence until 1979. It is recognized for its historical, architectural and environmental value and was designated as a Federal Heritage Building in 1994. Building 18 was converted into the Blair House Museum and was opened to the public on May 29, 1981. The museum showcases the history of Nova Scotia's apple industry and the past and present research of the centre.

#2 CHURCHILL HOUSE: Churchill House is a historic house and community centre located in Hantsport. The house was built in 1860 by noted Hantsport shipbuilder Ezra Churchill as a gift for his son John Wiley Churchill. The well-preserved example of an Italianate house today serves as a museum and community centre owned by the nonprofit corporation Hamtsport Memorial Community Centre.

#3. COSSIT HOUSE: Built in 1787, Cossit House is one of the oldest surviving houses in Sydney and possibly one of the oldest buildings on Cape Breton Island. Named for its original owner, Reverend Ranna Cossit, the house depicts 18th-century life and serves as the cornerstone of the city's North-end Heritage Conservation District. Following the American Revolution, Rev. Cossit was assigned to the British colony in Cape Breton that, at the time, was separate from mainland Nova Scotia. Accompanied by his wife Thankful and their growing family, Rev. Cossit became the region's first Anglican minister and assumed a key role in Sydney's social and political development.

#4. HALIBURTON HOUSE MUSEUM: The Haliburton House Museum is part of the Nova Scotia Museum system and is located in Windsor. It was originally built in the 1830s for Thomas Chandler Haliburton, a Windsor native who was one of Canada's first famous authors. His *Sam Slick* stories won him acclaim around the English-speaking world of the 1840s and, though Haliburton's famous character was fictitious, the home has also been informally referred to as the Sam Slick House for many years. The house was added to during Haliburton's time, but successive owners also made major changes to the house until the 1920s. In 1939, the province acquired the home and in 1940 opened the site as the Haliburton Memorial Museum. Though Haliburton auctioned off the property and the contents of the home when he left for England in 1856, the museum does have some furniture and artifacts that belonged to him, including his writing desk. Most of these items were procured by donation to the Nova Scotia Museum to coincide with the 1940 opening. The rest of the museum is furnished in period pieces from the museum's collection.

#5. KNAUT-RHULAND HOUSE MUSEUM: Knaut–Rhuland House is a historic 18th-century house located in Lunenburg. It is a designated a National Historic Site as well as a Provincially Registered Property. It is located within the Old Town Lunenburg World Heritage Site and is owned by the Lunenburg Heritage Society, which operates a museum in the house open to the public during the summer. The house is named for its first two owners. The first owner, Benjamin Knaut, had the house built in 1793. Knaut was one of the town's first sheriffs, a trader and a privateer. The second owner, Conrad Rhuland, was also a trader and a ship owner and, during the War of 1812, was a privateer's prize master.

#6. LAWRENCE HOUSE MUSEUM: Informative and entertaining guided tours include an indoor exhibit depicting the community of Maitland, a scale model of the "great ship" and 23 period rooms that highlight heirlooms collected by the Lawrence family during their world travels. The site is an interesting introduction to Nova Scotia's first municipally designed Heritage Conservation District, Maitland. Photographers and birders alike will enjoy the Ducks Unlimited Canada Wetland area adjacent to the museum. A large deck over-looking the pond provides a unique opportunity to experience the natural wonders of some of the Bay of Fundy's winged inhabitants.

#7. PERKINS HOUSE MUSEUM: Colonel Simeon Perkins (February 24, 1735 – May 9, 1812) was a militia leader, merchant, diarist and politician. Perkins led the defence of Liverpool from attacks during the American Revolution, French Revolutionary Wars and Napoleonic Wars. In the 1770s, Liverpool was the second-largest settlement in Nova Scotia, next to Halifax. Perkins also funded privateer ships in defence of the colony. He wrote a diary for 46 years (1766-1812) that is an essential historic document of this period in Nova Scotian history. Perkins' home was preserved through the efforts of the Queens County Historical Society in 1949 led by the author and historian Thomas H. Raddall. It opened as a museum in 1957 and became part of the Nova Scotia Museum system, the oldest building owned by the province.

#8. PRESCOTT HOUSE MUSEUM: Prescott House Museum is a historic house and gardens located in Starr's Point, which is part of the Nova Scotia Museum system. Built between 1812 and 1816 by Charles Ramage Prescott as the centrepiece of his country estate called "Acacia Grove," it is one of the best-preserved Georgian houses in Canada. The house explores Prescott's life, Georgian architecture, the apple industry and the lives of the Prescott sisters. Fully restored rooms depict both the Georgian period of Charles Prescott's time and the later era of the 1930s and 40s, when it was restored by the Prescott sisters.

#9. ROSS-THOMSON HOUSE AND STORE MUSEUM: Travel back in time to discover 1780s Nova Scotia and the recently settled town of Shelburne, where thousands of Loyalist refugees began new lives after the American War of Independence. It is in this historic store that seasoned merchants George and Robert Ross carried on international trade in tea, coffee, rum, port and wine, offering both necessities and luxuries to the town's residents. Stroll Ross-Thomson House and Store's gardens; step up to the store's counter and ask the clerk about the kinds of goods the Ross Brothers once bartered and sold; spend time inside the living quarters, furnished in the sparse but elegant style of the period; and visit the Militia Room above the shop where you might meet a 1780s militia guard.

#10. SHAND HOUSE MUSEUM: The Shand House Museum is part of the Nova Scotia Museum system. Located in Windsor, it was built in 1890-91 for Clifford and Henrie Shand. It is a Queen-Anne style late-Victorian Era home and most of its elaborate machine-made trim features are still intact. It contains most of the original family's belongings including furniture, dishes, artwork, toys, photos and books, which date to the turn of the century. Many pieces of the home's furniture were made at the nearby Windsor Furniture Factory, which was in operation in the late 19th and early 20th century Windsor. Unusually for its time the home was constructed with indoor plumbing, central heating and electric lighting within a year of its completion. While the family were noted local figures, the house is primarily maintained not as a memorial to the Shand family but rather as a very well preserved example of the architectural, economic and social history of 1890s Nova Scotia. The home was opened as a Museum in 1985.

Chris Mills' List of the Top 10 Most Important Lighthouses in Nova Scotia

#1. LOUISBOURG (FIRST LIGHT): Canada's first lighthouse, and North America's second, still lights the way for traffic entering and leaving Louisbourg's harbour on the wild east coast of Cape Breton. Today, the light comes from a state-of-the-art LED array, but in 1734 the source was a circle of wicks fed by cod-liver oil. The original stone lighthouse survived a fire in 1736 but it was no match for the second British siege of 1758, falling into ruin after the attack. A wooden tower/dwelling went up in 1842, set on a massive foundation of cut stone. It burned to the ground in 1922 and the current, ornate concrete tower replaced it a year or so later. Interestingly, it has a twin, on Georges Island, in Halifax Harbour. Unfortunately, the fine dentils, cornices and keystones still visible on the Louisbourg tower have been covered on Georges Island, due to deteriorating concrete. Roy Forgeron was the last keeper at Louisbourg light. In the 1980s, his job consisted of general maintenance and keeping an eye/ear on the light and horn. By this time the keeper's house was a prefab home situated in the nearby woods. Roy retired in 1990 and the light was left on its own. Today, the tower draws tourists from around the world. Folks come to enjoy unparalleled views of the rugged eastern shore of Cape Breton and of the grand reconstructed Fortress of Louisbourg across the harbour.

#2. BRIER ISLAND (MY FIRST LIGHT): Brier Island lighthouse (locally known as "Western Light") has marked the southern approaches to the Bay of Fundy since 1809. It's marked my own "approach" to lighthouses and lightkeeping since 1969. When my parents purchased a cottage just up the road from Western Light that year, they soon became friends with assistant lightkeeper Donald Wickerson "Wick" Lent. Wick's bearded countenance, deep voice, omnipresent pipe and his prosthetic leg all conspired to make him, to my young eyes, an almost mythical figure. During our evening visits, Wick held court in his recliner, regaling us with great (and small) stories about lightkeeping and life on Brier Island, while just up the hill, the light sent its revolving spokes into the gathering dark. On foggy days, the mighty diaphone foghorn near the tower hurled its body-shaking blasts into the murk. That diaphone scared the crap out of me, and during one memorable afternoon, the very idea that it might let loose its horrendous "moo" was enough to send me running from the fog-alarm building to fall face-first in the grass outside. Wick got a real charge out of that. He'd only been flicking a light switch on as we entered the building. There's been no lightkeeper at Western Light since 1987; of the half-dozen or so buildings that once made up the station, only the tower remains. Wick passed away in 2005 at the age of 85. But Western Light, and Wick, are what inspired me to become a lightkeeper in 1989. And I love foghorns now!

#3. SAMBRO ISLAND (THE OLDEST): The massive stone tower on Sambro Island has stood guard at the approaches to Halifax Harbour since Halifax was just a fledgling nine years old. Begun in 1758, workers completed the granite structure two years later. It was a tough slog. Men hauled the heavy granite blocks to the top of the island to lay the bottom layers of the tower, which is almost two metres thick. They completed the masonry by late 1758 and in April of the next year Captain Joseph Rous became the light's first keeper. Early oils used for illumination weren't too reliable and there were numerous complaints that if the light happened to go out, the keeper would often let the tower stay dark, especially if there weren't any ships in sight. This didn't go down well with naval authorities in Halifax, who noted that the fatal loss of the sloop Granby on the Sambro Ledges in 1771 occurred "… for a want of light being kept in the lighthouse, for it is most notoriously and shamefully so, the King's ships bound into Halifax are frequently, nay, almost constantly obliged to *fire* at the lighthouse to make them show a light…"! Better lights installed in 1772 helped, and for the ensuing 216 years, diligent keepers kept the light burning and, when necessary, sounded all manner of fog signals, from cannon, to whistle, to explosive charge, to diaphone and finally a solar-powered electronic horn. In a case of perverse irony (considering early complaints from ship-owners looking for a light), complaints from a local resident helped put an end to the horn a few years ago. But Sambro Light has its friends too and years of lobbying by the Sambro Island Heritage Society led to the restoration of the stalwart tower, inside and out, in 2016. Sambro Light continues to mark the dangerous Sambro Ledges and light "the sea road to Halifax."

#4. SEAL ISLAND (THE INSISTENT MARY HICHEN'S LIGHT): Lighthouse Heroines: England has Grace Darling; the U.S. has Ida Lewis. And we have Mary Hichens. Mary and her husband Richard were among the original settlers of Seal Island in the late 1820s. Located about 18 nautical miles west of Cape Sable Island, the island claimed dozens of ships beginning in the early 18th century. Vessels still occasionally come to grief on its sand beaches and granite shores, most recently in 2009. In the early days it was a nasty business. Shipwreck victims fortunate enough to drag their weary bodies ashore soon realized that there was no shelter or food on the uninhabited island. Every spring, preachers and residents journeyed from the mainland to find and bury the dead — in one heartbreaking case, 21 in a single day. According to stories handed down by generations of Seal Islanders, it was thanks to the insistent and relentless urging of Mary Hichens that the colonial government constructed a massive timber tower on the island's southern end. On November 28, 1831, Mary Hichens gave birth to a daughter, as the tower's fixed light sent its first beams seaward. Richard and lightkeeping partner Edmund Crowell kept the light. The two also maintained a lifesaving station on the island, which drew its crew from stalwart islanders who saved dozens of lives with the help of an open lifeboat. Until October 17, 1990, keepers and their families — and at the end, bachelor crews — tended Seal Island light. Although hands-on rescues waned after the war years, there is no doubt that Seal Island's powerful light, foghorn and, later, radiobeacon, kept thousands of lives safe at sea. Today, the 1831 tower still stands, along with a few abandoned outbuildings and a solar-powered foghorn near the rocky beach below the tower. Inside the tower, the massive 47' hand-hewn uprights remain in amazingly good condition, as do the natural-growth knees below the lantern. And, the smell remains — a heady collage of kerosene, paint, diesel and age. A small plastic lens atop the tower still rotates and shines by night, keeping Mary Hichens' life-saving legacy alive.

#5. CAPE SABLE (THE TALLETS): Cape Sable is home to Nova Scotia's tallest and most beautiful lighthouse. Okay, beauty is a subjective thing, but the Cape's 101-foot (just shy of 31-m) tall, classically-inspired concrete tower is graceful and commanding. It stands on the outer Cape, south of The Hawk on Cape Sable Island, guiding shipping and fishing traffic around Nova Scotia's treacherous southwestern tip. It contains one of our most powerful remaining lenses and a horn that still sounds for four seconds out of every 60. The government of the day built the first, short wooden tower on the Cape back in 1861. In 1923-24 the Canadian government put up the present tower, which gave a much stronger light thanks to its increased height and the installation of a beautiful 3rd-order Fresnel lens. The Cape was a busy station, with its big tower and light to maintain, and a foghorn that blared hundreds of hours each year in frequent pea soup fogs. Keeper Benjamin Smith landed on the Cape with his family in 1931 and stayed until 1945. He was back for another go in 1952. As his son Sid said, "I remember him saying to my mother, 'You know, I thought I needed a change, but I guess all I needed was a rest!'"

Sid worked as assistant to his father. Both men were consummate lightkeepers, revelling in maintenance of the light, the mighty diaphone horn and everything else that demanded their attention. As Sid remembered, living in the old duplex near the tower was an adventure in itself. "After an easterly storm," he laughed, "perhaps the wind would start breezin' up from the west'ard and after a while you'd hear this awful crunch! The whole house had gone that three inches or so to the eastward because of the west wind and all the doors that normally would open, now wouldn't open, and all the others would fly open!" Benjamin retired in 1970 and Sid took over as principal keeper, living at the station with his family until 1979. Lightkeeping was a family affair in many ways, with kids Bev and Locke pitching in to help with lightkeeping and livestock duties. The lightkeeping way of life was a natural fit for Sid's wife Betty June as well: her father Morrill kept nearby Bon Portage (Outer) Island from 1929 to 1964 and her mother, Evelyn Richardson, wrote the classic *We Keep A Light*. The last keepers left Cape Sable in 1986. In 2016 workers completely restored the tower, which continues to lift its 101' "skeleton finger" above the ever-changing seas of sou'west Nova Scotia.

#6. CAPE GEORGE (THE HIGHEST): While Cape Sable can claim title to being the tallest lighthouse in Nova Scotia (actually, the tallest in the Maritimes), Cape George, near Antigonish is the loftiest. The concrete tower shows a light from 123 m (just shy of 404 ft) above St. Georges Bay. It's an area early mariners sought to avoid; shallow water extends at least half a kilometre from the base of the cape. On the night of November 1, 1861, the first keeper climbed the wooden steps and ladders in the tower attached to his house to light the oil lamps in the lantern. Thanks to the use of polished metal reflectors, the light proved to be useful to shipping as far offshore as 25 nautical miles — an impressive distance for the day. The station's elevation made it a target for almost constant harassment by the wind, and within five years the superintendent of lighthouses noted it might be prudent to change the rotating apparatus to a fixed light. Gales often made the building vibrate so badly that the revolving light would not work properly. Wire stays fitted to the tower helped but even so the wind continued to badger the tower and dwelling.I In 1908, a new beacon went up. Its beautiful rotating Fresnel lens could be seen as far away as Cape Bear on PEI — a healthy distance of 30 nautical miles. Today, a little acrylic lens rotates atop the current concrete lighthouse. You can see the previous tower's glittering Fresnel lens at the Bluefin Tuna Interpretive Centre in Ballantyne's Cove, just down the road from Cape George.

#7. THE SALVAGES (THE LOWEST): Well, technically it may not be the absolute lowest, but The Salvages light, on the Half Moons, off Port LaTour, is about as close to the water as a lightkeeper would want to get without actually swimming in it. The place is a low strip of granite ledge and cobble beach, completely at the mercy of the open Atlantic. Families moved into the fortress-like bunker in 1915, where their only company was the sea, wheeling gulls and the bawling diaphone foghorn with its droning compressors — attached directly to the living quarters. The Salvages was one of several Nova Scotia light-stations that started out as a fog signal establishment without a light — it wasn't until the 1960s that the Coast Guard plunked a red lantern (the metal and glass enclosure which protects a lighthouse lens) and light atop the massive foghorn bunker. Jim Guptill spent 10 years on The Salvages in the 1970s and 80s. By then it had become a "bachelor" station, with two teams of two lightkeepers each, working rotating 28-day shifts. Jim remembered the massive portholes set in the lower level of the engine room building. He recalled pressing his face against the heavy panes of glass, almost mesmerized by the massive seas rushing in to cover. "You could look out almost any area out of this basement in bad weather," Jim said, "and be looking right into the sea. Literally. It was fascinating. Scary, but I couldn't help looking, right? It was like watching somebody get hit on the highway with a car. I'd get in one of these portholes and say, 'Holy crap, this one's gonna be it! And it would SMACK! against the side of the house. It was a crazy experience!" That crazy experience ended with automation and de-staffing in 1987. The Salvages' brooding bunker remains today, although its functions have been taken over by a light on a small skeleton tower bolted to the wave-washed granite.

#8. BON PORTAGE ISLAND (THE "LITERARY LIGHT"): Until Evelyn Richardson wrote We Keep A Light, no Atlantic Canadian woman had ever written about lighthouse life. Well, no one had really written about lightkeeping in detail and today Evelyn's engaging and descriptive work stands as a Nova Scotia classic. Evelyn and her husband bought Bon Portage Island, off Shag Harbour, in 1929. They also became its keepers, remaining on the island until 1964. The Richardsons raised a family of three children in the drafty old tower, with its attached dwelling. The family also raised sheep and pigs, kept a cow and oxen, farmed the land around the lighthouse and by all accounts revelled in the experience. Evelyn, always busy with lighthouse and family chores, snatched precious moments over the years to set down the family's life on the island on a treasured typewriter. In 1945, Ryerson Press in Toronto published We Keep A Light. Much to the family's surprise, and delight, the book won a Governor General's Medal. Evelyn went on to write half a dozen or so books, setting down the social and natural history of the area.Today, Acadia University owns Bon Portage, maintaining the Evelyn and Morrill Richardson Field Station in Biology in the former keepers' homes. It's a fitting tribute to Evelyn's legacy as an early historian and naturalist in Nova Scotia, and to her family's love for Bon Portage. As her daughter Anne later recalled, "Where do people today go, to find a place without people, where there's just themselves and nature? I mean as a family, or as an individual. In a great many lives it can't be done. I have always prized the fact that I had that on Bon Portage. And frankly, I miss it yet."

9. SAINT PAUL ISLAND (THE GNARLIEST): To be fair, every lighthouse in Nova Scotia has had its share of storms and shipwrecks. But some stations stand out. Photos of Saint Paul Island northeast light, taken during the calm summer months, belie the real nature of the place. The moniker "Graveyard of the Gulf" is more to the point. Until the government of the day built lights on the southwest and northeast ends of the island (about 13 nautical miles NE of Cape North, Cape Breton), dozens of vessels and thousands of people came to grief on its jagged cliffs. The worst of all was in the winter, when ice choked Cabot Strait between Cape North and Saint Paul. It was gruesomely common for residents in Aspy Bay to watch, powerless, as fires burned on the shores of St. Paul. As the days passed, the fires dimmed and finally went out. As on Seal Island, men from northern Cape Breton would travel to the island in the spring to bury the dead. Often, they found bodies clustered near the cold remains of their fires. In 1815, 799 people died when troop ships Royal Sovereign and Viceroy of India struck the island. A lighthouse finally went up on the southern end in 1831.

The next year, the governments of New Brunswick and Nova Scotia established two lifesaving stations, one on each side of the island. Apparently neither crew was aware of the other! In 1839 the colonial government built a beefy wooden light on a nub of rock across the tittle at the island's north end, and from then until 1991 a series of keepers and their families hunkered down at Northeast Light. Shipwrecks continued, but between the keepers and the lifesaving crews, many fewer people died. By the mid-20th century, shipwrecks were pretty well a thing of the past, but the keepers still lived through horrific weather. Lightkeeper's wife Adalene McSheffery remembered a winter storm that brought chaotic water racing up the rocks to the house, a full 35 m (115 ft) above sea level. The wave smashed into the side of the house, knocking the family's Christmas tree over. At its peak, the island had a population of about 50, but towards the end, with lifesaving station closed, and the sou'west light destaffed, only four keepers remained, working 28 rotations at

Northeast Light. The Coast Guard sent them home in 1990. Today, a solar-powered light still stands guard over The Graveyard of the Gulf.

10. CAPE FORCHU (THE LAST): In the summer of 1993, Yarmouth's iconic Cape Forchu lighthouse became the final Nova Scotia beacon to lose its keepers, ending more than two centuries of lightkeeping in this province. Established in 1839, its first keeper, Commander James Fox, was a direct ancestor of Evelyn Richardson. The Department of Transport tore down the old wooden tower in 1961, replacing it with the current "apple core" structure, with its tall, slender tower and flared lantern deck. By the early 1990s, Cape Forchu was one of the few stations in the Maritimes to retain resident keepers. Their job had evolved from guardians of flame and steam whistle to long-distance lightkeepers, monitoring computer links to 20 or so automated lighthouses in the area. This duty too passed into history in the summer of 1993, when the last keepers packed up and left Cape Forchu. In 2001, a new era began at Cape Forchu when the federal government transferred the station to the care of The Friends of the Yarmouth Light Society. Today, the striped lighthouse, foghorn building and two keepers' houses make up a top-notch tourist attraction and provide a welcome sight to vessels passing in and out of Yarmouth Harbour.

Chris Mills built his first lighthouse when he was six. Modelled on (but not necessarily resembling) the lighthouse down the road from his family's cottage, it helped spark his interest in becoming a lighthouse keeper. Flash forward almost two decades and Chris decided to forsake a budding career in journalism for a much less-certain career as a relief lightkeeper. One shift led to nine years spent on 11 lightstations in Nova Scotia, New Brunswick and British Columbia. In 1997 he moved back east, working in marine search and rescue and in radio news for the CBC and private radio. Today, he works as a lifeboatman on a Canadian Coast Guard lifeboat. In his spare time he still visits and researches lighthouses, as well as hosting a weekly radio show on Seaside FM in Eastern Passage. A founding member of the Nova Scotia Lighthouse Preservation Society, Chris is the author of Vanishing Lights: A Lightkeeper's Fascination With A Disappearing Way of Life *and* Lighthouse Legacies: Stories of Nova Scotia's Lightkeeping Families. *He lives in Ketch Harbour, NS with his wife and daughter.*

A List of 10 Famous Ships Built in Nova Scotia

As shipbuilding played such an integral part of Nova Scotia's history and economy, many of the vessels built here have made nautical history for various reasons. The following is a list of 10 famous ships built in Nova Scotia.

#1 BLUENOSE: Designed by the legendary William Roué, *Bluenose* was built by the famed Smith and Rhuland shipyards and was launched in Lunenburg on March 26, 1921. She was captained by Luenburg-born Angus Walters. *Bluenose* became a provincial icon for Nova Scotia as well as an important Canadian symbol in the 1930s. She was built to be a racing ship and fishing vessel and in over 17 years of racing, no challenger—American or Canadian—could wrest the International Fishermen's Trophy from *Bluenose*. The schooner was in its last race in 1938. Fishing schooners became obsolete after the Second World War. In 1940, Walters retired as a fisherman and started a drive to save *Bluenose* and preserve it as a piece of Nova Scotian history, but in 1942 Walters had to sell the schooner to the West Indies Trading Company. On January 29, 1946 *Bluenose* struck a reef off the coast of Haiti and sank. Walters lived to sail on the maiden voyage of the *Bluenose II* in 1963 and to see his ship appear on the Canadian dime.

#2. BLUENOSE II: A replica of the famed *Bluenose,* she primarily serves as Nova Scotia's sailing ambassador. Built to original plans and by many of the same workers, *Bluenose II* was launched in Lunenburg on July 24, 1963, from the same shipyards where he namesake was built. The original *Bluenose* captain Angus J. Walters took the helm of the new replica for her maiden voyage. *Bluenose II* was built by the Oland Brewery for $208,600 as a marketing tool for their Schooner Beer brand. Her popularity led to the schooner being sold to the Nova Scotia government for the sum of $1. *Bluenose II* serves as a goodwill ambassador, tourist attraction and provincial symbol in Lunenburg. During the summer, she visits ports all around Nova Scotia and frequently sails to other ports on the eastern seaboard. In honour of her predecessor, *Bluenose II* does not officially race.

#3. THE BOUNTY: The *HMS Bounty* is one of the most famous ships in the world. It is known for the storied mutiny that took place in Tahiti in 1789 on board the British transport vessel. In 1960, at the request of MGM Studios, Smith and Rhuland Shipyard in Lunenburg built a replica of the famous vessel to be used in the motion picture *Mutiny on the Bounty* starring Marlon Brando. The *Bounty* remained the property of MGM until 1986 when she was bought by television mogul Ted Turner during his purchase of the company's film library. In 1993 Turner sold the boat to the Fall River Chamber Foundation, which kept the *Bounty* for eight years before selling her to the HMS *Bounty* Organization LLC. Sailing out of Greenport, New York, the historic vessel made the occasional return to its Lunenburg roots spending time at another local shipyard, Scotia Trawler Shipyard undergoing repairs. *HMS Bounty* appeared in many documentaries and was featured in films such as *Pirates of the Caribbean: Dead Man's Chest*, with Johnny Depp, in which *Bounty* stood in for the *Edinburgh Trader*. *Bounty* sank off the coast of North Carolina during Hurricane Sandy on October 29, 2012.

#4. PICTON CASTLE: Picton Castle, based in Lunenburg, is a tall ship employed in sail training. The vessel undertakes 13-month round-the-world voyages, among a variety of shorter voyages along the east coast of the Americas. *Picton Castle* was originally built as a motorized fishing trawler in 1928, along with four other trawlers for the same company, and operated out of Swansea, Wales. In August 1939, the Royal Navy requisitioned the trawler for use in the Second World War and refit her as a minesweeper. Following the war, the ship was renamed *Dolmar* and worked as a freighter in the North Sea and Baltic Sea. During the early 1990s, Daniel Moreland, the ship's current captain, acquired her while seeking a vessel to convert to a barque. In 1996, she was taken to Lunenburg to begin a two-million-dollar refit. A clipper bow was welded in place, three steel masts were added and she became a square-rigged barque. The ship has space for roughly 50 people, consisting of about 12 professional crew and 40 sail trainees.

#5. THE ROSE: Today's "HMS" *Rose* is a replica of a mid-18th century Royal Navy frigate, which figured in the colonial and revolutionary history of the United States. While she is a replica of a British Colonial-era vessel, today's *Rose* is an American ship. Although she is sometimes referred to as "HMS" *Rose*, her official documented name is simply Rose. The original *HMS Rose* was built in Hull, England in 1757. *Rose* was built in Lunenburg in 1970 by Newport historian John Fitzhugh Millar, using original construction drawings from 1757, which were obtained from the National Maritime Museum in Greenwich, England. He intended her as a project to celebrate the forthcoming bicentennial but she spent the first 10 years of her life in Newport, Rhode Island, largely as a dockside attraction. In 1985, already in serious disrepair, she was purchased by Kaye Williams and brought to Bridgeport, Connecticut. Williams formed the "HMS" *Rose* Foundation, a private, nonprofit group, to restore and administer the ship. After extensive rebuilding, the ship is once again in sailing condition. In 1990 she toured the Great Lakes and in 1991 she sailed the east coast from Maine to Florida while displaying Rhode Island's original draft of the Bill of Rights. In September of 1991 *Rose* was certified as America's first Class-A size Sailing School Vessel by the U.S. Coast Guard, making her the largest sailing school vessel in the United States. In 2001 *Rose* played the *HMS Surprise* in the film Far Side of the World. She still visits Lunenburg on occasion.

#6. THE SHERMAN ZWICKER: Built in 1942 at the Smith and Rhuland Shipyard, Lunenburg, the *Sherman Zwicker* was among the last of her type. She is a slightly modified traditional Banks-schooner design with a large marine diesel engine fitted as a prime mover. The hull and lower mast rig owe more to the sailing era than to contemporary powered fishing-vessel design. Vessels of her type were used in the Grand Banks dory fisheries out of Lunenburg and other ports until the mid-60s. The *Sherman Zwicker* made her last trip to the Banks in the early 60s. As a museum the schooner represents scores of sister vessels which sailed to the Banks in the salt-fish trade. The vessel also represents, in a meaningful manner, the fishermen and their trade. Today the *Sherman Zwicker* sails the Atlantic waters of the northeastern United States and Canada to ports such as Lunenburg and Halifax, various ports along the south coast of Newfoundland and American ports such as Boston, New York and her home port of Boothbay Harbor, Maine. She is cared for by the Grand Banks Schooner Museum Trust.

#7. THE THERESA E. CONNOR: The last of the saltbank schooners to operate from the port of Lunenburg, the *Theresa E. Connor* represents a way of life for generations of fishermen along the Atlantic coast. She is now the flagship for the Fisheries Museum of the Atlantic in Lunenburg. The *Theresa E. Connor* is an authentic reminder of an age of schooner fishing that lasted for almost 100 years in Atlantic Canada. The schooner was launched in Lunenburg on December 14, 1938 at the Smith and Rhuland Shipyard. A sister ship, the schooner *Lilla B. Boutilier*, was launched in October of that year. The *Theresa E. Connor* was originally owned by Maritime National Fish Company, Halifax. Captain Clarence Knickle was the first master of the schooner. In 1952, Maritime National sold the vessel to Zwicker and Company Limited. The Lunenburg Marine Museum Society purchased the *Theresa E. Connor* and opened the vessel to the public in 1967. As a Museum vessel, the *Theresa E. Connor* has undergone extensive restoration work, but with few physical changes to suit the preferences of visitors.

#8. THE RESEARCH: The ship *Research* was built on the shore of Yarmouth's waterfront in 1861 for Thomas Killiam. At 1,459 tons, she was the largest ship built and owned in Yarmouth at that time. On November 10, 1866, she was commanded by Captain George William Churchill of Yarmouth. On this voyage with the *Research*, Captain Churchill had with him Aaron Flint Churchill, his nephew, who had just passed his 16th birthday. The *Research* sailed from Quebec, lumber-laden, for the Scottish port of Greenock. After a stormy passage through the Straits of Belle Isle, she ran into a vicious nor'west gale. A heavy sea struck the rudder and parted the chains, breaking it just below the case. Captain Churchill rigged a jury rudder and young Aaron, stripped nearly naked in freezing winter weather, on a ship that was at times almost on her beam-ends, with a rope about his waist, was lowered over the stern. He managed to rig the jury rudder and was pulled back onto the deck, half-frozen. However, the gear soon parted and was lost. Aaron went over the stern eight times. With the determination of the Nova Scotian skipper and his crew, another was made and it worked. The weather moderated and the *Research* was brought to the entrance of the Firth of Clyde in Scotland after a passage of 88 days from Quebec. In recognition of the determination and courage of the captain, Aaron and the crew, the famed House of Lloyds of London awarded vellum certificates. This voyage was christened "The Voyage of Many Rudders," and Captain William Churchill became known as "Rudder Churchill" for the several jury rudders he made, his heroic nephew going over the side to rig them.

#9. WILLIAM D. LAWRENCE: The full-rigged sailing ship, *William D. Lawrence*, was built in Maitland, along the Minas Basin in the Annapolis Valley, and named after her builder, the merchant and politician William Dawson Lawrence (1817-1886). Built in 1874, she was the largest wooden sailing ship of her day, one of the largest wooden ships ever built anywhere in the world and the largest sailing ship ever built in Canada. Launched on October 27, 1874, she undertook her maiden voyage during 1874-1875.Initially planning to build a smaller vessel, William Lawrence deliberately increased the size of *William D. Lawrence* to create a landmark vessel for the province's shipping industry. The vessel defied critics who claimed that a wooden vessel of its size would be unmanageable and lose money. After several profitable years, the ship was sold to Norwegian owners in 1883 and renamed *Kommader Svend Foyn*. She was stranded in the English Channel in 1891 and converted to a barge, later sinking in Dakar, Senegal.

#10. I'M ALONE: Used as a rumrunner during Prohibition in the United States, this auxiliary schooner was built in Nova Scotia in 1923 and for six years she transported contraband alcohol. She was registered in Lunenburg. *I'm Alone* was intercepted in the Gulf of Mexico off the coast of Louisiana by *USCGC Wolcott* on March 22, 1929, as the schooner was returning from Belize with liquor. The crew of *I'm Alone* disobeyed orders to stop and was shelled and sunk by *USCGC Dexter*. Seven of the ship's eight crewmembers were rescued. The eighth, a French-Canadian boatswain, Leon Mainguy, died. The surviving crew members, including Captain John "Jack" Randell, were arrested and jailed in New Orleans. The sinking caused tensions in Canadian-American relations and the Canadian government sued for damages. Coast Guard intelligence personnel, led by Elizabeth Friedman, were able to demonstrate in international arbitration that the owners of *I'm Alone* were Americans, despite the ship's Canadian registry. As a result, the U.S. paid a fine much lower than the amount initially requested by Canada. Captain Randell and Amanda Mainguy, the widow of the crew member who died, both received restitution.

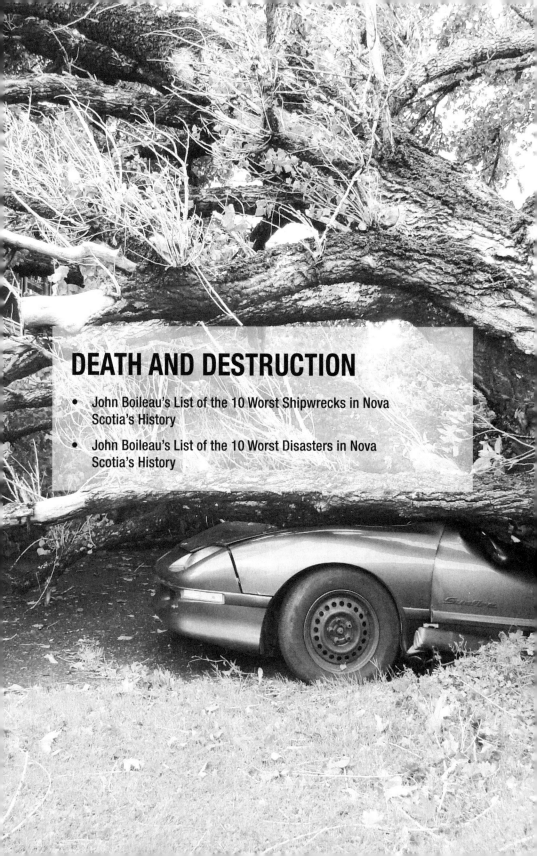

DEATH AND DESTRUCTION

- John Boileau's List of the 10 Worst Shipwrecks in Nova Scotia's History

- John Boileau's List of the 10 Worst Disasters in Nova Scotia's History

John Boileau's List of the 10 Worst Shipwrecks in Nova Scotia's History

Given its position projecting into the North Atlantic Ocean, closeness to major shipping routes, rocky shores and frequent fog banks, it is no wonder that Nova Scotia has as many shipwrecks as it does. Halifax's Maritime Museum of the Atlantic maintains an online searchable database of some 5,000 shipwreck records, one-fifth of the estimated 25,000 shipwrecks along the province's shores.

In creating this list of the 10 worst shipwrecks off Nova Scotia, I have used a very simple criterion — the number of deaths (which are shown in brackets for each ship). Where the exact number of deaths is unknown, an estimate is shown, indicated by *est.*

#1.RMS TITANIC: White Star liner that sank 1,300 kilometres southeast of Nova Scotia, April 15, 1912 (1,517 in total — 40 Canadians). Purists may not agree that *Titanic* qualifies as a Nova Scotia shipwreck, but I have included her because of the recovery operation mounted out of Halifax, which resulted in 209 bodies being brought to that city, where 150 are buried.

#2. RMS ATLANTIC: White Star liner that ran aground and sank near Prospect, April 1, 1873 (562). This was the deadliest civilian maritime disaster in the North Atlantic Ocean prior to the loss of *Titanic*.

#3. CHAMEAU (OR LE CHAMEAU): French Navy armed transport ship that sank off Louisbourg, August 27, 1725 (216-316 est.; 180 bodies washed ashore).

#4. SIBYLLE: Immigrant ship that sank off St. Paul's Island (known as "The Graveyard of the Gulf" with more than 350 recorded shipwrecks), 23 kilometres northeast of the northern tip of Cape Breton Island, September 11, 1834 (300+).

#5. HMS TRIBUNE: Royal Navy frigate that sank off Herring Cove, November 16, 1797 (238).

#6. SS HUNGARIAN: Allan Line steamship wrecked off Cape Sable Island, February 19, 1860 (205).

#7. SOVEREIGN: British troop transport stranded on St. Paul's Island, October 18, 1814 (202).

#8. HMS ACORN: Royal Navy 18-gun sloop wrecked off Halifax, April 4, 1828 (115).

#9. MARIA: Immigrant ship that sank in Cabot Strait, 80 kilometres from St. Paul's Island, May 10, 1849 (109).

#10. HMS FEVERSHAM: Royal Navy 32-gun warship wrecked on Scatarie Island off the east coast of Cape Breton Island, October 7, 1711 (102).

And for any purists who do not consider *Titanic* a legitimate Nova Scotia shipwreck, one more:

#11. HANNA: Immigrant ship that sank in the Gulf of St. Lawrence, April 29, 1849 (49 est.)

Retired army colonel John Boileau is the author of more than a dozen books of historical non-fiction, as well as more than 500 magazine and newspaper articles on a variety of subjects, book reviews, op-ed columns, travelogues and encyclopedia entries.

John Boileau's List of the 10 Worst Disasters in Nova Scotia's History

In compiling this list of the 10 worst disasters in Nova Scotia's history, I have excluded shipwrecks, which are contained in my other list of the 10 worst shipwrecks in Nova Scotia. But like the shipwrecks list, I have used a very simple criterion — the number of deaths (which are shown in brackets for each incident).

Other disasters caused more property damage — $100 million by category-two Hurricane Juan in September 2003, for example — but killed fewer (six in the case of Juan). Additionally, I have not differentiated between natural and human-made disasters; the impact of a disaster is the same, whether caused by nature or humans. Where the exact number of deaths is unknown, an estimate is shown, indicated by est. Interestingly, half of these disasters were coal-mine accidents (three in Springhill alone), while another three were hurricanes.

#1. HALIFAX EXPLOSION: A massive explosion, which was the result of the *SS Imo*, a Belgian relief ship travelling in ballast, colliding with the French ship *Mont-Blanc*, laden with more than 2,500 tonnes of high explosives, in the narrowest part of Halifax Harbour. It remains the largest human-made, non-nuclear blast in history, December 6, 1917 (1,950 recorded names; total could be as high as 2,500).

#2. GREAT NOVA SCOTIA CYCLONE: A hurricane that was reduced to category two by the time it paralleled the province's coastline. It never made landfall here; most of those killed were sailors at sea, August 24, 1873 (500 est. plus another 100 est. in Newfoundland and Labrador).

#3. SWISSAIR FLIGHT 111: A scheduled international passenger flight from New York City to Geneva, Switzerland, in which the airplane, a McDonnell Douglas MD-11, experienced a total loss of power due to a fire and plunged into the Atlantic Ocean eight kmes from Peggy's Cove, killing all onboard, September 2, 1998. It remains the second-largest loss of life of any air disaster in the country, while its investigation became the largest and most expensive transport-accident investigation in Canadian history (229).

#4. 1927 GREAT AUGUST GALE: A category-three hurricane that made landfall near Yarmouth and then travelled across the province, which was not only the deadliest Canadian hurricane since at least 1900, but also the strongest tropical storm ever to strike the country, August 24, 1927 (173-192 est.).

#5. 1891 SPRINGHILL MINING EXPLOSION: Springhill's first mining disaster — and its worst — occurred in No. 1 and No. 2 Collieries, which were joined by a connecting tunnel 400 m below the surface. In addition to those killed, dozens were injured, with many of the victims 10- to 13-year-old boys, February 21, 1891 (125).

#6. 1958 SPRINGHILL MINING "BUMP": The most severe underground earthquake, or "bump," in North American mining history not only hit No. 2 Colliery (one of the deepest in the world) but also injured town residents and destroyed Springhill's economy; the mines were never re-opened. Rescue operations continued for a week, with 99 trapped miners saved, October 23, 1958 (75).

#7. DRUMMOND MINE EXPLOSION: Actually a series of explosions that were likely caused by a fire in Canada's leading colliery at the time, Westville, Pictou County, May 13, 1873 (70).

#8. 1926 GREAT AUGUST GALE: A category-one hurricane whose remnants hit Cape Breton Island after having sunk several ships and boats offshore, including two Lunenburg fishing schooners that crashed onto Sable Island, killing 49 fishermen, August 8, 1926 (55-58 est.).

#9. 1956 SPRINGHILL MINING EXPLOSION: Several cars from a mine train hauling a load of fine coal dust to the surface of No. 4 Colliery broke loose, derailed, hit a power line and caused an arc that ignited the dust at 1,700 m below the surface. Heroic rescue operations resulted in 88 miners being saved, November 1, 1956 (39).

#10. WESTRAY MINE EXPLOSION: Underground explosions at Plymouth, Pictou County, initially caused by methane gas and subsequently coal dust, which were the result of unsafe working practices, after only eight months of operation, May 9, 1992 (26).

Retired army colonel John Boileau is the author of more than a dozen books of historical non-fiction, as well as more than 500 magazine and newspaper articles on a variety of subjects, book reviews, op-ed columns, travelogues and encyclopedia entries.

THE ECONOMY

- Pam Wamback's List of the Top 10 Lobster Experiences in Nova Scotia
- A List of the 12 Outstanding Business People From Nova Scotia's Past Who Changed the World
- Angus Bonnyman's List of 11 Interesting Facts About the Nova Scotia Christmas Tree Industry
- A List of 12 Facts About Nova Scotia's Blueberry Industry
- A List of 12 Facts About Apples and the Nova Scotia Apple Industry
- A List of the Top 10 Most Expensive Residential Homes Sold in Nova Scotia
- A List of the 10 Largest Maple Syrup Producers in Nova Scotia

Pam Wamback's List of the Top 10 Lobster Experiences in Nova Scotia

If you haven't eaten lobster in Nova Scotia then you haven't really eaten lobster! This popular crustacean is still the lifeblood of many of our working fishing communities. While lobster is available fresh and fished around the province 365 days a year, the lobsters caught in Districts 33 and 34 in southwest Nova Scotia account for approximately 40 percent of all lobster caught in Canada. That's why the Municipality of Barrington has dubbed itself the Lobster Capital of Canada. So if you are looking for the best places to experience or taste fresh lobster, here are a few suggestions:

#1. Visit the Hall's Harbour Lobster Pound and pluck a fresh lobster from the tank then, while you wait for your lobster to be cooked, stroll the wharf and watch lobster boats navigating the narrow harbour when the tide is in. If it's a fair weather day, eat your lobster on the picnic table on the wharf next to the boat that may very well have caught it.

#2. Learn firsthand about the lobster industry and how lobsters are caught with tour operators who focus on the lobster experience: Gillis Lobster Tours, Cape Breton Lobster Tours, Peggy's Cove Boat Tours or Shelburne Harbour Boat Tours.

#3. Adopt a baby lobster at the Lobster Hatchery at the Northumberland Fisheries Museum and release it back to the Bay (you get an official adoption certificate too!).

#4. Visit one of the many Living Wharves in the Yarmouth and Acadian Shores region where real-life fishermen tell a few tales while helping you try your hand at fishing. Imagine yourself there, splicing rope for lobster traps while facing the salty ocean breeze.

#5. For a traditional Nova Scotia lobster supper, chow down at The Shore Club in Hubbards, Baddeck Lobster Suppers or Beaux Vendredis Lobster Suppers in Clare.

#6. Try some different dishes, like lobster poutine or lobster fondue at Capt. Kat's Lobster Shack in Barrington; lobster mac & cheese at the Salt Shaker Deli; lobster Cobb salad at Pictou Lodge Resort; or a good old-fashioned lobster sandwich at Liscombe Lodge. (*BONUS*: Capt. Kat's Lobster Shack's lobster roll was voted as the BEST at the 2018 South Shore Lobster Crawl Lobster Roll Challenge.)

#7. Have you ever wanted to learn how to perfectly boil a Nova Scotia lobster? Join the Argyler Lodge for a lesson that will leave your taste buds tingling — just in time for dinner!

#8. Get a taste of the world's largest lobster fishery at the Great Canadian Lobster Fishing Feast at White Point Beach Resort. Join a crew of Nova Scotia lobster fishers for a morning at sea, returning to your resort with the freshest lobster and ultimate bragging rights. Meet at the beachside bonfire, as Chef prepares today's catch for your cozy dinner party inside.

#9. The Good Cheer Lobster Feast in Annapolis Royal combines authentic Acadian and Mi'kmaw music with local flavours and more than 400 years of stories in this exclusive dinner party, held after hours at Port Royal National Historic Site, one of North America's first European settlements. Host Samuel de Champlain brings good cheer right to your table!

#10. We are the festival province so there are plenty of lobster-themed festivals: the South Shore Lobster Crawl (February), Shelburne County Lobster Festival (June), Digby Lobster Bash (June), Pictou Lobster Carnival (July) and St. Peter's Lobsters R Us Seaside Lobsterfest (July), just to name a few.

Pam Wamback is a Media Relations Specialist (Editorial) with the Nova Scotia Department of Tourism and Culture.

A List of the 12 Outstanding Historical Business People from Nova Scotia Who Changed the World

#1. ALEXANDER KEITH: Alexander Keith's was founded in 1820, making it one of the oldest commercial breweries in North America. It was founded by Alexander Keith, who emigrated from Scotland in 1817. Today, the brewery is under the control of Labatt, a subsidiary of Anheuser-Bush InBev. Alexander Keith was born October 5, 1795 in Halkirk, Scotland, where he became a brewer. He immigrated to Canada in 1817 and founded the brewing company in 1820. Alexander Keith died in Halifax on December 14, 1873, and was buried at Camp Hill Cemetery across from the Halifax Public Gardens. His birthday is often marked by people visiting the grave and placing beer bottles and caps on it.

#2. O.E. SMITH: Morse's Teas is a six-storey brick-and-stone commercial property located on Hollis Street in Halifax. A landmark of the downtown, the large trapezoidal building is one of Halifax's oldest commercial properties and is situated on the northern end of the block bounded by Hollis, Duke and Water Streets. The designation extends to the building and the land it occupies. Morse's Teas is valued for its association with early trade in Halifax, its associations to J.S. MacLean and

J.E. Morse and Company Ltd. and for its Georgian architectural features. It is also valued as Canada's first tea company.

In 1855, J.S. MacLean, a New York businessman, purchased the building and based his grocery store there. Importing products from overseas, his business specialized in tea, which he transported in small sailing vessels and horse-drawn wagons to communities throughout Nova Scotia, New Brunswick and Prince Edward Island. After 30 years in business, he sold the building to another local merchant, Cyril H. Gorham, and in 1910 Gorham sold it to O.E. Smith, president of J.E. Morse and Company Ltd. Under Smith's direction, tea was blended, packaged and shipped to wholesalers and retailers, establishing the property as Canada's first tea business. Most sales were to Atlantic Canada, though tea was also shipped to destinations in the U.S. and West Indies. The building remained in the Smith family until the late 1970s. In 1973, the building was threatened with demolition to make way for a proposed superhighway but Halifax City Council saved the building along with several other heritage structures in the vicinity. In 1989, Morse's Teas became part of the campus for the Nova Scotia College of Art and Design (NSCAD). In 2004, a Toronto-based developer purchased the property. The building is distinguished by its unusual trapezoidal footprint.

#3. WILLIAM CHURCH MOIR: The earliest reliable records of Moirs Limited date back to 1830, when Moir, Son and Company began when Benjamin Moir, a native of Scotland, started a bakery in the heart of Halifax. Benjamin Moir's son, William Church Moir, inherited the business in 1845. The younger Moir turned his father's business into a powerhouse. At the time of his death in 1896, the factory he had built employed more than 260 workers, produced more than 11,000 loafs of bread daily, and made more than 500 types of confectionery (a business he got into in around 1873 with his son, James William), all sold across Canada. The biscuit operation was added in 1862, when a five-storey building was built on the original site. In 1873 James William Moir, grandson of the original founder, experimented in the manufacturing of confectionery and developed a line of chocolates. In 1903 the company took the name of Moirs, Limited, and in 1927 a nine-storey structure for manufacturing candy was added to the facilities. In 1928, Moirs introduced the now-famous Pot of Gold brand of chocolates to the world and in the early 1930s a chocolate processing plant was established in Bedford. The Dartmouth factory opened in 1975 and in 1987 candy giant Hershey purchased Moirs, along with the Halifax-area facilities and Pot of Gold. The Dartmouth factory closed in December 2007.

#4. CHARLES E. STANFIELD: Stanfield's Limited based in Truro is one of Canada's leading garment manufacturers. With approximately 550 employees, the company's products are sold throughout Canada and around the world. The company started in 1856 when Charles E. Stanfield and his brother-in-law Samuel E. Dawson founded Tryon Woollen Mills in Tryon, Prince Edward Island. Charles sold his interest to Samuel a decade later and moved to Truro. In 1870, Charles Stanfield established the Truro Woollen Mills on Brunswick Street, Truro. The Truro Felt Works were later established east of the woollen mills and Stanfield finally established the current textile mill on the south bank of the Salmon River in the town in 1882. Charles Stanfield sold his business interests to his two sons, John and Frank, in 1896. The Truro factory was renamed Truro Knitting Mills Limited. Their company was innovative and sold many products in the form of shrink-proof heavy woolen underwear that were used by workers during the Klondike Gold Rush in the late 1890s. This early success led to the 1906 establishment of Stanfield's Limited. In 1910, Stanfield's bought out Hewson Woollen Mills in Amherst, which was renamed Amherst Woollen Mills.

#5. ENOS COLLINS: Born on September 5, 1774, in Liverpool, Nova Scotia, Enos Collins was a merchant, ship owner, banker and privateer. Upon his death on November 18, 1871, Collins was acclaimed as the richest man in Canada. As owner of the privateer schooner *Liverpool Packet*, he made his main fortune through shrewd wartime trading and careful peacetime investments. He moved to Halifax during the War of 1812. When the merchant Charles Prescott retired in 1811, Collins purchased Prescott's wharf and warehouse on Upper Water Street in Halifax, later expanding it by purchase and foreclosure to become the headquarters of his commercial empire. He cofounded the Halifax Banking Company in 1825. One of the first Canadian banks, today it is known as the Canadian Imperial Bank of Commerce. He built a large stone estate house called Gorsebrook in the South End of Halifax. The estate is the site of Saint Mary's University, although the Collins mansion was demolished in the 1960s. However Collins' bank and warehouse buildings on the Halifax waterfront were rescued from demolition by Nova Scotia's Heritage Trust in the 1970s and form the most distinct part of a waterfront revitalization known as Historic Properties.

#6. AARON FLINT CHURCHILL: Born in 1850, Aaron Flint Churchill was one of Yarmouth County's most prominent native sons. At age 16 he had become a hero by jury-rigging a rudder on the vessel called Research eight times in a November gale at sea to bring the vessel safely to port. Both he and his uncle, George Churchill, the ship's captain, were recognized for the feat with gifts from Lloyd's of London, who insured the vessel. By age 21, Churchill had become a sea captain himself, but at age 24 he quit the sea and opened a stevedoring business at Savannah, Georgia. Later, he established the Churchill Steamship Line at Savannah and also gained a reputation as an inventor. He was later a director of the Savannah Bank and Trust Company and owner of the Churchill Compress Company with headquarters in Memphis, Tennessee. He also became one of the most prominent and wealthiest Canadians working in the United States at the turn of the 20th century. In 1899-90, Churchill built a stately mansion he called Anchorage. A summer residence for Churchill and his wife, Lois and other family members, it is located at Darling Lake on the outskirts of Yarmouth. When Churchill died on June 10, 1920 he was buried in the family cemetery on a hill not far from his well beloved Anchorage.

#7. EZRA CHURCHILL: Born in Yarmouth on May 18, 1806, Ezra Churchill was a 19th-century industrialist, investing in shipbuilding, land, timber for domestic and foreign markets, gypsum quarries, insurance companies and hotels, among other interests. As a politician he held positions in the Nova Scotia legislature and was appointed to the Canadian Senate as a representative for the Province of Nova Scotia. Churchill was also a Baptist lay preacher. In 1824, Churchill married Ann Davidson and subsequently, after Ann's death, married Rachel Burgess. His move to the eastern end of the Annapolis Valley came with the purchase of a 66-acre lot at Hantsport in 1841. He enlarged his landholdings in the area and over the years sold lots to workmen and their families who were moving to Hantsport for the jobs being created by the shipbuilding boom. Although Hantsport and area had been the location of a number of shipbuilding ventures, Churchill was the catalyst that transformed a small gathering of farms along the confluence of the Halfway and Avon rivers into a major shipbuilding port. Nearly 200 vessels were built in the Hantsport area shipyards. Churchill became one of the largest shipbuilders and ship investors in Nova Scotia, launching dozens of large sailing vessels from his yards at Hantsport. Among his many vessels was *Hamburg*, the largest three-masted sailing barque ever built in Canada. Churchill died in Ottawa on May 8, 1874.

#8. SIR SAMUEL CUNARD: Shipping magnate Samuel Cunard was born November 21, 1787, in Halifax. The son of a master carpenter and timber merchant who had fled the American Revolution and settled in Halifax, he founded the Cunard Line in 1840. Cunard's business skills were evident at an early age and by age 17 he was managing his own general store. He later joined his father in the family timber business, which he expanded into coal, iron, shipping and whaling. Cunard was a highly successful entrepreneur in Halifax shipping and one of a group of 12 individuals who dominated the affairs of Nova Scotia. Early investments in steam included co-founding the steam ferry company in Halifax harbour and an investment in the pioneering steamship *Royal William*. Cunard went to the United Kingdom, where he set up a company with several other businessmen to bid for the rights to run a trans-Atlantic mail service between the UK and North America. It was successful in its bid, the company later becoming Cunard Steamships Limited. Sir Samuel Cunard died at Kensington on April 28, 1865, and is buried there in Brompton Cemetery.

#9. CYRUS EATON: Born December 27, 1883, on a farm near the village of Pugwash in Cumberland County, Cyrus Eaton was an investment banker, businessman and philanthropist, with a career that spanned 70 years mostly in the U.S. For decades Eaton was one of the most powerful financiers in the American Midwest. He was chiefly known for his longevity in business, for his opposition to the dominance of eastern financiers in the America of his day, for his occasionally ruthless financial manipulations, for his passion for world peace and for his outspoken criticism of United States Cold War policy. He funded and helped organize the first Pugwash Conferences on World Peace in 1955. The Pugwash Conferences and their chairman, Joseph Rotblat, were awarded the Nobel Peace Prize in 1995. Eaton died in Ohio on

May 9, 1979, and had his ashes were buried in Blandford, Nova Scotia, where his family had a summer home.

#10. ALFRED FULLER: Alfred Fuller, who was born January 13, 1885, on an Annapolis Valley farm in Welsford, Kings County, made his mark on the world as the original "Fuller Brush Man." In 1903, when Fuller was 18, he moved to Boston, Massachusetts to live with his sister. Three years later, in 1906, with a $75 investment, he started the Fuller Brush Company in Hartford, Connecticut. Selling brushes door to door, Fuller became a household name and by 1919, the company had achieved sales of more than $1 million per year. Fuller Brush went on to be recognized throughout North America, even inspiring two comedy films —*The Fuller Brush Man* (1948) starring Red Skelton and *The Fuller Brush Girl* (1950) starring Lucille Ball. The company remained in the Fuller family's hands until 1968, when it was acquired by Sara Lee Corporation. Fuller died on December 4, 1973, in Hartford, Connecticut and is buried at Pleasant Valley Cemetery in Somerset, in his native Kings County where he was born.

#11. IZAAK WALTON KILLAM: Izaak Walton Killam, who became one of Canada's most eminent financiers, was born in Yarmouth on July 23, 1885. By the mid 1890s, Killam rose from a paperboy to become one of Canada's wealthiest individuals. Born into a family of merchants and shipowners, Killam had little formal education but great entrepreneurial drive. He joined the Union Bank of Halifax as a clerk in 1901 and was transferred to head office two years later. He befriended Max Aitken and moved to Montreal. From 1909 to 1913 Killam managed the London office of Aitken's Royal Securities Corp. In 1915 he became president and four years later bought out Aitken, remaining president until 1954. Killam built an investment empire in Canada and Latin America with holdings in publishing, utilities (International Power, Calgary Power, Ottawa Valley Power Co), pulp and paper (BC Pulp and Paper and Mersey Paper in Brooklyn, Queens County), construction and films. In 1922, Killam married Dorothy Brooks Johnston. After his death on August 5, 1955, she more than doubled her $40-million inheritance and carried out her husband's wishes to assist the arts, education and sciences. Initial funding for the Canada Council (1957) was largely provided from some $50 million in inheritance taxes on the Killam estate, with a similar amount from the estate of Sir James H. Dunn. Mrs. Killam left $30 million to Dalhousie University and $30 million to be divided among three other universities, $8 million to the Izaak Walton Killam Hospital for Children in Halifax, $4 million to the Montreal Neurological Institute and a further $15 million to the Canada Council. The Killam Memorial Prize honours Canadian scholars, and Killam research fellowships are presented to Canadian scientists and scholars.

#12.JOHN W. SCOBEY AND FRANK H. SCOBEY: The grocery-store conglomerate known as Sobeys was founded in Stellarton by John W. Sobey in 1907 as a meat delivery business. In 1924, his son Frank H. Sobey convinced him to expand into a full grocery business, serving Pictou County. From that point until his death, Frank was the driving force behind the business. Sobeys opened its first self-serve supermarket in 1949 and the chain eventually expanded throughout Atlantic Canada. During most of the second half of the 20th century it was the region's dominant grocer. In the 1980s, Sobeys expanded into southern Ontario, challenging Loblaws on its "home turf," thereby igniting what came to be a nationwide battle for market supremacy. Today, Sobeys Inc. is the second largest food retailer in Canada with over 1,500 supermarkets operating under a variety of banners. Headquartered in Stellarton, it operates stores in all 10 provinces and accumulated sales of more than $16 billion in 2012.

Angus Bonnyman's List of 11 Interesting Facts About the Nova Scotia Christmas Tree Industry

The Christmas tree industry is worth millions of dollars to the Nova Scotia economy but here are 11 interesting facts that you may not have known about the industry:

#1. THE BEST YEAR EVER FOR SALES: Approximately 95 percent of the Christmas trees produced in Nova Scotia are exported around the world. Numbers suggest that 2016 was the best year for sales of real Christmas trees. In terms of numbers sold, the industry peaked in 1957 with 3.8 million trees exported.

#2. OLDEST TREE EVER CUT: There is a record of a 72-year-old tree being cut, but no other records found.

#3. TALLEST TREE EVER CUT: The world's tallest cut Christmas tree was a 67.36-m (221-ft) fir erected and decorated at Northgate Shopping Center, Seattle, Washington, USA, in December 1950.

#4. MOST EXPENSIVE TREE EVER CUT? Worth an incredible 41,329,531 United Arab Emirates dirham (approximately 11 million dollars U.S. or seven-million pounds), this blinged-out tree was displayed in the grand lobby of the Emirates Palace in Abu Dhabi during the holiday season in 2010. What makes this tree so pricey? Perhaps the lavish décor; in a stunning 13.1-m (43.2-ft) exhibit of gold and silver, it was covered in 181 items of jewelry.

#5. NUMBER OF CHRISTMAS TREE FARMS IN NOVA SCOTIA: Nova Scotia has roughly 1,200 families producing an estimated 1.3 million balsam fir Christmas trees on 30,000 acres of land. Although Christmas comes but once a year, a lot of work goes into cultivating the perfect tree!

#6. THE WACKIEST WAY A CHRISTMAS TREE WAS EVER USED: Every year we hear of new and exciting ways people are recycling their trees after Christmas. Some of those include providing homes to animals recovering from injury, as a refuge for fish or preventing shoreline erosion. That said, the wackiest way I've seen a Christmas tree used was at the breakfast table, on toast! (Check out the balsam fir jelly recipe at *iloverealtrees.com/why-real/recycling-options*.)

#7. THE MOST FAMOUS NOVA SCOTIAN CHRISTMAS TREE: The Tree for Boston, which annually commemorates the support received from the people of Boston in response to the Halifax Explosion, is the most famous of our province's Christmas trees.

#8. THE FIRST TREE EXPORTED FROM NOVA SCOTIA: The first Christmas trees exported from Nova Scotia was probably shipped by Arthur Manual of Chester Basin in 1922 or 1923.

#10. THE FARTHEST A NOVA SCOTIA TREE WAS EVER SHIPPED: Each year, a tree travels from Halifax to Japan, a distance of some 10,000 kms.

#11. THE PROVINCE'S LARGEST CUSTOMER: Our neighbours to the south, the United States, import more of our trees than any other nation. However, real Christmas trees grown in Nova Scotia travel all around the world.

This list was compiled by Angus Bonnyman, executive director for the Christmas Tree Council of Nova Scotia.

A List of 12 Facts about Nova Scotia's Blueberry Industry

The blueberry was officially designated our provincial berry in 1996. Nova Scotia is Canada's top producer of blueberries. The town of Oxford calls itself the Blueberry Capital of Canada. Wild blueberries became a commercial industry in about 1940, but since then worldwide demand has grown. In fact, according to provincial information, the world loves our blueberries and the economic value of the industry in Nova Scotia is estimated at around $100 million, making it our number one fruit crop in acreage, export sales and value.

Blueberry farming is a family tradition in Nova Scotia. Many of the 1,100 or so producers are family owned and wild blueberries are key ingredients in fuelling other entrepreneurial ventures in our province. The Wild Blueberry Producers Association of Nova Scotia provides this list of facts about the industry:

#1. The entire year's crop is harvested in a little over three weeks. Fresh blueberries are available locally only during this time.

#2. The majority of the blueberry crop is frozen and sold year-round to domestic and international markets.

#3. 2014 was a record year for wild blueberries with a harvest of 62-million pounds.

#4. The 2014 harvest would have been enough to provide every Nova Scotian with more than 60 pounds of wild blueberries.

#5. The industry creates and sustains approximately 1,500 direct year-round jobs in the province. During the harvest season that number increases by hundreds more.

#6. The oldest fields in the province have been in production for 100 years.

#7. The wild blueberry is Nova Scotia's provincial fruit.

#8. Oxford Frozen Foods in Oxford is the world's largest supplier of frozen wild blueberries. The town is well known as the Wild Blueberry Capital of Canada.

#9. There are approximately 44,000 acres of blueberry fields in the province.

#10. Wild blueberries grow in two-year cycles, so half the crop is harvested every year.

#11. Wild blueberries are fat-, sodium- and cholesterol-free.

#12. Wild blueberries are one of the most anti-oxidant rich fruits. These anti-oxidants fight harmful free radicals in our bodies.

A List of 12 Facts about Apples and the Nova Scotia Apple Industry

Every February Nova Scotians observe Apple Month, a month-long celebration of a fruit that has become one of the pillars of the provincial economy. The industry pumps millions of dollars into the economy but here are 12 things you may or may not about apples and their history in Nova Scotia.

#1. The Acadian settlers brought apples with them to our province in the 1600s.

#2. English Planters brought new varieties in the 1700s.

#3. Today, more than 40 varieties of apples are grown in Nova Scoita.

#4. According to farm-census data and provincial agriculture statistics, Nova Scotia has the largest acreage of apples of all the provinces in Atlantic Canada and apples are the number one fruit grown on Nova Scotian farms.

#5. The apple is the second highest value crop grown in Nova Scotia, second only to blueberries.

#6. In addition to being sold as a fresh crop, apples are also important ingredients in other local products including juice, cider, vinegar and commercial baked goods.

#7. The Town of Berwick is known as Nova Scotia's Apple Capital.

#8. Hundreds of Nova Scotian farms earn income from apple production. When you purchase local apples at a grocery store, farmers' market, roadside farm stand or at a u-pick, you help support an industry that represents the fabric of our beautiful province.

#9. Apples are actually part of the rose family. That's why they have a rosy aroma.

#10. Apples float because they are 25 percent air.

#11. The McIntosh is Canada's national apple.

#12. The fear of apples is known as Malusdomesticaphobia.

This information is from the Nova Scotia Fruit Grower's Association.

A List of the Top 10 Most Expensive Residential Homes Sold in Nova Scotia

The top 10 most expensive residential homes sold in Nova Scotia from 2002 (when our current system of collecting data began) until 2017 range in price from 2.7

million dollars and 6.1 million dollars in Halifax Regional Municipality and Lunenburg County (including Chester).

Here are the top 10 residential sales prices:

#1. $2,757,500   **#6.** $4,333,110

#2. $2,800,000   **#7.** $4,400,000

#3. $3,100,000   **#8.** $5,000,000

#4. $3,795,000   **#9.** $5,288,000

#5. $4,000,000   **#10.** $6,100,000

This list was provided the Nova Scotia Association of REALTORS®.

A List of the 10 Largest Maple Syrup Producers in Nova Scotia

The maple syrup industry is worth approximately two-million dollars to the Nova Scotian economy. The Maple Producers Association of Nova Scotia (MPANS) is an active group of producers in the province. One of the association's main goals is education for producers, which includes everything from production through to packaging with the goals of increasing production, quality and profitability of its membership.

There are approximately 50 producers who are members located throughout Nova Scotia. They range in size from just a few taps to many thousands. The following is a list of the 10 largest producing members of MPANS:

#1. WENDELL SMITH: Located in Leicester with 55-thousand taps.

#2. AVARD BENTLEY: Located in Westchester with 40-thousand taps.

#3. KEVIN MCCORMICK: Located in Rodney with 37-thousand tap.s

#4. KEITH CROWE: Mapleton enterprises, located in Mapleton with 25-thousand taps.

#5. DAVID DICKINSON: Located in Southampton with 18-thousand taps.

#6. JOHN GOODWIN: Located in Mapleton with 17-thousand taps.

#7. JASON HAVERKORT: Located in Antigonish with 12-thousand taps.

#8. JIM GALLAGHER: Located in Mapleton with 11,500 taps.

#9. HAROLD LANGILLE: Located in South Brook with 10-thousand taps.

#10. PETER GRANT: Located in Earltown with 8,500 taps.

List of Contributors

The author would like to extend a sincere thank you to the following list of contributors who made this book possible:

Joe Canada (Jeff Douglas) • Brent and Sara (from Dashboard Living) • Donna Hachey Hatt • The Traveller (Leigh McAdam) • Darryll Walsh • Gerry Doucet • Pam Wamback • Len Wagg • Blackrattle (Dave Brown) • The Kilted Chef (Alain Bossé) • Tristian Glen • Angharad Wylie • Patricia Nelder • Astro Wayne (Wayne Mansfield) • Scott Cunningham • Joshua Peters • The Halifax Adventurer (Cheryl Campbell) • David Currie • Michael Haynes • Adam Barnett • Lindsay Bunin • Rick Howe • John Boileau • Denyse Sibley • Richard Crouse • Sheldon MacLeod • Heidi Petracek • Halifax Mayor Mike Savage • Dr. Tim J. Fedak • Yarmouth Mayor Pam Mood • Joan Dawson • Pete Luckett • Joan McEllman • Elain Elliot • Ian Robinson • Kempton Hyson • Todd Beal • Jared Hochman • The Pizza Queen (Dana Thompson) • Elisabeth Bailey • The Bologna Lover (who wishes to remain anonymous) • Virginia Lee • Moira Peters • Andrew Macdonald • Dr. Melissa Grey • Dan Soucoup • John G. Leefe • Dan Conlin • Brian Tennyson • Mr. Know-It-All (Bruce Nunn) • Michael Melski • Hugh Creighton • Natalie MacMaster • Jimmy Rankin • JC Douglas • Sandra Phinney • John Tattrie • Cruise • Dr. Allan Marble • Laurie Lacey • Philip Croucher • Bill Spurr • Patrick Hirtle • Michael de Adder • Graham Steele • Lowell R. DeMond • Andrew Hebda • Donna Barnett • Bridget Thomas • Allan Billard • Chris Mills • Angus Bonnyman • Kevin McCormick • Tanya White • Special thanks as well to copy editor Chris Benjamin, designer Greg Tutty and publisher John MacIntyre.